A STUPENDOUS EFFORT

A STUPENDOUS EFFORT

THE 87TH INDIANA IN THE WAR OF THE REBELLION

Jack K. Overmyer

INDIANA UNIVERSITY PRESS
Bloomington and Indianapolis

The paper used in this publication meets the minimum requirements of American National Standard for Information Sciences—Permanence of Paper for Printed Library Materials, ANSI Z39.48-1984.

Manufactured in the United States of America

Library of Congress Cataloging-in-Publication Data

Overmyer, Jack K.
A stupendous effort : the 87th Indiana in the War of the Rebellion / Jack K. Overmyer.
p.   cm.
Includes bibliographical references and index.
ISBN 0-253-33301-6 (cl : alk. paper)
1. United States. Army. Indiana Infantry Regiment, 87th (1862–1865).
2. Indiana—History—Civil War, 1861–1865—Regimental Histories.   3. United States—History—Civil War, 1861–1865—Regimental Histories.   I. Title.
E506.5 87th.094   1997
973.7'472—dc21   96-54581

1   2   3   4   5   02   01   00   99   98   97

Dedication

To my wife, Marge, for her unfailing love and
support, and without whom there would
be no reason to do anything.

CONTENTS

MAPS

by Deana Gottschalk

Illustrations follow page 72.

PREFACE

This is the story of young men from the farms and small towns of northern Indiana and of their precarious journey through some of the Civil War's most momentous campaigns and battles.

At a time of imminent peril to their state, 945 of them became the 87th Infantry Regiment of Indiana Volunteers and went off to preserve the Union of American States. Over a fourth of them died while achieving it.

Their story does not presume to be a history of the Civil War, for I am not a historian. However, the 87th Indiana's performances are placed within the larger context of the war's strategy and tactics so that the reader can understand the purposes for which the regiment strove during nearly three years in the field.

This narrative had its origin, I suppose, 56 years ago when the Civil War first pierced my imagination in Miss Rena Wright's American history class at Rochester High School. It was there that the grandeur of this monumental national struggle first enthralled me. Ever since, its abiding presence has kept me exploring its exhilarating, inexhaustible record.

Beyond the fascination of the Civil War's memorable battles and captivating leaders lie the beguiling stories of the volunteers in the ranks, those whose dedication to their oaths and their principles sustained a frightful national upheaval for four long years.

I often wondered how this searing experience had affected those who at that time inhabited my own city and county. I began to find an answer when, five years ago, a reader brought into our newspaper office an evocative photograph.[1]

In it are ghostly images from the past, 63 survivors of the 87th Indiana Regiment who have become aged and gray-whiskered. They stand with military precision in four rows, proudly erect and gazing into the camera with a bit of their old wartime defiance. One man in front is missing a leg but balances firmly on his crutch, an unmistakable symbol of the regiment's sacrifices.

The grizzled veterans were gathered at the Fulton County Courthouse in Rochester for one of their regular regimental reunions. It was September 19, 1907, the 44th anniversary of deadly Chickamauga where the 87th had distinguished itself at the price of many of its lives.

Here, suddenly, were the men whom I had yearned to discover and never expected to find in such an intimate setting. I was captivated by the sight of them and I determined to learn more about their experiences. I soon found that while the 87th Indiana participated in the war's most decisive actions in the West, its part never had been thoroughly chronicled.[2] I began seeking written memories of these warriors for there, I thought, I also might know their personalities.

Four years of research have disclosed diaries, journals, letters and memoirs of the regiment's men, some never before revealed, others largely forgotten since their conception.[3] If my story of the 87th Indiana's contributions to the Union victory is of any interest or importance, it is because of these personal recollections. My greatest hope is to be able to show the regiment's human qualities along with its military achievements.

One account was discovered that described the 87th Indiana as being among the war's most versatile regiments: good at front line fighting as at Chickamauga; good at building (or tearing up) roads, railroads and bridges as it did from Kentucky to North Carolina; and, finally, good at living off the country as it was required to do on the epic marches through Georgia and the Carolinas.[4] High praise, indeed, and reason enough for its story being told if that were all.

This telling, though, tries to show more: how the rural Hoosiers of the 87th rose to the supreme test of their lives, a nation-threatening war; how their hearts were touched by the fires of that war's intensity and how their steadfast devotion to the Union cause earned them the empathy and gratitude of succeeding generations.

LAKE MANITOU
ROCHESTER, INDIANA
AUGUST, 1996

ACKNOWLEDGMENTS

In particular: to Jack Hogan, who brought forth the photograph that started it all; to Judge Wendell and Jean Tombaugh, whose inspired newspaper research led me to so much of value; to Robert Bailey and David Bailey, for allowing me to share Great-Grandpa Jonas Myers' diary and letters, and to the late Marguerite Miller, who almost 90 years ago had the good sense to capture and preserve those priceless memories of Fulton County's pioneer settlers.

And also, Fulton County Historian Shirley Willard, David Ewick, Leslie Damas, and Krystal Smith of Fulton County Library, Joanna Smith, Mary Moore, Mr. and Mrs. Fred Keim, all of Rochester, Ind.; Ruth Davis, Talma, Ind.; Janece Rouch Herrold, Grass Creek, Ind.; George Sweet, Miami, Fla.; John Palmer, Local History, St. Joseph County Public Library, South Bend, Ind.; Carol Pickerl, Copshaholm Museum, Northern Indiana Historical Society, South Bend, Ind.; A. Wilson Greene, executive director, Pamplin Park Civil War Site, Petersburg, Va.; James Ogden III, chief historian, and Doug Towne, assistant, Chickamauga National Battlefield Park, Ga.; Barney Thompson, reference desk, Indiana State Library, Indianapolis; Eric L. Mundell, Paul Brockman and Alexandra S. Gressitt, William Henry Smith Memorial Library, Indiana State Historical Society, Indianapolis; Glenda Brown, Jasper County Public Library, Rensselaer, Ind.; Jan Handy, LaPorte County Museum, LaPorte, Ind.; Mildred Kopis, Miami County Museum, Peru, Ind.; and Rodger Green, Whitehouse, Ohio.

You each helped me on this absorbing passage into a wondrous past.

The Journey of the 87th Indiana Into War and Back

A STUPENDOUS EFFORT

1
The Rebels Are Coming!

"We shall confidently expect to meet you on the Ohio," Gen. Braxton Bragg wrote to Maj. Gen. Edmund Kirby Smith, and from his lean and ragged Confederate soldiers Bragg exhorted determination: "Should the foe retire, we must follow him rapidly to his own territory and make him taste the bitters of invasion."[1]

With such ambitious rhetoric did two separate Southern armies invade Kentucky in August of 1862. Their object was twofold: secure this neutral border state for the Confederacy and gain an Ohio River base from which to take the war into Indiana and Ohio.

Out of such immediate peril to its state was created the 87th Infantry Regiment of Indiana Volunteers, which until war's end served the cause of the Union's preservation with high distinction but has not received the attention it deserves. Charting its course and analyzing its place in the momentous events of the ensuing 34 months are the objects of all that follows.

The Kentucky invasion notwithstanding, the time had arrived in the mid-summer of 1862 for the North to take seriously this Secession of the Southern States. Not many were calling it the Civil War; that would be for more dispassionate observers. On the Indiana home front, it was simply The Rebellion, perpetrated by "fiendish traitors who forced this issue upon us," whose treason should "be forever crushed" to deliver the nation from "overthrow and destruction."[2]

In this second August of the 16-month-old conflict, the military situation of the North was bleak. The Confederate Army of Northern Virginia had taken on a new commander, Gen. Robert E. Lee, and under his direction it had driven back the North's Army of the Potomac from the very gates of Richmond, the Southern capital. Union forces, directed so irresolutely by Maj. Gen. George McClellan, were huddled against the banks of the James River, awaiting transport back to Washington. Soon Lee, in his turn, would threaten the Northern capital.

Within the vast reaches of the war's Western theatre, Brig. Gen. Ulysses S. Grant had emerged from obscurity in February with his capture of Forts Henry and Donelson in western Kentucky. In January another of the Union's rising field commanders, Brig. Gen. George H. Thomas, won the battle of Mill Springs in eastern Kentucky. Together, these two victories cleared Kentucky of Confederates, opened the Tennessee capital of Nashville to Federal occupation and gave the Union access to the South's interior by way of the Cumberland and Tennessee Rivers.

Optimism turned to horror in early April, however. Gen. Albert Sidney Johnston gathered the scattered Rebel forces and surprised Grant's army near the log church of Shiloh on the Tennessee River near the Mississippi border. Two days of savage bloodletting ensued in which Grant's men barely escaped with victory. Each side counted more than 10,000 in killed, wounded and missing; Johnston himself was among the dead. Those were more casualties than the country could count from all its previous battles. The nation was shocked and the idea of a negotiated peace vanished. Neither side would speak any longer about an easy conquest.

President Abraham Lincoln confirmed the rising belief that putting down the stubborn insurrection was going to be a grim task, for on July 2 he called for 300,000 volunteers to serve for three years.

In northern Indiana that was welcome news to many. Corydon E. Fuller, publisher of the *Rochester Chronicle,* wrote that "the government is at last awaking to the stupendous proportions of the rebellion and to the effort necessary for its suppression. . . . War is to be the Nation's profession for the next few months. . . . It becomes every man to immediately place his business in such a situation that he can leave it."

Despite their setback at Shiloh, the Confederates were not finished with their designs upon Kentucky, a state that while officially neutral was composed of a bitterly divided populace whose young men were wearing both blue and gray. Kentuckians were an exotic mix of the two sides' warring principles. They possessed a strong leaning toward the Union but a contented acceptance of slavery and a deep aversion to any trend toward racial equality.[3]

Kentucky was the bedrock of the Federal government's Border State concerns. To lose it, said President Lincoln, "is nearly the same as to lose the whole game . . . we would as well consent to separation at once, including the surrender of this capital (Washington)." He meant that Kentucky's loss very likely would cause the other slave-holding Border States of Missouri, Maryland and Delaware to leave the Union.

The stakes were high in this particular game and the South still had one card left. Braxton Bragg would play it and thereby bring Indiana's 87th Infantry Regiment into its first battle action.

Bragg's Mexican War comrade and good friend, Confederate President Jefferson Davis, gave him command of the Army of Mississippi after its Shiloh defeat. A 45-year-old West Point graduate and native of North Carolina, Bragg won three citations for bravery as a captain of artillery in the Mexican War. Between wars he became a plantation owner in Louisiana. Tall and bearded with a grizzled, ungainly appearance, he was such a harsh disciplinarian that few of his troops either admired or respected him. Irritable and quarrelsome, he was unpopular with his peers and had few friends. Perhaps this failing partly was due to his chronic migraine headaches. In any case, these frictions with fellow officers often affected execution of his usually well-laid military maneuvers. Historian Bruce Catton described Bragg "as singular a mixture of solid competence and bewildering ineptitude as the war produced."[4]

Now, as August began, Bragg was in Chattanooga to meet Edmund Kirby Smith and organize the thrust into Kentucky by their two armies. Kirby Smith, 38, from Florida, also was a West Pointer and a decorated veteran of the Mexican War who served with the Old Army on the Texas frontier. He had led a brigade at First Bull Run and was wounded in action. Smith had an independent command at Knoxville in East Tennessee but was so optimistic of success in the coming Kentucky campaign that he offered to serve under Bragg's command.[5]

Kirby Smith's 21,000-man Army of Kentucky moved out first, on August 13, advancing through Cumberland Gap and into eastern Kentucky.

The alarm bells rang.

Learning of the advance, Maj. Gen. Don Carlos Buell sent messages to the governors of Indiana, Illinois and Ohio to send new levies of troops to the defense of Louisville and Cincinnati.

Buell, the third major player in the drama now unfolding, had been a hero at Shiloh where he arrived with his Army of the Ohio in time to help Grant turn threatened defeat into victory on the second day.[6] He was an Ohioan who spent his boyhood at an uncle's home in Lawrenceburg, Ind. Like Bragg and Kirby Smith, he was a West Pointer cited for bravery in Mexico, where he was severely wounded. Still in the Army when the Civil War erupted, Buell was 44 years old and considered one of the Union's most able generals. The impending campaign, however, would destroy his reputation and end his military career.[7]

When word of Kirby Smith's march into Kentucky reached the Northern governors, fear spread throughout the Ohio River towns in Indiana, Illinois and Ohio. Martial law was declared in southern Indiana and in Cincinnati. The militias were called out and earthworks were thrown up hastily by merchants, clerks and laborers. Artillery was assembled and supplies gathered.[8]

Oliver P. Morton, Indiana's wartime governor, reacted with his usual decisiveness to Buell's call for troops to oppose the invaders. On August 15 his General Order 71 directed that one regiment be organized in each of the state's 11 Congressional Districts "from such men as may offer." Within three weeks all 11 regiments, numbered from the 79th through the 89th, had been mustered in and sent off to the fronts.[9]

Some of these untrained and poorly equipped Hoosiers were rushed to the Cincinnati defenses at Covington across the river in Kentucky. These were the 80th, organized at Princeton; the 84th, from Richmond; the 85th, from Terre Haute, and the 86th, from Lafayette. Their presence was needed for on August 30 at Richmond, Ky., 110 miles south of Cincinnati, a hastily assembled army of 6,500 similarly green troops, mostly other Hoosiers,[10] were crushed by Kirby Smith's invaders.

It was perhaps the most decisive victory ever scored in the entire war. Maj. Gen. William Nelson, himself wounded, suffered casualties of 1,050 in killed and wounded along with 4,303 captured, an astounding loss of 75 percent of his force. Their sacrifice bought time to build up Cincinnati's defenses, however, as Kirby Smith moved north to the Bluegrass country at Lexington and ever closer to the river.

On August 28, the exact day that the 87th Indiana Infantry Regiment was organizing at South Bend, Bragg left Chattanooga with 36,000 men of the Army of Mississippi and headed for the Bluegrass State. Buell had allowed the Rebels to launch their two-pronged invasion of Kentucky by keeping his Army of the Ohio stationary 35 miles southeast of Nashville.

It now was a race for Louisville, and Buell was not at all certain that he could win it.

Another of those 11 quickly raised Indiana regiments would give him some help. The 89th, organized at Wabash, was hurried off to Munfordville, 65 miles south of Louisville, to join the force of Col. John T. Wilder, owner of a foundry at Greensburg, Indiana. At Munfordville in mid-September, Wilder's 3,500 new recruits held off the Rebels for three days before surrendering.[11]

Bragg became more cautious. With Buell approaching him from the south, his provisions gone and none to be found in that barren region, he moved off northeast to Bardstown for the food his men so badly needed.

The way to Louisville was opened for Buell. There he headed, and there among his reinforcements would be the 87th Indiana Infantry Regiment, now formed and ready for its journey into Civil War distinction.

2

An Army
of Volunteers

T he 87th Regiment of Indiana Volunteers represented six of the 14 counties in the Ninth Congressional District of northwest Indiana: Fulton, Jasper, LaPorte, Miami, Pulaski and St. Joseph.[1] Nine of its 10 companies came together and were placed into regimental order at South Bend on August 26, 1862.[2] On the war's Eastern front that day a large Union army under Maj. Gen. John Pope was about to engage Gen. Robert E. Lee's Army of Northern Virginia near Washington. By August 30 this Second Battle of Bull Run had become just like First Bull Run, a Union disaster.

The 87th's men were needed more urgently on the Western front at Louisville, however. They were dispatched immediately to Indianapolis where, on August 31, they were mustered into Federal service for three years and then sent to Kentucky.

A total of 1,262 men served in the regiment, 945 of them present at its formation. At war's end 34 months later, 466 were casualties or 37 percent of the total. Of that number 268 died in the field and only 313 of the original muster, almost an exact third, were present at the mustering out.[3]

Who were they and how were they organized?

As in all infantry regiments, the 87th was composed of 10 companies identified by the letters A through K. The letter J was not used because its similarity to the letter I in writing dispatches and records would cause confusion.[4] Each company was led by three commissioned officers of captain, first lieutenant and second lieutenant, and 13 non-commissioned officers of first or orderly sergeant, four duty sergeants and eight corporals.[5] Companies, by and large, were recruited from the same city or county so the men could serve with friends or acquaintances.

The 87th's soldiers came from small towns or from farms, for the Indiana of 1862 still was a rural society with no city over 20,000 and just three with 10,000 or more. Indianapolis, the state capital, had but 18,611 inhabitants in the 1860 census, followed by New Albany with 12,647 and Evansville with 11,484. LaPorte was the largest city in the six counties that produced the regiment and its population was only 5,028.[6]

The men of the 87th were young, as are most of those who fight in wars, but not as young as those cocksure youths who volunteered with a rush of patriotic fervor in '61. The volunteers of mid-1862, by and large, were the community's more substantial citizens, having become soberly convinced of the nation's danger of disintegration and who were leaving wives, children and businesses to help thwart it. Many were articulate as well as literate, as we shall learn when they speak to us through their diaries, journals and letters.

A majority of the 87th was right off the farms, to be sure, since fully one-third of all Northern farmers went into uniform, but there also were physicians, attorneys, newspaper editors, building contractors, grocers and real estate agents. Tradesmen such as coopers, butchers, shoemakers, millers, harnessmakers, stonecutters, printers and carpenters also put on uniforms, as did laborers, draymen and clerks. The 87th Regiment mirrored all of America's wartime armies in that it was a cross-section of its society.[7]

Company A was recruited in Jasper County and was captained by Edwin Hammond of Rensselaer. The enlisted men came from county seat Rensselaer and from Pleasant Grove, Francesville, Valparaiso, Brook, Kokomo, Adriance, Cathcart, Remington, Monticello, Monrovia, Canada, and Frankton in Indiana, and also from Joliet, Ill.; Peekskill, N.Y. and Black Rock Falls, Wis.

Company B originated in Pulaski County; its captain was James Selders of Winamac, the county seat. Hometowns of the men in ranks were Winamac, Star City, Francesville, Oak, Logansport, Bruce Lake, Columbus and Maxinkuckee.

Company C came out of Miami County with Henry Calkins of county seat Peru as captain. Its enlisted men were from Peru, Mexico, Chili, Xenia and Gilead.

Company D was made up entirely of Rochester area men with William Wood of that Fulton County seat town as captain.

Company E also originated in Fulton County; Alfred Jackson of Kewanna was its captain. The enlisted men came from Kewanna, Bruce Lake, Logansport, Winamac, Blue Grass, Star City, Metea, Fulton and Plymouth.

Company F was the second to be entirely recruited from Rochester with Asa Plank as captain.

Company G was recruited in LaPorte County and had Alanson Bliss of LaPorte, the county seat, as captain. Its men were from LaPorte, Michigan City, Door Village, Rochester, New Carlisle, Callao, New Durham, Waterford, New Carlisle, Plainfield, Rolling Prairie, Peru, South Bend, Tyner City and Williamsport in Indiana, and also from Almond, N.Y.

Company H also originated in LaPorte County. Richard Sabin of Union Mills was its captain. Hometowns of its enlisted men were Union Mills, Chili, Westville, Pawpaw, Unionville, Brookston, Bradford, Monticello, Rensselaer, Peru, Burnettsville and Logansport.

Company I was the third company to be organized in LaPorte County. Its captain was James Crawley of LaPorte. The soldiers came from LaPorte, Hannah Station, Lowell, Wanatah, Bigelow's Mills, Knox, Tippecanoe, Francesville, Washington, Crown Point, Morgan Station, Rolling Prairie, Union Mills, Westville, New Carlisle and North Bend in Indiana, and also from Kankakee City, Ill.

Company K, the last, came out of St. Joseph County with John Wheeler of Mishawaka as captain. Its men were from Lawrenceburg, Mishawaka, Elkhart, county seat South Bend, Rensselaer, Nineveh, Goshen, Bremen, Tyner City, Deep River, Logansport, North Liberty and New Carlisle in Indiana, and also from Marion, Iowa; Adrian, Mich.; Pleno, Ill.; and Hillsdale, Mich.[8]

Some of these small towns were mere villages or settlements and have since disappeared.

Regimental field officers were colonel, lieutenant colonel and major. Staff officers were a surgeon with major rank, two assistant surgeons and a chaplain as captains, and an adjutant and quartermaster as first lieutenants. The adjutant was the colonel's administrative aide, while the quartermaster was in charge of maintaining the regiment's food, clothing and equipment. The non-commissioned staff consisted of a sergeant-major, quartermaster-sergeant, commissary-sergeant, hospital steward and principal musician.[9]

At authorized strength a regiment consisted of 39 commissioned officers and a maximum of 1,025 enlisted men to a minimum of 845. Since it was the Union's Civil War practice to organize recruits into new units, the strength of a regiment during its service steadily declined from death, disease and desertion.[10]

The 87th Indiana entered the war with a blustery 52-year-old Rochester attorney, Kline G. Shryock, as its colonel. He had no previous military experience but neither did any of his peers. However, his county of Fulton supplied the regiment with 300 men in three companies (D, E, and F), the largest number of any of the six counties involved. Also, Shryock at the time was judge of the common pleas court for five counties and thus possessed some political clout that came in handy in his selection. The petition for his appointment, in the end, was signed by all captains and lieutenants of the regiment except three who were absent.[11] Newell Gleason of LaPorte was appointed lieutenant colonel, and Thomas Sumner of Plymouth was named major. The regiment, like all others, would see extensive changes among its officers, from lieutenants up to colonel, during the course of the war.

This was a regiment of volunteers as, indeed, the Union Army was an army of volunteers, unique not only for that but also because its recruits came forth to defend an abstract principle of government. Only later did slavery's abolishment become a war aim that was accepted by some, but by no means all, Federal soldiers. During the war's four-year course there were more than 2.3 millon three-year enlistments, some encouraged by the cash bounties first offered in this year of 1862. At the South's surrender in April 1865, the Union army numbered over one million, of which only 52,000 had been drafted. It was an exceptional achievement in enlistments for the North's 23 million population.[12]

By joining Indiana's volunteers, the 87th Regiment was helping Indiana compile a record of manpower contribution to the Union cause that was unequalled by any other Northern state. At war's end 196,363 Hoosiers of military age had served, an astonishing 65.5 percent of the 300,000 eligible. Deaths among them totaled 26,672 from all causes, or 13.6 percent; 7,243 of those were in battle.[13] Indiana raised 140 regiments over the course of the war, 126 of which were infantry.[14]

This performance wiped out the stain that had marred the history of Indiana's military volunteers, transforming it into an obscure historical footnote. At the 1847 Battle of Buena Vista during the Mexican War, the Second Indiana Infantry Regiment was accused by Commanding General Zachary Taylor of retreating in disorder in the face of the enemy. A court of inquiry later found this to be substantially untrue, but Taylor never retracted or modified his report and Hoosiers were indignant at this "dishonor of a whole state." Their reaction may have played a part in Taylor's loss of Indiana in his successful presidential campaign of 1848.[15]

The facts of the matter appear to support the volunteers, if not their officers, and the story contains some unusual aspects. Although it was a Northern state not influenced by the economic motives that pushed Southern states to support the war with Mexico, Indiana in four weeks provided enough volunteers to staff five regiments. (Indiana's volunteer regiments in the Civil War thus began numbering with the Sixth).

Only the Second and Third Regiments got into any action in Mexico. Their principal officers were political creatures who either were incompetent or passionately hated each other. Just before the Buena Vista battle, for example, the colonel of the Third Regiment, James Lane, formed his regiment on the parade ground. His enemy Joseph Lane (no relation), the brigade's commanding general, was present and the two soon got into a shouting match. It ended with a fist in the face of the general, who left to get a loaded rifle and go after the colonel. The men in the ranks rose to the defense of their colonel and threatened to shoot down the general, who finally was pacified. Neither officer was disciplined.

The Second Regiment was sent into the Buena Vista action. Its colonel, William Bowles, was a physician who was spending more time collecting botanical specimens than drilling his troops. The regiment of 360 was coolly returning the Mexicans' fire when Bowles inexplicably ordered them to retreat. He repeated it twice until the men finally began falling back, in small groups and then in a rout. The colonel had become hysterical, pure and simple. Later, he was so humiliated by his act that he picked up a rifle and fought as a private.

Eventually all but 15 or so of the shattered Second Indiana recovered and fought hard to save the day for the Americans. Serving with distinction on that field were Col. Jefferson Davis and his Mississippi Rifles regiment and Capt. Braxton Bragg and his artillery batteries. Their friendship would carry over to the Confederacy, with ominous results.

Gen. Taylor maintained afterward that only a handful of the Second Indiana had remained on the field to fight. The court of inquiry absolved Col. Bowles of cowardice, found that most of the Second Indiana had indeed been rallied and that the Third Indiana came on to help repel a final charge by Mexican lancers. The crusty Taylor still would not take back his remarks, some say because he wanted Davis, his son-in-law, to have all the battle's credit.[16]

Leaving aside such lingering Mexican War controversies, in the Civil War no Northern state exceeded the zeal or the performance of Indiana's sons and in their passion lies the riddle of man's irresistible attraction to war. It stems from many sources: patriotism, boredom, a manifestation of one's courage, commitment to home, family and to a way of life and, as mentioned, a dedication in our Civil War to the abstract principle of national union.

There are other reasons to consider, too.

Oliver Wendell Holmes, Jr. survived a bullet through the neck at Antietam to become one of the U.S. Supreme Court's most eminent jurists. Speaking at a Memorial Day address in 1884, Holmes explained to his audience that he and his fellow Civil War veterans "shared the incommunicable experience of war. We have felt, we still feel, the passion of life to its top. Our hearts were touched with fire." Justice Holmes' eloquence brings us close to the core of the question. A powerful motivation must have been, in that popular phrase of the day, the chance "to see the elephant," to live life's most personal adventure, to have war's incommunicable experience.

There is a less romantic, but perhaps more realistic, view of why Civil War soldiers enlisted in such numbers. Thousands of men in the 1860s were filled with a pent-up emotional energy, almost animalistic in nature, that could find no outlet. Their America was a troubled land and did not offer the boundless opportunities that later came to be identified with it. Only in the war did such men see their chance for fulfillment.[17] For many of the men this yearning for fulfillment was driven in large measure by its companion, ambition. If one could attain significant personal achievement during this great national crisis, unlimited postwar prominence and success might follow.

Sometimes sudden impulse propelled a man into uniform, too. Jacob Wright was plowing at his family's farm in Fulton County on August 11, 1862, when he reached the end of a furrow. He tied his horses to the fence and was on his way to the house when he saw a wagonload of volunteers going to camp at South Bend. The 29-year-old Wright got into the wagon, went along and joined Company D of the 87th Regiment. He did not see his team or his home again until war's end.[18]

There were those like George Morgan, too young to enlist but so determined to do so that they lied about their age. Morgan was 14 1/2 when he sauntered up to the recruiting officer at Rensselaer and announced that he was 18 years old. The officer handed him an enlistment blank, probably with an indulgent smile, and Morgan was taken into Company A. He served the rest of the war without injury, wound or sickness. The young man also developed a talent at dice and card games, returning home with a snug bankroll.[19]

Public meetings where speakers appealed to young men's patriotism also could be effective. Henry Clay Green, an 18-year-old farm boy from near Kewanna in Fulton County, attended such a rally in the county seat of Rochester in August 1862 and "became convinced that nothing would conduce me so much to my happiness and boyhood pride as the life of a soldier. I then and there made a promise to myself that at the very next opportunity I would volunteer my services to my country." That he did, on August 9, enlisting as a private in Company E.[20]

Whatever personal motivation was impelling them, recruits began to fill nine companies of what would become the 87th Indiana Infantry Regiment during the first week of August 1862. They came from a variety of sources. Some already had joined military units and were sworn into state service under the reorganized Indiana militia law of 1861. They elected their officers and had begun drilling when the army called. Other men were attracted by their acquaintance with or by the reputation of a capable local person who was organizing a company and would be its captain. Recruiting stations often were set up at the local post office from where the martial music of a fife and drum attracted crowds and stimulated enlistments.

Although the Northern states were responsible for raising the first troops, Congress quickly offered its help by voting in July 1861 to pay bounties for three-year enlistments. These three-year men, such as the 87th Indiana, received $100 that was paid over a period of time rather than in a lump sum.

Over the four-year course of the war, the six counties which supplied men for the 87th Indiana Regiment produced 12,317 volunteers. That represented 16 percent of their total 1860 population of 77,368, but 70 percent of those in the military age bracket of 18 to 45.

Following Gov. Oliver P. Morton's August 15 order for the immediate formation of 11 regiments to help repel the Confederates from Kentucky, nine of the 10 companies that would make up the 87th Indiana began assembling. They were summoned to Camp Rose, the organizational point for the Ninth Congressional District's contribution to this manpower call.

Camp Rose was a mile northwest of the center of the small town of South Bend, occupying the St. Joseph County Fairgrounds. During the war two other Indiana regiments were organized there, the 73rd and the 99th.[21]

Companies trickled in over the course of the month. Transportation of troops to any given point in the Indiana of 1862 could be a complicated matter because the construction of the state's railroad network was in its infancy, having begun only 14 years before.

Peter Keegan, a 29-year-old Irish immigrant and shoemaker, enlisted as a private with Company C at the Miami County Seat town of Peru. His company first traveled west to Logansport on the Wabash Railroad, then boarded the Great Western to South Bend. The company arrived at the camp at midnight and had no blankets, so Keegan started his military career with a severe head cold.[22]

Daniel Bruce, 26, left a wife, daughter and farm at Bruce Lake near the Pulaski County seat of Winamac on August 11 when he enlisted in Company E at nearby Kewanna in Fulton County. The company included many of Bruce's friends and seven of his relatives, including brother-in-law Alfred Hizer and six cousins: the Troutman brothers, Peter, John and James; Hiram and Henry Rairick and Philip Obermayer.[23]

A neighbor and staunch Union man, John Shelton, provided dinner for all 94 of the company, after which friends and neighbors drove them to Winamac in 65 wagons. There they boarded the train that took them north through Valparaiso to spend the night at the junction of Ainsworth near Lake Michigan. No supper was offered, so Bruce and his buddies did their first foraging (which Bruce always referred to as "drafting") and solved the problem by appropriating a calf and 12 geese and chickens. Armies were not bashful in such matters, North or South.

Tuesday, August 12, was the same story. There was no breakfast when Company E returned to the rail cars at 8 A.M. for the four-hour trip to South Bend. The men marched into camp, were bivouacked at an Oddfellows Hall but got no supper, either. The realities of army life were beginning to sink in.

The two-week stay at Camp Rose while the regiment was filling up apparently proved pleasant enough in the end. Pvt. Keegan thought so, particularly remembering speeches of congratulations and good wishes that were made to the troops by prominent local politicians, among them Republican Congressman Schuyler Colfax of South Bend and Charles Cathcart of LaPorte, a former Congressman and a Democrat.

Bruce diligently kept a diary until war's end with entries almost every day. It gives a personal glimpse into the recruits' first days as soldiers. Examinations for those wishing to become sergeants were held the day after arrival and by Saturday of that week the company was sworn into service for "sustaining the government." By now there was plenty to eat and on Saturday they even enjoyed a picnic provided by South Bend women. "The amount of folks I never saw before," wrote a marveling Bruce. Monday, August 18, officers began drilling the men in military maneuvers and tactics, three hours of it. Two more companies arrived Monday night, when Bruce was put on night guard duty for the first time, two hours on and four hours off. Folks from home sent along a wagonload of clothing and quilts and blankets. Letters were written and received, Sunday sermons given.

Passes into town were possible after a few days. Bruce got a haircut there and also with a friend had his silhouette image cut by a paper artist. The military life was not agreeing with everyone, for by Sunday, August 24, there were 25 from the camp in the hospital. Philip Anderson of Bruce's company went to the guard house for "drafting" some honey, but evidently was the only one of several to get caught at it.

Many friends and relatives from Winamac and Kewanna were among the large audience of admirers Tuesday, August 26, when the regiment was marched in parade style and then told to be ready at 5 o'clock the next morning to depart for Indianapolis. Afterward the men engaged in various kinds of sporting activities for the rest of the day.

The regiment was up at 2 A.M. and on the cars at 6 A.M. on Wednesday, August 27. The train chugged westward to Michigan City, went south on the Monon Railroad to Lafayette and then via the Big Four to Indianapolis where the 87th slept in the carbarn without having had dinner or supper.

Thursday, August 28, found the regiment north of downtown Indianapolis at Camp Morton, which had been transformed from the Indiana State Fairgrounds.[24] Tents were put up, tables constructed and, at last, a meal of meat, bread and coffee was passed out.

Saturday the regiment marched into Indianapolis and in solemn ceremony was presented with the American flag made for it by women in South Bend. The equally new 89th Indiana Regiment, out of Wabash, had departed for its sacrificial holding action and capture at Munfordville, so the 87th was given the 89th's vacated barracks.

There was yet one loose end for Daniel Bruce to tie up. His father, Abraham, came to spend the night at Camp Morton and discuss arrangements for Daniel's farm, which Abraham agreed to oversee during his son's absence. The Bruces were among the first settlers in the Fulton-Pulaski County area; Daniel's grandfather, Stephen, brought his family there in 1837.

Sunday, August 31, nine of the regiment's 10 companies were mustered into Federal service for three years (Company I, the 10th, was not mustered until September 12).

The regiment was paid its bounty money, $25 toward the $100 promised, plus $1.50 for enlistment. Bruce also received his first month's private's pay of $13. He gave Abraham $10 to pay off some debts back home, then went into Indianapolis to buy a revolver, two pairs of socks, and needle and thread for the inevitable mending.

The 87th now was dispatched to the war front. The men spent all night Sunday in their railroad cars south of Indianapolis; it rained and there was no place to lie down. Early in the morning the hungry troops found boxes full of crackers in a warehouse and "drafted" all of them.

The journey began at 5 A.M. and ended nine hours later in Jeffersonville at 2 P.M. The regiment marched through the town to steamboats awaiting them on the Ohio River. Crossing to Louisville, the 87th tramped south for four miles on the dusty Lexington Turnpike and bivouacked on the Jefferson County Fairgrounds. They slept in the open because their baggage wagons had not yet arrived.

It now was Monday, September 1, and the 87th Indiana Infantry Regiment was near the war. The pitifully few Union troops who escaped August 30 from the disaster at Richmond 90 miles eastward were streaming back toward Louisville. What future plans the victorious Confederates of Edmund Kirby Smith were making was unknown. On that same day, Braxton Bragg's other invading Southern army was halfway through Tennessee, at Pikeville. Its destination most certainly was expected to be Louisville.

Daniel Bruce seemed awed and a little bit puzzled by his new situation. "The town (Louisville) seemed about half colored folks. We are now in rebel country." Not quite, for Louisville was prosperously pro-Union. Its slave-holding culture, however, did match the impression which these Indiana farmers, clerks and mechanics held of the Deep South.

The infantrymen of the 87th Indiana are about to be launched into their Civil War travails and triumphs. Before we accompany them, let us examine more closely the times and the society from which they came.

3
The Life
They Left Behind

Much later John Troutman remembered with keen nostalgia the abundance of wild game there was around his Fulton County home when he left it in 1862 to go to war as a corporal in Company E of the 87th Indiana Regiment.

The wide prairie extending westward from the county seat of Rochester to Troutman's Kewanna home teemed with ducks, geese, sandhill crane, prairie chickens and quail. There were six to 10 coveys of quail on almost every farm. Deer were almost everywhere and wild turkeys roamed in droves through the plentiful woods, which often resounded with the chatter of red, black and gray squirrels, the barking of foxes and the drumming of pheasant wings. In the autumn came the passenger pigeons, darkening the sky for hours before roosting in such numbers in the willow trees that branches broke from their weight. They were killed joyously and recklessly, by clubs as well as guns, in flight or while roosting. Fish were so plentiful they clogged mill wheels at Lake Manitou and were seined by the bushels from the Tippecanoe River.[1]

Troutman was not embellishing his memories. At that point in the 19th century northern Indiana had moved beyond its pioneer beginnings but still was a rural, agrarian and unsophisticated society whose development was lagging behind the state's central and southern portions. Its tier of 20 counties had an 1860 population of 286,000, roughly half that of each of the other sections. While commercial activity and manufacturing were putting some bustle into the villages and towns of the north, none of these were large; Fort Wayne, the biggest, had fewer than 10,000. Railroads did not yet reach into all counties. Wagon roads left much to be desired on the best of days and were virtually impassable in some seasons.

Farmland was being cleared steadily but still, in 1862, vast forest expanses of beech, walnut, oak and ash remained to shelter the wild game that Troutman remembered. Another impediment to the region's internal development was the huge swamplands of northwest Indiana; it would take 57 years, 8,200 miles of tile and 17,500 miles of drainage ditches to transform them to productive cropland.[2]

Northern Indiana was largely settled by immigrants from New York, Pennsylvania and Ohio whose political roots gave the region a pro-Union stance. In the six northern counties that produced the 87th Indiana, for example, 70 percent of the eligible men enlisted in the Union Army during the Civil War.

Fulton County's 9,416 inhabitants made it the fourth smallest of the 87th's six counties. However, it contributed almost a third of the regiment's 945 original volunteers: the entire companies of D and F, and all but 17 in E. That amounted to 300 men, who were followed into the 87th later by 56 more county citizens. LaPorte County, largest of the six with 22,784 population, also organized three companies but they were not filled as exclusively with local recruits as were the three from Fulton.

Being midway in size among the six counties while foremost in manning the regiment make Fulton County the proper choice, then, for a representative examination of the life and times of these soldiers who we are to follow through a convulsive war. Fulton County's location is midway among the group of six; LaPorte and St. Joseph are north at the Michigan border, Miami immediately south, Pulaski and Jasper to the west.

Fulton County was only 26 years old when its 87th Indiana recruits marched off determined to save the Union. It was organized in 1836, six years after the first white inhabitants arrived in the area of Lake Manitou and the nearby site of Rochester, which became the county seat. Construction of the Michigan Road from Indianapolis to Michigan City made the county accessible after 1832; removal of most of the indigenous Potawatomi Indians to Kansas in 1838 opened its lands to settlement by large numbers of immigrants from the East. Its 1840 population of 2,000 tripled by 1850 and by 1860 grew another 50 percent to 9,416.[3]

Seventeen percent of those 9,416 answered the nation's crisis call, an impressive ratio almost identical to that in each of the other five counties of the 87th Regiment. Fulton's 1,566 soldiers were made up of 1,510 volunteers and 56 who were drafted.[4] Nine companies of recruits eventually were organized in the county, the first leaving four months after Fort Sumter. Fulton County soldiers fought at Shiloh, Perryville, Vicksburg, Stones River, Chickamauga, Missionary Ridge, Mansfield, Atlanta, March to the Sea, the Carolinas, Franklin and Red River.

There was a local tradition for such patriotic, martial spirit. In 1847, only 11 years after Fulton County's founding, enough young men were eager to fight in far-off Mexico that a company was formed under the command of a local medical student, 18-year-old Albert Brackett. He and his remarkable family are a paradigm for 19th-century dedication to military service.[5]

Albert was one of seven Brackett brothers whose English Puritan ances-
tors fled to Massachusetts in the 17th century and whose two grandfathers
fought in the Revolutionary War. He had come to Rochester early in 1847
to study medicine with brother Lyman, the county's second doctor. Lyman
died of pneumonia at age 28 in the spring of that year and by June Albert
was caught up in the Mexican War fever. He recruited the aforementioned
company and took it to Mexico as its first lieutenant, joining the Fourth
Indiana Regiment that missed all the major actions.

From the family home in Cherry Valley of central New York, two other
Brackett brothers came to Rochester to succeed the late Lyman in the practice of medicine. They were James and Charles.

In April 1861, immediately after the outbreak of the war, Charles recruited a company of 80 men from Fulton County and became its captain
at age 37. The state's volunteer quota was full by the time the company
reported, so Charles became assistant surgeon of the First Indiana Cavalry
in order to get into the fight. He later joined brothers Albert and James in
the Ninth Illinois Cavalry, serving as surgeon in Missouri and Arkansas
until his death from illness at Helena, Ark., in February 1863, refusing to
the last to leave his post.

Albert was made for a military career. His regiment served in Mexico
with Lane's Brigade, commanded by the same Joseph Lane of Indiana who
was involved in the parade ground fisticuffs earlier in our story. After
Mexico, Albert became a fourth Dr. Brackett and practiced a few years in
Logansport, south of Rochester. Curiously, however, he asked a superior
in 1862 to omit from his biography any reference to his involvement in
medicine. "It is unsoldierlike and I do not like it," he wrote. Brackett left
his despised medicine in 1855 to return to the army and became captain of
the newly formed Second U.S. Cavalry that was sent to Texas to fight Indians, which he did with distinction.

Albert Brackett's colleagues in the Second Cavalry during those prewar
days included many who later were prominent on both sides of the Civil
War. His commander was Col. Albert Sidney Johnston, who was killed com-
manding the Confederates at Shiloh. The second in command was Lt. Col.
Robert E. Lee of enduring Confederate fame. Other officer comrades were
the future Confederate generals William Hardee, Edmund Kirby Smith,
Earl Van Dorn and Fitzhugh Lee; and Union generals George H. Thomas,
George Stoneman and Innis Palmer.

Albert became colonel of the Ninth Illinois Volunteer Cavalry soon after
the Civil War began, serving with brothers James and Charles as we have
seen. He later wrote books about his Mexican War experience and of the
history of the U.S. Cavalry. Albert died in Washington in 1896 and was
buried at Arlington National Cemetery.

An older brother, Capt. John E. Brackett, was a graduate of West Point
who had resigned his commission when President James K. Polk recalled

him for a singular mission: captain of a New York regiment to be sent to California before the end of the Mexican War and become somewhat of an army of occupation there when that war was successfully concluded. After the war ended, John made many friends among the native Mexican landowners. At the 1849 state convention to decide if California would seek admission to the Union as a free or a slave state, his influence with the Mexican delegates helped hold them firm and tip the balance toward freedom. Such was the credit given him in a family memoir written by his U.S. Army nephew, also a John and a physician. Capt. Brackett died at age 43 in 1855.

These, to be sure, were men of value and if few families could match the Bracketts in family military performances, Jacob Strong of Akron could surpass them in quantity. He sent all four of his sons into the Union army and got all four of them back. There also were plenty of individuals ready to show they had the Bracketts' kind of mettle.

William Wood, a 43-year-old farmer near Akron east of Rochester, had been of a military mind since 1856 when he organized and drilled the county's first militia. [6] In the spring of 1862 he captained another such militia, the Rochester Home Guards, which became the core of Company D of the 87th Indiana. Wood served as its captain through the battle of Perryville, after which he resigned because of an illness that caused his premature death in 1866.

Peter Troutman, 29, had given up farming for teaching school when he joined Company E of the 87th at Kewanna in Union Township, where members of his family had been the first settlers. Troutman was elected first lieutenant of the company but by November had become its captain upon the resignation of Alfred Jackson. His courageous leadership at Chickamauga, during the Atlanta campaign and on the March to the Sea was outstanding.

Horace Long, a Rochester shoemaker like his father, was 25 years old when he enlisted as a musician in the 36th Indiana in September 1861. Four months later he was discharged when all regimental bands were eliminated by Maj. Gen. Don Carlos Buell. Six months afterward he joined Company F of the 87th as first sergeant, advancing to lieutenant and then to captain. He led the company through Chickamauga and at Missionary Ridge in exemplary fashion.

Asa Plank, 35, was Rochester's first druggist and although his business was thriving, he felt a duty to join the fight. He recruited Company F of the 87th and was its captain through Perryville. Company F's roster reflected the seriousness of the community's attitudes toward the war by mid-1862. Wrote the *Rochester Chronicle:* "We think this company contains much the largest proportion of men in the prime of life of any (of the six) that has left us. Many of our best citizens are in its ranks as privates, men who have left a good business and pleasant homes for the privations of camp." [7]

Life could be pleasant, even if its comforts were primitive by today's standards and diseases such as typhoid fever, scarlet fever, ague, smallpox and diphtheria were ever-present threats to one's existence. The times were simpler than today, but friendships perhaps were more gregarious. The future seemed bright to most people if only the damnable question of secession and slavery could be settled.

Rochester, the county seat, had been incorporated as a town only nine years before and contained 650 inhabitants; not counted were six colored.[8] Even smaller were the county's villages of Kewanna, Akron, Fulton and Bloomingsburg; other settlements such as Tiosa, Green Oak, Bruce Lake, Mill Ark and Blue Grass served some of the needs of the isolated rural areas. Rochester was still a wooden village, had not yet taken on much refinement and without a railroad still was rather remote. Cows, pigs and horses roamed at will among its streets, which were choked in many places with uncontrolled weeds. There was but one brick building in the town, the Fulton County Courthouse at the central square, and south of it were cornfields. Fire was an ever-present threat to property; when one broke out, citizens by the scores tried to keep it from spreading by throwing on buckets of water. Public health controls were a thing of the future; drinking water often was contaminated and sewers or septic systems didn't exist.

Commerce was beginning to thrive. One could buy almost anything at the several general stores, from groceries to clothing to hardware—even fresh oysters. There were jewelers, shoe merchants, druggists and saddle-harness makers. Industrially, there were an iron forge mining its own ore, a woolen factory, flour mills and grist mills and small factories making wagons, buggies, buckboards, plows, kettles and iron castings of many kinds. [9]

Professionally, the citizens had a choice among attorneys and physicians; dentists came through from time to time, as well. No banks had been started yet and most people kept their wealth in gold coins. These were hidden at home and not always successfully. One Sunday robbers took $980 in gold from the Henry Bohls family east of town. Henry had hidden it in a chest of clothing.[10]

There was also entertainment. The Wallace House on the north side of town held weekly dances with such lively steps as in the cotillion and schottische; even in the rural precincts the neighbors got up a dance once a week, particularly in the winters. Tickets at the Wallace House affairs were 50 cents a couple, there were refreshments available in an adjoining ice cream "saloon," and at midnight supper was served. Men amused themselves with horse races, fist fights and dog fights and brewed themselves something they called "40-rod whiskey." It was said that this rotgut was made 10 years old in 10 days and was "brewed with dogleg tobacco, apple cores, copperas and other filth."[11] Whether anybody died from drinking it was not recorded.

Men yearned for such relaxation because work on the farm was hard and unrelenting. It was no wonder that when youths left home, they never got homesick, said one who recalled those days. Women's lives were filled with the drudgery of keeping house, helping on the farm when needed, cooking meals and raising children, but the women also found time for church and for visiting neighbors. This was a period of intense religious feelings and close friendships; people knew their neighbors intimately for miles around.

In the countryside the farmers planted wheat, corn, buckwheat, pumpkins, vegetables and flax, mainly with teams of oxen. Harvesting 20 bushels of wheat per acre was considered good. Grain was cut with a sickle or cradle, then threshed with a flail or tramped out by horses. Wild fruits of cranberries, swamp huckleberries, blackberries, strawberries, plums and grapes were plentiful. You could kill all the squirrels you needed in a couple of hours over a few acres.[12]

Land still was being cleared and board fencing erected. The Parish Stump Machine had been developed to help rid the ground of these stubborn obstacles; in that year in Union Township west of Rochester 800 stumps were taken out by June. There still was a wildness in the country, although by then most of the wolves and the droves of wild hogs that used to be so frequent in the thick woodlands were gone. Still to be accomplished, however, was the reclaiming of large areas of wet ground in the prairie southwest of Rochester. Not until after the war did extensive ditching finally end the battle with mud that mired cattle and horses and in springtime became a flood from which fish were speared.

The citizenry's major preoccupation was securing a railroad, a project the war interrupted and that would not be consummated until 1868 when the county first was connected with Plymouth and then in 1869 with Peru, hence with South Bend and Indianapolis. One of the leading promoters of extending the railroad was the chief engineer of the Cincinnati, Peru and Chicago line who visited Rochester several times before the war to conduct public meetings on the subject. As fate would have it, this was Newell Gleason of LaPorte who enlisted with the 87th Indiana Infantry as its lieutenant colonel and later became its colonel, leading it to the end of the war so capably that he won a brigadier general's star.

The outside world first reached Rochester and Fulton county in 1856 with the telegraph lines that were strung along the Michigan Road. There also was a daily mail coach at noon and the town had two weekly newspapers, the Republican-oriented *Chronicle* and the Democratic-slanted *Sentinel*. The 87th's soldiers pined for their newspapers' delivery at camps and thought the papers' news of home "worth gold."

Otherwise, travel was slow, not always dependable and sometimes dangerous. The road to Peru, for example, was uneven and rough; 2 1/2 hours was a good time for the 25 miles. Stagecoach lines reached Peru or Plymouth, from where trains headed south or north. The Peru stage left Rochester twice a week at 7 A.M., returning the next day. Hacks were for hire as well. You could get one to take you to Logansport for $2 but it also would result in "the jolting of all the breath from you." Highwaymen were another danger. Two attempted to stop the Plymouth stage in which Mrs. Charles Shryock and her infant son were riding in 1859 as it slowed to negotiate a swampy stretch. Vigorous whiplashing by the driver overcame the robbers that time.[13]

A new schoolhouse was built but funds were lacking to buy a bell for it. There also were select schools with independent teachers and private lessons for vocal or instrumental music, but some children attended neither. Those who did received a sound fundamental education in the three R's, as attested by letters home from the 87th Indiana soldiers.

Patriotism was in public vogue those days. Consider how Rochester enthusiastically celebrated the Fourth of July in 1862. The grand day was begun at 4 A.M. with the ringing of bells at the Courthouse, Firehouse and the Presbyterian and Methodist churches. At sunrise, a salute of 13 guns was fired. Citizens were asked to bring their contributions of food to the Methodist Church until 8 A.M. when all would be transported to the Fairgrounds on the town's south edge. The procession formed at 10 A.M. with band and colors in the fore, followed by officers of the day, the featured orator, reader and chaplain, then veterans of the War of 1812 and Mexican War. Last came the townspeople—men, women and children. The pomp, ceremony, orations and feasting consumed the rest of the day.[14] 'Such Independence Day panoply had begun in 1847 during the Mexican War and on that occasion even featured a Revolutionary War veteran, John Johnson.

Later in 1862, however, patriotism became a matter of interpretation when the nation went to war with itself. After the first rush of volunteering, enormous casualties from the Union army's disastrous defeats had an effect on morale at home and stiffened Democrats in their opposition to how the conflict was being conducted. Some Democrats agreed to end partisanship and joined Republicans to support the government. Most Democrats backed the war to preserve the Union but believed Republicans were threatening individual liberties by expanding government's powers. Then there were those Democrats flat-out against the war, favoring instead an armistice and reconciliation with a separated South, for in Southern Indiana were many citizens who were natives of states now in the Confederacy.

Indiana as a whole reflected these divergent opinions. In 37-year-old Gov. Oliver P. Morton, however, Indiana had one of the nation's most decisive and resourceful war governors, one who used any governmental means, legal or not, to defeat the Confederates. In October of 1862, just after the 87th Indiana emerged from its coming battle baptism in Kentucky, Democrats rode this tide of dissatisfaction in Indiana and into control of the General Assembly. However, when the Legislature convened in January 1863, Gov. Morton defied the Democrats, devised a series of loans from bankers and Washington to finance government, and for the next two years ruled the state as a benevolent dictator, standing firm for the war and for the Union.[15]

In Fulton County, where the entire Democratic county ticket was elected in 1862, it quite naturally followed that since most volunteer soldiers were Republicans, many of the men who stayed home were Democrats. They were found most generally in the rural areas of the county, particularly in Newcastle Township and its village of Bloomingsburg (now Talma). Their political deviltries and disturbances brought considerable anguish and anger to soldiers at the front when they learned what was happening back home. One 87th Indiana private called them "freedom-hating poltroons" upon hearing of the three incidents which follow.

In February 1863, the body of F.C. Hamlett of Newcastle Township arrived home for burial, three months after his death from illness with the 29th Indiana Regiment. What happened afterward exposes the animosity that existed between the two political factions.

The *Chronicle,* the Republican newspaper, was the first to report. "Cowardly Copperheads" of Newcastle Township, it wrote, believed Hamlett's coffin was not opened before its burial because it contained "arms for the Abolitionists." So 30 or 40 "cowardly Newcastle hyenas" took up rifles, dug it up and split it open with an axe despite remonstrances from the dead man's wife and brother. No arms were found. The *Chronicle* published names of the alleged offenders and sent the story to papers as far away as Nashville, Toledo and Chicago.

The *Sentinel,* a Democratic organ, responded that Hamlett's widow wanted the coffin opened but his brother had objected. She had no suspicion of arms being contained therein. This created so much interest that a delegation of Democrats, Republicans and Abolitionists removed the casket and found it did contain the soldier, according to The *Sentinel.* "It was not split by an axe, but was opened by a Republican," the paper reported, blaming the unreasonable and unexplainable opposition of the brother for the incident.

The widow settled the matter with a letter to the *Chronicle,* shaming the Southern sympathizers who had involved themselves. She wrote that she had wanted to see her husband's body but the casket could not be opened without damaging it so she agreed to burial. Later, a rumor did arise that the coffin contained arms but Mrs. Hamlett said she refused consent to disinterment, as also did her brother-in-law. "I said that if Gov. Morton would send us firearms, we could find a better place to put them than in the graveyard," she wrote. The deed was done anyway, despite the sign and flag the widow placed on the grave imploring them to desist. "They came to the graveyard with guns in their hands shouting for Jeff Davis and now they have the impudence to say it was all done through friendship." She named Ellis Strosnyder and Orange Meredith as the ringleaders. Such hostility outlasted the war many years.[16]

In the Betzner school neighborhood in eastern Fulton County southeast of Akron, young Levi Gaerte announced in early 1863 he would join the Union army. That aroused the Copperhead element thereabouts, whose members told Levi they'd kill him before they would allow him to enlist. An empty threat, Gaerte thought, until the night before he was to leave when a freshly dug grave appeared in the schoolyard with a note stating Levi would fill it in the morning. His entire family, with friends, stood guard all night at the Gaerte residence. Either it was a bluff or the show of force worked; the next day Levi went off to war unmolested.[17]

Then in June of 1863 came a rebellion in the county against the draft of soldiers. John Mow of Rochester, recently discharged from the 87th Indiana, arrived in Bloomingsburg as draft commissioner to register eligible men in Newcastle Township. He was met with angry opposition and two men confiscated his registration books. A telegraph message to Indianapolis brought quick reaction, for Gov. Morton did not brook such antagonism to the law or to the war. A company of the 71st Indiana Infantry was dispatched to Rochester, where its 100 soldiers arrived on a Tuesday and stopped at the Courthouse to load their muskets. But it was all sham resistance; when the company marched into Bloomingsburg, it was met with friendly townspeople and farmers. The soldiers remained on the scene until Sunday morning before returning to Indianapolis, being entertained meanwhile with a banquet and a ball.[18]

Those who opposed the draft made trouble needlessly, for Indiana was among the Northern states in which there were so many volunteers in 1863 that conscription was not necessary.

Nevertheless, opposition to the war remained so vigorous in Fulton County and its inhabitants became so polarized over the issue that by July 4, 1863, two separate Independence Day ceremonies were conducted. It was as if the nation already had split into two parts. Capt. Long of the 87th Regiment's Company F, who we shall come to know quite well, became indignant when he learned of it in a letter from his wife. In late July he replied to her from the regiment's camp in southern Tennessee with scorching words:

"I would have liked to come along with Company F and cleaned out both parties. I think that Fulton County is full of butternuts if they are bold enough to hold a celebration by themselves and do think the Union people real foolish and weak to let them. If it were not for a few, I wish Fulton County would sink down to the lower part of H--l."

Long went on to write that he had welcomed news of Confederate Gen. John Hunt Morgan's July cavalry raid into southern Indiana. "I hope that he (Morgan) will just raise Ned there and maybe it will bring some of the butternuts to their milk. And I wish (if it were not for my folks) that he would get up in Fulton County and burn about half of it up and see what kind of effect it would have on them. Maybe the people would feel like doing something then."[19]

Soldiers of the 87th Regiment kept a constant wary eye on how folks at home were supporting their efforts at putting down the rebellion and, as we shall learn as this narrative unfolds, were not backward in voicing their opinions and objections.

There is little evidence that Abolition was being discussed publicly in Fulton County at the time the regiment was organized, but assistance to runaway slaves through the Underground Railroad system was an accepted fact and had been going on since the late 1840s. One route through Fulton County to Canada for these frightened, hunted Negroes was over a secluded trail, after which they stayed overnight beneath straw in Dr. Joseph Sippy's barn at Akron. Another route took them toward Plymouth along the Peru road, stopping for the night in the basement of a house at Green Oak just south of Rochester.[20]

Public support for the Union was shown 10 days after Fort Sumter's bombardment at a mass meeting in the Courthouse at Rochester, where Judge Kline G. Shryock's resolution supporting the Union, its Constitution and enforcement of Congressional laws was passed without dissent. Three days later, at another such meeting, it also was resolved to support families of all who enlisted for the Union. Similar meetings were held about the same time in Akron, Kewanna and Fulton.

Aid became a critical issue for the many women who were to suffer during the absence of husbands, fathers and sons. Their valor in operating the family farm or business and caring for the children with little or no income often equalled the courage of men in uniform. Fulton County's able-bodied homefolks tried to help. In January 1863, volunteers hauled 83 loads of firewood to the families of absent soldiers, an exercise that was to be repeated yearly.[21] The county also established a relief agency to which such families could apply for assistance, but most had to be encouraged to do so; the concept of public welfare was unknown and acceptance of charity was considered ignoble.

Lt. Mark McAfee of the 87th's Company D, while in Rochester on furlough, was disturbed to learn that many of his regiment's families were destitute but were unwilling to accept relief and be thought of as being among the county's poor. McAfee considered such relief an honorable thing when it was necessary and he spent much of his time while at home trying to convince others.

The husbands and fathers in the 87th Indiana Regiment, now in Louisville and apprehensively awaiting their first combat, must have taken some comfort in knowing that their wives and children were not forgotten at home in their absence.

4
Soldiering
in Louisville

As far as Jerome Carpenter of the 87th Indiana was concerned, his first two weeks of the war at Louisville had produced very little of the glamor of soldiering but a whole lot of its discomfort and aimless marching.

This Rochester private in Company F finally found some time on September 16 to write a letter home but, ironically, he was back in Indiana when the opportunity arrived. On that day Col. John Wilder was surrendering his small force of 3,500 new recruits at Munfordville, 65 miles south of Louisville, after holding up Gen. Braxton Bragg's oncoming Confederates for three days. Among those green Federal troops laying down their arms was the 89th Indiana out of Wabash, whose vacated barracks the 87th had occupied in Indianapolis.

Wilder's stubborn stand deflected Bragg from his direct course, enabling Maj. Gen. Don Carlos Buell's Army of the Ohio to win the race to Louisville. It also provided the city with time to strengthen its defenses against the Rebel onslaught, now anticipated from Bragg in the south and Maj. Gen. Edmund Kirby Smith on the east. Events involved in these preparations would directly affect the 87th Indiana's role in the subsequent campaign.

Pvt. Carpenter neither knew nor cared about such matters. He was preoccupied with trying to understand the reason, after being hurried into Kentucky, that "we have been marched and counter-marched through the city of Louisville, in particular, and Jefferson County, in general." Carpenter was at a loss to grasp "why we have been thus used," but he guessed it might be some sort of a "hardening process which soldiers very much need in order to get them ready for all the duties they are called upon to perform."

Upon arriving in Louisville, the 87th Indiana was placed with two other Indiana regiments recruited in the same troop call, the 81st and 82nd. They were brigaded under the command of Brig. Gen. Stephen Burbridge, a 31-year-old Kentucky lawyer and farmer who had fought at Shiloh but whose military career would end disgracefully. Given civil and military powers in Kentucky in early 1864, his harsh, dictatorial rule over his fellow citizens earned him such hatred that he and his family were driven from the state at war's end.[1]

Pvt. Carpenter would have sympathized with the Kentuckians' dislike of Burbridge after he had submitted to the general's grueling and seemingly capricious march orders. He wrote a vivid account of one of these marches to the folks back home in which he expresses the soldier's traditional incomprehension of army life.

On Monday, September 8, a week after arriving in Louisville, Carpenter wrote, the regiment still was at Camp Oakland four miles southwest of Louisville at the Jefferson County Fairgrounds, along the Lexington Turnpike.

"We were ordered to prepare two days' rations and be ready to march next morning at 4 o'clock. Well, we got ready by that time and started. When I say we, I mean the whole brigade, which consists of the 81st, 82nd and 87th Indiana Regiments, all their tents, Commissary's and Quartermaster's and Sanitary stores. To give you some idea of what it takes to move this concern, I will say that each company in a regiment (10 companies in all) has a six-mule team and a large, heavy wagon. The Surgeon's, Commissary's and Quartermaster's departments have from three to five, making in all 40 or 50 six-mule teams for the whole brigade. Add to this four six-horse teams that were attached to our artillery and you have some idea of what it takes to move a small brigade.

"This was our second tramp with our knapsacks. It soon became evident to us that we were to travel on the (turn)pike. I must give a description of this pike. It is made of stone, broken up into pieces about the size of hulled walnuts. By constantly riding and driving over this, the stones on top become pulverized and the result is a superfine dust, from one-half inch to two inches deep, covers this road from one side to the other and from (one) end to the other. Now imagine 3,000 men, four abreast, walking in this dust for six hours at a time, sweating as much or more than we would in a harvest field, and you can form some idea of what we would look like. But this is part of the soldier's glory.

"We traveled on in this way about 12 or 13 miles and then came to a halt, pitched our tents, got supper and laid down to rest; but alas! the hour of midnight had scarcely come when we were aroused from our pleasant slumbers by the cry of 'To arms! The rebels are advancing on us!' We did not need twice telling, for in a few minutes our tents were all struck, our provisions and cooking utensils packed into the wagons and the teams started on the back track and we after them. We retreated in good order—indeed, it was a masterly strategic movement—for about a mile to a good position and formed into three distinct lines of battle; the 82nd Regiment fronting the enemy, the 81st about one-fourth of a mile in the rear of the 82nd and the 87th still in the rear of the 81st.

"Here we waited with intense anxiety till day began to dawn but not a rebel dared advance on so formidable an army. I must say for the credit of both officers and privates of the 87th that they conducted themselves in a way that would not disgrace an old, tried, true and well-drilled regiment. And I verily believe from the coolness manifested by the boys on that occasion that they would have fought with that determination that would have insured success.

"But enough of this. We now commenced to retreat without any breakfast and kept on retreating till we arrived at our starting point, which took us until late in the afternoon. It commenced to rain when we were within about five miles of our camp and we got just as wet as rain could make us. But then that would have been nothing if we had been going to a comfortable home and a good warm fire with plenty of dry clothes to put on. But instead of that we were going into an open field, drenched with rain, without anything to eat since the evening before except a few hard, dry crackers. But we soon pitched our tents, made fire, got supper—what I mean by getting supper on such an occasion as this is making some coffee, dipping it out in a tin cup, sweetening it and drinking it with our hard crackers— laid ourselves down on the ground and soon lost our troubles in 'nature's sweet restoring, balmy sleep.'"[2]

Carpenter was right; the marches were part of the training process, exercises preparing the brigade for the complicated procedure of moving its mass of men and equipment across country to confront an enemy. As for the alarm of approaching Rebels on that occasion, it too was a drill; Bragg's army wasn't even in Kentucky yet and Kirby Smith's forces were 80 miles away in Lexington.

Marches like this were repeated several times during the following days until suddenly the 87th and its brigade found themselves aboard a steam ferry, crossing the river to Indiana. The men cheered with delight when the ferry pushed off from Louisville, Carpenter reported, and cheered again when it landed at Jeffersonville "and we stepped on the free soil of Indiana." These Hoosiers had seen enough of the slavery that Kentucky's loyal Unionists tolerated. Some may have put on their uniforms to defend the Constitution; many of the 87th's small-town soldiers were out to eradicate slavery, too.

Such was Pvt. Carpenter's view, anyway. "Our boys hate Louisville and Kentucky in particular and if permitted they would burn the secesh hole of Louisville." He described Kentucky as "this rebellious land . . . only loyal when you will protect and defend the accursed and hell-begotten institution of slavery," and said that he looked "with disgust and pity" upon any man in the North who would "uphold the institution . . . either in thought, word or deed."[3]

The brigade marched to its bivouac at Camp Gilbert, established on the riverbank at a former brickyard a mile east of Jeffersonville, and there on

Sunday, September 14, it was joined by the 104th Illinois Regiment just in from Ottawa.[4]

The same afternoon companies D, F and G of the 87th were ordered to prepare all the rations they could carry and be ready to move instantly. After the companies had waited many hours under a hot sun, the order was countermanded and another issued for 3 A.M. Monday. All three companies decided this was a fool's game, so stayed in their bedrolls only to find that they had been mistaken again and must march off without breakfast. They boarded a train and started north toward Indianapolis, then were divided into squads of 15 that were left to guard railroad bridges against destruction by Southern Indiana's Rebel sympathizers.

Pvt. Carpenter's squad drew the bridge over Muddy Fork, 10 miles north of Jeffersonville. It was good duty under a considerate commanding officer, Lt. David Mow from Rochester. The lieutenant made friends with a nearby resident, "a good Union man by the name of Ash," who provided the entire squad with a warm, satisfying supper at his home. "May his shadow never grow less," the grateful Carpenter said of their benefactor.[5]

The squad's release from the routine of camp life ended abruptly two days later when the brigade was ordered back to Kentucky. The return began on the morning of Wednesday, September 17, but it was late afternoon before all four regiments were across because of too few ferry boats. Cpl. Joseph Wheat of the 104th Illinois recalled the brigade's subsequent march to Camp Robinson, also called Camp Grasshopper, three miles past Louisville. This camp was located on the plantation of Rebel Brig. Gen. Simon Bolivar Buckner, who now was invading his native state as a division commander in Bragg's army.[6]

There the brigade remained until the morning of Monday, September 22, when it was ordered to Louisville to man the city's defenses. The march went on until 2 A.M. Tuesday, being delayed repeatedly by a horde of people fleeing for the river and safety in Indiana. The crisis of invasion was approaching its climax.

Newly raised Union regiments such as Indiana's 87th had been arriving in Louisville daily from Indiana, Ohio, Illinois and Wisconsin to confront the Confederate threat and by this time these levies totaled almost 40,000 troops. Bragg's army, it was learned, was approaching Bardstown only 40 miles away. Louisville's citizens began yielding to panic.

On that September 22 the Union general in command of the city, William Nelson, ordered women and children to evacuate the city immediately. The wharf became clogged by people with wagons, carts, buggies, horses and on foot, all trying to cross into Indiana. They were loaded onto ferries and flatboats, many carrying all their belongings with them.[7] It's little wonder the 87th's brigade had difficulty breasting this human tide to reach its post.

Maj. Gen. Nelson the next day conscripted male citizens of Louisville

for defense and assigned Brig. Gen. Jefferson C. Davis, a Hoosier, to organize them. It was to be a fateful decision for Nelson and, ultimately, for the
87th Indiana.

Nelson constructed a semicircle of trenches around the southern and
eastern edges of the city. Soldiers of the 87th and other regiments were
given 25 cents a day extra pay for laboring on them; impressed citizens
and slaves worked for nothing. Nelson planned to hold these works long
enough for Buell to come up and strike Bragg in the rear, for he fully expected the Rebels to arrive first. If overwhelmed at the trenches, he seriously considered burning the city before retreating to Indiana on two pontoon bridges across the Ohio.[8]

It was not to come to that. Buell arrived in Louisville Thursday, September 25, his bedraggled and footsore Army of the Ohio following over the
next three days. Louisville relaxed; it now was garrisoned by 81,000 soldiers including the new levies. Buell announced to all that he would quickly
reorganize the troops and move south to drive Bragg and Kirby Smith from
Kentucky.

Remarkably, the reorganization was performed in just four days, by
Monday, September 29. Buell integrated one new regiment with every three
of his veteran regiments to form a brigade and then divided the whole into
three corps under Major Generals Alexander McCook, First Corps; Thomas Crittenden, Second, and Nelson, Third.[9]

And thus it came about that these Hoosiers of the 87th Indiana Regiment were introduced to comrades they would get to know and depend
upon during the next two years. Col. Kline G. Shryock brought his 87th
into its new bivouac besides four, not three, veteran regiments. They were
the Second Minnesota led by Col. James George, the Ninth Ohio of Col.
Gustav Kammerling (Lt. Col. Karl Joseph in temporary command), the 35th
Ohio of Col. Ferdinand Van Derveer and the 18th U.S. Regulars under Maj.
Frederick Townsend.

The Regulars would be detached later; otherwise, volunteers of the 87th
Indiana and Second Minnesota will be a part of this brigade until the end
of the war in 1865, while the 35th and Ninth Ohio will remain until mustered out in mid-1864. Together the four regiments will merge into a formidable marching and fighting brigade exceeded by none other in the armies
in which it served.

All three of the brigade's veteran volunteer regiments enlisted for three
years shortly after war's outbreak. The Second Minnesota, originally intended for service in the East, was sent to Kentucky instead and remained
in the Western army thereafter, reenlisting to finish the war. The Ninth Ohio
was formed in Cincinnati as the Union army's first all-German regiment.
Its members were German-speaking and mostly German-born. The regiment was organized along German lines and commanded in the German
manner. The 35th Ohio was recruited at Hamilton, north of Cincinnati.[10]

Two of the three regiments already had been battle-tested at Mill Springs (also known as Logan Cross Roads and Fishing Creek). That fight, on January 19, 1862, was the Union's first battle triumph and drove the Confederates out of eastern Kentucky for the first time. Mill Springs came nearly a month before Brig. Gen. Ulysses S. Grant freed western Kentucky with his victories at Forts Henry and Donelson. The prize of these two achievements was Union possession of a Confederate capital, Nashville, as a base for further penetration into the South.

At Mill Springs the Ninth Ohio, supported by the Second Minnesota's furious rifle fire from the center, attacked with fixed bayonets from the right and broke the entire Rebel line, finishing the action.[11] Mill Springs is remembered also for the curious death of the Southern commander, Felix Zollicoffer, who went into battle wearing a white raincoat that made him a perfect target when he mistakenly rode up before a Federal regiment.[12]

Coming into camp alongside such experienced soldiers, the 87th's newcomers had to endure the veterans' jibes and taunts, such as "Fresh fish!" and "Welcome to the ball; you'll be dancin' soon enough!" Shryock counseled his men to bide their time and await their chance to earn the brigade's respect by performance in the field.

This brigade, incidentally, had a special relationship with Maj. Gen. George H. Thomas that continued throughout the war. Thomas, at this time second in command of Buell's army, trained the brigade in its earliest days and commanded it at Mill Springs, which was his first military triumph. The brigade's dependable and aggressive conduct in that action earned for it the general's enduring respect. With the Confederates back in Kentucky, the job of repelling them had to be done once more; this time, it was hoped, for good.

The 87th's brigade was officially the Third and it was commanded by Brig. Gen. James Steedman, a giant of a man with an aggressive temperament but an inspirational leader to the raw farmboys he led into many bloody fights. A Pennsylvanian by birth, the 45-year-old Steedman had but little formal education but he overcame his lack of schooling by sheer determination. He learned the trade of printer, served in the Mexican War, was a Forty-Niner in the California Gold Rush, then moved to Ohio to become a state legislator and owner of the *Toledo Times* newspaper. Steedman was an active Democrat who received his commission despite supporting Stephen A. Douglas in the 1860 presidential race. He will be heard from often as this story unfolds.[13]

Steedman's Third Brigade was a part of the army's First Division. Its commander was Brig. Gen. Albin Francisco Schoepf, 40, a Pole who was an Austrian army captain when he defected to Hungarian revolutionists and then escaped Austria's retribution by emigrating to the United States in 1851. He had commanded a brigade at Mill Springs. Schoepf's command over volunteers was handicapped by his inflexible belief in the rigid discipline of European armies, a principle not suited to the democratic attitudes of the American soldier.[14]

Artillery attached to the First Division were the Fourth Battery of Michigan Light, Capt. Josiah Church; Battery C of First Ohio Light, Capt. Daniel Southwick, and Battery I of Fourth U.S., Lt. Frank Smith. In addition, a detachment of the First Ohio Cavalry under Col. Minor Milliken was under division command.

Steedman's brigade of Schoepf's division was a part of the Third Corps of Buell's reorganized Army of the Ohio and that corps was assigned to the command of Maj. Gen. William "Bull" Nelson.[15]

Nelson was a 38-year-old Kentuckian whose brother was a longtime friend of President Lincoln. He was a midshipman in the Navy during the Mexican War but opted for the army when the Civil War began and had led a division at Shiloh. Nelson was a huge, muscular man, 6 feet 4 inches and 300 pounds. Prone to sudden and towering rages that overwhelmed his normally boisterous geniality, he also was somewhat of a bully. His flamboyant nature led him to recklessly expose himself to enemy fire trying to inspire his raw troops at the Richmond debacle. That foolishness earned him a couple of bullet wounds from which he only now was recovering.[16]

For all his faults, Nelson was an aggressive commander whom Buell considered to be one of his most valuable officers. He had performed valuable service preparing Louisville's defenses and Buell now was counting on Nelson's corps leadership against Bragg. But Nelson would not live to take command. His unexpected death was one of two surprising events occurring on Monday, September 29, that would seriously impact Buell's army and his plans for the coming campaign, including the 87th Indiana's part in it.

The first of these events occurred about 8:30 that morning in the Galt House, a prominent Louisville hotel, when Nelson was shot to death by a fellow officer, Brig. Gen. Jefferson C. Davis.

Nelson was overbearing and Davis was touchy in matters affecting his personal honor. The result was a clash of personalities that ended tragically. Davis, a Hoosier from Memphis in nearby Clark County, had come to Louisville to help out while on sick leave from another assignment. On September 23, it will be remembered, he was assigned by Nelson to organize the city's male citizens as soldiers. A couple of days later Nelson asked how this was progressing but received no specific answers or information. Nelson's anger flared; he told Davis, "I have made a mistake in selecting you for this duty," and in an abusive manner ordered Davis from his presence. Davis stiffened, demanding the respect due him from one general officer to another, but Nelson was relentless. He ordered Davis to report to Cincinnati and when the latter questioned his authority to do so Nelson turned to his adjutant general and said, "Captain, if General Davis does not leave the city by 9 o'clock tonight, give instructions to the provost marshal to see that he is put across the Ohio."

Davis went to Cincinnati only to be ordered by a superior to go back to Louisville. First he detoured to Indianapolis where he told his troubles to an old friend, Governor Oliver P. Morton. When Davis arrived back in Louisville, Morton was with him. The Indiana governor was never shy about interfering with Union generals over their treatment of Hoosiers and he yearned to confront Nelson about what he believed was Nelson's mishandling of green Indiana troops at the Richmond disaster. Davis and Morton agreed to demand an apology from Nelson.

The two men met Nelson in the lobby of the Galt House just after breakfast. Davis demanded satisfaction for the rudeness to him. Nelson sneered, placed his hand to his ear and asked Davis to speak louder. Davis raised his voice, accusing Nelson of exceeding authority in threatening to arrest him. When Nelson called him "an insolent puppy," Davis flipped a crumpled piece of paper into Nelson's face, whereupon Nelson raised a ham-sized hand and struck him twice in the jaw.

Davis fell backward. Nelson then accosted Morton, asking if the governor had come to insult him, too. Morton said he was there only as a witness. Nelson turned on his heel and walked up a staircase, shouting to an acquaintance coming down, "Did you hear that damned rascal insult me? I suppose he don't know me, sir, I'll teach him a lesson, sir."

Davis, in a cold fury, went among the several bystanders seeking a weapon. A certain Capt. Gibson supplied him with a pistol, whereupon Davis went up the stairs, discovered Nelson walking down a hallway and shot him in the chest from about 12 feet. The 300-pound general dropped to the floor and was dead within 30 minutes.[17]

Nelson's blood had not dried on the hallway floor when the second jolt came. A courier from Washington arrived with orders relieving Buell and placing Thomas in command of the army. Lincoln had insisted on the change, blaming the Confederate invasion of Kentucky upon Buell's failure to confront the Rebels in Tennessee. Buell prepared to depart but before he could do so, he was restored to command. Thomas had refused it, wiring Washington that "General Buell's preparations have been completed to move against the enemy and I therefore respectfully ask that he may be retained in command. My position is very embarrassing, not being as well informed as I should be as the commander of the army on the assumption of such a responsibility."

The embarrassment was more Buell's, however. Suddenly he was commander by default, a rejected general about to conduct the Union's most important Western offensive. His military career was on the line and the possibility of failure would influence his every decision; one wrong move or misjudgment would be fatal. Bragg had to be destroyed, not just defeated.[18]

Furthermore, Buell now had lost in Nelson the corps commander in whom he had the most confidence. An immediate replacement was needed, for the campaign was about to begin. Buell's choice was Charles C. Gilbert, a 40-year-old career Army officer from Ohio. Buell thought Gilbert a major general but actually he still was a mere captain. In the chaotic conditions following the Union's rout at Richmond and Nelson's wounding there, Gilbert had the rank of acting major general thrust upon him when others refused it; the commission never was confirmed.

Now Gilbert would direct in battle the entire Third Corps of over 22,000 men—including the 87th Indiana—when he had not before taken into action anything larger than a company.[19] Yet, it must be admitted, nobody else was available.

Davis never was charged or brought to trial for Nelson's murder. With a battle soon to be fought, there was no time to appoint a court of inquiry and the Lincoln administration, for some inexplicable reason, let the matter drop altogether; Morton may have had a hand in that. Ultimately Davis was punished only by refusing him promotion to the full rank of major general, despite his distinguished later service in division and corps command. He remained in the army after the war, retiring as a colonel. His reputation as one who should not be unnecessarily provoked stayed with him to the end.

Nelson's killing did not go unnoticed by the troops, although some, like diarist Daniel Bruce of Company E, took it rather matter-of-factly. His entry for September 29 notes that "General Davis shot General Nelson" but relegated that news secondary to "Wrote letter to mother." Men in the ranks, after all, had limited interest in and an imperfect understanding of the rarified world inhabited by their generals.

Bruce was curious about his own world, however.

The day after the 87th Indiana arrived at Louisville on September 1, Bruce noted that the regiment began drills with its newly issued Springfield muskets. Like Carpenter of Company F, he recorded strenuous marches of 10 miles or more in dust reckoned as three and four inches thick, creating discomfort that was leavened only by the "drafting" of fruit along the way. Bruce found "the best grapes I ever ate" on one occasion but on another discovered the dangers in such foraging because "two soldiers (were) poisoned with peaches." In the regiment's training marches around the Louisville countryside, one night was spent in a clover field on the farm of John Hunt Morgan, the legendary Confederate cavalry leader. Bruce also was bemused by having to wash his own clothes for the first time in his life and after one march wrote that "my feet is awful sore. I can't scarcely walk."

Suddenly his walking problem was solved. On Saturday, September 7, Bruce was made regimental teamster for the 87th Indiana, an assignment that meant driving a heavy army wagon pulled by six mules. He never had handled mules before but he had considerable native intelligence and soon became proficient at this vital job of supplying the regiment with the food, equipment, ammunition and animal fodder without which it could not function. He will perform this task until war's end, for other regiments as well as the 87th and often under dangerous conditions miles away. He always returns to his friends in the 87th and in Company E.

The wagons that kept an army from starving were usually pulled by six mules in three spans of two each. The two largest mules, called wheelers, were hooked to the wagon; the teamster rode the one on the left, or nigh, side that was called the saddle mule. Ahead were two mules of medium size, the swing team. The smallest two mules, known as leaders, were in front. The teamster directed all with a single line attached to a bit on the nigh leader, which he handled with one hand. In the other was a whip with a long, stinging lash that sounded like a pistol shot when expertly snapped. A good teamster, it was said, could pick a fly off the ear of a swing mule four out of five times with the tip of his lash.

Teamsters also were known throughout the army for the power of their lungs and the unearthly shouts, snorts and creative profanity these men hurled at their teams to get them over stony hills, swamps and corduroy roads. Without such curses, supply trains never would have reached the front, many claimed.[20]

Just before the Mill Springs battle in January, a facetious rumor was started that agents of the Christian Commission had promised "$100 in gold to the man who should for 30 days drive a six-mule team without the use of profane language." Col. Judson Bishop of the Second Minnesota reported that the prize never was claimed, even though there was some brief competition. "As a wicked wagon master explained, the war must go on and the wagons had got to get into camp and his drivers were too loyal to be corrupted by a hundred-dollar bribe," said Bishop.[21]

There is no written evidence that Daniel Bruce ever resorted to profanity while driving his mules, but he certainly must have raised his voice, at least, to urge them along.

During the first three weeks with his mules, Bruce frequently had to appropriate corn for them where he could find it. He loaded tents, oats, pork and picks and shovels, twice crossing the river to Jeffersonville for these supplies and often spending the night under his wagon. Wednesday, September 11, was a bad day, one on which he considered "a soldier's life is the worst life a man ever seen." That day he had accompanied the regiment on an 18-mile march that began at 2 A.M. and ended with 16 of his company sick from the heat and two of the regiment dead. "Cannot tell what it was done for, but to make sick men," Bruce declared.

Whatever it was done for was about to begin. Buell had to forget Washington's distrust of him and put aside the killing of Nelson. He now had half again as many men as Bragg and Kirby Smith, even though the Confederates were lean veterans while a third of his troops knew little more than the manual of arms. Nevertheless, there could be no more procrastination; the Rebels had to be destroyed.

Buell called his corps commanders together the night of Nelson's death and outlined his plans to confront Bragg at Bardstown. The Army of the Ohio would move out early in the morning of Wednesday, October 1.

The 87th Indiana was about to go into its first battle with only one month's training. That, however, was a great deal more than many other regiments had received before being thrust into the fratricidal combat of this war.

5

The Walnut Crackers
Find a Fight

The 87th Indiana Infantry Regiment left Louisville on Thursday, October 2, 1862, beginning marches that would take it 1,400 miles over the next 19 months. Within their first week in the field, these month-old soldiers would experience the tumult of combat and the shock of enemy fire.

The Army of the Ohio had begun moving out the day before. Maj. Gen. Don Carlos Buell detached 19,000 troops toward Frankfort as a feint to keep Kirby Smith occupied. The main force of 58,000 advanced on Gen. Braxton Bragg at Bardstown, the three corps using separate roads that converged there. The 87th with Maj. Gen. Charles C. Gilbert's Third Corps of 22,000 went by way of the Shepherdsville Road on the right. Maj. Gen. Alexander McCook's First Corps of 13,000 was on the left by the Taylorsville Road, with Maj. Gen. Thomas Crittenden's Second Corps of 23,000 in the center on the Bardstown Road.

Buell and his staff accompanied the Third Corps. He expected problems there because of Gilbert's inexperience at this command level, a shortcoming that Gilbert was trying to hide with an aloof, uncompromising disposition that ignored needs of men in the ranks.[1]

The 87th Indiana marched out at 5 A.M. that Thursday, Company E's men leaving a "Secesh house," which they had appropriated for lodging along with its chickens, geese and peach preserves. The family had two sons in Rebel uniform; that gave takeover of the house a legitimacy as far as Company E was concerned.[2]

It was not an easy march. The day became extremely hot and dust hung thick over the road, making progress difficult, particularly for new recruits such as the 87th. Soon extra equipment from knapsacks littered the road as the men lightened their loads. They cared little whether teamsters or citizens picked up the discards, wrote an Ohio soldier. The 87th Indiana moved along carefully in the presence of Confederate cavalry but experienced no serious resistance and arrived in Shepherdsville at 10 o'clock the next night,

Friday, October 3. Camp was made on grounds Rebel troops had left only the night before.[3]

Meanwhile, the Third Corps was beginning to have problems with its commander. Gilbert discovered men of the 36th Illinois stealing apples during a rest stop. He threatened to have them shot by his escort if they did not leave the orchard. Other men in the regiment sprang to their feet, loaded their muskets and warned the escort that carrying out such an order would mean their own deaths. Gilbert backed down. On another occasion, he humiliated an Illinois colonel by taking the officer's sword for allowing one of his men to climb a persimmon tree along the road. Gilbert's air of self-importance, his inflexibility and his disdain of the common soldier was opening a breach between him and his men.[4]

Saturday, October 4, the Third Corps with the 87th began the 18-mile march to Bardstown where they arrived in mid-afternoon Sunday, still with no opposition from the Confederates. "The Rebels are skedaddling," wrote teamster Daniel Bruce, noting that 25 were captured.

The Confederates, it was learned, had retreated southeastward on the Springfield Road and might be headed for Danville. Gilbert's Corps was ordered to Springfield. Approaching that place early in the morning of Monday, October 6, Gilbert found Col. Joseph Wheeler's Confederate cavalry in position on the other side of town. Here, at last, was some opposition. It turned out to be just a skirmish, for when the Third Corps infantry formed in line of battle, Wheeler's men soon withdrew toward Perryville.

The 87th Indiana got off its first hostile rounds, however, and took credit for one enemy dead, 12 wounded. Teamster Bruce was present for the action, reporting that "our boys heard the bullets whistle over their heads and the cannon balls sing over them for the first time." Fortunately, they had no casualties then but in a brief skirmish the next day one of the regiment was shot in the ankle.

By now both armies were beginning to suffer from thirst, for this part of Kentucky was in the midst of a prolonged drought that had dried up streams, creeks and springs. One soldier described the water as "so thick and stagnant you cannot see an inch into it. A deep sediment remains in the bottom of your cup." When Union soldiers found the infrequent pool of water, often there were dead Confederate mules lying in it.[5] The campaign was to develop into a dash by each army to secure its water supply and that in turn would precipitate a battle at Perryville.

The topography in which the armies were maneuvering also would affect the conduct and outcome of the impending battle. The troops were marching up and down constantly, traversing Kentucky's wooded hills and narrow hollows, its tight and twisting roads. The hills were small but endlessly repetitive, more like folds separated by slim creases. In such broken terrain it became almost impossible to see major enemy movements. Confederates had the advantage of knowing the country; often their infantry could hide its presence almost until attacking.

As the march progressed, the four veteran regiments of the Third Brigade were watching the performance of its newest unit and thinking the 87th Indiana might be a bit too soft. Rigors of their first hard march began to tell on the newcomers. Some of the time it was at "double quick" pace, sleep was comfortless and taken on the ground wherever night found them; many still were without blankets. As a result, the 87th's beginners were becoming footsore, weary and complaining loudly about their discomfort. This brought them no sympathy from the old soldiers, only derision of teasing and taunts. "It's the breakin' in that hurts, like the old horse that was fed on sawdust. Just as he was gettin' used to it, he up and died. Hope it doesn't work that way for you fellas."

Soon the 87th was being called "The Walnut Crackers" for its habit during rests in the march of clustering under walnut trees in the bluegrass pastures to hull and crack nuts, recalling a Hoosier pastime.[6]

On the morning of Tuesday, October 7, Gilbert's Third Corps with the 87th Indiana moved eastward out of Springfield toward Perryville, where Confederates just then were setting up a battle line around that small town. Wheeler's cavalry brigade appeared again in the late afternoon but was driven back by Gilbert's infantry. Here bad luck continued to dog Buell. His horse suddenly reared, throwing him to the ground and inflicting a painful cut on his thigh. Unable to ride, he climbed into an ambulance to find a headquarters at the Dorsey farm, four miles west of Perryville.[7]

By 11 P.M. the 87th and its Third Corps all were in camp around the Dorsey House. No fires were allowed, no rations issued; Gilbert characteristically enforced the order so strictly that there was no chance to get food of any kind and water was almost non-existent. The men awaited the morrow anxiously.

Buell's three corps had become separated by their search for water. He ordered the other two to concentrate on Gilbert; only then would he fight what he mistakenly believed were the combined forces of Bragg and Kirby Smith. Bragg, on his part, thought the main Federal force was far to the north at Frankfort, Buell's feint with part of the army in that direction having deceived him. But in war armies develop their own momentum and that now was to produce the Battle of Perryville.

Col. Daniel McCook was one of the famous 17 "Fighting McCooks" of Ohio and had shared a prewar law practice in Leavenworth, Kansas, with a future Union general, William Tecumseh Sherman. His brother, Maj. Gen. Alexander McCook, commanded the First Corps which now was preparing to answer Buell's summons. These two McCooks will play key roles in the battle.[8]

Before dawn on this Wednesday, October 8, Buell ordered Daniel McCook to take his Third Corps brigade to the high ground called Peters Hill and protect several pools of water along Doctor's Creek that were vital to the army.

Confederate units were there for the same reason. Thus, Daniel McCook's appearance began a confrontation between the two forces that steadily escalated until his brother's First Corps arrived on the Federal left in the early afternoon, bringing about a general engagement. Bragg, still believing he faced only a part of the Union army, sent in all 16,000 men of his Right Wing under command of that Episcopal Church bishop, Maj. Gen. Leonidas Polk.

Alexander McCook's 13,000-man corps had marched nine miles with empty canteens and only parched corn to eat. His troops, mostly new and untrained, had barely gone into line when the Rebels made the first charge about 2 P.M. Many of the bluecoats gave way and two Union generals, William Terrill and James Jackson, were killed trying to rally them. More Confederate attacks broke McCook's right flank and threatened to overwhelm the entire corps.[9]

Around 4 P.M. Alexander McCook sent a frantic message to Buell, telling him that he was about to be driven from the field unless he received reinforcements. Buell could hardly believe it, for although he was just 2 ½ miles away he had heard no musketry or artillery. He ordered two brigades to be sent to McCook's aid, little enough help if what McCook said was true. Yet this decision, so indifferently made, would decide the battle.[10]

With one of the two brigades, Brig. Gen. James Steedman's Third, the 87th Indiana Infantry went into the Battle of Perryville.

The heaviest price there would be paid by the other brigade, Col. Michael Gooding's veteran 30th from Brig. Gen. Robert Mitchell's Division. It was sent off first and Steedman's regiments followed sometime after. It was past 5 o'clock before Gooding reached Alexander McCook's position because nobody seemed to know exactly where to find it among the hills that were suppressing battle sounds. Finally, the chaos of combat suddenly appeared in an open field along the Mackville Road northeast of the brigade's starting point.

Gooding's men went into the front line and were immediately engaged in a fierce exchange of volleys with the assaulting Rebels, who were checked. Steedman's brigade soon followed through the thick dust and formed into reserve behind Gooding, near the edge of a woods on a terrace-like ground. The 35th Ohio and Ninth Ohio were formed in front with two artillery batteries; behind were the 87th Indiana and Second Minnesota.

The 87th, last of Steedman's regiments to arrive, nearly caused a disaster. This was a new, nervous experience for the Hoosiers as they came up through the woods behind the Second Minnesota in the gathering darkness. They expected to find the enemy immediately in front of them and seeing the shadowy figures of the Second Minnesota ahead, they halted, cocked their muskets and awaited an order to shoot. This ominous sound got the attention of the Minnesotans, who suddenly feared being shot in their backs by their own men.[11] "A prompt and vigorous introduction of the two regiments by name probably saved us from what would have been a sad misfortune," wrote Col. Judson Bishop of the Second Minnesota in his postwar memoirs. He added that "we had no experience in the whole war so startling as that cocking of muskets behind us."[12]

Once in line, Steedman had his men lie down and ordered them not to fire unless they could see the enemy, which they never did. During the ensuing minutes, however, three Rebel batteries tried to locate them. The oncoming shells were "deathly music . . . some sounded like a threshing machine cylinder when they went through the air and the (walnut-sized) grape shot sounded like hail in the trees and leaves," a Second Minnesota corporal wrote home.[13] Meanwhile, Minié balls overshooting Gooding's men dropped "like the falling of nuts on a frosty morning under a heavy windstorm," according to a recollection from a 35th Ohioan.[14]

Astonishingly, Steedman's casualties would be just six wounded, two severely from the 87th Indiana, neither of whom was identified. Gooding's losses in stopping the Rebels on the front line were much greater: 185 killed or missing and 314 wounded, 30 percent. This resolute brigade, composed of the 22nd Indiana and 59th and 75th Illinois, had arrived just in time to thwart the Confederate onslaught and to hold off subsequent attacks until darkness forced a halt to four hours of fighting. Alexander McCook had been saved by this reinforcement but sustained 25 percent casualties, including 1,097 killed or missing.[15]

Gooding's exhausted survivors withdrew from the front line and Steedman's brigade with the 87th moved up in their place. The men laid on their arms the entire cool, moonlit night, expecting resumption of the fight with even greater fury in the morning. There was good reason to expect this, for Bragg had outfought Buell with an army more than a third smaller. Over 7,600 men had fallen, 4,200 Federals and 3,400 Confederates.

But Bragg at last realized that he was vastly outnumbered and could be annihilated if he chose to continue, so he ordered an immediate retreat. By the time Buell had all his men up and ready to fight the next morning, Bragg had summoned Kirby Smith and was gone, taking with him, as it turned out, Buell's career.

The Union commander lost his chance to destroy Bragg's army because he was too cautious, too patient and totally oblivious to what was happening on the battlefield. This partly was due to a quirk of physics known as acoustical shadow, or the "silent battle" phenomenon. It results in sounds being inaudible a short distance away but easily heard 100 miles distant in another direction. At Perryville the cause was folds in the ground; dense woods caused the same thing to happen the following May at Chancellorsville.[16]

If he had heard, Buell might have put all of Gilbert's Third Corps (instead of just two of its brigades) and all of Crittenden's Second Corps into Alexander McCook's fight and thereby smashed Bragg. As it was, only nine of the 24 Union brigades saw action. Crittenden's entire corps of 23,000 men was two miles away on the right and never was committed.

Buell's staff also served him ill, but none worse than the inexperienced Gilbert, who for the most part remained at the Dorsey House instead of at the front, so ignorant about the field and the battle's progress that he allowed a whole Rebel brigade to move across his front to attack Alexander McCook's line. Certainly, the aggressive William "Bull" Nelson would not have acted so; Nelson's absence contributed to Buell's failure, just as the latter feared. The 87th Indiana would have been more deeply committed to action under Nelson than it was under the indecisive Gilbert, of course, and for the Hoosiers it was a stroke of luck.

In the midst of the fierce fight along Gooding's front at dark, Confederate Gen. Polk saw men he took to be his own firing obliquely into the flank of one of his brigades. Having no staff nearby, he decided to correct the matter himself and rode up to the offending commander, demanding in angry tones why he was shooting his own friends.

The colonel, surprised, replied: "I don't think there can be any mistake about it for I am damned certain they are the enemy." The 55-year-old Polk, an imperious man with a leonine shock of white hair, was astonished at this insolent reply. "Enemy!" he said. "Why I have just left them myself. Cease firing, sir! What is your name, sir?" The colonel quickly replied, "My name is Colonel Keith of the 22nd Indiana, and pray, sir, who are you?"

Polk suddenly realized he was in the rear of a Yankee regiment. He decided that the fading light, his dark blouse and a bluff might get him out of this blunder. He shook his fist in Keith's face, ordered him to cease fire, shouted toward the Yankees to do the same and cantered slowly down the line until he reached a small copse of trees, when he spurred his horse and reached his own lines. There he ordered up a brigade to pour a volley into the Union regiment that he inadvertently had just reconnoitered. Many Yankees fell, including the aforementioned Colonel Squire Keith with a mortal wound. The 22nd paid heavily altogether in its relief of Alexander McCook, with 159 killed and wounded.[17]

And so, a two-pronged invasion of the North by the Confederacy ended finally in failure in Kentucky. Three weeks earlier, on September 17, Gen. Robert E. Lee's Army of Northern Virginia had been stopped at Antietam in its attempt to rally Maryland to the Southern cause. Now, with Bragg's abject retreat, Kentucky was lost forever to the Confederacy. Because of these two results, wrote historian Bruce Catton, the Confederates' jaunty optimism about ultimate victory disappeared. The war was about to turn into one of grinding attrition.

The 87th Indiana's teamster Bruce and his Company E cousin James Troutman went to a field hospital to see Perryville's wounded. "It was horrible," Bruce wrote, "men groaning and moaning, some with arms and legs cut off. Wounded in every place (of their bodies) that can be imagined. The awful scene that it is cannot be told."[18] The 87th Indiana's men were lucky this time, to be sure, but many now knew the awful truth of what could be in store for them.

And some were questioning their leadership. "The boys stood it very well as long as we were in pursuit of Bragg," wrote one 87th correspondent. "We followed him 175 [*sic*] miles and overtook the gentleman but that was all the good it did as we let him go again and all through the ill management of our generals. At least that is the opinion of our officers and soldiers as a general thing."

The 87th joined in the tramp after Bragg for almost two weeks, eastward through Danville and Lancaster and then south to Stanford and Crab Orchard where, on Wednesday, October 22, Buell called off his pursuit. He detached the two corps of Gilbert (with the 87th Indiana) and Alexander McCook, ordering them back north to Stanford and then west to Bowling Green. There they were to assemble and move to the protection of Nashville. That Union supply base was too important to lose and Buell was fearful the Confederates were headed there.[19]

It was Buell's last decision. Two days later, on Friday, October 24, he was removed as commander of the Army of the Ohio. Buell's failure at Perryville and his refusal to follow Bragg into East Tennessee was enough for Lincoln; the President gave up trying to motivate him into aggressiveness. Buell was accused officially of dilatory tactics but a military commission investigating the matter made no recommendations. It mattered little; he received no more orders for duty and resigned his regular commission before war's end. The same military commission condemned Gilbert, however, for failing to support Alexander McCook's corps and he never again held a field command.

The 87th Indiana Infantry Regiment had seen battle close up at Perryville and did not flinch from its duty, but still it could not yet claim to have been bloodied in action. Now the men were marching to Nashville and, likely, to more deadly clashes with these fellow Americans they now knew as Johnny Rebs, or Johnnies.

Or as butternuts. Many Southern soldiers wore the brownish-gray homemade clothing, popular among the South's rural poor of the time, that had been dyed with extract from the butternut or walnut tree, or with a copperas solution. For Union soldiers the word butternut had a meaning beyond "rube" or "hick;" it was more contemptible, similar to "white trash." For the Confederates in their turn, the term Yankee bore all these connotations, and more.[20]

Soon, the 87th would exchange the feckless Gilbert for a corps commander of legendary fame who they would follow for almost two years and there find their military glory.

Teamster Bruce was too ill to care about any of this. He was sick, riding on his own wagon with 16 or 17 others from his company who also were ailing. The mail had caught up with him at last, though, and he had seven letters from home to keep up his spirits.

6
Campaigning in Tennessee

It was Saturday, November 15, five weeks since the Perryville battle, and Sgt. Lewis Spotts of Rochester had lost his enthusiasm for military adventuring, as had many others in Company D.

"I can tell you most of the boys are willing to acknowledge having seen enough of the elephant to distinguish his ears at least and think if we have to serve out our three years he will be visible without the aid of an opera glass. And I am of the same opinion. The soldier's life is a little harder than I supposed. Our rough grub is what takes most of the boys. To think of a pudding or a chicken pie just makes me sick."[1]

Spotts and his 87th Indiana Infantry Regiment were encamped in Tennessee, at South Tunnel on the Louisville railroad, 25 miles north of Nashville. They arrived three days before, following an arduous march of 185 miles from Crab Orchard, Ky., where their Third Corps had broken off pursuit of Gen. Braxton Bragg and started for Nashville to protect that major Union military base.

It was not an easy journey and the 87th's green troops had suffered from it. So many were sick or otherwise absent, according to Sgt. Spotts, that "only 400 guns are stacked at night." That was less than half the starting number; clearly, the 87th was undergoing the necessary "seasoning" that all new regiments must endure before their true campaigning strength was determined. Communicable diseases, coupled with the hardships of camp life, were taking their toll. It was not unusual for a third of a regiment's strength to be lost by illness; some recovered, some did not.

Col. Kline G. Shryock was among the disabled, having taken sick leave on the march at Franklin, Ky., and just now rejoining his men. Peter Keegan, the Company C private from Peru, became ill with dysentery on the march and a physician gave him a potion of opium on cayenne pepper. It only made him nauseated, so he wore out the sickness himself. The coming of cold weather made as many as 150 of the regiment sick at one time. Officers once issued whiskey to some in the ranks "who got beastly drunk and caused much commotion," wrote Keegan. When the march began, this Irish immigrant had been much taken with the majesty of the experience, thinking "a military camp at night a grand scene, grander than any fireworks display." By now Keegan's feet were "sore as boils and ached clear up to his knees," so he no longer spoke of such exhilaration.[2]

The first 50 miles of the march from Crab Orchard carried the 87th and its corps through Stanford, Danville and Perryville to Lebanon, where there was a pause until tents and overcoats could be brought up. The weather was beginning to cool, four inches of snow covering the ground one morning. Water still was scarce or often putrid and rations were short, mainly hardtack and coffee. Soldiers were taking all the provisions they could from protesting farmers along the way. The tents and coats finally arrived and the march was resumed toward Bowling Green Wednesday morning, October 29. The pace quickened, 12 to 20 disagreeable miles a day, so "soldiers had no time to think of friends or anything else save the big day's march before them," wrote Sgt. Spotts.

The country still was so rough and hilly that teamster Daniel Bruce found it hard at times to sit his mule. The weather was windy and dusty as their route took them through Campbellsville and Greensburg to Cave City, where the smoother Louisville-Nashville turnpike led to Bowling Green. There, at last, they found a pleasant camp in a woods with plenty of good water, enough even for washing clothes and bodies.

At Bowling Green the 87th Infantry caught up with the news that its army had been reorganized as the Army of the Cumberland and given a new commander. George H. Thomas, who had been offered Maj. Gen. Don Carlos Buell's job before Perryville, was passed over this time in favor of Maj. Gen. William Starke Rosecrans.

"Old Rosy," as his troops knew him, was 43 years old and a West Point graduate from Ohio who had an undistinguished career as an engineer before resigning his commission. Returning to service after Fort Sumter, he commanded the Union forces in western Virginia which drove out Confederates led by Robert E. Lee and resulted in the formation of the state of West Virginia. Rosecrans (Rosenkrantz in the family's original European spelling) was a man with a cranky, hot-tempered disposition. He would prove to be a master at maneuver but less confident when the shooting began.[3]

The 87th Indiana's brigade remained intact in the new organizational scheme except that the 18th U.S. regiment was given duty elsewhere. The 18th's departure was not lamented by any of the remaining four regiments, for relations between volunteers and regulars never were cordial in this army.

Gen. James Steedman retained brigade command and Col. Gustav Kammerling came off sick leave to resume his post with the Ninth Ohio. The brigade continued as the Third, now in the Third Division led by Brig.

Gen. Speed Fry. He replaced Brig. Gen. Albin Francisco Schoepf, who was discredited at Perryville along with Maj. Gen. Charles C. Gilbert. Fry was a 45-year-old Kentucky lawyer and graduate of Wabash College in Indiana who fought as a volunteer in Mexico. Fry took part in the Mill Springs battle but at Shiloh was criticized for bringing his division to the field too late to fight; he would not be long in this command.[4]

This new Army of the Cumberland was divided into three wings, Thomas Crittenden and Alexander McCook retaining two of them as at Perryville. To replace the ineffectual Gilbert, Rosecrans chose the capable Thomas. The 87th Indiana now found itself under his leadership of the Center Wing.[5]

And happily so, for George Henry Thomas, 46, was destined for greatness. He was a native Virginian, having been raised in the middle of southern Virginia's slave territory of Southampton County. When he was 15, his family was in the midst of Nat Turner's 1831 slave rebellion and fled their home, hiding in woods to escape the murderous blacks. A West Point classmate of William Tecumseh Sherman, Thomas was a career military man who served with the artillery in the Seminole War in Florida and then earned two brevets for bravery in Mexico. He later transferred to the cavalry and was stationed on the Indian frontier in Texas (with the Second Cavalry and Rochester's Albert Brackett) when the war came.

Thomas was a staunch Unionist and flatly refused Virginia's offer of high command when Secession came. For this, his sisters disavowed him until the end of their lives. Thomas, as we have seen, won the Union's first battle victory at Mill Springs and also led a division at Shiloh before joining Buell. His soldiers admired him as "Old Pap," for he never forgot their needs nor their performances. A stocky, deliberate person, Thomas in action was imperturbable, decisive and fearless.[6] He was to become one of the Union's three greatest generals, along with Ulysses S. Grant and Sherman. The 87th Indiana would follow him for two years and find its own glory in his.

Artillery for the brigade remained the same in the reorganization: Capt. Josiah Church's First Michigan, Capt. Daniel Southwick's First Ohio and the Fourth U.S. of Lt. Frank Smith.

On Wednesday, November 12, the 87th ended its grueling march from Kentucky at South Tunnel and that day at roll call discovered 217 of its number were in various hospitals. One of those incapacitated by disease, Pvt. William Miller of Union Mills and Company H, died November 19. The regiment now got hard labor to replace marching. The vital supply railroad from Louisville to Nashville had been cut by blocking South Tunnel five miles north of the town of Gallatin. The brigade camped on the hill above the tunnel and set to work clearing the track.

Confederates had filled the 800-foot-long tunnel with dry wood which then was fired. The intense heat scaled off slatelike rock which cascaded to a depth of seven to 10 feet. The 87th and its brigade worked night and day to remove the rock. After 20 men from the Second Minnesota and 35th Ohio were injured by a collapse of the tunnel roof, escaped slaves, or "contrabands," were brought in to help. Two of them were killed by the falling rock before the job was done on Thanksgiving Day, November 27, and cars once again began running to Nashville. The regiment then was sent northward a few miles to repair track from another Rebel depredation.[7]

There was more than hard work to make the regiment grumble. Mail was a month past due. "If there is anything in the world calculated to keep up the spirits of a poor soldier, it is the thought of being remembered by near and dear friends at home. It inspires them with new hope and courage and better enables them to endure the hardships incident to a soldier's life."

So wrote Jerome Carpenter of Company F, freshly advanced to commissary sergeant for the regiment. In the same letter, Carpenter reported on the illnesses of some company members: Cpl. Banner Lawhead of Rochester in his tent with lung fever, George Loomis of Rochester at Gallatin with inflammatory rheumatism along with James Barrett, also of Rochester. Lt. David Mow of Rochester soon was to resign, "his health being so poor he cannot stand the exposure of camp life."

Also resigning and returning home were three captains, William Wood of Rochester and Company D, Alfred Jackson of Kewanna and Company E and Asa Plank of Rochester and Company F. Promoted from lieutenant to replace them were Lewis Hughes of Rochester in D, Peter Troutman of Kewanna in E and George Truslow of Rochester in F. Orderly Sgt. Horace Long of Rochester became a second lieutenant in Company F, beginning a rise that would carry him quickly to captain.

Carpenter had been told some in the regiment were writing home with "some hard yarns" about life in the field. Those who spread such tales are "ungrateful," he thought, for the food is ample, clothes are woolen and warm, all have overcoats and the reason some have no shoes "is because they have provided themselves with good hightop boots."

Carpenter and Sgt. Spotts obviously had a difference of opinion about life in the infantry.

Bruce's teamster duties kept him from lugging rock so he had no complaints about his stay at the tunnel. In fact, he found his time there to be pleasant, noting that he was able to take his pants off for the first time in many weeks and sleep in a warm bed. His meals were improving, too. Breakfast was boiled rice, fried meat, coffee, molasses, sugar and crackers. Sometimes there even were oysters and fried apples. "As good food as I was used to at home," he confided to his diary, noting that for supper he had pickles, tomatoes, sweetcakes and butter.

Bruce often was sent with his mules and wagon to forage for supplies among the surrounding farmsteads. He found some families to be poor and hungry, such as a mother of five children with nothing to eat and almost no clothing, the father gone to the Rebel army. Another time he returned with two loads of corn and three loads of hay appropriated from two farms five miles out of camp.

Quartermaster Robert Rannells and Adj. Fredus Ryland made a trip to Nashville and Rannells came back convinced of the Confederates' determination. "If anyone can show him where the war would end in less than three years he would like to see him," Bruce reported in his diary. People in Nashville speak boldly as "Secesh" (pro-Confederate) and say they will vote Democratic this year, Rannells reported.

Whiskey and women were causing troubles, too. A couple of 35th Ohio soldiers got drunk on some illicit liquor, began quarreling and one clubbed the other on the skull, killing him instantly. Brig. Gen. James Steedman finally cracked down on prostitution, arresting seven of the hookers and sending them to jail at Gallatin. "They have ruined many a brave soldier," thought Bruce, "and there are many such women in this country following the army."[8]

Following South Tunnel the 87th spent two weeks guarding a ford at Pilot Knob on the Cumberland River, a few miles south of Gallatin, throwing out pickets on either side of the ford. For the last three weeks of 1862 the regiment was at Gallatin for still more picket and guard duty, watching for signs of any Confederate movements. It was cold and boring duty, but dangerous. Who knew how many butternut cavalrymen were skulking about?

The hardness of military life continued to plague the regiment. At the Pilot Knob camp one morning only 210 were present for roll call, according to Pvt. Solomon Deacon of Marion, Iowa, and Company K, many being in hospitals at Gallatin and Nashville.[9] That number was a shocking reduction from the 945 who had left Camp Rose in South Bend four months before and almost 200 less than Sgt. Spotts had counted a month earlier. The regiment's "seasoning" obviously was not yet completed. Weather was cold; snow covered the ground.

There were occasional bright spots in the soldiers' lives, such as the return of an officer from home furlough. Lt. Mark McAfee of Company D came back from Rochester early in December, bringing a huge sack of articles from the men's families. Pvt. Kline Wilson got the gloves he had requested but was delighted when an unexpected new pair of boots also rolled out.

The gifts lifted the gloom from an otherwise bad day, for the men that morning had watched Pvt. James Quigg of Rochester die. Wilson wrote of it in a letter to his father and mother:

"He died about 7 o'clock in the morning, lying in his tent on the ground. It was a hard sight. He was perfectly crazy all night; it took three men to keep him still. The last words he said were that he wanted us to go for Charley Brackett (his hometown physician) as fast as we could. We made a box and buried him by the side of two other soldiers. James was a first rate civil boy and was loved by all the company. Also, (Sgt.) John Newby (of Rochester) died in the hospital at Gallatin last week. He was a stout, rugged man when we came out. About two hours after we had buried Quigg, McAfee came and he brought a good pair of boots for him and sundry other articles; also some things for Newby. It made us all feel bad to think they were not here to enjoy them."[10]

The regiment's chaplain, Joseph Albright of South Bend, died about the same time at Gallatin, where four field hospitals had been set up in commandeered private homes and public buildings. "He was a good man and tried to do his duty under all circumstances," wrote a comrade.

In mid-January 1863 came the attack on "Fort Lard," as the 87th's soldiers termed it to their great amusement. Three companies of the 87th and three more of the Second Minnesota were rousted out at 3 A.M. one cold and rainy morning. They marched to the Cumberland River which was crossed on flatboats and canoes, then marched three more miles into a cornfield and ordered to begin digging at a ravine.

"Then began a general assault on Fort Lard," wrote Pvt. Henry Clay Green of Company E, "and an upheaval of the ground." Union officers had learned the Confederates had buried many barrels of lard at that spot. The number uncovered is conjectural; Pvt. Green put it at 5,000; Cpl. D.B. Griffin of the Second Minnesota thought it 900. Regardless, it all was taken to Nashville by every kind of rickety conveyance that could be requisitioned in the surrounding countryside.[11]

Although the 87th Indiana brigade and division were removed from Rosecrans' pursuit of Bragg's army, they still were not out of harm's way. Bragg had turned loose Brig. Gen. John Hunt Morgan's cavalry to wreak havoc on the Union supply lines while he prepared for an assault on Nashville.

Morgan was one of the Confederacy's three legendary cavalry leaders, along with J.E.B. Stuart and Nathan Bedford Forrest. His series of raids into Kentucky and Tennessee, at this stage of the war, and into Indiana and Ohio in mid-1863 tied up many Union regiments like the 87th Indiana. He became the scourge of the North, winning official thanks from the Confederate Congress and the unceasing enmity of countless Yankees.

A 37-year-old Alabaman, Morgan had the romantic streak that fit well with his swashbuckling military image of gay cavalier. His new wife could testify to that. She was a local belle of Murfreesboro, southeast of Nashville, who became enamored of Morgan while reading of his celebrated raids on the Yankees. When Federal troops for a time occupied Murfreesboro, she was asked her name by a tormenting officer and replied, "It's Mattie Ready now, but by the grace of God one day I hope to call myself the wife of John Morgan." The story was repeated to Morgan who later made it a point to make her acquaintance, found her to be "as pretty as she was patriotic" and, after a whirlwind courtship, married her in the winter of 1862. Morgan's two sisters also married Rebel generals, A.P. Hill and Basil Duke. He fought at Buena Vista in Mexico and was a Lexington, Ky., businessman when the war came.[12] Morgan would lead his most famous raid into Indiana and Ohio in mid-1863, when his adventures will be chronicled again.

Morgan's first raid came when he took his horsemen into Kentucky in July of 1862 to harass Buell's army after Shiloh. In 24 days he traveled 1,000 miles, captured and paroled 1,200 prisoners and lost fewer than 100 men. This torment of Buell began that general's troubles that would continue through Perryville.

In the Perryville campaign Morgan accompanied Kirby Smith to Lexington and retreated with him on October 9. At Crab Orchard, however, he was given 1,800 troopers for another bold raid back into Kentucky. He circled around to Lexington, captured it on October 18, and continued through Bardstown, Elizabethtown and Hopkinsville, finally stopping at Gallatin after destroying several railroad bridges and meeting insignificant opposition.[13]

T.F. Rannells of Rochester, licensed as a sutler for the 87th Indiana, found himself in the midst of the latest Morgan maelstrom. Sutlers were private contractors approved by the army to sell food, drink and supplies to troops in the field "at a reasonable price." It could be a profitable private enterprise but also rather dangerous, as Rannells found out. He left Louisville with his wagon teams for the 87th's camp at Lebanon, where it had paused on its march toward Nashville. On the way he met the two resigned, homeward-bound captains of the 87th, Wood of Company D and Plank of Company F.

At Bardstown on Sunday, October 19, the Federal commander told Rannells to go no further, handed him a musket to help defend the city and promised to guard his teams. Morgan's men were in front and rear of the town, the officer said, and might soon attack. That proved untrue for on Monday 1,000 Union cavalry dashed through the town in pursuit, returning with 100 prisoners. Rannells later learned he was lucky to have been safely in Bardstown. Morgan divided his men, some heading toward Louisville. At Cox's Creek, six miles north of Bardstown, the Rebels surprised 72 government wagons and 28 sutlers' wagons. They took what they could from them, set fire to the rest and marched the drivers in double-quick time 26 miles to Elizabethtown. There a citizen named Price, lying sick in a government wagon, was shot through the head when he couldn't leave the wagon as ordered. Rannells confirmed this atrocity with Price's parents on his way back.

Even though some of Morgan's raiders were seen galloping toward Springfield, it was decided to send a government train of wagons in that direction Wednesday evening under heavy guard; Rannells tagged along with his teams, to more trouble.

Six miles out the train halted for men of the guard to fill their haversacks. A young soldier from the 135th Illinois jumped into Rannells' wagon, first throwing in his gun. A few minutes later the musket accidentally discharged, smashing one of the soldier's legs. He was left in the care of a kindly citizen at a nearby house. Then a few miles further a government wagon overturned down a steep bank, burying a half-dozen men under it. Everybody pitched in, but it took an hour to get moving again. Rannells walked the entire 18 miles to Springfield, the better to guard his teams, and said he was so tired when he arrived at 1:30 A.M. that he wrapped himself in a blanket, fell onto a stone pavement and slept as soundly "as if I had slept on a feather bed."

Rannells located the 87th Regiment nine miles away at Lebanon Thursday morning, finding that Col. Shryock was thriving in command but that quite a few of the men were unfit for duty during this pause of their rigorous march.[14] The intrepid sutler, having survived his immersion into the war, is not heard from again. Perhaps he felt he had used up his luck.

Morgan's third raid of this period came while the 87th Indiana was on picket duty at Gallatin. He left Alexandria, east of Nashville, on Sunday, December 21, to disrupt Rosecrans' lines of communication in Kentucky. He had 4,000 men in two brigades under A. R. Johnson and brother-in-law Duke; when he returned 10 days later, only two had been killed. This time Morgan destroyed $2 million in Union property, took 1,887 prisoners and captured Elizabethtown. A brigade was sent from Gallatin and attacked him near Elizabethtown, but Morgan got away from it and from another Federal force at Lebanon with forced night marches.[15]

Now, in late December 1862, he was at Columbia, west of Nashville, making Union generals jittery about where his horsemen would appear next. It also was on the minds of many of the 87th Infantrymen as they stood on their picket posts. They were aware that their part of the Army of the Cumberland was stretched excessively thin guarding the war sector between Louisville and Nashville, allowing Morgan to strike almost at will with little fear of a concentration against him. He could be devious, too. Once 900 Union troops were surrounded and captured along with two cannon when his men got the countersign from a mail deliveryman and used it to surprise the camp at daybreak.[16]

The Hoosiers of the 87th preferred the uncertainties of Morgan's attacks, nevertheless, over the horrors of the next big Western battle at Stones River near Murfreesboro, 30 miles southeast of Nashville. It began on the last day of 1862, a Wednesday, and the 87th could hear the rumble of distant cannon clearly from their camp at Gallatin. Rosecrans and the major portion of the Army of the Cumberland, 41,000 men, finally had brought to bay Bragg and his own new Army of Tennessee, now 35,000 after absorbing Kirby Smith's forces.

The fight along the river's banks, on December 31 and again January 2, was conducted with the usual ferocity of the Western armies. Bragg once again was the aggressor and after the first day could claim a tactical victory. Rosecrans refused to quit the field, however, and after the second day's action Bragg lost his nerve and retreated into southern Tennessee. In the end Stones River was a strategic victory for the North; Kentucky was safe forever and Nashville was made secure as a base for future operations. The cost, as usual, was high: 25,000 casualties, almost evenly divided.

Bragg's army no longer threatened Nashville, to be sure, but it still was intact and an 1863 confrontation with it further south was inevitable. Rosecrans began moving his forces in that direction, which meant a change of scene for the 87th Indiana and its brigade.

Their first move was to Nashville. The 20-mile trip was attempted on Wednesday, January 14, only to have the weather turn foul with rain that became sleet and then six inches of snow. The brigade was ordered back to Gallatin. Finally, on Thursday, January 29, their baggage was sent ahead by wagon and the soldiers were given a train ride. They pitched tents at Nashville and expected to stay awhile, but at 11 A.M. the next day marching orders were issued again.

On south they went, along the Nolensville Pike some 12 miles to Concord Church, "a very pretty place." There was plenty of wood and fence rails to burn "and the boys always prefer the latter for they burn much better than green wood." Camp was made by the regiment in a nice grove, but "the boys are just slaying the timber; they cut the trees down, I guess, just to see them fall."[17]

Concord Church was midway between two railroads, one leading to Chattanooga, the other to Decatur, Ala. Both were vital to supplying the Federal army in its upcoming campaign and the brigade was well positioned to strike at Confederate cavalry threatening the tracks. The 87th would be sent out frequently in pursuit of the butternut horsemen; Company E once brought back two deserters as captives.

While at Concord Church, 1st Lt. Jacob Leiter of Rochester and Company F got himself into a bit of trouble while commanding a foraging company into the countryside. He and the men had plenty of Confederate money with them, of both official and counterfeit variety. Leiter stopped at a farm to purchase chickens, ham and anything else available, the woman owner agreeing beforehand to take Confederate money in exchange. The next day she appeared at headquarters to show Gen. Steedman the counterfeit scrip she had been given. Steedman, anxious to remain on good terms with the inhabitants, sent the phoney money to Col. Shryock with the admonition that if the amount were not made good "in the course of 30 minutes," he would have the entire company arrested and sent to Murfreesboro in irons.

Naturally, Shryock passed the buck down to the next in line, so Leiter borrowed the money immediately from the regiment's sutler. The lieutenant, uneducated and unable to write, was popular with the men who had elected him to his post and this unfortunate incident likely would have happened to any other commander on the same mission. It did not affect Leiter's military career. He remained with the company and regiment until near the end of the war, receiving an honorable discharge April 25, 1865, because of disability from wounds received in action.

A significant change in the Third Brigade's command was made before the march to Concord Church began. Fry was relieved after only three months and Steedman was advanced from brigade to replace him at division. The new brigade commander was the 35th Ohio's Col. Ferdinand Van Derveer.

It was a fortuitous choice, for Van Derveer was a citizen soldier of exceptional merit who would lead the brigade, and the 87th, through its most momentous actions with courage and initiative. Col. Charles Long replaced him at the head of the 35th.

Van Derveer was 39 years old, a lifelong resident of Butler County, Ohio, north of Cincinnati, onetime county sheriff and a lawyer in the city of Hamilton. He enlisted in the Mexican War with the First Ohio Volunteers, rose from sergeant to captain and led one of the storming columns at Monterrey. He had been colonel of the 35th Ohio since its inception in September 1861.[18]

The 87th's own Col. Shryock was back with the regiment after some time in Louisville. It was Shryock's second sick leave since Perryville. One of his soldiers said the colonel was "looking tolerably well but complaining a little." The early February weather had become "nice and warm and the boys are capering around as gay as larks. It has been very muddy for some time past but is drying off and is very pleasant again."

Down in the ranks, the 87th's men had time to analyze the reasons they were off fighting this war and to comment on the lack of support they were receiving from some of those at home. The Federal government's proposal at that time to create armed Negro regiments for the Union army prompted these remarks in a letter sent to the *Rochester Chronicle* from a writer identified only as "W."[19]

"I see by the proceedings of Congress that they are going to arm the Negro. And why not? Is he any better than we are? Is it committing a sin to set him up for a mark to be shot at any more than us? 'Oh, yes,' some of these Negro-loving men of the North will say, 'you must not arm them, if you do we will secede.' Well, all I have got to say to those kind of men is, secede, and come down here in Dixie and you will get enough of seceding to last you for awhile.

"I am sorry, very sorry, to hear of some of our citizens making such a pitiful howl about arming the Negro. I say arm them; put them in the front rank if need be. I would as soon have one of them killed on the battle-field as to have my brother or father. I say shame on such men, they know not what they do.

"I am sorry indeed while we are down here trying to put down this rebellion that we have men at home that oppose every effort that is put forth for a speedy termination of this war. But I suppose they propose to settle it themselves. How? By armistice; yes, no doubt of it. They will never get any leaders of the rebellion to meet them to settle this thing until they are whipped, and I say pitch in and do it, and the quicker the better. Use every means that can be used to suppress it, and if it takes all the Negroes in America, why not take them? I see no reason why we should not."

When it came to fighting the Rebels, "W" was what we today would call an equal opportunity employer.

Four days after that letter was written, on February 13, Capt. Truslow of Rochester and Company F took advantage of a rainy, miserable day to compose what he called "a scribbling production" in which he sought to define a sinister source of the nation's current difficulties, straining overmuch with the effort:

"Our business is to assist in putting down this infernal rebellion, which I believe at this time is regarded by all parties as a 'big thing.' But notwithstanding its huge proportions, if the North will but be true to herself and true to the Government in this the hour of her greatest trial, it can be successfully put down. The great danger to be apprehended is from that large class of political demagogues who have so long been permitted to disgrace the councils of the nation, and judging their actions in the future by the past, it is to be feared that some of them at least would be willing to sell this glorious land of liberty as did Easau his birthright, simply for a mess of *greens* (money).

"However widely men may differ in regard to the causes which have produced this sad state of affairs they should with a degree of patience at least, wait until 'these calamities shall be overpast' and when it has become a settled fact that the nation is safe then, and not till then, should such things be mentioned. But some are so blinded by party prejudice, and so greedy for the loaves and the fishes, that one is led to presume that they can stand by with indifference, and after witnessing the death struggle and listening to the expiring groans of the nation can, like one of old, wash their bloody hands and declare their innocence to the last. But such wanton neglect and shameful indifference on their part will, as surely as the sun shines in the midday heavens, call down upon their guilty souls the vengeance of an angry God. It is to be hoped, Mr. Editor, that you have none in your vicinity who would take upon himself the responsibilities of acting the part of Judas, and for such a reward.

"With perhaps a few exceptions this part of the army is made up of those willing if need be to offer up upon the altar of their country their lives, in order to perpetuate those time-honored principles for which our fathers 'pledged their lives, their fortunes and their sacred honor.'"[20]

As it developed, Capt. Truslow was one of the exceptions. On March 16, he resigned his commission and returned home.

By March the Confederates began to appear in the 87th's brigade front as Bragg took up positions to block Rosecrans' anticipated drive on Chattanooga. On Thursday, March 5, the 87th and its brigade was sent on a two-day scout west toward Columbia where it surprised a Rebel cavalry force under Forrest, wounding seven and capturing 60. They suffered no losses but returned with 120 sick, prompting teamster Bruce to comment that it's "too hard on them to march all day and lay out in the cold rain all night. Philip Obermayer (his cousin) is very sick." Obermayer later was returned home on sick leave and died there October 16.[21]

The Federals began to concentrate their forces. And so, the 87th and its brigade broke camp at Concord Church on Sunday, March 8, moving 10 miles further south on the Nolensville Pike to the village of Triune. There they joined other Union units and began to dig rifle pits and construct breastworks to repel any Southern attack. Signs of spring appeared soon after their arrival, making the work a bit more pleasant. Woods were greening, peach trees were blooming and the regiment's health was improving; 400 were present for duty by March 23.

One who was not healthy, however, was Col. Shryock. He yielded to his physical disabilities and resigned on March 21, five days after Company F's Capt. Truslow quit. Truslow's replacement was Horace Long, who thus completed an ascension to captain from first sergeant in only seven months.

Shryock's place at the head of the 87th Indiana was taken by his second in command, Lt. Col. Newell Gleason of LaPorte, now promoted to colonel. Once again, the 87th was favored in the choice of a new commander. Like Van Derveer, the strapping 6-foot, 3-inch Gleason was a resolute and daring officer who honored his men and led them by example in their forthcoming ordeals. Like Van Derveer, too, Gleason was an untrained but natural military leader.

A native of Vermont, the 38-year-old Gleason was educated at Norwich University there, taught school and then entered the country's burgeoning railroad construction industry as a civil engineer. He moved to LaPorte in 1854 as chief engineer of the Cincinnati, Peru and Chicago Railroad.[22] Gleason had been a frequent visitor in Fulton and Miami Counties during prewar years, promoting expansion of the railroad from LaPorte to Peru. Friendships made then with many future regimental comrades would serve him well in the months ahead.

Deacon of Company K was not sorry to see the old colonel go, saying Shryock "got too confounded lazy to get out of his tent." Officers in general gave Deacon a bad taste in his mouth. Only two captains still were with their companies of the 10 who came out at enlistment according to Deacon which, he sneered, "shows how much they think of the boys."

Deacon was nearly right. Actually, three of the 10 captains who started with the regiment still remained: Alanson Bliss of LaPorte, Company G; Richard Sabin of Union Mills, Company H, and James Crawley of LaPorte,

Company I. Replacements in Companies D, E and F already have been mentioned. The other four new captains were George Payne of Pleasant Grove for Edwin Hammond of Rensselaer, Company A; George Baker of Star City for James Selders of Winamac, Company B; Milo Ellis of Peru for Henry Calkins of Peru, Company C, and James Holliday of Mishawaka for John Wheeler of Mishawaka, Company K. None of the 10 companies ended the war with its original captain; Company I even reached into Company H's private ranks on July 1, 1864, to find its final captain, John Catlin of Union Mills.

Since the army soon was to advance, the 87th and its brigade in early April were gratified to receive Enfield rifled muskets to replace their older Springfield smoothbores.[23] The Enfield was the general infantry weapon of the British army, weighed just over nine pounds with bayonet and fired a .577 calibre bullet like the Minié ball accurately at 800 yards and fairly accurately at 1,100. The smoothbore's range disappeared rapidly after 100 yards. The Union imported a half-million Enfields until its own production caught up with rifle needs.[24]

The North was phasing out smoothbores rapidly by this stage of the war for the more effective musket with rifled barrel. Also in wide use was the U.S. Springfield rifled musket with 300-yard accuracy. Its bullet, called the Minié ball after its French inventor, was conical in shape with a hollow base that expanded when fired, grabbing the grooves of the rifling and spinning when it left the barrel. The .58 caliber, ounce-sized Minié was smaller in diameter than the gun's barrel, making it easier to load and allowing two to three shots per minute if the shooter was efficient.

All muskets were muzzle loading. The breech-loading, repeating rifle had been developed but was not yet in mass manufacture and never got into wide use during the war. Special sharpshooting units, some cavalry and mounted infantry were equipped with the repeaters, such as the Sharps or Spencer.

Muzzle loaders were difficult to load unless one was standing. It took a complex series of nine movements before such a gun could be fired. The soldier first tore open a paper cartridge with his teeth, poured its black powder down the barrel, dropped in the bullet followed by the cartridge paper, then rammed the whole into the barrel with his ramrod. The gun then was cocked, a percussion cap taken from the cartridge box carried on his belt and placed on the nipple at the breech. Only then was it ready to fire, which occurred when the trigger was pulled and the hammer hit the cap, exploding its small bit of powder which ignited the charge in the barrel.

Performing the procedure in the fright of battle was another thing, for a lot of shooting was needed to hit somebody and it often was said it took a man's weight in lead to kill him. Often two or more loads would be found in rifles after a fight; one actually had 13 crammed in. Either the trigger wasn't being pulled or a percussion cap was not being put in place. Excitement, fear and confusion were responsible. Tearing off the cartridge's top smeared the soldier's face with black powder after a time, caused him to swallow some of it and left his mouth even drier than fear made it. The rifled musket also could not be fired for too long a time, for residue of black powder built up in the barrel and ramming became impossible. Unless cleaned, it was then unusable.[25]

Griffin of the Second Minnesota recorded delivery of the Enfields with obvious pleasure: "They are not as heavy as the muskets were and are better guns, so you see we are fully armed and equipped for the summer campaign."

In mid-May the 87th Indiana received a new division commander, the third and final change in its command structure before the campaign began. Steedman was given a new assignment and was replaced by Brig. Gen. John Schofield. However, Schofield shortly was sent to Missouri and Brig. Gen. John M. Brannan took over the Third Division, Army of the Cumberland. For the third time the 87th Indiana "lucked out" in a new commander, for Brannan was to prove masterful at battlefield maneuver and improvisation.

Brannan is listed as a Hoosier in some accounts, but he was born in Washington, D.C. While serving as an 18-year-old page in the House of Representatives, he became so popular with congressmen that 114 of them approved sending him to the U.S. Military Academy. The actual appointment was made by Rep. Ratliff Boon of Indiana, likely giving rise to an assumption of his Hoosier origin. Brannan, 54, became a career army man who won two citations for bravery in the Mexican War. He had served creditably on the South Atlantic coast prior to this assignment, which was his first in which he was in charge of a division.[26]

Brannan quite likely welcomed the challenge; it could help him put aside the recent sensational, scandalous end to his marriage. His wife, the former Eliza Crane, suddenly vanished. Fearing she had met with foul play, Brannan advertised her disappearance throughout the country and had lakes dragged for her body. All the time, it eventually was discovered, she was living in Italy with her lover. He turned out to be the socially prominent Powell T. Wyman, an army officer who later was killed in the war.

Brannan went to court for a divorce and took some satisfaction in the rapid granting of his plea and the presiding judge's accompanying remarks:

"During all this time she (the wife) was coolly speculating in prostitution on the other side of the Atlantic. I look upon this as one of the most aggravated and one of the most cruel instances of infidelity on record."[27]

Troops continued to mass at Triune through May and into June, by which time at least 20,000 were there. During all this time fortifications continued to be improved; troops were told to expect an attack any time. Trees were cut down all around the breastworks to present a field of fire; every company was ordered to have a barrel of water in the entrenchments at all times.

There was time, nevertheless, for card playing, washing and "bodyguard (lice) killing," according to John Stevens of Francesville and Company B, who also reported a rousing fight that broke out at a company poker game. And there were accidents, sometimes amusing if one wasn't involved. George Dunlap of Valparaiso, a musician from Company A, shot himself in the toe getting out of bed one morning, also hitting nearby George Knowles in the leg.[28]

Benjamin Hooten, a 25-year-old musician from New Carlisle in Company G, tried to do some business with a sutler at Triune but found the prices too rich for his blood: 35 cents a dozen for eggs, $1 a pint for canned fruit and $2.50 a pound for tobacco. Writing in late May, he reported the soldiers organizing horse races and cockfights but assured wife Harriet that he was not a party to such evils. While he was "minding the flies" off a sick man, a letter came from his wife and he found someone else to take over so he could read it right away. When he returned, the man was dead but the attender hadn't even noticed.[29]

Death had become commonplace at Triune, to be sure. Dr. Samuel Higginbotham of South Bend, a physician with the 87th only three months, died of typhoid fever May 29 at the Triune hospital. Three weeks before, illness also had claimed Jacob Woolf of Peru and Company C.[30]

The many weeks in camp brought more introspection among the troops of this citizen army. Our unknown correspondent "W" wrote home that in his view the army was "in good order and ready to meet the enemy again." Peace, however, should not come at any price. He continued:

"Our men appear to be more determined than ever to put down this rebellion. We all want peace and would be glad if such a thing could be done, but we want an honorable peace. Give us an honorable peace or let us fight them for 20 years. I am not in favor of letting them make the terms to suit themselves. We must have a hand in it, or no go.

"It is not very pleasant, it is true, to be away from home and friends, but what would they be if we had no country? My God first, my country next. Who can think of dividing this glorious old Union that our fathers fought for! Let us both in the army and at home try and maintain the institutions that were handed down to us by our fathers."

"W" knew that there were many back in Fulton County opposing the war and trying to get others to do the same. But he was puzzled:

"What do they want? Do they want war in Indiana? God forbid. It does appear to me that they are blind to their interest. Just let them come down here in Tennessee and pass over the grounds that the armies have passed over and see if they would want the State of Indiana cursed with the ravages of war. They certainly will see the error of their ways and turn before it is too late.

"If they only knew it, the soldiers in the army do not sanction their way of doing business. It is surprising to me that they should act so. Why not go heart in hand and help put down this rebellion! It is certainly as much to their interest as it is to ours to have the Union restored and I am in hopes that they may ere long rally together and may the voice of the North come up as the voice of one man, saying, 'the Union must, and shall be, preserved.' Send on your 500,000 more men and by the heavy tramp of that 500,000 we will make the Rebels weak in the knees and I do not think it would be long until they would cry peace, peace!

"Then we ask those Southern sympathizers to forsake their treasonable purposes and come out on the Lord's side. Many of you have friends in the army and do you want to sacrifice them by your treasonable acts at home? Then I say again, come out and help us, and soon all may return to our homes and families, there to live under the protection of the Star Spangled Banner, knowing that we have put down the most unholy rebellion that ever cursed this earth."[31]

About the same time at Triune, Cpl. Henry W. Hoober of Blue Grass and Company E exercised some of his scorn of the homefront "traitors" and at the same time testified to his pride of soldiering:

"It would be very gratifying to soldiers generally to see those traitors at home brought down here and put in the ranks. We are all with but few exceptions 'down upon' them and are we to blame? I do not use epithets or I would not know any too bitter to apply to them. We are commanded to 'love those who hate us' and 'pray for those who despitefully use us.' Now ... if ever a poor deluded people needed our love and our prayers I think these traitors do for we know that they hate us and their actions prove that they are despitefully using us.

"If they knew the destruction that follows an army and see the horrors of war they would not court it at home as they are now doing. I have seen both the horrors and destructions of war and I say God forbid that our fair state of Indiana ever be scourged by it. Do not construe this into a regret on my part for having joined the service. I do not and never have regretted that I came into the service of my country; I shall be happy to serve my three years if my life is spared and longer if required. It is true that we have a great many hardships to suffer and no one can say that it is a pleasant life to live but then what are a few hardships when compared with our liberty, that which every freeman loves."[32]

In early June Col. Van Derveer took the brigade on a reconnoitering expedition toward Franklin to scatter a Confederate cavalry detachment from Forrest's command. It was easy duty, for the gray riders dispersed as soon as the brigade went into battle formation.

About this time a new organization of the Army of the Cumberland announced by Rosecrans became official. Thomas' center wing became the XIV Corps, a designation it was to retain for the rest of the war. Brannan led its Third Division and Van Derveer the Third Brigade, which was made up of Indiana's 87th, Ohio's Ninth and 35th and Minnesota's Second.

Alexander McCook and Crittenden retained corps commands as they had at Perryville and at Stones River: McCook the XX, Crittenden the XXI. In addition, a Reserve Corps was created under Maj. Gen. Gordon Granger and was called the Army of Kentucky.[33]

By then the signs were inescapable that something big was about to happen. Brigades were to be ready to march with 10 days' provisions. All nonessential baggage and equipment was being sent to Nashville. Troops of Granger's corps arrived in camp at Triune. Daily drills now were of brigade size, or even division strength, as would be required in battle.

Rosecrans was about to launch one of the most ambitious and perilous campaigns of the entire Civil War. D-Day, as a future war would call it, was set for Tuesday, June 23.

The winter's wait was over. The 87th Indiana Infantry was heading for Chattanooga.

7

Over Mountains
to a Georgia Creek

In the summer of 1863 Chattanooga had a strategic value for the Union far beyond what its population of 3,500 might suggest. It was the gateway to the Deep South that opened onto a path to victory in the Western sector of the war. If the Federals could seize and hold Chattanooga, they could invade Georgia and Alabama, gain easy access to the pro-Union eastern third of Tennessee, appropriate coal deposits and ironmaking essential to the Southern cause and possess the hub of three critical railways that led into the deepest recesses of the Confederacy, clear to the Gulf of Mexico.[1]

And so from Murfreesboro on Tuesday, June 23, Maj. Gen. William S. Rosecrans launched 58,000 men in his Army of the Cumberland toward this mountainous city tucked into the loops of the Tennessee River just north of the Georgia line.

Merely traversing those 100 miles might be more difficult than defeating the 37,000 men of Gen. Braxton Bragg's Army of Tennessee. The first 40 miles were over foothills to Tullahoma, where Bragg had his headquarters and advance supply base. Once there, the audacity of Rosecrans' campaign plans would be revealed.

Between Tullahoma and the Tennessee River, just slightly more than 30 miles, the army would face the lofty Cumberland Mountains. Rugged and wild with little forage or water and few inhabitants, the Cumberlands were a desolate area of oak and cedar in ridges, thickets and gorges. The ground would become no less formidable on the east side of the wide river than it had been on the west. Paralleling the river on the east were long, high mountain ridges. Nearest the river was Sand Mountain of 2,200 feet, called Raccoon Mountain at its northern end just west of Chattanooga. It was parched and barren with only a few miserable roads. East of Sand-Raccoon was 1,000-foot Lookout Mountain, beautiful but wild, and between them was Lookout Valley.[2]

The 87th was embarking with the Army of the Cumberland upon one of the Civil War's most ambitious campaigns, one that epitomized the uniqueness of war in the Western theater. Fighting in the West was conducted over a vast area between the Appalachian Mountains and the Mississippi River. It was a war of extensive movement, much different from the war in the East where armies fought mainly in the 100 miles of territory from Washington to Richmond.

Lacking the roads and railroads of the East, the still-developing West made up for this military deficiency with its many navigable rivers. They flowed both north and south and east and west, enabling Union troops and supplies to reach deep into the Confederacy. Eastern streams mainly ran east and west and were only partly navigable.

The great distances confronted in the West contributed to a difference in the war's conduct there, too. Remote from the Eastern capitals of both Union and Confederacy, Western armies often were considered secondary and their needs treated with indifference. The more visible Eastern armies got first choice in manpower and supplies. Thus Western commanders frequently had to improvise in their campaigns, a trait that developed aggressiveness and a Western reputation for relentless fighting.[3]

The Western armies, both North and South, drew their soldiers from a rugged society whose young farmers, woodsmen, mechanics and laborers were inured to physical hardships, accustomed to handling guns and in battle exhibited self-reliance and an innate fierceness unmatched in the East. These young men simply enjoyed fighting, for the violence that always marked frontier society in America had not entirely disappeared from the Western states in the 1860s. The coming of war provided a natural, acceptable and even heroic outlet for this tendency.

Claims of Western distinction would be substantiated over the next 22 months by Rosecrans' ambitious campaign and by the three campaigns of his successor, William Tecumseh Sherman. The 87th Indiana was to take part in all four.

As it swung out of its Triune camp at 7 o'clock that Tuesday morning to join the XIV Corps at Murfreesboro, the 87th was displaying a new confidence. The regiment numbered close to 400, its peak strength after undergoing the "seasoning" of the past 10 months. Those still in the ranks had survived illness, homesickness and acclimatization to harsh military life and could be counted on to stay the course.

The Hoosier soldiers by now were comfortably uniformed in their Yankee blues—light-colored pants, darker coats and visored French kepi caps with distinctive flat, circular tops. When enlisting, each got pants, coat, overcoat, shoes, socks and underwear. Some who had come from a hardscrabble existence in the newly opened northern Indiana farmland knew nothing about underwear and had to be told how it was worn, and why. The government's shoes left something to be desired. They were not shaped for left or right feet but made identically, with squared toes, and were quite uncomfortable, particularly on the march. It' not surprising that many quickly became footsore and that letters home begged for a good pair of boots by mail. Pants and coats were issued randomly, without concern as to the recipient's size, so it took a good bit of trading before the proper fit was found.[4]

The uniforms were 60 percent wool and 40 percent cotton, a material good in the chill of winter but less than comfortable in the heat of summer such as was beginning. Wool did wick away the body's perspiration, but at what cost to one's sense of smell is not difficult to imagine. In any event, frequent bathing was a rare practice in the society of that day; the American fetish with personal hygiene came much later. Perhaps, since almost everyone exuded the same odor, nobody particularly noticed.

Long campaigning, sleeping on ground and in woods, rarely being able to wash clothing brought an aggravation that did get everyone's attention, however: insects. Particularly annoying were body lice, the affliction of all armies that is oblivious to rank. The Yankees usually called them "graybacks" and spent much time in camp, stripped almost naked, picking them from clothes to kill. The only permanent solution was boiling the clothes in water and there never was time or enough water for that, so the pests had to be endured. The louse wasn't the only soldierly irritation in camp or on the march, though; there were chiggers, fleas, black flies, mosquitoes, tarantula spiders and woodticks.[5] Marching through the South was worth a lot more than the private's $13-a-month pay, to be sure.

Men of the 87th strapped to their backs the knapsacks into which were crammed extra clothing and other necessities, including a wool blanket, overcoat and a poncho or "gum blanket" for rain protection. There also might be extra socks, perhaps a shirt or two or another pair of shoes. Around their waists were strapped the haversacks, made of canvas that was white when new but soon turned a deep shade of black from use. The haversack was the soldier's pantry, the place he carried his food. Within it might be chunks of bacon, fresh meat and damp sugar tied up in a rag, or such things as potatoes, vegetables and fruit picked up along the way; blackberries were particular favorites of the men, who gathered them at every opportunity. Every haversack became rather malodorous in time, but on the march or facing the enemy a man learned not to be fastidious. Knapsacks often were left behind for wagons to carry during strenuous marches and sometimes took days to catch up with their owners; haversacks went along everywhere.[6]

The Union soldier had plenty to eat most of the time, but not all of it good. The Union army had no interest in enlisting cooks or bakers. At first the soldiers were expected to prepare their own food but many objected to this, so company cooks were appointed and they could be either capable or dreadful. Either way, the food had to be eaten for there was no alternative. On the march the Hoosiers pulled salt pork or bacon from their haversacks, along with hardtack that was a large, thick soda cracker made tough enough to survive until used in the field. Reported to be good enough when fresh, hardtack was old by the time it reached the men and often infested. Hardtack often was crumbled and mixed with bacon or other meat into a meal that sounds quite indigestible. The sugar was kept by the men for their coffee, an absolute essential to a campaigning soldier. Each carried a tin container of some kind to boil whole beans issued by the army. The beans were ground in a bucket or on a rock with a rifle butt.

Completing the Yankees' regular equipment were a canteen and a cartridge box, the former slung over a shoulder, the latter attached to his belt. The canteen was made of cloth-covered tin and was designed for water but might carry milk, cider, molasses or even, clandestinely, liquor. When a canteen leaked and was replaced, the old one was separated and the halves used for wash basins and frying pans or even to dig rifle pits.

Such was the condition of the 87th Indiana Infantry Regiment as it started on the most splendid, perilous march of its war service.

Rosecrans conducted the first phase of his plan, called the Tullahoma campaign, with a bold brilliance that thoroughly deceived Bragg. Within a week the Confederate commander's forces had been so thoroughly outflanked that he abandoned his base at Tullahoma and retreated to Chattanooga, leaving the way open for the Federals to envelop the city.

The entire Tullahoma campaign was carried out under extremely difficult weather conditions because extraordinarily heavy rains fell incessantly for two weeks.[7]

Rosecrans sent out his army in five columns to deceive and confuse the Rebels. We shall follow the route taken by George H. Thomas and the XIV Corps where Indiana's 87th was marching. Their first action came the morning of Wednesday, June 24, at Hoover's Gap 15 miles south on the turnpike from Murfreesboro. There Maj. Gen. Joseph Wheeler's cavalry screen was scattered with no more damage than a few bullet holes through some coats. This put infantry into the Confederates' rear, precipitating one of the series of retreats that would force Bragg to give up Tullahoma.

Marching 35 miles further southeast on the turnpike without opposition, the regiment reached Manchester on the south bank of the Duck River. It then turned southwest to occupy Tullahoma with the rest of Thomas' corps at noon on Wednesday, July 1, eight hours after Bragg abandoned it. The city was almost deserted, barely two dozen inhabitants seen on the streets. The regiment's march from Manchester to Tullahoma was peaceful, not a gun being fired nor a butternut seen. Rosecrans took over the house Bragg had left and the 87th's brigade camped around it.

That night Union cavalry brought in a number of Rebel deserters who said if Bragg was retreating to Georgia, they would not fight because they were Tennesseeans and, besides, they had not been getting anything to eat.[8] If any Yankee soldier thought this meant Bragg's army was going to be a soft touch, they would be greatly mistaken. Bragg, in fact, had sent many men out to act as deserters and plant just such an impression.

Kline Wilson of Richland Center and Company D had vivid impressions of his Tullahoma experience, which he wrote home to Fulton County:

"We captured two tons of tobacco, three siege guns and a lot of prisoners. They were fortified at that place and I should have thought they would have made a stand there, but I guess Old Bragg began to think that Rosy was at the head of too many Yanks for him. I understood that our men captured a telegraph office in Tullahoma and a dispatch from (President Jefferson) Davis to Bragg that the woods were full of Yanks and that the best thing he could do was to make himself scarce, which he did on double-quick I assure you and the Stars and Stripes were soon floating where the Rebs had left their rag which was torn down in a trice.

"Three miles on the other side of Tullahoma while we were skirmishing there was a cannonball struck a mare in the breast that the surgeon of the 35th Ohio was riding and went clean through her, killing her instantly but did not hurt the surgeon any more than it knocked him about 20 feet and stunned him for awhile. I did not exactly see it done but saw the mare in a few minutes afterward and I see the doctor every day. Pretty narrow escape, wasn't it? But then a miss is good as a mile, of course. The colonel of the 29th (Indiana) Regiment was shot in the eye while fighting at Shelbyville."[9]

Teamster Daniel Bruce's mule team was one of 300 sent 25 miles to Shelbyville immediately after the occupation of Tullahoma to resupply the army. Roads in the area were so sandy, Bruce recorded, that he began using eight mules instead of six. His saddle mule became ill and had to be rested and another mule died. Bruce wasn't feeling so well himself, once writing of being "sick and scarcely able to be about." Like always, he recovered, this time with the help of "some medicine." He did complain, for the first time, of being "bothered by clothes lice."

Thursday morning, July 2, the rains let up long enough for the 87th and its brigade to leave Tullahoma in style, which it did by marching out at daylight with colors flying and band playing. That mood soon ended when their route encountered swampy country reaching the Elk River eight miles southeast of Tullahoma. Confederates had burned the bridge there so the brigade was forced to ford the deep swift-running water. This was not attempted until Friday noon, July 3, when there was another short cessation in the interminable rains. It took all afternoon for the brigade to cross, the men holding onto two thick ropes stretched across the banks.

A. L. Thompson of the 10th Indiana, also in the 87th's division, remembered the difficulty of the crossing. The water was armpit-deep, the current swift enough to knock men over even holding onto the ropes. Seven or eight in the First Division drowned, he reported. Some men stripped themselves, tied their clothing into a blanket and held the bundle and their guns on their shoulders. Others scorned dry clothing, hanging their cartridge boxes on their guns and holding guns above their heads; many lost their ammunition anyway.[10]

On the Fourth of July, Friday, Brig. Gen. John M. Brannan halted the entire division until rations could be brought up. The brigade went into camp where they had the first good view of the towering Cumberland Mountains now in their path, 10 miles away. There the news came down from Rosecrans of the Union victory at Gettysburg the previous day and a salute was ordered to be fired. Cpl. D.B. Griffin of the Second Minnesota described how it went:

"Our battery fired 24 rounds and it speaks louder than an old anvil, I tell you. I stood off about 20 rods (110 yards) and the shocks would fairly make the ground tremble and then there is five or six brass bands here and they kept a playing with them until late in the night and thus passed away the 4th of July 1863."

Two days later came news of Vicksburg's capture, opening the Mississippi River to the Union, which brought more artillery salutes.

Kline Wilson of Company D wrote his father that "the way our old 12-pounders spoke was a caution; I expect if you had listened you could have heard them in Rochester. Now if this news is true I think the Southern Confederacy is about played out and there must be something of it, for I think Old Rosy would not have had so much firing unless our armies had met with a brilliant success somewhere. Still, I am afraid the news from Vicksburg is too good to be true." Pvt. Wilson had his eye on souvenirs. He described a visit to the nearby settlement of Decherd where he saw a lounge that Bragg reportedly had slept on or, as Wilson wrote, "laid on, rather, for the old woman who kept this place said he was too uneasy to sleep." Wilson wished he had cut off a piece of it to send home.

The regiment, Wilson reported, was in good spirits "and although we have pretty hard times to contend with, yet we think it is all for the Union and go ahead with a stout heart and a more determined step than ever."[11] This cheerful young farmer did not survive the war, dying while on duty in Georgia December 6, 1864.

And still the rains came. By July 8 it had rained for 16 consecutive days and the army was immobilized by muddy roads and broken bridges. Supply trains could not reach the troops and for a week they had to make do with one hardtack cracker a day. Knapsacks also had been left with the wagon train some days before, so there were no clean shirts to replace the messy ones.

The solution to the laundering problem could be found among the many Negroes who had begun to collect around any Union army camp. News of the Emancipation Proclamation, in effect since January 1, had reached into the deeper parts of the war regions, giving hundreds of slaves the courage to leave their masters and take up the uncertain joy of freedom on the road.

They were drawn particularly to the troops in blue, who they considered to be their saviors, and offered to do all kinds of chores and services for them. Bruce recorded often in his diary of hiring Negroes to wash his clothes, usually for 20 cents, and once he gave a woman's dress he had confiscated to "a darky" to have it made into two shirts. It was the officers, however, who benefitted most from this new labor pool.

Three months before, ex-slave John Patton had come into Company F's Triune camp selling greens. At Capt. Horace Long's request Patton stayed as his personal cook/servant as well as the company's occasional handyman. Long found much comfort in the arrangement, as he described in a July 5 letter to his wife:

"My negro is one of the most faithful servants you ever saw and I would have seen a much harder time if it hadn't have been for him. Some nights he has been up most all night fixing things for me, preparing rations for me and bringing me water. He always finds out some way to get holt of something for me to eat. I never have to run around to hunt up water. These hot days he always fetches me cool water every chance he gets. Most every time we halt he is on hands with a cool drink for me. He does all this without one saying a word to him.

"He got lost for the regt. and could not find it for a day or two, but when he did find us he was real tickled. He said that he was scared for fear that he would not find me. I was afraid that he was lost. I would hate to loose him, and he is a real clean boy, keeps everything nice and clean, never picks up a plate or cup but what he wipes it off again before he lays it down. Well, I could not do well without him. He says that he would rather be with me than any place that he has been."

Long explained to his wife in another letter what kind of bed he had those days in camp. Four stakes were driven into the ground three feet high. Shortened fence rails were put between each of the ends and other rails then placed perpendicularly on which to lay. There was no straw for the rails but there were a buffalo robe and a couple of blankets for the occupants' cover. The captain called it "my rail featherbed."[12]

On Saturday, July 18, the regiment finally moved with its brigade three miles and into camp near Winchester at the foot of the Cumberlands, where it would remain until crossing those mountains. The rains finally ended, but the weather was hot and drills were being conducted twice a day. Death remained a familiar visitor to the regiment. John Wesley Carter of Kewanna and Company E died on Monday, July 20, of "disease of the lungs and mortification[13] of the bowels," wrote Bruce.

The 87th's Hoosiers became absorbed at this time in reading the details of Brig. Gen. John Hunt Morgan's surprising raid into southern Indiana from the newspapers that followed the troops along with the mail. They had no inkling then of the part their former colonel had taken in chasing the daring Confederate cavalry commander.

Morgan took off on his most famous raid with 2,460 men and four guns in two brigades, again commanded by A. R. Johnson and Morgan's brother-in-law, Basil Duke. He crossed the Ohio River near Mauckport on Wednesday, July 8, and the next day captured Corydon after handing the Indiana Home Guards 360 casualties.

Morgan's appearance created near panic in the state. Gov. Oliver P. Morton's patriotic call for citizens to leave their jobs and repel the invader was answered within 48 hours by 65,000 men. They were organized quickly, if haphazardly, into 13 regiments and one battalion of artillery and rushed south.

Morgan, meanwhile, learned that he had aroused the militia of Ohio as well as of Indiana and that there was Federal infantry around Cincinnati. He decided to get back to Kentucky, if he could. Continuing east in Indiana, he rode through Salem, Vienna, Lexington (where Federal cavalry almost captured him in his sleep), Paris, Vernon, Dupont and Sunman. Early in the afternoon of Monday, July 13, five days after entering Indiana, he crossed into Ohio at Harrison with his force now reduced to 2,000 and his tired mounts changed for captured but unshod horses.

Force-marching near the river, Morgan finally was cornered and captured in eastern Ohio on Sunday, July 26. His raid may have been a reckless endeavor, but it was a feat of remarkable endurance: 21 hours a day in the saddle for 18 days after crossing the Ohio. He and some of his officers were jailed in the Ohio state penitentiary, from which he escaped in late November and rejoined the Confederates. Morgan's effectiveness to the Southern army was ended, however.[14]

The part played in this event by the 87th Indiana's former colonel, Kline G. Shryock, brought him no credit. After quitting the 87th with ill health in March, Shryock returned to Rochester where in December he was appointed provost marshal of the Ninth Congressional District to replace Capt. W.W. Wallace of LaPorte.

When Morgan's raid precipitated the huge outpouring of men to oppose him, officers were needed and Shryock was given command of the hastily organized 105th Infantry of 713 eager but untrained volunteers. He took command July 12, the day before Morgan entered Ohio. This was not known immediately, of course, and Shryock's regiment left by rail for Lawrenceburg, where it heard all kinds of alarming rumors from the panicked citizenry. The next day the regiment marched to Sunman and was near Harrison, Ohio, when it learned that Morgan had left the state.

About 10 o'clock that night a frightened courier rode into camp with news that Morgan had been headed off in Ohio and had turned back to Lawrenceburg, desolating the countryside. Reacting immediately to this alarming, but false, report, Shryock formed up his men and started them on the highway. These men soon learned what was afoot and being just off the farms and out from behind counters, they were frightened, apprehensive and undisciplined.

Approaching Lawrenceburg in the darkness, the head of the column was halted. The order was not heard in the rear ranks and the men suddenly closed upon one another. Suddenly, all was confusion. Word flew from rank to rank that the enemy was near. Some were heard to say "this is as good a place to start fighting as any" and firing began without an order. A company on the flank, supposing this fire came from a suddenly appearing enemy, poured a volley into the mass of men still on the road. Before Shryock and other officers could restore order, eight had been killed and 20 wounded. The regiment returned to Indianapolis and was mustered out after six days of service.[15]

Shryock did not soon put behind him this ignominious end to his military field career. Around both Fulton County and the Ninth Congressional District, his Democratic political foes reminded the public of the Morgan fiasco for many years, to the detriment of Shryock's political career.

Back in southern Tennessee with the 87th Indiana, the tempo slowed in bivouac near Winchester, now called Camp Thomas. While waiting for Rosecrans' order to climb the mountains and reach Chattanooga, the 87th's division was reviewed by the commanding general himself on Tuesday, August 11. "Old Rosy" rode down the lines, speaking kindly to every regiment and shaking hands with every commanding officer. Stopping at the 87th Indiana, the general greeted them with "How do you all feel, boys?" It was the first time any of the division's regiments had been reviewed by such a high officer.

That same day those of Company E who had been recruited from the Union Township areas of Fulton County got together to mark an anniversary. Exactly one year before they had left Kewanna for regimental organization at South Bend's Camp Rose. The company had volunteered to suppress the Rebellion and they believed they had done it, "if long and continued hard marches have any bearing. The history and position of the regiment at Springfield, Perryville and Hoover's Gap are too well known to need comment." That day, also, Hamilton McAfee resigned as first lieutenant of the company and was replaced by John Vandever of Plymouth.[16]

Pleasant days and idle hours while in camp gave the men time to pursue interests other than military. Three of them—Jonas Myers, Clark Heikman and George Toothman—volunteered to help their Company F captain, Horace Long, improve his abode. They constructed a bower in front of the captain's tent, weaving evergreen cedar boughs among its slats to create a shady oasis in the hot Tennessee sunlight. The men liked the results of their creation so much that they proceeded to put up similar bowers along both sides of the company's tent street.

There was time for an occasional pass to leave camp, too. Capt. Long, accompanied by Cpl. James League, took a horseback ride into the countryside to make friendly calls on some of the homes surrounding Camp Thomas. Stopping at most of the houses they came to, they found people friendly but "crying for bread." Giving them all they had, the two soldiers went along not knowing how they would eat themselves. They came upon a brick house just at dinner time when they heard a church bell pealing in distant Winchester. Considering the bell a timely, mystical signal, they knocked at the door and asked for dinner. Their instincts were right; the family obliged by sharing its own slim fare of "good" string beans, potatoes, corn bread made from meal and water, and sweet milk. Payment by the guests was refused, but accepted were two teacups full of brown coffee, the first the family had seen in a year.

Long's empathy for the plight of these civilians caught in the merciless grip of war was heightened later when he and League called on a woman of about 24 whose husband had been killed at Stones River. Her two small children reminded the captain of his own at that age but differently, for these were "running around with starvation staring them in the face." The best the two Yankees could do was give the youngsters the few sticks of candy which Cpl. League had brought with him.[17]

In August came a few command changes in the 87th's brigade. Col. Judson Bishop took over the Second Minnesota, Lt. Col. Henry V.N. Boynton the 35th Ohio. Another battery was added to the brigade's artillery, C of the First Ohio Light, Lt. Marco Gray in command.[18]

At last, clear and concise orders came from Rosecrans of how each corps was to advance. Sunday, August 16, began the ascent of the mountains that would take the army first to the Tennessee River, then to Chattanooga. Thomas was given the simplest mission. His XIV Corps was to move directly toward the river as quickly as possible. Thomas sent Brannan's Third Division (with the 87th Indiana) toward the narrow Battle Creek Valley along with Maj. Gen. Joseph Reynolds' Fourth Division. At the creek's mouth with the Tennessee, boats would be built for the crossing. Thomas was ordered to advance with utmost secrecy.[19]

The 87th left camp near Winchester at 11 A.M. that Sunday and waited at Decherd, four miles northeast, wrapped in their gum blankets, for the passing of a torrential rain. The regiment then camped for the night further east to allow another of Thomas' divisions to clear the road before it tackled the Cumberlands, the first of three mountains in its path.

On Tuesday, August 18, the climb began at 6 o'clock in the morning. The summit was 1,960 feet above the point where the regiment struck the mountain. According to George Martling of Mishawaka and Company K, it was "very steep climbing but scenery on looking from top grand." Many like him in the regiment, accustomed to the prairies of northern Indiana, would remark on their unusual, exciting mountain experience of the next few days.

Henry Clay Green of Company E remembered the snakes; all rocks and stumps "seemed to be full of them." The soldiers exterminated as many as they could with rifle fire, wrote Green, who recalled that three of the rattlesnakes he shot were from four to six and a half feet long.

Reaching the summit, the 87th pitched its tents beside good water near present-day Sewanee, site of today's University of the South. The university's cornerstone was laid with much pomp and ceremony in October 1860, by Episcopal Bishop Leonidas Polk who helped organize it in the hope of educating a Southern ruling class.[20] We have met the bishop before in his role as a lieutenant general in the Confederate Army. When the 87th arrived on the proposed campus, construction had been stopped by the war. Capt. Peter Troutman of Kewanna and Company E saw only two large workers' sheds and a row of log houses.

Teamster Bruce drove his six-mule team with the wagon train all the way to the top, arriving at dark after a seven-mile trip that he described as "stopping, stalling and breaking wagons."

Wednesday, again at 6 A.M., the regiment crossed 12 miles of the mountain's tableland over an easy downgrade march on a good road. That gave Solomon Deacon of Company K time to see Winchester and the valley far below as "a vast garden beautifully arranged . . . some of the most beautiful scenes I ever saw before in my life." The descent was difficult, on a rocky road that continually switched back onto itself. Bruce called it "very steep" and unloaded baggage before starting.

The road came out finally into Sweeden's Cove where the regiment camped at dark. A narrow valley (cove, in the local vernacular) of some five miles long, Sweeden's Cove was a half-mile wide and beautifully picturesque, surrounded by high and heavily timbered mountains. There were some small cornfields in the valley and the size of the corn astonished the many farmers among the men from Indiana; some stalks were 20 feet high.[21]

Friday, August 21, the regiment moved down the valley, found Battle Creek tumbling from its mountainous source and followed it to its mouth on the Tennessee River. Amid high weeds, the men made a camp that they soon named Fort Thomas.

Here the 87th's brigade got on speaking terms with the Johnny Rebs, whose pickets on the other side of the river first began taking shots at the bluecoats. That didn't last long, however, for soon boys in blue and gray were trading jokes, insults and good-natured ribbing across the water. A few Yanks got the Johnnies' agreement not to shoot while they were swimming and hundreds subsequently dived in. Pvt. Martling went to the riverbank to talk with these Southerners, speaking to one who begged him for coffee that Martling did not have. Some of the Rebs' jokes were quite amusing, according to Capt. Troutman, but he said that "they don't believe us when we tell them Morgan is in the penitentiary." Such front-line camaraderie was not uncommon in this uncommon war.[22]

Fraternization could not last, however, and on Friday, August 28, a week after arriving at the Tennessee River orders came to begin organizing the brigade's crossing. Col. Newell Gleason of the 87th Indiana was put in charge of erecting a bridge for access from both sides of Battle Creek; he picked 80 men from the regiment for the task. Boats and rafts also were constructed and activity became so frenzied that the Rebel pickets, alarmed at the Yanks' overwhelming numbers and intentions, disappeared.[23]

Sunday, August 30, the entire brigade crossed. One raft, made from logs from vacant houses, was 50 feet long and 16 feet wide. It held two companies at a time. All along this section of the river Brannan's troops were getting onto the other shore. Those who couldn't find a boat ride stripped, bundled their clothing, tied their rifles to fence rails and swam the 400 yards, pushing everything ahead of them if they were strong swimmers or drifting with the current to the opposite bank if they were not. Confederates could have picked them off easily.[24]

With the whole army across, the advance continued but Brannan's division with the 87th Indiana stopped to catch its breath for a few days. The march resumed on Saturday, September 5, reaching the huge Nickajack Cave where saltpeter had been mined for many years. There was time to explore its seven-mile depth, an unfortunate pause for two Company K men who got lost and had to be rescued by a local guide. The cave is at the exact spot where the state lines of Georgia, Alabama and Tennessee meet.[25]

Sunday, September 6, the 87th marched three miles up Raccoon Mountain west of Chattanooga. It was a rough, steep climb; artillery teams had to be doubled. At the top, camp was made near immense, abandoned coal mines. The scenery from 2,200 feet once more stunned Hoosier flatlanders. Monday, September 7, the regiment continued down into Lookout Valley.

Bruce and his mules rejoined the regiment for the Raccoon climb, having spent almost three weeks on foraging and supply expeditions for corn, hardtack and other rations from army depots at Bridgeport and Stevenson, west of the river in Alabama. On these trips, he slept on the ground with his mules or on the sacks of corn in his wagon and once spent a whole day fruitlessly searching for his nigh swing mule that "somebody" had stolen.

The country that the 87th had just passed through was the roughest its soldiers had yet encountered; one of them spoke of "immense cliffs of rock heaped one upon the other, forming innumerable barriers."[26] No letters written about this achievement mention anyone of the regiment faltering along the way.

Once in Lookout Valley, the 87th and its brigade turned southward for 10 miles and stopped at Trenton on Tuesday, September 8. They now were in Georgia. After a pause to regroup, they turned their attention on Saturday, September 12, to climbing their third mountain. Martling of Company K was glad to get the rest. He was stricken by rheumatism, a soldier's affliction coming from constant exposure, and he kept up with the regiment only by spending a day in an ambulance, another riding a horse provided by a kindly officer.

Climbing mountains no longer was a concern for the 87th Indiana, so

Lookout Mountain's 1,000 feet were covered in the first two hours after daylight. The final barrier to an attack on Chattanooga from the south, Lookout was impassable except at scattered gaps which meant that Rosecrans' army would be widely separated as it came down. The 87th headed for Stevens' Gap and from there emerged into McLemore's Cove, an almost pristine forested meadow tucked between Lookout Mountain and one of its spurs called Pigeon Mountain.

It was there on September 12, for the first time, that the northern Indiana Hoosiers looked upon a sluggish, muddy creek that rose out of the valley. It was named Chickamauga by the Cherokee Indians, first inhabitants of this still-remote frontier region. In English the word meant "River of Death." It was the Indian word, however, that would be forever remembered by those who survived the next eight days.

In McLemore's Cove the 87th waited with its brigade while Thomas gathered all four divisions of his XIV Corps. By Wednesday, September 16, that was accomplished and the 87th joined the corps as it began a march up the valley toward Chattanooga. Rebel drumming and artillery sounds indicated that the Confederates were concentrating to confront the Yankee army now spilling over Lookout Mountain into the woodlands south of Chattanooga.

After only a short advance to the north, a halt was called and a line of battle formed. But it proved a false alarm and after awhile the order came to stack arms.[27]

Thursday morning, September 17, the 87th was in line of battle again at its campsite when, about 8 o'clock, Rebel artillery began randomly bombarding the brigade from Pigeon Mountain. The fire promised to become too effective, so the regiment was ordered to strike tents, shoulder knapsacks and move to its left. Quartermaster Robert (Newt) Rannells and teamsters began loading the wagon transports.

The regiment marched off into a road that "for acute angles, excelled anything of the kind I have ever seen, before or since," according to a Company D sergeant. The sharp angles, Rannells noted, would separate the transport wagons into segments of two six-mule teams, each out of sight of the other.

Col. Gleason threw out a strong skirmish line a hundred yards to the right as a precaution against surprise attack and ordered the regiment to move out, leaving Quartermaster Rannells to finish loading the wagons. Just then, a regiment of butternut cavalry appeared in a timberline about half a mile to the front. This spooked Rannells, who began rushing the work to get underway before the Rebs could intercept him.

The regiment marched off along the twisting road and had gone about a mile when a courier from the quartermaster dashed up to Col. Gleason. Rannells was asking that the regiment be halted until the wagons could come up, for the train was in danger of capture.

Col. Gleason was a bit irritated, for he and Rannells had developed a dislike for one another that often brought reprimands from the colonel and responsive anger from the quartermaster. However, Gleason moved the column by right oblique off the road, dismounted with his staff and waited.

Soon Rannells on his roan charger came galloping into view around one of the sharp bends in the road, followed in frantic and disorderly fashion by one after another of the six-mule wagon teams. As Rannells pulled up the roan and dismounted in front of the colonel, Gleason's displeasure at the unruly scene erupted into the brisk comment: "Mr. Quartermaster, I want you to keep those teams closed up and straight in the road, sir."

Quartermaster Rannells was not to be so summarily chastised. Straightening himself and crossing his hands behind his back in characteristic fashion, he replied in a voice that rose steadily from beginning to end of the sentence: "Colonel, how in the hell are you going to keep teams closed up and straight in a crooked road, by God!"

Everybody within earshot broke into a laugh; except, that is, Col. Gleason, who turned on his heel and walked away. The strained relationship between the two men ended nine weeks later, on Nov. 24, when the quartermaster resigned his commission and returned to Rochester.[28]

With the transportation train now in place, the 87th Indiana continued its march up the valley without further interruption and joined the rest of Col. Ferdinand Van Derveer's Brigade in bivouac at Pond Spring. By now, every man was aware that a big fight was coming soon.

Daniel Bruce of Bruce Lake who filled four diaries with his daily experiences as a teamster with Company E. He drove a six-mule team pulling a wagon to supply the regiment with its essential food, equipment, ammunition and animal fodder.

Lt. Col. Edwin P. Hammond of Rensselaer, commander of the 87th Indiana during its March to the Sea through Georgia. He became an outstanding Indiana jurist after the war, rising to a seat on the Indiana Supreme Court.

Peter S. Troutman, a Kewanna schoolteacher who became captain of Company E and led it through Chickamauga, Missionary Ridge, the Atlanta campaign and the March to the Sea. He was an articulate correspondent from the war fronts.

Kline Shryock of Rochester, the 87th Indiana's first colonel. Later, he led another Indiana regiment during its ill-fated campaign against Brig. Gen. John Hunt Morgan's invasion of southern Indiana.

Asa Plank, the Rochester druggist who recruited Company F of the 87th and became its first captain. He resigned his commission after the Battle of Perryville.

Dr. Charles Brackett of the redoubtable military Bracketts. He recruited a company from Fulton County at the outbreak of the war, became a surgeon in the First Indiana Cavalry and later joined two brothers in the Ninth Illinois Cavalry where he served until his death.

William Wood of Akron, captain of Company D at the Battle of Perryville. He resigned afterward because of ill health and died in 1866. Wood organized and drilled Fulton County's first militia in 1856.

Horace C. Long, the Rochester shoemaker who rose steadily from sergeant to captain and commander of Company F. He reported graphically on the company's battle performance at Chickamauga and wrote frequently about its subsequent experiences.

Benjamin Franklin Brown of Rochester, sergeant in Company D. He left his sickbed in the regimental ambulance to rejoin his company for the Night March that brought the regiment into Chickamauga's opening battle action.

Jonas Myers, the Rochester carpenter who entered the war as a Company F private and ended it as a second lieutenant for the Grand Review in Washington. His expressive diary entries give an evocative sense of Civil War soldiering with the 87th Indiana.

John B. Apt of Fulton, on the left, served until war's end as a private in Company F. He struck this harmonious pose with a former Confederate foe while attending one of the many annual reunions that were held in Chattanooga by veterans from both of the armies who fought at Chickamauga and Missionary Ridge. (Olive Apt Herrold collection)

Reunion 87th. Ind.Vol.
Rochester, Ind.
Sept. 19-20, '07.

SURVIVORS OF THE 87TH, 44 YEARS AFTER CHICKAMAUGA

Veterans of the 87th Indiana Infantry Regiment favored September 19 and 20 as the time to gather for their postwar reunions. It was on those days in 1863 that the 87th performed so gloriously, and at such sacrifice, in the frightful woodlands of Chickamauga. The regiment's reunited survivors posed for the above picture 44 years after the battle, on September 19, 1907, at the Fulton County Courthouse in Rochester. No contemporary identification of the photo has survived. However, the author believes Sgt. Jonas Myers of Company F is in the third row, third figure to the right of the flagstaff, wearing a hat with pointed crown, and Sgt. Albert Pugh, also of Company F, is fourth to the right of the flagstaff in the first row. The unexpected appearance of this photo inspired the author's research which led to the writing of A Stupendous Effort.

8
The Night March

Friday, September 18, Sgt. Benjamin Franklin Brown of Rochester was beginning to feel better. Ten days earlier he was stricken by "something like a bilious attack," probably a gallbladder disturbance. Since then he had been riding in the regimental ambulance during the 87th's advance northward out of McLemore's Cove, a cul-de-sac valley with Lookout Mountain on the left, Pigeon Mountain on the right. Yankee soldiers knew the valley by various other names: Chickamauga, Chippewa, Pigeon.

The sergeant figured it was time to rejoin his Company D, because "we were expecting to get into a muss with the Rebs."

The regiment had been ordered to move out at 7 P.M. Friday for a night march which Brown was told would be about five miles; he believed he could make it that far. So he got his rifle from the ordnance wagon and took his place at the head of the company. He couldn't abide the thought of a cartridge box buckled around his tender middle, so he put it in his knapsack after pocketing 10 rounds of cartridges and some percussion caps.[1]

Sgt. Brown guessed right about a number of things that day. He did complete the march even though it took all night. He was wise to have his Enfield musket's ammunition handy, considering what was ahead of him. And, most significantly, there certainly was a "muss" coming with the Confederate army, although that was a puny description for the impending Battle of Chickamauga, bloodiest of the Western theatre and worst two-day loss of life in the entire Civil War.

Three months of maneuvering and marching by the two armies were coming to an end. From Hoover's Gap, to Tullahoma, to the Tennessee River, Maj. Gen. William S. Rosecrans had outflanked the Rebels brilliantly, forcing them further and further southward. Finally, unable to cover the Union's widespread envelopment of Chattanooga, Gen. Braxton Bragg had evacuated the city September 7 and retreated into north Georgia. Rosecrans thought Bragg would continue to backpedal.

Confederate President Jefferson Davis, however, knew that loss of Chattanooga would open the South's heartland to the Union hordes, so he decided to reinforce Bragg with two divisions of Lt. Gen. James Longstreet's First Corps from the Army of Northern Virginia. Longstreet's arrival would give Bragg 66,000 men to Rosecrans' 58,000. Davis ordered Bragg, his long-time personal friend, to smash the Federal army as it emerged into the Georgia woodlands from behind Lookout Mountain.

By this Friday, Bragg's intention to turn and fight had become apparent to Rosecrans; there were ample signs the Rebels were moving to flank the Union left. Confederate skirmishers already were across Chickamauga Creek to the east and large clouds of dust denoted infantry moving north toward its bridges. Rosecrans knew that he must secure routes to his Chattanooga base and get ready for a Confederate assault westward from Chickamauga Creek.

He ordered his entire army to shift northward along the line of the La Fayette Road, which would become the axis of the battlefield.[2] That order is what got Sgt. Brown out of his ambulance and back into the ranks.

Sgt. Brown was not the only one anticipating an impending "muss" with the Rebels, for signs of a fight were obvious to all. The day before, an oppressively hot Thursday, the 87th's Third Brigade had moved north from its camp at Pond Spring, filling the air with fine dust from underfoot. All the while there was a corresponding dust cloud moving in the same direction on the other side of Pigeon Mountain, less than a mile away on the right. The two armies were moving on parallel paths, certain to converge somewhere to the north. Thursday night the Confederate campfires were visible clearly on the east. The Third Brigade, which had advanced but three miles, was ordered to "sleep on its arms" in case of an attack.

The day's experiences clearly had affected the troops. Judson Bishop, colonel of the brigade's Second Minnesota Regiment, recalled that "all day a feverish, mysterious, nervous foreboding had seemed to pervade the camp; everyone was conscious of it."[3]

For the men of the 87th Regiment the expectation of battle must have been particularly engrossing. They all realized that what was coming would be no Perryville, where they also had slept with their arms awaiting an attack, one that never came. This was going to be a very big fight and they had not been in one like it, had not been tested by the torments of battle that now loomed ever more fearsome in their imaginations.

To accomplish his army's northward movement, Rosecrans chose Maj. Gen. George H. Thomas and that meant the 87th Indiana. Thomas' XIV Corps would jump over Maj. Gen. Thomas Crittenden's XXI Corps and extend the Union line five miles to the north, thus outflanking the flanking Confederates. There was a mutual esteem between Rosecrans and Thomas that had begun during their days as fellow West Point cadets. Thomas, the Virginia Yankee, was loyal, cool, tenacious and resourceful; he could be depended upon to hold the left.

Thomas' corps was made up of four divisions: Brig. Gen. Absalom Baird's First, Maj. Gen. James Negley's Second, Brig. Gen. John M. Brannan's Third and Maj. Gen. Joseph Reynolds' Fourth. We'll hear from all of them during accounts of the next two days but it is Brannan's division that will stand out and it, of course, included the 87th Indiana of Col. Ferdinand Van Derveer's Third Brigade. Two other brigades completed Brannan's division, the First led by Col. John M. Connell and the Second led by Col. John T. Croxton.[4]

Brannan, and his division, will take significant and crucial roles in the development and final resolution of the impending battle. The importance of this division's performance must not be overlooked nor minimized in any balanced account of Chickamauga.

Crittenden was to realign his divisions to allow Thomas to pass through from the south. Subsequent orders were misinterpreted, or reversed, or ignored; delay and confusion resulted. The hours slipped by; when darkness came Friday, it was apparent that a night march, possibly lasting until sunrise, would be necessary to get the army into its new positions.

Rosecrans pondered the decision at his headquarters in the Gordon-Lee mansion at Crawfish Springs, south of Crittenden's position. Although concerned how effective the men would be after a night without sleep, he realized that unless Thomas reached the La Fayette Road to confront the Confederates in the morning, there would be the devil to pay. So he told Thomas to push on with all possible speed.[5]

The march would be five miles long from Crawfish Springs, where all the Union troops filled their canteens in passing for it was the only source of drinking water on their side of the lines. For the 87th and its Third Brigade, the march would be seven miles from bivouac at Owen's Ford on the Upper Chickamauga. It would not be a speedy walk.

Soldiers of the Civil War remembered night marches with a shudder, for they were the worst. They usually began before supper, as did this one, and they always were particularly tiring of body and mind. This march would be forgotten by few who made it. The deep and dark forest closed in on the columns; the temperature fell to near freezing. To light the way, scouts rode ahead and set fence rails on fire but there was no time for soldiers to do the same. It went on all night with little persistent progress.[6]

The Second Minnesota's Col. Bishop remembered that "we moved about a quarter of a mile per hour through the whole night, halting every few rods just long enough to get stiff and cold, but never long enough to build fires and get warm. Many of the men would fall asleep, sinking down in the road and some standing on their feet, but strict orders were given not to leave the column and to follow closely those leading us."[7]

Not unexpectedly, other memories of the tiresome march vary widely. Among the 87th Sgt. Brown and Pvt. Henry Clay Green thought that the regiment marched almost without stopping for rest. Pvt. Peter Keegan of Company C came off picket duty at 6 P.M. to find the regiment packing to move out. After 30 minutes there was a three-hour halt, he said, and then a march until 3 A.M. when the regiment lay down until daylight. Progress was very slow, Keegan confirmed, because the road often was blocked with troops and artillery that was moving along with them. Keegan's diary, unlike Col. Bishop's narrative, reports that troops "burned all the fences along the way to keep warm, as it was very cold." Keegan thought the march was 14 miles long, twice its actual distance, and to one who was there it very well might have seemed that long.

Company E of the 87th Regiment was camped in a woods next to Company F that was in a cornfield. Peter Troutman of Kewanna, Company E's captain, was surprised when the march continued through the night for he understood it was to be a short one. A letter he wrote eight months later recalled that everything he saw on the march "showed that an engagement was inevitable."[8]

Horace Long of Rochester, captain of Company F, also remembered a 15-mile march in a letter he wrote two months later. The regiment got a precautionary marching notice at noon in their cornfield camp, he said. Soldiers packed their baggage and waited, probably not as patiently as Long remembered, until the final order came at 7 P.M., by which time some of the men "was about to commence to fix up for the night." Just at daybreak, Long recalled, the regiment passed Rosecrans' headquarters at Crawfish Springs.[9]

As dawn lightened the eastern skies, men of the 87th saw brigades and batteries leaving La Fayette Road in line of battle, moving east into the woods toward Chickamauga Creek. The pieces of the puzzle were falling into place. The 58,000-man Union army was getting into position for the great struggle about to take place; the tedious progress of the night march suddenly became more understandable.

The 87th and its other three brigade regiments finally were halted at 8 A.M. along La Fayette Road, near the wretched little cabin and stubbled cornfield of Elijah Kelly. The men filed out of the road and stacked arms, hearing the welcome words "20 minutes for breakfast." Within five minutes hundreds of small "can kettles," the small fruit cans carried by all soldiers, were filled with canteen water and set to boil over hundreds of small fires. The men paired off; one got coffee in the cans, the other sliced and broiled bacon from haversacks. In another five minutes, the coffee was ready, the bacon browned, hardtack moistened and toasted.[10]

Suddenly, on the dusty La Fayette Road appeared an aide in a frantic gallop. He rode up to Col. Van Derveer, handed him an order and dashed off. In an instant the bugle blew to fall in. Sgt. Brown had only half his coffee downed, Capt. Long just had taken a sip of his but Capt. Troutman was more efficient. He had downed "an excellent breakfast of broiled meat, coffee and crackers."

There also was much "sulphurous profanity" heard as hungry, angry men filed back into the road to await orders. Years later numerous survivors of the brigade would call this lost breakfast one of their most enduring war memories. Each man was not sure at that moment if he'd ever eat another.

Many wouldn't, for Croxton's brigade from Brannan's division had opened the Battle of Chickamauga nearby and needed help. Brannan sent for Van Derveer's brigade, and there was no time to lose.

As the 87th Indiana Infantry stepped off onto La Fayette Road, it was marching to its destiny. Chickamauga was its ultimate war experience, the inevitable test of its courage, resolution and skill. By performing in harmony with their brigade, the 87th's survivors would emerge from the two-day holocaust in Georgia's tangled woodlands with enough fame and satisfaction for a lifetime and beyond.

There was to be a frightful cost for it. The 87th entered Chickamauga's firefights Saturday morning with 366 officers and men, only a third of its original strength 13 months before. When darkness fell Sunday, only 174 were present to answer roll; 192 had been killed, wounded or were missing. That 52 percent casualty rate was the greatest of all 28 Indiana infantry regiments engaged in the battle and the eighth highest of all 131 Union foot regiments in action.[11]

Capts. Long and Troutman, Sgt. Brown and Pvt. Keegan of the 87th could not know on that Saturday morning they would live to write their memoirs, nor could they imagine what an astonishing two days were ahead of them.

On this opening morning their brigade would repulse four Confederate charges, the last time saving the Union left flank from envelopment. Sunday morning it would perform the same task again, throwing back a Rebel assault that was about to envelop Federal breastworks on the left. Finally, on Sunday afternoon and evening the brigade was to be among those heroic few who rallied on a hillside and held off the victorious, exultant Rebels for five hours, thereby saving the Union army from total destruction.

The 87th's unpleasant night march was over, but the morning's prospects were even more dreadful.

9

"We Waded in without Flinching"

C hickamauga Creek's name, from a Cherokee Indian word that means "River of Death," was quite appropriate for the murderous battle that occurred west of its sluggish waters.

Chickamauga has been called a battle of soldiers, not of generals, and so it was, for the terrain made generalship nearly impossible. Most of the rough and broken ground west of the creek was a dense, mixed-wood forest and within its surrealistic depths much of the fighting took place.

Today the woods are choked with undergrowth because the National Park Service has allowed the battlefield to achieve its natural appearance. This was not so in September 1863. North Georgia resembled a wilderness. The few farm families who inhabited the Chickamauga forests closed in their yards and fields with split-rail fences. Their livestock roamed freely in the frontier's open ranges outside these fences. Over time the animals had trampled and grazed the shrubs, brambles and wild grasses, leaving much of the space between trees free of underbrush.

The densely packed trees with their overhanging limbs and vines remained, reducing visibility inside the forests to 50 yards in many places, 150 yards at most. Passage was obstructed by rotting tree trunks, fallen dead trees with snarled branches, earthen hillocks overgrown with brush and heavy tangles of vegetation. As the day progressed and sunlight faded, vision was obscured further in the battle's gunpowder smoke that was trapped by the tree canopy. There were often fires in the underbrush started by sparks from the guns.

Fighting in such frightful woodlands created command and control problems that almost were insurmountable. Regimental battle lines were at least 400 yards wide, often longer, and alignment was crucial. But commanders could see only fragments of their line and could not know whether it was being maintained or being enfiladed or flanked. So when they were sent into

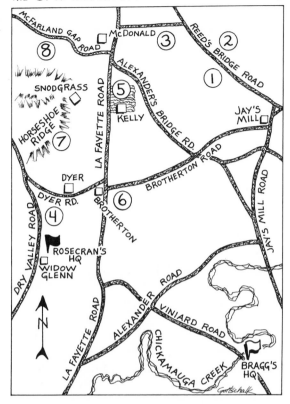

KEY TO MAP 2

1 Where the 87th Indiana and its brigade engaged the Confederates at the opening of the battle, Saturday morning, September 19, turning back three Rebel assaults.

2 Quickly changing fronts to this position, the 87th and its brigade then met and defeated the Confederates' flanking movement, saving the left wing of the Union Army from being enveloped.

3 Location of the cedar glade where the 87th Indiana and its brigade rested after Saturday morning's actions, until summoned in late afternoon to reinforce the Union center.

4 Where the 87th and its brigade bivouacked without fires Saturday night to await resumption of the battle on Sunday.

5 Kelly Field, where the 87th's brigade was summoned quickly Sunday morning, arriving in time to demolish a Rebel attack that once again threatened to outflank the Union's left wing.

6 Where Longstreet's wing of the Confederate army broke through the gap in the Union line later Sunday morning and sent most of the Federal army into panicked retreat.

7 Horseshoe Ridge, alongside the Snodgrass House, where the 87th and its brigade arrived mid-afternoon on Sunday and took part in the heroic stand that held off the triumphant Rebels long enough for most of the Union army to reach safety.

8 McFarland Gap Road, the route to Chattanooga for the 87th with its brigade at nightfall Sunday, after the defense of Horseshoe Ridge.

action, soldiers stepped into a personal world and the outcome depended upon each man's combat against those indistinct figures he saw in the haze or smoke, who were dodging from tree to tree, bush to bush. The soldier's initiative combined with his training, instincts, resourcefulness, determination and bravery would determine his fate, and that of his comrades.

This Chickamauga nightmare had "no generalship in it," declared Col. John T. Wilder of Indiana much later. "It was a soldier's fight purely, wherein the only question involved was the question of endurance. The two armies came together like two wild beasts and each fought as long as it could stand up in a knockdown and drag-out encounter. If there had been any high order of generalship displayed, the disasters to both armies might have been less." Wilder and his mounted infantry, the "Lightning Brigade" that was armed with Spencer repeating rifles, fought with high distinction at Chickamauga.

There was a ferocity to this struggle from its very beginning, a fury that made it stand out even among the Western theatre's clashes that as a rule were conducted with a greater animosity than were their Eastern counterparts. An Alabama Confederate described the battle as "one solid, unbroken wave of awe-inspiring sound . . . as if all the fires of earth and hell had been turned loose in one mighty effort to destroy each other." A Union officer thought of it as a "mad, irregular battle, very much resembling guerrilla warfare on a vast scale, in which one army was bushwhacking the other."[1]

The 87th Indiana Infantry Regiment's ordeal at Chickamauga now began. When the Hoosiers followed Col. Ferdinand Van Derveer up La Fayette Road shortly after 8 o'clock Saturday morning, they were answering an order from Brig. Gen. John M. Brannan, their division commander. The ball was about to open, as veteran soldiers liked to describe the start of a battle.

Earlier in the morning the 87th's corps commander, George H. Thomas, had just arrived at Kelly Field when he was told by Col. Daniel McCook of Maj. Gen. Gordon Granger's reserve corps that a single brigade of Rebs was west of the creek and could be gobbled up. McCook was wrong. Only some dismounted cavalry from Brig. Gen. Nathan Bedford Forrest's command were there, screening Maj. Gen. William Walker's infantry division that had begun crossing the creek.

To develop the enemy's strength, Thomas selected a brigade from Brannan's division, that of 26-year-old Col. John T. Croxton, a lawyer and loyal Kentuckian who would end the war as a major general.[2] Croxton's men also gave up their breakfast to advance into the dense woods eastward from La Fayette Road toward Jay's Mill, a steam sawmill at a dirt crossroads about two miles away. Short of the mill they were attacked by elements of Forrest's horsemen but drove them back with two volleys. The brigade moved on and soon was engaged with more of Forrest's dismounted cavalry and elements from Walker's infantry moving up from the creek.

Croxton sent back word of his encounter; Brannan responded by ordering Van Derveer's brigade to turn the Rebels' right flank by way of Reed's
Bridge (Ringgold) Road. It intersects La Fayette Road north of Kelly Field,
running due east and then southeast to the site of Croxton's action. The
battle now truly was joined and the 87th's brigade was to be in the thick of it.

Van Derveer led his men up La Fayette Road to the McDonald farm at
the Reed's Bridge Road intersection, but 100 yards short of the crossing he
turned his force eastward along a wagon trail. Van Derveer was a courageous, but not foolhardy commander. He had no guide and no knowledge
of where he was going, so quickly after leaving La Fayette Road he formed
the brigade into two lines, its left along Reed's Bridge Road, skirmishers to
the front.[3]

The men moved cautiously, all the time hearing brisk firing on the right
from Croxton's engagement. A mile out the road bends to the southeast
and ascends a hill. Reaching its crest, Van Derveer was ordered to make an
attack to relieve the pressure being put on Croxton's force.

Only three of his four regiments were present; the Ninth Ohio was on
the way from guarding the division ammunition train. Van Derveer sent
out skirmishers and behind them quickly formed a battle line with the 35th
Ohio on the right and the Second Minnesota on the left. Lt. Frank Smith's
artillery battery of four 12-pounder Napoleons was placed in the center
and right. The 87th Indiana, still untested in battle, was put in reserve behind the battery and 30 yards to the rear.

The brigade then moved 500 yards southeasterly into the forest to the
base of the hill, where Van Derveer ordered his men to lie down to escape
fire from the unseen skirmishing going on in their front. Those bullets began coming hot and heavy, many of them passing over the front line into
our unfortunate 87th Regiment laying in wait. Several were killed or
wounded when the balls "showered about us . . . thick as hail."[4]

The skirmishing continued for 15 minutes, drawing ever closer to the
waiting battle line. Finally the brigade's skirmishers rushed in and "over a
little rise in the woods in front appeared the heads of a solid line of men in
gray." It was the dismounted Tennessee cavalry of Col. George Dibrell,
who had been searching for the rear of Croxton's force and found Van
Derveer's instead. With their piercing Rebel yells splitting the forest air,
the Tennesseeans attacked and were met with a volley from Minnesota
and Ohio muskets. Dibrell's first line disappeared and the second line came
up. For 30 minutes the furious firing went on. Van Derveer's line held but
the 35th Ohio was losing men rapidly. Finally, about 9:30 A.M. the fire slack-
ened as the butternuts backed away. The woods fell silent.[5]

The hush would last barely half an hour before there came a second
attack, this time by the Texas brigade of Brig. Gen. Matthew Ector. The
tramp of their feet preceded them by a full minute and so Van Derveer's
line was ready with a volley when they emerged from the smoke. The Rebels
halted and the Texans returned fire, but their line was decimated by canis-

ter from Smith's battery. It was an unequal contest and Ector withdrew after 30 minutes, or about 10:30 A.M. Once again the unlucky 87th Indiana had suffered silently, taking more casualties in reserve on the crest of the ridge, this time from Confederate artillery overshooting its mark.[6]

The 87th's passivity finally was at an end, however. Van Derveer ordered it into the front line to relieve the badly mauled 35th Ohio. Col. Newell Gleason led the regiment forward and the movement, according to Van Derveer's official report, "was executed with as much coolness and accuracy as if on drill."[7] The regiment moved smartly within a few paces of the 35th. The men lay down "in the midst of a shower of lead to allow the Buckeyes to pass to the rear and as soon as the front was clear of bluecoats we let fly at the butternuts," reported Capt. Peter Troutman of Company E. Prisoners afterward told Troutman that the 87th's fire had raked them badly, unlike many previous volleys that were too high.[8]

"It was our first regular engagement and we waded in without flinching," recalled Capt. Horace Long of Company F, for the regiment opened right away with a volley on a largely unseen enemy that was returning fire from behind trees and brush.[9]

Clearly, men of the 87th could be counted on in battle.

Some already were lost, though. Company D's Corp. William Ewer of Rochester, in position to the left of Sgt. Benjamin Franklin Brown, did not rise when the regiment was ordered up; he had been mortally wounded while lying in reserve and died in a few minutes.

Company F's men barely had let off their first volley before Pvt. James Babcock of Rochester was shot in the knee; he fired once in return before hobbling off the field. Capt. Long's pride soared as he watched his men in their first battle action.

"After the first round or so our boys never paid any attention to (the enemy) but stood up, loaded and fired. . . . I heard another of my men say 'I am hit,' and looking around I saw it was Simeon Frear. 'Where are you shot?' I said, and he replied 'in the foot.' I told him to go to the rear and he hobbled off. I returned to the head of my company and had no more than got there when a tree top was cut off by a cannon ball above my head, falling on me and several others but not hurting me, only covering me up with the leaves and smaller branches but hurting Sgt. Albert Pugh so badly as to compel him to leave the field.

"The next man of my company who was hit was Sgt. Clement Clay, in the right leg by a rifle ball just grazing it below the knee but not bad enough to make him leave the field. We stood there in our tracks and fired 50 or 60 rounds to the man."

Long's admiration for his company's performance under fire was epitomized by two sergeants, Jonas Myers and the aforementioned Clay. They were detailed as file closers, the sergeants or officers who were posted during battle behind the double ranks of soldiers. Their duties were to keep the lines closed as casualties occurred or if men wandered from proper position. File closers normally were not involved in the action, but that was not the case that day with Myers and Clay.

"When the fight was the hottest," Long said, "I had to laugh to see Sergeants Myers and Clay, they being file closers and in the rear of the lines, they would load, stoop down, pick out their man, grit their teeth and fire, then step back into their places, load and repeat the same over during the engagement. Better and braver men they do not live."

Capt. James Holliday of Mishawaka and Company K was lost during this opening action of the regiment. A Minié ball in the forehead killed him outright, reported Pvt. Henry Clay Green of Company E who was standing at the captain's side.[10]

The enemy became quiet for a time, allowing Col. Gleason to put out a few skirmishers, replenish ammunition, send some prisoners to the rear and take care of the 87th's wounded.

During the lull at Company E, Lt. Franklin Bennett of Kewanna walked toward the front, saying he'd like to find some battlefield relics, but returned shortly without souvenirs or comment. It was his last act. Sporadic firing resumed and Bennett was hit. Capt. Troutman was 10 paces to Bennett's right and heard the bullet strike distinctly, the firing not being regular at the time. "I run to him," said Troutman, "raising him up and found the ball had taken effect in that region of the heart. I had him carried to the rear but, alas, the work was too well done and the noble and patriotic Frank was another martyr to his country's cause."

Over at Company E's position during the pause in the firing, some prisoners were brought in who identified themselves as Lt. Gen. James Longstreet's veterans sent to reinforce Gen. Braxton Bragg. The 87th learned it was up against seasoned, formidable soldiers.

The new battle line which Van Derveer formed put the Second Minnesota on the left, then Smith's battery with the 87th on its right. Next came the Ninth Ohio, which had just arrived on the scene, and still further on the right were reinforcements sent by Brannan: a section of Capt. Josiah Church's battery and the 17th Ohio Regiment out of Col. John M. Connell's brigade. The 82nd Indiana Regiment from Connell was put in reserve with the 35th Ohio.[11]

Van Derveer was content to hold his position and see what the butternuts next had in mind. Firing soon broke out all along the line. The 87th again was in the midst of it and began to take more casualties. Corp. James Moore and Pvt. Josephus Collins of Company D went down, Collins to die from his wounds a month later. Both were from Rochester.

All at once the explosive sound of regimental file firing was heard from the forest to the brigade's right. Then lines of men in blue appeared out of the trees, coming toward Van Derveer's line. They were Brig. Gen. John King's U.S. Regular brigade from Brig. Gen. Absalom Baird's division which had been flanked by Rebel infantry and was in pell-mell retreat, with three of Brig. Gen. Edward Walthall's Mississippi regiments firing and yelling triumphantly in pursuit. "I do not remember any more appalling spectacle than this was for a few minutes," recalled the Second Minnesota's Col. Judson Bishop.

These Regulars had stood fast at Stones River but this morning they were wild-eyed and panic stricken, shouting at the Volunteers to save themselves and retreat. The Volunteers were disgusted at the sight; one artilleryman from Smith's battery flattened a retreating officer with his sponge for having disturbed his cannon. "And Regulars think we Volunteers won't fight," Capt. Troutman shouted in contempt.

The 87th and its comrades would show the army's career soldiers what Volunteers were made of. Not a man left the ranks. Although they had to endure the Rebels' pursuing fire until the "flying Regulars" were out of the way, this was done calmly and when the Mississippians drew within 40 yards, the entire line rose up to deliver a volley that stopped the butternuts in their tracks. They returned the Federal fire but then the 10 cannons of Smith and Church raked the field with canister and the attackers began to back out of range.

At this moment Col. Gustav Kammerling of the Ninth Ohio, who had been "chafing like a wounded tiger" because he had missed the opening of the engagement, took matters into his own hands. Yelling something about "them got tam rebels," Kammerling ordered his regiment up to attack the disappearing enemy. This German-speaking outfit was anxious to follow whatever orders its colonel gave. The 87th Indiana joined in for a few yards but Van Derveer called the Hoosiers back; his shouts at Kammerling to return were drowned out by the Teutonic cheers of the 500 Germans. On they went, at the cost of 50 killed and wounded, smashing into the tiring Mississippians and retaking six guns of a battery that had been lost just minutes before.[12]

In this engagement Lt. Sloan Martin of Westville was killed as he encouraged his men to "be steady and fire low." Peter Balder of Bremen and Company K also died here. Peter Keegan, the Peru private in Company C, saw his captain, Milo Ellis of Peru, go down with a Minié ball in the side; Keegan lost hearing in his left ear and partial hearing in the right ear from the artillery concussions.[13] Three from Capt. Troutman's Company E fell at this time and two, Richard Liming and John Yagle, both of Star City, did not survive their wounds.

Van Derveer had good reason for wanting to keep everybody, including Kammerling's Germans, on hand. A fourth Confederate attack was coming, from an unexpected direction.

Forrest, still in charge of the dismounted troopers in Van Derveer's front, ordered Col. Dibrell and Brig. Gen. H.B. Davidson to take their two brigades north along Reed's Bridge Road and turn the Union left and rear. The move-

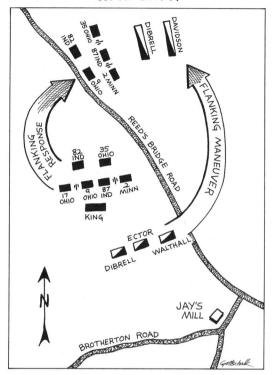

ment was detected, but almost not in time. Van Derveer ordered his brigade to change front from the south to the north and move at the double-quick to Reed's Bridge Road by which they had come. It became a foot race to see which side would get into position first. Van Derveer's men won.

In a few minutes the brigade's three regiments had moved back up the hill, crossed the road and into the forest, forming a northward-facing line with 10 pieces of artillery. On the right was the Second Minnesota, next a section of Smith's battery, then the 87th Indiana, flanked by Church's battery and the other section of Smith's, with the 35th Ohio on the extreme left. The 82nd Indiana still was in reserve. Van Derveer had lost 250 men in repulsing three Confederate attacks; he now had 1,800 to hold off this fourth assault. The line formed a lazy V with the opening toward the enemy. It now was noon.

The Confederates came steadily out of a ravine in two disciplined lines, earning the waiting Yankees' respect. Discipline and drill would not be enough, however. The Union artillery belched double-shotted grape and canister, mowing down swaths in the ranks, and the Federal infantry's volleys exacted a still greater price. The butternuts had superiority in numbers and the 35th Ohio began to give way on the left, but this exposed the attackers to murderous enfilading fire from the right by the 87th Indiana and Second Minnesota. The Ninth Ohio came up from its impetuous charge in time to help out. At 60 yards the Confederates began to waver and at 40 they broke, dashing through the smoke and brush back into the forest.

The left of the Union line had been saved from envelopment.[14]

In the final action Franklin Smith, a private in Company D, was killed instantly by a ball through the head and Sgt. Clay took his second and third wounds of the day, one ball grazing him under the right arm, another hitting him below the left knee. Still he would not leave the field. Sgt. Brown's only brush with a battle wound came there when a ball "left the size of it on my arm" but wounded Pvt. John Robbins who was standing just behind him.

George Martling of Mishawaka and Company K was detailed to carry wounded after this action and never forgot "the mangled remains of men and horses" covering the field and "all the timber mowed down by artillery."[15]

By now it was 1 P.M. Saturday's work was over for the 87th Indiana and the Third Brigade. A remarkable day it had been. They had repulsed four separate Confederate attacks in four feverish hours over a forested area of only 50 square acres and in so doing preserved the left wing of the Army of the Cumberland.[16]

The 87th Indiana proved its valor, but 11 of the regiment lost their lives on Saturday. Chickamauga was exacting a price and it was not yet fully paid.

Three of the 11 dead were officers: Capt. James Holliday of Mishawaka, Company K; 1st Lt. Sloan Martin of Westville, Company H; and 2nd Lt. Franklin Bennett of Kewanna, Company E.

Eight deaths came from among enlisted men.

Company A (one): Sgt. Elijah Israel of Rensselaer.

Company D (two): William Ewer and Franklin Smith, both of Rochester.

Company G (three): Henry Baker of LaPorte, Michael Gilfoyle of New Carlisle and Amos Prince of Rochester.

Company H (one): Eugene Pratt of Union Mills.

Company K (one): Peter Balder of Bremen.

None of the 11 bodies ever were recovered by their families although those of Bennett and Israel later were identified near where they fell, as we shall see. It is possible that some of them were buried immediately on the battlefield.

Van Derveer ordered his medical aid station to be set up in the rear of the brigade when it went into action Saturday morning. That rear turned out to be the front when he was flanked and had to shift almost 180 degrees. Thus, the final Confederate assault passed over the Union wounded because there had been no time to evacuate them. Such are the horrors of war.[17]

When the fight was over, officers agreed to Van Derveer's suggestion that the dead be buried before moving on. That this did occur was confirmed when a 35th Ohio grave was opened sometime later. Many of the Union dead, however, lay exposed for three months until Federals recaptured the battlefield and gathered them for nameless burial in Chattanooga National Cemetery. In 1867 when more bodies were sought for transfer to the cemetery, a grave was found in this vicinity containing eight to 10 bodies from the 87th Regiment. Those very well might have included the men listed above.[18]

The 41 from the regiment who were wounded on Saturday were collected and dispatched by ambulance to Col. A.C. Cloud's Third Division field hospital, located in a church and adjoining cooper's shop three miles away on Missionary Ridge.[19] By the time of Chickamauga, the Union army's method of evacuating wounded by ambulance had become quick and effective, although the jolting ride over rutted roads could be excruciatingly painful to those who had to endure it.

Once deposited at the field hospital, the wounded soldier often was in for an even more terrifying experience. Bullets of the time were fired at speeds too slow to purify them, so when entering the body, they contained germs from the hands of those who fired them along with bits of the dirty clothing they happened to strike. Surgeons knew nothing of bacteria and so their dirty hands and instruments, unsterile cleansing and bandaging brought more deadly microbes. Thus recovery from the wound quite often was secondary to fighting off the infections. Those who could survived; those who couldn't wasted away in a lingering death.

Then there were the amputations, performed on three of every four of the wounded, sometimes with chloroform but often without. "Brave was the man who submitted to unanesthetized surgery," wrote one scholar of the war's medical history, "but braver still were those detailed to hold him still." One of the most macabre sights at any field hospital was the pile of amputated arms and legs, steadily growing and in plain view.

Union hospital conditions continued to improve. By the time of the 1864 campaign into Georgia, large mobile hospitals kept pace with the forces and remained near the railroad for easy transport to Chattanooga for recovery.[20]

Meanwhile, back with the 87th Indiana on the morning's battle line, the Third division's ammunition train arrived to refill cartridge boxes. When that was completed, the brigade marched back up Reed's Bridge Road toward La Fayette Road.

Halfway there it turned southward into the woods and halted at a large cedar glade, gaining a short respite to replenish body and soul in this relatively serene enclosure. The glade's alkaline soil kept the high ground there clear, dry and soft.

About the time the brigade had swung around to meet its last assault on the left, Maj. Gen. William S. Rosecrans decided he'd better leave the Gordon-Lee mansion at Crawfish Springs and find new headquarters closer to the coming action. He knew by then that the Confederates were west of Chickamauga Creek and that the battle would be fought on his left, as Thomas had been telling him by courier all morning. Rosecrans ordered reinforcements to Thomas and galloped off furiously with his staff.

He stopped at the Widow Glenn house, a small log cabin perched near Dyer Road on the northern slope of a high hill, behind what would become the center of the Union line. There were good sight lines north and east, making it an ideal location to direct the battle. Or so it seemed at the time.

Eliza Glenn lived there with her two-year-old son and an infant daughter. Her husband, John, had died in a Mobile, Ala., hospital two months after enlisting in the Confederate army. Rosecrans took the time to advise the young widow to move with her children to a place of safety. This she did.[21]

From its sanctuary in the cedar glade, the 87th Indiana and its brigade could hear occasional battle sounds southward but they were not summoned until late in the afternoon. There was trouble in the Union center, near the Brotherton House on La Fayette Road. Brannan ordered Van Derveer and Connell out of the glade and they were on the way by 4:30 P.M. but Brotherton's was almost two miles away. By the time they arrived, around 5:30, the situation had stabilized. Maj. Gen. Alexander Stewart's division of Tennessee, Alabama and Georgia troops crossed La Fayette Road to threaten the Widow Glenn house when Maj. Gen. James Negley's fresh bluecoat division arrived from the right in time to push Stewart's unsupported men back across the road.[22]

Brannan posted Van Derveer's brigade at the center as his division's reserve for the night. The four regiments went into bivouac in a sloping field westward on Dyer Road immediately west of the Dyer House and north of Widow Glenn's. The men needed a rest because since noon of the day before they had received no sleep and meager food.

As soon as the 87th regiment had settled in, distribution began of letters and packages. Even in the midst of a battle this was not considered unusual, for Civil War commanders understood that contact from home was the most important part of a soldier's morale. Each regiment had its mail clerk and the mail was distributed as quickly as possible after it came. Pvt. Keegan received a towel and handkerchief, he recorded.

It was the autumnal equinox, traditional time of north Georgia's first frost, and it arrived heavily on that clear night. Many of the regiment had no cover for they had lost their knapsacks and blankets during the day's hectic events. Even worse, though, after their suppers were eaten orders came down from Gen. Thomas: all campfires were to be doused and none lighted the rest of the night. That side of the hill was next to the enemy. So for the second night in a row there was no sleep, this time because of the bitter cold. Everyone was up often to walk about and get warm, Col. Gleason included.

The Hoosiers took macabre solace that they were better off than the thousands of wounded men of both sides whose shrieks for help, for water or for a quick death sundered this dark night unceasingly. Those who tried to reach the wounded were targeted by the pickets. A private of the 72nd Indiana wrote in his journal of yearning to "drown this terrible sound." A Texas cavalryman said "we literally walked on dead men all night" and in the light of a permitted campfire finally saw "hundreds of ghastly corpses mangled and torn . . . scattered around us. I can sit here by my little glimmering light and count a score of Federals, dead and dying. . . . I have not had a particle of sleep, nor do I want any while this bloody work is going on."[23]

The dense woodland was dark and gloomy, the prevailing sense of horror almost palpable. With so much death already present on this killing field, a soldier could not help but contemplate the imminence of his own.

Horace Long of the 87th's Company F had another matter on his mind. He was pleased by the memory of his good supper of coffee, hardtack and salt pork. He relished it, he said, "as much as the fine suppers of our friends at home, I mean those young able-bodied men strutting the streets who are too cowardly to come out and give us a hand in putting down this unholy rebellion and saving their country."

Capt. Long could have another go at delivering the country's salvation in the morning, for he and everyone else on that field knew the issue had not been decided. The clanging of axes and the sound of falling trees to the east, where Thomas' troops hurried to construct breastworks, confirmed that anyone who expected Sunday to be a day of rest was going to be badly disappointed.

10

The Bravest Deed in the Entire War

The 87th Indiana Regiment's momentous Sunday of September 20, 1863, began with sunrise at a quarter to six. White frost blanketed the ground, smoke still lingered in the forest, fog and mist rolled in from the Chickamauga Creek bottoms. A surprising, eerie stillness enveloped the four-mile-long battlefield stretching along La Fayette Road. The quiet was like a grave and most oppressive, one recollection has it.[1]

Stiff and tired from their uncomfortable passage through the cold and fireless night, men of the 87th kindled their small cooking fires for coffee and bacon, then waited for orders. Some additional hours of rest would be granted before fate summoned them at 10:30 o'clock to prove their military valor once again.

The factors that would bring this about were put into motion during the dark and foreboding night that now had changed to an apprehensive daylight. After a full day of vicious bloodletting all along La Fayette Road, the armies were about in the same positions where they began except that Maj. Gen. William S. Rosecrans had at last concentrated the three Union corps of his Army of the Cumberland.

The Federals' connections to their base in Chattanooga lay behind their left. Gen. Braxton Bragg was certain to assault that end of their line in the morning to cut off their supply routes and then attempt to destroy them with his superior numbers. Rosecrans, knowing that Lt. Gen. James Longstreet's corps had arrived from Virginia, felt that Bragg would attack aggressively.

Rosecrans was so worried about the coming day's outcome that he had lost some confidence. He agreed to send more help to Maj. Gen. George H. Thomas on the left, but told the loyal Virginian to "defend your position with utmost stubbornness. In case our army is overwhelmed it will retire on Rossville and Chattanooga." These must have been daunting words to hear from one's commander just before a battle.

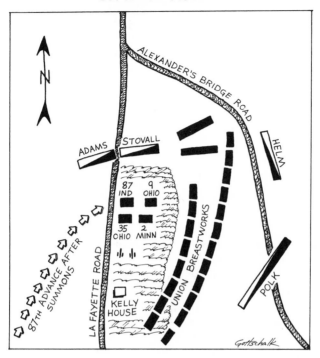

Thomas harbored no thoughts of defeat, for during the night he ordered a line of breastworks built surrounding the forest salient of Kelly Field. The soldiers went to it with a will, for such cover gave them an inestimable advantage against attack. They used fence rails, rocks, fallen trees, branches, literally everything they could find that might absorb or deflect a bullet. They used the trees they chopped down to clear a field of fire in front. The barrier was put up three feet, high enough to squat or lie down behind. These works when completed looped for almost a mile around Kelly Field on the east.

On the Confederate side Bragg, to the dismay of his commanders, reorganized the Army of Tennessee during the night into two wings. He put the right wing under command of Lt. Gen. Leonidas Polk, the Episcopal bishop who had blundered into Yankee lines at Perryville. The left wing would be led by Longstreet, a West Point roommate of Rosecrans, who had arrived from Virginia too late to direct his troops Saturday. Polk's wing was to attack the Federal breastworks at dawn and Longstreet's left wing would follow to provide a continuous assault of the Union line.

But Bragg issued no written orders and some of his key staff members did not learn his intentions. There would be no dawn beginning of Sunday's fight.

Such were the machinations in progress that would impact Indiana's 87th Infantry, which at Dyer Field still was shaking the kinks out of tired bodies from a cold night on the hard Georgia ground.[2]

At 8 o'clock the 87th was posted with Col. Ferdinand Van Derveer's brigade as Brig. Gen. John M. Brannan's reserve northeast of its bivouac site, behind the brigades of Col. John M. Connell and Col. John T. Croxton. Brannan had moved Connell and Croxton into line Saturday evening to reinforce the Union center shattered by Maj. Gen. Alexander Stewart's Confederates. The position was along La Fayette Road near Poe Field, south of Kelly Field.

Van Derveer formed his brigade into double column. The 87th had won his respect with its staunch performance Saturday and was placed in the front line on the left with the Ninth Ohio on the right; the 35th Ohio and Second Minnesota made up the second line.[3] There they waited in formation when shortly after 9:30 A.M. they heard the Rebels "open the ball" east of nearby Kelly Field.

Soon the fearful sound of infantry file firing was heard and enemy bullets began passing over the Union battle line, dropping among Van Derveer's idled men "in a very disquieting manner." The rest of the brigade understood how the 87th Regiment had felt Saturday when, in reserve at the action near Jay's Mill, it had to undergo a rain of Minié balls.

The men began to make light of their predicament with jokes and facetious comments that fit perfectly into a sudden occurrence nearby. Stragglers began appearing out of the woods, crossing the road near the brigade and passing into the field beyond. Some were wounded but most were the "cowardly skulkers" found in every battle who got out of harm's way as fast as they could. Most had thrown away their guns with their courage, so early efforts to stop them were abandoned. Then six men with guns emerged from the woods carrying a man in a blanket with his face covered. It appeared to be a wounded general officer, being carried to the rear by a guard detail. Suddenly a shell came shrieking through the trees and landed near them. "They dropped the blanket and their guns and took the double-quick to the rear; the man in the blanket got up and ran after them."[4]

This gave the brigade comic relief from the tension that soon would be transformed into action.

The Rebel attack was begun at 9:30 A.M. by the division of Kentuckian John C. Breckinridge, a former Vice President of the United States now a Confederate major general. It also was a Kentucky brigade that led the first charge. Commanding was 32-year-old Brig. Gen. Benjamin Helm, married to the sister of President Abraham Lincoln's wife Mary; he would not survive the morning's conflict. By 10:30 o'clock the Confederate pressure was beginning to tell. Especially weakening was the left of the breastworks line held by Brig. Gen. Absalom Baird's division that included the U.S. Regulars who had fled so disgracefully on Saturday.

Brannan's division was summoned to Baird's assistance by Thomas, who did not know that two of Brannan's brigades had been put into line at the center. Brannan answered in the only way he could, releasing Van Derveer from reserve and hastening him on.[5]

The 87th's brigade moved northeastward through the forest paralleling La Fayette Road and emerged from the woods onto the road at about midpoint of the half-mile-long Kelly Field. Brig. Gen. Henry V.N. Boynton said long afterward that what Van Derveer's men did next was the bravest deed he saw in the entire war. Boynton saw it at close quarters, for at that moment he was a lieutenant colonel in charge of the 35th Ohio.[6]

Here is Boynton's description of the action that now ensued:

"As (Van Derveer's) front line emerged from the forest it entered a thicket of low pines which fringed the western side of the Kelly Field. The flags, the bayonets and the mounted men of the front line could be seen above the thicket. The soldiers in the pines could see nothing. Just at this moment two Confederate brigades of Breckinridge's division, which had passed around the Union left and wheeled southward, burst into the field from the northern border, full into the Union rear. Its lines covered the western half of the field, extending into the woods from which Van Derveer was emerging, and were marching directly on his flank which was not more than 200 yards distant.

"The Confederate lines, seeing the flags and horsemen in the pines, which with the glittering of bayonets clearly marked the Union lines, opened a hot and destructive enfilading fire upon it. Van Derveer, who was riding in advance, took in the situation at a glance. Sending staff officers to each regiment with orders, he rushed his lines forward into the open field, wheeled them to the left on a run and under a rapidly increasing fire, until they fairly faced the approaching line.

"The distance to Breckinridge's front had meantime been reduced by its advance to a hundred yards. Van Derveer's men had not fired a gun. Under orders, his lines dropped on their faces and waited until the enemy was within 75 yards when the front of two regiments (87th Indiana and Ninth Ohio) rose and poured a volley into the faces of the enemy, effectually checking his advance. Van Derveer's second line (35th Ohio and Second Minnesota) sprang up under succeeding orders, passed over the front line on a charge (and was) followed instantly by the front line, both dashing at a run toward the enemy's front. It fired once, then broke, and was rapidly pursued by the charging brigade and driven back around the Union left.

"Van Derveer's loss was about 20 percent in 30 minutes. Every horse in the brigade but two was killed or wounded."[7]

The brigade pushed the Rebels at bayonet points into the woods at the north edge of the field for a hundred yards or so, then held them back with steady rifle firing for an hour until other Union units arrived on the right to relieve them. The enemy by this time was almost silenced, reported Van

Derveer, and he ordered a return to the open Kelly Field behind. This was done smartly by passing the lines of two regiments to the rear, each line firing as it went.[8]

Two Confederate brigades had been routed by this astonishing response of a single Union brigade. The Rebels were the Louisiana and Alabama regiments of Brig. Gen. Dan Adams and the Georgia, North Carolina and Florida troops of Brig. Gen. Marcellus Stovall. They had broken around the Union breastworks and were about to have the XIV Corps surrounded. It was a close escape from calamity.

Brig. Gen. William Hazen, whose brigade was at the breastworks nearby, commented later that this repulse of Breckinridge "was the only occasion in the war on which I saw two opposing lines deliberately advance to close quarters and fire in each other's faces. The first shots of the enemy came from 25 degrees from our rear and left and except for the repulse, the battle must have ended then."

He concluded: "It was the most anxious moment of my life."[9]

In this firefight the 87th Indiana Regiment found itself immediately in front of the fire from all of Adams' five regiments. The Hoosiers, said Col. Newell Gleason, were "exposed to a terrible crossfire from an artillery battery." Capt. Peter Troutman's account agrees but adds that "our boys poured it into them at left oblique and were the victors." In this mix with the immovable 87th, Adams and his adjutant, Capt. Emile P. Guillet, both were wounded and captured while Maj. Loudon Butler was killed.[10]

Capt. Troutman helped take the wounded officers to the Union field hospital, where Adams later praised the stubbornness with which the 87th's brigade fought his larger force. Brannan, who left conduct of the engagement entirely in the hands of Van Derveer, told the men afterward in Pvt. Peter Keegan's presence that they were the Iron Brigade "for we had to be composed of such material to stand up under such fire."[11]

Victory was not accomplished without a heavy cost; surviving accounts speak of dead and wounded everywhere around Kelly Field. Capt. Troutman's Company E lost three killed. Simon Fall of Kewanna and Robert Tribbett of Rochester both were shot in the head, Aaron Smith of Blue Grass in the breast. Two died later of wounds: Sgt. Jonas Clark of Blue Grass, shoulder, on September 23, and John Ferrell of Kewanna, head, on October 14. Four had severe wounds: Walter Soper of Bruce Lake, groin; John Rush of Blue Grass, side; Robert Smith of Kewanna, arm; and James Thomas of Bruce Lake, heel and leg. Slightly wounded in the head was George Kiplinger of Fulton.

Wrote Troutman: "While our loss was terrible, yet it was light when compared with the great work accomplished. It is a settled fact that if the enemy had succeeded in effectually turning our left, the main part of the invincible 14th Corps would have been captured. The credit of holding this point justly belongs to the Third Brigade, Third Division, 14th Army Corps, of which the 87th was a conspicuous part."

Capt. Horace Long reported that when the action opened, Company A was on the right of the regiment and in Kelly Field, his Company F was in the open road and Company D extended partly into the road. "We had a clear front to the rebels, as clear as in the streets of Rochester, but there was no flinching, every man stood up to the work like old veterans."

Long believed the musketry firing there must have been one of the heaviest of the war. The Rebels came at them four lines deep and "the balls came so thick amongst us that it seemed like a swarm of bees were flying about." Soon he began to see one after another of his men go down. "Corporal Polk McMahan was hit, he staggered and whirled around and grabbed me as I was standing near him. He was wounded in the right eye and wrist. I told one of our boys to help him back and get him out of danger as much as possible. Now John House fell, a ball breaking his neck; then Corporal (Isaiah) Webb was wounded. About this time Lieutenant (Joseph) Beeber was shot through both legs just above the knees. One after another fell until 10 of my men were killed or wounded; right there (Alfred) Goodrich, (William) Farry, (Peter) Hoffman, (John) Robbins, (Harper) Rodgers, (Jonathan) Clay, Joseph Taylor and about 20 paces to my left fell Adjutant (Fredus) Ryland; still closer fell Captain (Lewis) Hughes of Company D. I did not know how soon my turn would come." While fighting in the woods north of Kelly Field, Cpl. John Roth and Harrison Stotler of Long's company were wounded. All the men mentioned were from Rochester.[12]

Mishawaka's George Martling of Company K, helping to carry off the wounded at this time, was sent back by his major with Lt. Beeber's horse to get the wounded officer. He hoisted Beeber aboard but then lost both man and horse while retrieving Beeber's sword as the regiment began falling back. Beeber survived. Martling also saw and spoke with Charles Long who had been shot in the leg and Nate Russ with a leg wound. John Sumstine came by on a litter, shot in his side and at his nose. He would die of the wounds Jan. 14. All three men were from Mishawaka and Martling's company.[13]

When the regiment rose up to fire its first volley, Sgt. Benjamin Franklin Brown of Company D thought Adams' butternuts were "as thick as I ever saw pigeons on a newly sown wheat field." His company lost 18 of the 35 men who went into the action. Not only Capt. Hughes was killed but also James Osborne, Brown's closest friend and a relative. Among the wounded were William Oliver, David Oliver, David Shelton, Benjamin Porter, Eli Strong, Henry Moore, David Moore, John Wright and Kline Wilson. Missing was Levi Sherow. All were from Rochester.[14]

When it all was over, the lines of the two forces were plainly marked by the rows of dead, said Keegan, who was unhurt although a ball passed through his knapsack and struck him on his waist belt. Keegan helped carry wounded Pvt. James Foss of Peru to Col. A.C. Cloud's division hospital on Missionary Ridge and took care of him all through the night. Keegan did not rejoin the regiment until Monday.

Keegan noted that in the two days of Chickamauga action, the regiment had only one instance of cowardice; it was a sergeant from Company K who later was reduced to the ranks.

Col. Judson Bishop of the Second Minnesota had a spectacular accident during action on the brigade's right wing. While Bishop was galloping around his regiment's flank in the open field, his horse was shot in the breast, dropping her to her knees and sending Bishop in a flying somersault over her head. He got up unhurt and abandoned his steed, thinking her fatally wounded. After the fight she was discovered by one of the wounded men and the two helped each other over the road to Rossville where they rejoined the regiment about midnight. Both survived and served until war's end.[15]

Van Derveer had gone into this action without his battery, which had been taken from him to join other artillery Thomas was massing behind the Union left on a ridge near the Snodgrass house. This thievery did not amuse Van Derveer at the time but in the fight he got excellent support from the First Ohio Light Artillery battery, which Capt. Wilbur Goodspeed set up just north of the Kelly cabin.

By 1 o'clock survivors of the 87th Indiana and its Third Brigade had moved south to the smoking ruins of the Kelly cabin, where they gathered up their wounded and flopped onto the ground to rest and regain their composure.

The Confederates could not put together another coordinated effort to flank the Union left. They continued assaulting the breastworks until late in the afternoon when, because of battle events that had transpired to the south and west, the blue troops were ordered out of the lines.[16]

By then, the 87th Indiana and its brigade had rushed off to perform one final, heroic service at Chickamauga, for while the regiment was resting at Kelly Field, not far away a calamity was about to strike the Union army.

11

Making a Stand
to Save an Army

The Battle of Chickamauga is a fascinating study. It offers the astounding coincidence that brought the Confederates not only victory, but also a chance to annihilate the Army of the Cumberland. From that came another improbability: the inflexible determination of a small portion of the defeated army to save the remainder from destruction. It is ironic that the Union's final performance in the face of its disaster is the most notably remembered event of this monumental example of 19th-century warfare.

These quirks in the battle and their development must be considered to understand how, for one last time, the 87th Indiana Infantry was brought into the cauldron of Chickamauga to share in its resultant glories.

At 11:30 o'clock Sunday, while the 87th was locked in its savage struggle at Kelly Field, there was relative quiet at the center of the Union line three-fourths of a mile south on La Fayette Road. Suddenly at the Brotherton farm there, 11,000 Confederates appeared out of the woods on a dead run over a 500-yard front, the blood-chilling yip-yip-yip of their Rebel yell filling the air. Leading the way were Brig. Gen. Bushrod Johnson's division of Tennessee, Texas, Arkansas and North Carolina regiments.[1]

Lt. Gen. James Longstreet was launching the spearhead of the 23,000-man left wing and there to meet it was . . . practically nothing.

Incredibly, a gap in the Union lines had opened at the precise point struck by Johnson's force. It was, in fact, the only true breakthrough of a defensive line in the entire Civil War.[2] The Federal center and right collapsed.

The explanation for the existence of such a gap is complicated and reflects the relationships and personalities of those involved. It should be noted for our story, however, that Brig. Gen. John M. Brannan's division was directly, though innocently, involved in creating the hole.

Brannan had pulled Col. John T. Croxton and Col. John M. Connell's brigades back into the cover of woods after they and Maj. Gen. Joseph

Reynolds' division on their left had repulsed an earlier attack that morning. One of Maj. Gen. William S. Rosecrans' staff officers, reconnoitering the line soon afterward, failed to see Brannan's troops among the trees and reported it as a gap to Rosecrans. Brannan, the aide said, had moved out at Maj. Gen. George H. Thomas' request to help the hard-pressed left. The commanding general was exhausted and preoccupied with the fast developments on that edge of the battle. He gave little analysis to his aide's excited report of the gap, quickly directing an order for Brig. Gen. Thomas Wood's division to close up to the left on Reynolds. Nor did he read the order after it had been written, or he might have seen that its wording neglected to make the movement conditional on Brannan's absence.

When Wood received the order at 11 A.M., he was startled; he knew Brannan was in position and there was no gap. Besides, his skirmishers were actively engaged with the Rebels, so something might be up with the enemy. That should have settled the matter; no gap, no order. Wood, however, had been reprimanded by Rosecrans in front of Wood's own staff just 90 minutes before because his division had been slow in complying with orders. Wood was a West Point professional and perhaps should have known better, but he was peeved. Anyway, he had Rosecrans' order in writing if anything went wrong. Wood ordered his division out of line.

So Rosecrans was creating a gap in his line where none existed. It was fate's cruel joke that at the very moment of its creation, Longstreet was marching upon that exact spot from 700 yards away.[3]

The Rebels were dazzled and momentarily disconcerted by this unexpected stroke of fortune, but quickly poured through the Union lines. Before long almost half of the Federal army was in headlong, panicked retreat. The terrified bluecoats headed for the rear toward Dry Valley Road which led to McFarland Gap of Missionary Ridge and thence to Chattanooga. The Yankees were in an appalling frenzy. Infantrymen abandoned rifles, ammunition and anything on their person impeding flight. Artillerymen jumped on their horses, cutting the traces and leaving their guns to the pursuers.

By noon Rosecrans decided to quit the field, accepting defeat. Joining him were two of his corps commanders, Maj. Gen. Alexander McCook and Maj. Gen. Thomas Crittenden, plus four division commanders. They had to force themselves through a human mob onto Dry Valley Road, where as far north as they could see was the wreckage of their army: frightened soldiers, angry officers, walking wounded and an endless chaos of wagons, limbers, caissons, ambulances. It was the worst Union rout since First Bull Run in July 1861.[4]

The Confederates formed up and turned northwesterly toward the same objective as the hysterical Union soldiers: Chattanooga. Brannan, whose division had been on the edge of the breakthrough, gathered his survivors and led them in the same direction, but toward a series of hills and ridges that ended at Dry Valley Road. Arriving at these heights about noon, Brannan began patching together a thin defensive line from his broken brigades of Connell and Col. William Hays, who had taken over for the wounded Croxton. Wood's division was taken in the flank while moving to its new position and disintegrated, but the brigade of Col. Charles Harker remained intact. It turned to confront the Rebels, holding them back long enough for Brannan to continue putting together his defensive line.[5]

Thus it came about that the final act in Chickamauga's appalling slaughter would be performed along a mile-long concave spur of Missionary Ridge, the rocky parapet that stretches 15 miles southward from Chattanooga. The spur was called Horseshoe Ridge, although it in no way resembled a horseshoe. Some called it Snodgrass Hill because it began with another spur in the cornfield near the cabin of George Snodgrass. Beyond that cabin the ridge consisted of three distinct hills thick with trees and underbrush, separated by ravines.

Here a valorous few would make their stand. They would run no more.

By 12:45 o'clock Brannan had completed a rather thin south-facing line along Horseshoe Ridge with remnants of his own brigades, stragglers and bits and pieces of other regiments that began appearing on the scene. These men quickly grabbed rocks, logs and fence rails for breastworks and rolled in all the batteries on hand. Harker's brigade, meanwhile, retreated from its holding action further down to establish the left of the line, on the hill in the Snodgrass cornfield.

About then Gen. Thomas, who as senior officer on the field succeeded to command of the army, rode into the cornfield with his staff. His stolid and confident demeanor amidst the haste and confusion had an inspiring effect upon the men. "You must hold this position at all hazards," he told them, to which a colonel replied, "We will hold this ground or go to heaven from it."

Word of "Old Pap's" appearance spread quickly from the Snodgrass spur down the Horseshoe Ridge line and greatly encouraged the defenders. Thomas was sincerely loved by his men, who believed they could not be whipped when he led them.[6]

This conviction was to get its most powerful test now, for at 1 o'clock the Confederates came up the slope to attack Harker on the left, or east. They were Brig. Gen. Joseph Kershaw's South Carolinians who 80 days before had taken the wheatfield and peach orchard at Gettysburg. They would not easily be denied, but denied they were, in three successive attacks.

This was the first of continual rushes up the hills by four Confederate divisions that would consume six hours until nightfall. There remains considerable confusion today exactly how many times Longstreet sent his butternuts up those wooded slopes; estimates range from 12 to 29. The General Staff College of the U.S. Army, which trains its officers in leadership and tactics at Chickamauga, puts the number at 25.[7]

Whatever the number, the attacks were furious and unrelenting. By 2 o'clock the west end of the line was in danger of being overrun only to be saved by the timely arrival of 3,700 men of Brig. Gen. James Steedman's two brigades from Maj. Gen. Gordon Granger's reserve corps. Granger risked his career by having sent them without orders from 3½ miles away, believing that Thomas badly needed help. Steedman's arrival was decisive in holding the Horseshoe Ridge line, although in doing so his mostly green troops took 1,788 casualties by sundown, almost 50 percent of their number.[8]

Decisive, too, was the appearance soon after Granger of Van Derveer's brigade with the 87th Indiana.

Col. Ferdinand Van Derveer was a commander whose imagination equalled his courage. He was not afraid to act independently on a battle-field when the situation demanded. By 2 o'clock while resting his brigade near the burned-out Kelly cabin, Van Derveer could hear the heavy firing going on to his right and learned that part of Brannan's division was engaged on the high ground in that direction. Van Derveer ordered up the 87th and the other regiments. The brigade went off through the woods, brushing aside elements of Col. Daniel Govan's Arkansas brigade, which had come into the Kelly Field area.

Sometime around 2:30 P.M. the Ohio colonel rode into the Snodgrass corn-field at the head of about 1,000 men of the Third Brigade, which became the last unit of its size to take up the defense. Brannan termed the arrival "most opportune" and after the battle called the 87th's brigade "gallant . . . one of the few who maintained their organization perfect through the hard-fought passes of that portion of the field." Thomas also greeted the brigade with enthusiasm, particularly the Second Minnesota and Ninth Ohio whose performance at Mill Springs had helped him win his first battle. He rode out to meet the brigade and sent them to the second and third hills to relieve Brannan's tired defenders.[9]

Indiana's 87th formed to the left of the Second Minnesota on the second hill. The Rebels came up the wooded slopes in repeated waves as the Yan-kees crouched behind their breastworks to deliver deadly rifle volleys and individual marksmanship. "From this time until dark we were hotly en-gaged," reported Van Derveer, beginning at 3 o'clock when assaults from Kershaw's brigade and the Mississippians of Brig. Gen. Patton Anderson were turned back.

Down among the 87th Indiana's riflemen, Company F had been reduced that morning to just four effectives: Capt. Horace Long, Pvt. Adam Rimenschneider and the two enthusiastic file-closers of Saturday morning's fight, Sgts. Jonas Myers and Clement Clay. Sgt. Myers rather playfully sug-gested that with such small numbers, it might not be worthwhile for the company to do anything more that day but the captain said they'd take their place with the regiment. Then the much-targeted Clay received his fourth Chickamauga wound, through the thigh, and this one finally put him down.

"Cap told me to take him to the rear," Myers recalled later. "We had gone but a short way when Clay fainted and I thought he was going to die. I pulled his knapsack up under his head to make him as comfortable as possible. Instead of dying, he laid on his back and prayed and I made up my mind that he was better than a half dozen dead men.

"When he was through praying, I opened my knapsack and pulled out a towel and bandaged his leg as good as I could. The Johnnies were crowding us back, so we had to move. I informed Captain Long that I could carry Clay no farther, so Rimenschneider assisted me and we carried him to where we thought him safe while I looked for a hospital. Finding one, we went back after our wounded comrade but he was gone. Someone had already taken him to the hospital."[10]

All four men survived the war.

Col. Judson Bishop described how the butternuts looked from behind the brigade's breastworks when their attacks came:

"The front ranks melted away under the rapid fire of our men, but those following bowed their heads to the storm and pressed on, some of them falling at every step, until the supporting touch of elbows being lost the survivors hesitate, halt, then turning, start back with a rush that carries everything with them to the rear. . . . This was all repeated over and over again until the slope was covered with dead and wounded men that looking from our position we could hardly see the ground."[11]

Bishop was not exaggerating. The brigades of Brig. Gen. Archibald Gracie Jr. and Col. John Kelly were sent up against Brannan's line about 4:15 o'clock with 2,879 men, Gracie's left reaching the 87th's position. In an hour 1,054 from Alabama, Georgia, Kentucky, North Carolina and Virginia had fallen. That time the sheltered blue defenders held their fire until 80 yards before blasting away at the exposed graybacks. It was one of the heaviest attacks of the war on a single point, according to Kershaw. Two Confederate divisions lost 3,000 in dead and wounded in the six hours of assaults against Brannan's fortifications. A Confederate officer later said that "the dead were piled upon each other, like cord wood, to make passage for advancing columns."[12]

At no time during the afternoon did Brannan's total force on the ridge exceed 2,500 men. Even counting the addition of Granger's 3,700 reinforcements, the total number of Union defenders probably did not exceed 9,000 and not all were on the line at the same time. There were 19 Union regiments on hand but some were represented only by remnants or stragglers. The Confederates committed fresh units as others became exhausted, using 11 different brigades or about 30,000 men before nightfall. This disparity in numbers was overcome by the Federals' excellent positions on the crests, coupled with failure of the Confederates to support or coordinate the assaults. Because of this weakness in command, many times the Rebels actually were outnumbered at the points of attack.[13]

Behind their breastworks, however, the bluecoats were running out of firepower. The XIV Corps ammunition supply train had vanished in the breakthrough and although Granger brought 95,000 rounds, it was all used up quickly. To understand how, consider that one Ohio regiment of 535 men fired 45,000 rounds that day, an average of 84 per man. Many of the men had no ammunition at all, so the dead or wounded nearby were searched for cartridges.[14]

By 5 o'clock, an hour before sunset and 2 ½ hours before darkness, Thomas knew that the ridge could not be held much longer with ammunition practically gone and the butternuts coming at them with ever-increasing ferocity. Van Derveer said the attacks late in the afternoon were being made "with unexampled fury, line after line of fresh troops being hurled against our position with a heroism and persistency which almost dignified their cause."

Thomas began the retirement toward McFarland Gap with the troops from the Kelly Field breastworks that had been holding out all day.

With Rosecrans and the retreating portion of the army by now safely inside Chattanooga, the heroism on the hills was about to conclude.

When sunset came at 6 o'clock, the ridges dissolved into ghostly, smoke-filled early darkness. Out of the gloom a Rebel officer, James Chenault, orderly to Col. Robert Trigg of Gracie's brigade, rode up to face the 35th Ohio that was lying in underbrush. Chenault challenged the soldiers in the bushes to identify themselves and when he learned they were Yankees, turned to flee. The Ohioans rose and fired, taking down both horse and rider, casualties of the last volley fired at Chickamauga.[15]

Soon after this event Brannan ordered the 87th and its brigade to move down into the Snodgrass field and assemble until Thomas gave the final withdrawal order. When that came, Van Derveer's was the last organized brigade to leave the field, as was the 35th Ohio the final regiment to fire a volley at the enemy.[16]

At 7 o'clock, as the darkness closed in, Col. Newell Gleason marched the 87th Indiana Infantry Regiment off the bloody field of Chickamauga with empty guns and 174 men, fewer than half of those he brought there two nights before. The regiment had lost 31 killed in its two desperate actions on Sunday, almost triple the 11 who fell on Saturday. Others would not survive their Chickamauga wounds.

Five of the 31 killed Sunday were officers: Adj. Fredus Ryland of Rochester, Capt. George Baker of Star City and Company B, 2nd Lt. Elisha Brown of Peru and Company C, Capt. Lewis Hughes of Rochester and Company D and 2nd Lt. Abram Andrew of LaPorte and Company I.

The toll of enlisted men was a grim 26.

Company A (one): Matthew Hopkins of Rensselaer.

Company B (four): Jacob Evans of Bruce Lake, Lewis Griffith, Alexander Waters and Maluff Williamson, all of Winamac.

Company C (three): William Haskell, Miles Petty and William Wickler, all of Peru.

Company D (one): James Osborne, Rochester.

Company E (three): Simon Fall of Kewanna, Aaron Smith of Blue Grass, Robert Tribbett of Rochester.

Company F (one): John House of Rochester.

Company G (seven): Sgt. Solomon Harding, William Pointer, John Rody and Peter Warberton, all of LaPorte; Abraham Leiper of Callao, Patrick McCarty of Plainfield and John Garner, hometown unlisted.

Company H (one): John Turner of Bradford.

Company I (two): Lewis Howe of LaPorte, missing in action, and Cyrus Hecox, hometown unlisted.

Company K (three): Sgt. Lewis Simpson of Elkhart, Peter Heminger of Mishawaka and Jacob Keifer of South Bend.

These men of the 87th now lay scattered with the other dead, Federal and Confederate, amidst the carnage of Chickamauga. The shocking sight that the battlefield presented to the victorious Rebels was described in vivid detail by Pvt. Sam Watkins of the First Tennessee:

"Men were lying where they fell, shot in every conceivable part of the body. Some with their entrails torn out and still hanging to them and piled up on the ground beside them, and they still alive. Some with their under jaw torn off, and hanging by a fragment of skin to their cheeks, with their tongues lolling from their mouth, and they trying to talk. Some with both eyes shot out, with one eye hanging down on their cheek. In fact, you might walk over the battlefield and find men shot from the crown of the head to the tip end of the toe. And then to see all those dead, wounded and dying horses, their heads and tails drooping, and they seeming to be so intelligent as if they comprehended everything. I felt like shedding a tear for those innocent dumb brutes."[17]

It may seem curious to express more remorse for the suffering of the animals than for that of his fellow humans, but without such callousness the soldier cannot proceed with the business of the killing of his own kind in war.

With the rest of the Federal army, the 87th Indiana Regiment fell back five miles to the hamlet of Rossville, where it entrenched in case the Rebels came after them. Monday failed to produce any significant pursuit, so the 87th continued with the army to Chattanooga during the night and arrived there about sunrise Tuesday, September 22. Then came the work of serious fortification against further attack.

"Never did men have a better relish for that rather disagreeable exercise," Capt. Peter Troutman remembered. "Both officers and men threw off their coats and pitched in and before the enemy recovered from the terrible shock he had received, we had rendered Chattanooga impregnable."[18]

The captain's defiant attitude was commendable and surely there was shock enough in passing through Chickamauga's inferno to affect even its victors. For the haggard survivors in the 87th Indiana Infantry Regiment, still tasting defeat's bitter pill, it was enough for the moment that they at last had put that nightmarish woodland behind them.

12

Reflections
on a Disaster

Chickamauga was the singular, most overpowering Civil War experience for survivors of the 87th Indiana Infantry Regiment. More fighting, more dying, more views of the elephant were to come but nothing would equal the fiery furnace from which they escaped near a Georgia woodland creek.

Chickamauga proved to be the bloodiest two days of the war; some scholars consider it the deadliest of all the battles. The two armies sent 124,548 men into the lines and when the carnage ended 34,624 were dead, wounded or missing, a staggering 28 percent. Only the three days at Gettysburg and the Seven Days battles around Richmond cost more casualties. Indeed, many have called the battle the "Gettysburg of the West." The Confederates, who generally were on the attack at Chickamauga, lost 18,454 of their 66,326 effectives. Union losses totaled 16,170 out of 58,222 engaged.[1]

The killing gave some validity to the Paris newspaper *Figaro*'s comments after the battle that "these Americans are fighting on a military system inaugurated by the Kilkenny cats. The two armies meet and fight and slaughter each other with the utmost fury. Then they (fall) back and reorganize for another general massacre. The war will end when the last man is killed."[2]

The price paid there by the 87th was a grim one: 192 killed, wounded or missing out of the 366 effectives who came onto the field Saturday morning. The 87th's casualty rate of 52 percent was the highest of all the 42 Indiana infantry, artillery and cavalry units engaged. Chickamauga was, in fact, the costliest battle of the war for Indiana; 3,000 of its sons were killed or wounded. Confederates suffered no less; the 10th Tennessee Regiment, for example, left 68 percent of its men on the field.[3]

The 87th Indiana lost eight officers and 34 enlisted men by death; in wounded, four officers and 138 from the ranks. Eight enlisted men were missing and could be counted as dead. Other regiments in Col. Ferdinand

Van Derveer's Third Brigade suffered proportionate casualties. The Second Minnesota had 35 killed, 113 wounded, 14 missing. The Ninth Ohio, largest of the brigade's regiments, lost 48 killed, 185 wounded and 16 missing. The 35th Ohio had 21 dead, 141 wounded and 27 missing. The brigade's Fourth U.S. Battery I's losses were one killed, 21 wounded. Altogether, the 87th's brigade took 812 casualties, 45 percent of those engaged.[4]

Glenn Tucker, in his 1961 study of Chickamauga, wrote that the 87th Indiana's Van Derveer brigade was one of the most heroic and omnipresent brigades in that battle.

Severe wounds reported on 22 men in three companies of the 87th illustrate how bullets struck at Chickamauga.

Sgt. David Shelton, Cpl. John Roth and John Robbins were hit in the neck. Shelton died three weeks later.

Cpl. James Moore, Joseph Taylor and Christian Rice all were struck in the leg. Moore did not survive.

William Cole died in March from a wound in the jaws.

Eli Strong and John Ferrell were struck in the head, Ferrell dying four weeks later.

David Oliver was wounded in the thigh and arm.

Sgt. Jonas Clark died four days after being shot in the arm and breast.

John Carter and Peter Hoffman took hip wounds.

John Rush had a side wound.

Lt. Joseph Beeber was hit in both legs above the knees; he was furloughed for treatment and rejoined the regiment four months later.

Sgt. Clement Clay and Richard Liming were struck in the thigh; Liming died two weeks later. Clay also was furloughed until his recovery; it was his fourth wound of the battle.

Cpl. Polk McMahan had eye and arm wounds.

Cpl. Isaiah Webb was struck in the heel and died in a month.

Simeon Frear's ankle was smashed.

Jonathan Clay was struck in the testicles, the bullet disabling him for life.

Harrison Stotler was hit in the arm.

Rush and Clark enlisted from Blue Grass, Carter from Kewanna and the rest from Rochester.

The same three companies reported 18 men slightly wounded during the battle but with the primitive medical treatment of the time, these often proved fatal, too. Death came in a month from what appeared to be the minor wounds taken by Josephus Collins, leg; Robert Smith, arm, and John Yagle, foot. Collins was from Rochester, Smith of Kewanna and Yagle of Star City. Isaac Townsend of Rochester was ill but fought throughout the two days without injury, only to die of chronic diarrhea in a Nashville hospital November 8.[5]

The Third Division of Brig. Gen. John M. Brannan comprised Van Derveer's brigade and the two led by Col. John M. Connell and Col. John

T. Croxton. The division suffered 2,191 in killed-wounded-missing, of which 325 lay dead on the fields and hills. The division lost 36.5 percent of its original 5,998.[6]

The performance of the 87th Indiana's Brannan division at Chickamauga was significant and timely to the Union army. Indeed, Brannan's instinctive selection of high ground around the Snodgrass cabin for a defensive stand after Lt. Gen. James Longstreet's breakthrough was crucial, as was the speed and efficiency with which he patched together a line from his own broken brigades and everyone else at hand.

One could say, in fact, that Brannan, and perhaps Brig. Gen. Thomas Wood, have as much claim to the "Rock of Chickamauga" title as does their senior commander who carries it, Maj. Gen. George H. Thomas. The line along Horseshoe Ridge and Snodgrass Hill was chosen and manned by Brannan before Thomas arrived from Kelly Field to assume command. Wood's actions were critical for holding the Rebels long enough to give Brannan the time he needed; Wood then moved to Snodgrass Field to become the left of Brannan's defense. It was quick redemption for Wood after having unwittingly created the gap.

Nor must the individual soldier be forgotten. Many non-commissioned officers and privates emerged out of the army's wreckage onto the ridge because pride would not allow them to run any longer and because they recognized it as the place to make their stand.

The imperturbability and confidence of Thomas, nevertheless, provided reassurance and the necessary command presence to maintain cohesion during the six hours of desperate fighting along those spiny ridges. Certainly without that the rear-guard stand might have ended much sooner. There are some who doubt that Thomas was everywhere on the ridge during the fight, exhorting his troops as legend would have it. One of our participants did recall such behavior, however. Capt. Horace Long of Company F, writing home a month later, said that during the furious butternut attack at 4 P.M. all officers "pitched in promiscuously to cheering and encouraging the men of all regiments alike. Gen. Thomas would jump off his horse, swing his hat, rush in among the men and encourage them by his own acts of valor."[7]

Whatever the truth of the matter, Thomas' immortal sobriquet will remain with his memory, even though at one time after the war a newspaper quoted him as saying Van Derveer's brigade deserved the title more than he.

Brannan's division was prominent elsewhere during the perils of those two days. It took part in the all-night march of Thomas' corps that outflanked Gen. Braxton Bragg's line. Then, early Saturday morning, his division opened the battle by clashing with Brig. Gen. Nathan Bedford Forrest's cavalry on the left. After throwing back a subsequent flanking threat there, the division was called upon to strengthen the center at nightfall. It thwarted another Rebel flank threat in Kelly Field Sunday morning and survived the gap breakthrough with enough force to anchor the defense on Horseshoe Ridge. The 87th Indiana Infantry had reason to be proud of fighting under such a commander and with the men of such a division.

This pride was reflected in post-battle comments of 87th survivors.

Col. Newell Gleason's official report stated that during the two days of battle "officers and men of my command behaved in the most gallant manner, giving strict attention to orders and keeping the ranks well closed." He regretted that some men became separated from the regiment, but pointed out that it was caused by his anxiety to have their large number of wounded taken from the field after actions had ceased. All those so separated rejoined the regiment at Rossville Sunday night.

Although he found it difficult to cite everyone who deserved mention after such an ordeal as the regiment had passed through, Col. Gleason had special words for a few. The bravery at their posts of Adj. Fredus Ryland of Rochester and Capt. George Baker of Star City, Company B, both killed on Sunday, was noted by the colonel, as was the fact that Capts. George Payne of Pleasant Grove, Company A, and Long of Rochester, Company F, left sick beds to lead their commands throughout the two days. Capt. Milo Ellis of Peru, Company C, was wounded in the first day's fighting but arose from his ambulance to take part in the second day's. The bravery of Capt. Peter Troutman of Kewanna in commanding Company E and Lt. Burr Russell of Peru for "gallantry and daring, exposing himself constantly," with Company C also drew the colonel's attention. William Agnew of Winamac, Company B, and Abel O'Blennis of Maxinkuckee, Company D, were lieutenants who succeeded to battlefield command of their companies. They were cited for exemplary conduct along with another lieutenant, James Burnham of Rensselaer, Company A.

Col. Gleason acknowledged the help he received from the only field officer present on his staff during the actions, Maj. Edwin Hammond of Rensselaer, and gave special mention to Capt. Richard Sabin of Union Mills. On Saturday Sabin had been the first to discover the enemy's approach on the left and quickly rallied his Company H to its feet to move against this flanking movement.[8]

Gleason's rank-and-file returned the compliments. Pvt. Peter Keegan of Company C spoke of his colonel's "cool bravery, unexampled by any field officer of the Third Brigade" which enabled the regiment to receive "highest style encomiums from commanders Brannan at division and Van Derveer at brigade." Capt. Long thought there were not many colonels like Gleason. "All day he was going from one end of the regiment to the other, regardless of the missiles of death flying about us."[9] Such leadership, heedless of its own safety, must inspire fighting men to similar heroism.

The brigade commander, Col. Van Derveer, also won the admiration of the 87th's men for his direction the previous two days. Capt. Long said Van Derveer was "everywhere cheering on the men" and considered him "one of the coolest and bravest men we have and hope that he may get the star that he so richly earned in the battle." (The star of a brigadier general would come, but not for another year.) Pvt. Keegan wrote of Van Derveer's "coolness" when the action was the heaviest.

Today three monuments among the 1,400 at Chickamauga mark locations where the 87th Indiana Regiment went into action. The largest is at Horseshoe Ridge, another is near Jay's Mill and the third is at Kelly Field.

On Horseshoe Ridge the 87th's tall memorial is at the front of the first parking spaces encountered when reaching the hill from the Snodgrass cabin. This is not, however, the place where the 87th Regiment fought during those momentous hours. One must walk 375 yards to the right, up the slope and onto the second hill. There, at the monument to the 84th Indiana Regiment of Brig. Gen. Walter Whitaker's reserve brigade, is the actual ground where Hoosiers of the 87th Indiana held back the charging Confederates. Vanity is responsible for the misplacement.

Congress established Chickamauga as a national military park in 1890 because of a campaign originated and led by battle veterans Ferdinand Van Derveer and Henry Boynton, who were in charge of monument placement. Both men served with the 35th Ohio and wanted their regiment's Horseshoe Ridge memorial to be in a prominent place, easily seen by visitors. So they placed it near the public access, up the hill from where the 87th's marker is today. Other Union regimental monuments also were moved eastward in their relative positions. The misplacements might never have been noticed if the Confederate monuments at the base of the ridge had been moved correspondingly. That they weren't was discovered by Southern veterans who noticed the Union monuments atop the ridge did not match the regiments that were met there.[10]

Thus was created one of the postwar controversies that arose between opposing veterans of the battle, this one spawning a 1911 book that discusses many of the other disputes. Titled "The Truth about Chickamauga," it was written by Archibald Gracie, son of the Southern brigade commander who led a charge up Horseshoe Ridge.

The other two monuments to the 87th Indiana, however, fairly represent its positions at Chickamauga.

The location of Saturday morning's struggle is deep in the woods where the regiment advanced from Reed's Bridge Road. Once there, though, the setting is perfect for the silent contemplation that can stir powerful, evocative images of how it must have been on that frightening, fateful September morning so long ago. It's worth the walk that is required.[11]

The Kelly Field monument to the 87th marks where the regiment emerged from the woods on the west to confront Maj. Gen. John C. Breckinridge's flanking maneuver Sunday morning. The three-foot-high stone is next to La Fayette Road about 175 yards from the field's northern tree line, 350 yards from the Kelly cabin on the south.

There were no such granite monuments about on Monday, September 21, 1863. Littering the ground instead were the dead and the dying, many of whom were being stripped of shoes, pants, shirts, jackets, muskets, knapsacks, haversacks, guns and ammunition by the jubilant Confederates. The Army of Tennessee finally had won its first battle against the Yankees and the Rebs wanted their booty; needed it, as a matter of fact.[12]

The human detritus of a battlefield is appalling and pitiful. Isom New of Rochester, a sergeant with Company D of the 29th Indiana, was shot through the right lung and right forearm Sunday. He lay on the field an entire week without care or attention, unable to move, until the Confederates finally picked him up. Remarkably, he recovered and was paroled and exchanged, surviving the war.

New was not alone among the wretched wounded that whole terrible week; later he said that enduring it and hearing the interminable cries for help from the dying was "the horror of horrors."[13]

Rochester's Peter Hoffman of Company F in the 87th lay on the field at Chickamauga all night with a bullet in a thigh which he carried the rest of his life. He was luckier than New for he was found quickly by the Rebels, exchanged after 11 days and served with the regiment for the rest of the war.[14]

No adequate system of battlefield first aid existed during the war and the hemorrhaging that followed a wound produced intense suffering before help arrived. At Chickamauga the dense thickets in which the battle was fought caught fire and many of the wounded burned to death before they were found. The plight of the Civil War's wounded astonishes. At Fort Donelson in February of 1862, for example, those who had fallen had to be pried from the mud into which they had frozen fast. One Union officer lay 24 hours with his head frozen to the ground while the opposing forces twice passed over where he lay. Miraculously, he survived because his bleeding wounds had frozen.[15]

Almost beyond belief, however, was the ordeal of Sheldon Judson of the Second Wisconsin at the Second Battle of Bull Run. It stands for all those determined to survive being shot on the battlefield. Wounded in the shin, Judson stopped the bleeding with a handkerchief and was taken by ambulance to some nearby woods and left with other wounded. There he promptly was attacked by a swarm of hornets. After a painful night he and his group were abandoned, taken prisoners by Confederate pickets who abandoned them again, whereupon Union artillery shelled them. Finally they were collected by Rebels who put them with a few hundred other Union prisoners. Judson remained there six days without treatment and one cracker a day to eat, lying two nights in a pool of water with no covering. Finally, a truce was called and he recovered in a Washington hospital. Another soldier from Judson's regiment crawled nine miles to reach a field hospital and have his shattered leg amputated.[16]

At Chickamauga, two days of brutal killings had come to an end and there was no question about the outcome. It was an unmitigated Union disaster and although Bragg had allowed the beaten Yankee army to escape into Chattanooga, there still was a chance to destroy it if he moved quickly.

The 87th Indiana Infantry was not yet free of Chickamauga's repercussions.

13
Redemption
at Missionary Ridge

George Martling, the Mishawaka private from Company K, spent a
week with his fellow 87th Indiana Infantrymen constructing Union
entrenchments around Chattanooga. Their section was on the left of the
Rossville Road by which they had escaped Chickamauga's killing grounds.

They worked all day, every day, Martling recorded in his journal, tearing down all the houses in the vicinity for campfires and to clear a field of
fire in front of the breastworks. Many in the regiment had thrown away, or
lost, tents and blankets during the two days of battle; the onset of cold
weather brought suffering in the ranks and a large increase in the sick rolls.
Horses and mules began to die for lack of forage; the number eventually
would reach 10,000.[1]

Eight days after the battle a truce was arranged for an exchange of
wounded. Martling counted 194 ambulances and five wagons of medical
supplies in the Federal wagon train that went through the Rebel lines. The
following day, September 29, the ambulances returned with 800 wounded,
Martling jotted in his diary.

Surrounded by their enemy and bereft of food, ammunition and supplies, the men of the 87th with 42,000 other survivors of Maj. Gen. William
S. Rosecrans' defeated army had every reason to expect more attacks from
the emboldened Confederates. A different Southern army might have continued pursuit of the disorganized, demoralized Federals. But not the one
led by Gen. Braxton Bragg.

Bragg considered his army too badly used up in its victory for immediate vigorous action. Anyway, now that he finally had won a battle, this
irritable and quarrelsome martinet was more interested in ridding himself
of those among his generals he considered to be his enemies. Particularly,
Bragg meant to cashier Lt. Gen. Leonidas Polk for being tardy in opening
Sunday morning's action. His efforts brought reaction in the form of a pe-

tition to President Jefferson Davis, signed by Lt. Gen. James Longstreet and 11 other of Bragg's generals, asking that Bragg be replaced as commander. Davis himself visited the army to investigate charges against his longtime friend but in the end he kept Bragg in place. Most of the petitioners were transferred to other sectors.[2]

One of those who was moved elsewhere was Brig. Gen. Nathan Bedford Forrest, whose dismounted cavalry had opposed Col. Ferdinand Van Derveer and the 87th Indiana so energetically Saturday morning near Jay's Mill. Bragg was highly critical of Forrest's actions following the battle, but this was a subordinate he could not cow. Considered the Civil War's most brilliant cavalry tactician, Forrest was an unschooled but intuitive leader whose ruthless courage was matched by an explosive temper. Bragg thought him a worthless military amateur, but pushed him too far with demeaning orders. Forrest rode to Bragg's headquarters overlooking Chattanooga, pointed his left index finger into the commander's face, coldly recounted the many insults he had borne from Bragg and concluded:

"I have stood your meanness as long as I intend to. You have played the part of a damned scoundrel, and are a coward, and if you were any part of a man, I would slap your jaws and force you to resent it. You may as well not issue any more orders to me, for I will not obey them, and I will hold you personally responsible for any further indignities you endeavor to inflict upon me. You have threatened to arrest me for not obeying your orders promptly. I dare you to do it and I say to you that if you ever again try to interfere with me or cross my path it will be at the peril of your life." He then turned on his heel and walked out of Bragg's tent without waiting for a reply.

The condition of command in the Confederate army was such that Forrest neither was court martialed nor censured for his conduct. He was given instead a separate, independent command in Mississippi by President Davis.[3]

And so, although they could not then know it, the busily entrenching 87th Indiana Infantry would face no immediate attacks. Instead, Bragg bottled up the Yankees with a vast overlooking semicircle of troops and guns beginning at the Tennessee River on the north. The Rebel line then ran along Missionary Ridge on the east, to Lookout Mountain on the south and back to the river again on the west. The wild, barren, mostly uninhabited country north of the river was untended, for it was nearly impassable to troops. Starvation might do in a couple of months what guns couldn't. Bragg's siege controlled all major accesses to the city: the river, a railroad along its southern side and roads that lay south of the river.

It was a picturesque situation, to say the least. From the heights of Lookout Mountain and Missionary Ridge the butternuts could look down upon the penned-up bluecoats, easily making out their movements. The Federals in turn had a good view of the Rebels' entrenchments and artillery. At night the great semicircle was outlined with the Southern campfires and with signal torches flashing messages from one height to another, messages whose code the Yankees soon cracked and passed on to their superiors.[4]

For a few days in late September the Rebs shelled the city with 20 long-range field guns hauled atop Lookout Mountain. The sounds of the cannon were spectacular; not so the results. Because of the inferior quality of the guns and ammunition, most of the shells exploded prematurely at these long ranges, or not at all. Union soldiers actually began to look forward to the booming of the guns. When the daily firing began, they would dash out of their tents and cheer as most of the shells burst high in the air.

One afternoon Peter Keegan of Company C left sewing chores to join such a cheer. Just after he vacated his tent, a shell burst over the 87th Indiana's camp and "a piece the size of a 2-oz. ink bottle passed through where I had just sat and buried in the ground." Keegan's luck would continue; he mustered out as a sergeant with the regiment in 1865.

On another occasion Col. Ferdinand Van Derveer of the 87th was walking in front of his tent, deep in thought, when a shell hit nearby with a shower of dirt and rolled to a stop right in front of him, unexploded. The colonel tapped it with a foot and commented that Longstreet would have to do better than that to keep his Eastern reputation alive in the West. Another time, a shell crashed through the roof of a hospital building and descended through two floors filled with sick and wounded. Mercifully, this one did not explode either.

An Ohio captain commented that the only damage he knew of from the bombardment was the killing of a mule that was about to die of starvation, anyway. After a week of it, the Confederates agreed that the shelling was a bad idea and called it off.[5]

Bragg left open only one route by which supplies could reach the besieged city: the one leading from the army's depot southwest in Stevenson, Ala. It was the longest and most demanding. Covering almost 60 miles, it extended by good road from Stevenson up the Sequatchie Valley but then turned to mount craggy Walden's Ridge and approach the city from the northeast. The 12 miles across the mountain involved steep crests and ridges, damaging both to the starving mules and their food cargoes. There was no forage for the animals and, in dry times, no water in the creeks. But when the rains came, the primitive road was a succession of bottomless pits of mud that trapped mules as well as wagon wheels.

Rains were falling on Friday, October 2, as a train of 800 mule-driven supply and sutlers' wagons was slowly making its way across Walden's Ridge, strung out 10 miles from the top of the ridge back into the valley. About 9 o'clock in the morning, Maj. Gen. Joseph Wheeler's Confederate cavalry suddenly appeared and fell upon the defenseless train. Supply wagons were ransacked for their food, sutlers' wagons for their whiskey; ammunition wagons were exploded with deafening roars. The Rebs' plundering went on for eight hours before they burned 400 wagons, killed 500 mules, and dashed off to the northeast with their prisoners.[6] Among the casualties was Pvt. Asa Marine of Peru and Company C, who died from the wounds he took there.

Daniel Bruce, the 87th Indiana's teamster, was a part of this train and escaped the disaster by unhitching one of his mules and riding pell-mell without hat, coat or blanket down the mountain and "through the brush and over the logs . . . and shooting on every side." He and his fellow teamsters later managed to save 14 mule teams and successfully herded them back to Stevenson, but it took five days of rugged traveling. Their only food was from two pigs that they killed and boiled; the mules had to do with two foraged sacks of wheat. On their way back down the valley, Bruce recorded, they passed the remnants of the wagon train returning to Stevenson with 1,500 wounded.[7]

As he reached safety, Bruce had no idea that his former commanding colonel of the 87th Indiana, Kline G. Shryock, also had been caught up in the calamitous attack and was a prisoner of the Rebels, forced to flee with them on a captured mule. His story, and how it ended, will have its proper place later in this chapter.

The absence of a dependable supply line forced the army to go on half rations of food and forage. By October 20 the 87th Indiana had moved camp a mile west of its entrenchments and Company K got the chance to occupy a house, no less. Martling was pleased to have a floor on which to sleep, but found the rats thereabout too abundant for his Hoosier taste. By the time of his 20th birthday, October 26, he was living on mule meat and ground wheat made into a sort of cake; there was no hardtack left. His accommodations were just as mean; the only lighting at night came from a rag wick in a sardine can of grease.[8]

But by the time Martling turned 20, matters also were turning in the besieged Union army's favor. For Chickamauga was the end of President Abraham Lincoln's patience with failures in the Western theatre of the war. He wanted results and Rosecrans obviously was not the man to produce them. Rosecrans' conduct after the battle, said Lincoln, "reminds me of a duck which has been hit on the head," a most evocative description of befuddlement.[9] Rosecrans was sent into the war's backwaters, from which he never emerged.[10]

Lincoln believed he had found his man in Maj. Gen. Ulysses Simpson Grant, the hero of Vicksburg's capture, who was given overall command of the Western armies and ordered to Chattanooga. Now began a play of forces that rippled from the Union's bewildering defeat at Chickamauga. This immense crisis brought forth a leader who would become this awesome war's most compelling, and triumphant, figure. Grant may never have gained the power he wielded so expertly without the fright that the Chickamauga defeat created in Washington. Furthermore, Lincoln was not about to suffer the further embarrassment of losing the besieged Army of the Cumberland. Reinforcements were ordered and 37,000 soon were on the way, from Virginia under Maj. Gen. Joseph Hooker and from Memphis and Vicksburg under Maj. Gen. William Sherman.[11]

Grant arrived in Chattanooga October 23 and, typically, got busy right away. His first move was to reorganize his forces, appointing Maj. Gen. George H. Thomas to succeed Rosecrans as head of the Army of the Cumberland. That put the XIV Corps under command of Maj. Gen. John Palmer, 46, an Illinois politician who would seek the presidency in 1896 as the Gold Democrats' candidate.[12] Brig. Gen. John M. Brannan was made chief of artillery and his Third Division given to Brig. Gen. Absalom Baird who had commanded the First Division at Chickamauga. A 39-year-old Pennsylvanian, Baird was a veteran of First Bull Run and the Peninsula campaign.[13]

The 87th Indiana remained in Col. Van Derveer's brigade, which added three regiments and became the Second Brigade, rather than the Third, still of the Third Division. Despite the additions, the brigade counted fewer numbers in seven regiments than it had in four before Chickamauga.

The newcomers were the 75th Indiana under Col. Milton S. Robinson, the 101st Indiana under Lt. Col. Thomas Doan and the 105th Ohio under Lt. Col. William R. Tolles. The brigade's artillery now consisted of three batteries under Capt. George Swallow, Seventh Indiana Light, Lt. George Repp; 19th Indiana Light, Lt. William Stackhouse, and I of the Fourth U.S., Lt. George Rodney.[14]

These organizing details completed, Grant moved fast to get relief from the siege. He approved a plan to float two brigades down the Tennessee around its long loop at Moccasin Point, and to surprise and overwhelm the Rebel forces at Brown's Ferry west of the city. This was done successfully, enabling Hooker's 20,000 reinforcements to arrive and also freeing the river as a supply line. On October 30 the steamboat Chattanooga arrived at the city's dock with 40,000 rations and tons of forage for the animals. "The Cracker Line" had opened and famishment no longer loomed.

Grant then waited for Sherman to arrive with his 17,000 men from Memphis and Vicksburg. As soon as they were available, he made his move to break Bragg's encirclement. The opening gambit came Tuesday, November 24, when Hooker's three divisions climbed the 1,100 feet of Lookout Mountain and drove off the besieging Rebels from its summit. A heavy fog covered this "Battle above the Clouds" most of the time and it was not until morning when the Stars and Stripes were seen floating from the top that the Federals below knew the attack had been successful. Their southern flank was secure.

That left the eastern Confederate line along the five miles of Missionary Ridge to be eliminated. Sherman was to take care of that by moving his newly arrived force across the river and attacking from the north, rolling up the Ridge line southward to meet Hooker's men coming across from Lookout Mountain. It looked like a perfect plan, but it didn't work out that way.

Sherman hadn't reconnoitered his ground too well and at Tunnel Hill was stopped cold by the divisions of Maj. Gen. Pat Cleburne and Maj. Gen. Carter Stevenson. Meanwhile, Hooker's men were delayed four or five hours at the other end by rebuilding a bridge the Rebs had destroyed while retreating from Lookout Mountain. The day wore on and there was no indication that Sherman's effort was going to succeed. Sometime after 3 P.M. Grant decided something had to be done. He ordered Thomas to take some pressure off Sherman by demonstrating up the center of Missionary Ridge. The regiments near the base of the ridge, including Indiana's 87th, heard Grant's orders repeated: take the first line of rifle pits, then stop to reorganize.

Waiting to go forward were four divisions of the Army of the Cumberland, including Indiana's 87th regiment, and they were plenty ticked off. For a month they had been taunted by Hooker's soldiers for having lost Chickamauga. Then Sherman's men arrived and joined Hooker's in sneering at them for needing to be rescued. The Cumberlands had had enough. This was an opportunity for payback, for redemption. Now it was their tormentors who needed rescue.[15]

At 4 P.M. six cannon shots boomed and the assault got underway along a mile and a half front. The first line of rifle pits, three-fourths of a mile away at the bottom of the 300-foot-high hill, were captured quickly but the men found they were exposed there to murderous fire from the crest. So upward they went, without orders. Suddenly it became another of those soldiers' battles; no generals needed. The Yankees could not be stopped, nor could Confederate cannon depress muzzles enough to halt them. Within an hour the summit had been reached, 37 guns and 2,000 prisoners captured after some desperate hand-to-hand fighting on top of the ridge. Bragg's army retreated into Georgia and the siege of Chattanooga was ended.

The next morning the 87th Regiment joined its brigade to go after Bragg's retreating butternuts. Suffering a great deal for lack of proper clothing, they reached Ringgold 18 miles away in Georgia before the pursuit was called off and they returned to Chattanooga.

Missionary Ridge is one of the Civil War's enduring legends, much as are Thomas' stand at Chickamauga, Pickett's charge at Gettysburg, Burnside's Bridge at Antietam, Jackson's foot cavalry in the Shenandoah and Sheridan's ride from Winchester.

Our 87th Indiana Infantry was in the midst of the Missionary Ridge assault and once again distinguished itself. Baird's division, with Van Derveer's brigade, was on the left of the attacking line, the 87th being the brigade's right.[16]

The division was sent about noon to assist Sherman on the left. On the way, however, Baird was met by a messenger telling him to return; Sherman had all the troops he could handle at the time. So the 87th was back in the center line in time to take part in the attack on Missionary Ridge.

The 87th Regiment lost three in the face of what Col. Newell Gleason called "heavy fire of shot and shell." Thomas Fisher of LaPorte and Company G fell somewhere in the dash up that slope. Solomon Deacon of Marion, Iowa, and Company K reached the top only to meet his death there. Deacon's company comrade, Andrew Chrisman of South Bend, was nearby when the two of them got to the summit. Said Chrisman: "Solomon was struck by a ball above the left eye halfway between the eyebrow and the hair, passing through his head and killing him instantly." The third casualty was 1st Lt. Burr Russell of Peru, Company C, who died of his wounds in four days. And 1st Lt. Jacob Leiter of Rochester, Company F, was among 13 from the regiment who were wounded.[17]

Regimental teamster Bruce hauled the bodies of Fisher and Deacon to their graves the next day—along with a load of beef.

Martling of Company K thought it took only a half-hour to reach the top. He saw the American flag planted there and the turning of their own batteries upon the Rebels as they fled down the eastern side of the ridge.

There are few regimental histories that do not claim to have planted the first flag upon the crest. This one will not attempt it, except to quote from Col. Gleason's official report that "the colors of the 87th Indiana, 35th Ohio, Second Minnesota and 101st Indiana were planted on the ridge at so nearly the same time that it would be difficult to designate the first one there." Col. Gleason also singled out a few of his men because of special performance that afternoon: Capt. Milo Ellis of Peru and Company C, who had been wounded at Chickamauga, and 1st Lt. John Vandever of Plymouth, Company E, who led charges along the top of the ridge amid desperate fighting, and "about 20 non-commissioned officers and privates of my regiment." His color bearer, Cpl. Henry Platt, carried the colors into the thickest of the fight despite the staff twice being shot with musket balls, wrote Gleason, who mourned the loss of the "dashing, gallant and very worthy" Deacon.

Grant reportedly showed considerable consternation when he saw the troops continue up the ridge without his orders. At the time he was immediately in their rear, at his observation post atop the eminence of Orchard Knob. Legend has it that he turned to Thomas and asked, "Who ordered those men up the hill?" There was no satisfactory answer and he said, "Someone will suffer for it, if it turns out badly."[18] So much for the elaborate plans of generals.

Plenty of heroes were discovered that day. One was an 18-year-old lieutenant from the 24th Wisconsin, Arthur MacArthur. He led his regiment to the top and planted its colors there, having seized them after two color bearers were killed. For his deed, MacArthur later would be given the Congressional Medal of Honor, an achievement later duplica ed by his more famous son, Gen. Douglas MacArthur of World War II fame.[19]

Watching from afar was Sgt. Jonas Myers of the 87th's Company F. He got his hand mashed in a work detail accident a few days before and was excused from handling his gun. Nevertheless, he said, "I could see Hooker's men fighting above the clouds and our men climbing Mission Ridge" and Myers could hardly contain his admiration. Myers went through the war without a serious injury or illness, writing later that "this was the first and last time the regiment left me."[20]

The 87th Indiana's hill-climbers emerged onto Missionary Ridge's crest where an Alabama battery of two six-pound bronze cannon and two 12-pound howitzers were stationed. Lt. William P. Hamilton was commanding, with Lts. C.W. Watkins and George D. Turner. Although firing rapidly at first, Hamilton could not depress the guns enough to stop the Federals as they neared the summit. The Confederates rolled one gun down the hill and tried to get the remaining three over the ridge in the rear only to lose them to the 87th's men on the slope of a ravine eastward.[21]

The Missionary Ridge example of soldiers taking over the tactics of a battle offers up an examination of the effect combat exerts on individuals. Officers who watched what was taking place on Missionary Ridge described the men as "completely and frantically drunk with excitement," operating as in a dreamlike state.[22] It was the kind of swelling exhilaration many Civil War soldiers felt when combat came upon them, an elevation of feeling that has been described as one of the enduring appeals of battle:

"Anyone who has watched men on the battlefield . . . finds hard to escape the conclusion that there is a delight in destruction. . . . Men who have lived in the zone of combat long enough to be veterans are sometimes possessed by a fury that makes them capable of anything. Blinded by the rage to destroy and supremely careless of consequences, they storm against the enemy. . . . The satisfaction in destroying seems to me to be peculiarly human, or, more exactly put, devilish in the ways animals can never be."[23]

Thus the campaign for Chattanooga ended as a Union victory after all, despite the horrible bloodletting of Chickamauga. The South's failure to follow up that battlefield triumph would prove to be a fatal mistake, for with Chattanooga's irretrievable loss the Southern heartland was opened to invasion. Chickamauga's mock victory was to haunt the Confederacy to its dying day and some thought that it was there that the butternut soldier sensed the futility of his cause.

Lt. Gen. Daniel H. Hill, who commanded a corps in Polk's right wing at Chickamauga, said 20 years later: "There was no more splendid fighting . . . than was displayed in those bloody days of September '63. But it seems to me that the elan of the Southern soldier was never seen after Chickamauga— that brilliant dash which had distinguished him had gone forever. . . . He fought stoutly to the last but, after Chickamauga, with the sullenness of despair and without the enthusiasm of hope. That 'barren victory' sealed the fate of the Southern Confederacy."[24]

Hill no doubt was on the mark, but as December came to Chattanooga in 1863, the 87th Indiana Infantry Regiment knew there was more killing to be done. Still, for the moment a new but welcome peacefulness descended upon its campground along the loops of the Tennessee River.

In their leisure, some from the regiment returned for a look at scenes of the 87th Indiana's violent confrontations at Chickamauga. Most of the regiment's officers and 40 of the men made up the party, including Capt. Peter Troutman and Pvt. Martling. Postponed from December 2 by rain, the nine-mile trip finally was made on Wednesday, December 16, almost three months after the battle's end. Troutman and Martling wrote afterward of their revulsion and indignation at what they found in the woods near Jay's Mill, at Kelly Field and on Horseshoe Ridge.[25]

The Rebels had buried most of their fallen but many of the Union's dead were stripped of clothing and left unburied "from mere brutality." Only skeletons remained of some of their comrades, one of which Martling identified as the Company H orderly, Sgt. Elijah Israel. The 87th's group buried as many as they could and were able to find all the regiment's officers who had been killed in the two days. Lt. Franklin Bennett of Troutman's Company E was found buried near where he was left by those who had carried him dead from Saturday morning's opening battle line. Troutman, who had been nearby when Bennett was shot, carved his friend's initials on two trees near the grave and "also left his initials and drove a post where he received the fatal wound."

At Kelly Field "near where our colors were when we repulsed the terrible charge of Adams' brigade on Sunday" the group found a grave that was said to contain the bodies of 19 Federals; Troutman believed most were from the 87th. The grim visitors enclosed the grave with timber and placed a suitable inscription on a nearby tree. Near there were found the graves of Adj. Fredus Ryland and Capt. Lewis Hughes, both of whom had fallen in the first exchange of volleys with Brig. Gen. Dan Adams' brigade. Their comrades also saw to the marking of their gravesites but, lamentably, neither was ever recovered for a proper reburial.

Troutman was astounded by signs left behind by the terrible fighting of September. He counted a hundred bullet holes in a tree only 18 inches in diameter, 81 in another and 75 in a third, each with its top shorn by cannonball. Similar sights were all around, a sobering, thoughtful experience for the 87th's surviving infantrymen.

A German from the Ninth Ohio of the 87th's brigade inspected the battlefield at the same time and left this description, which likely could apply to all of the war's killing grounds:

"The battlefield was a shocking sight. Putrefying corpses, detached arms and legs, and skeletons with dried skin clinging to the bones, lay scattered everywhere. Our brigade had used as a hospital a log cabin near Snodgrass Hill. The cabinside well the Rebels had obviously filled with corpses, for a foot and a skull protruded from the thin layer of earth thrown over them. At the Snodgrass house itself, where our brigade stood for hours and beat back Rebels storming the hill in assault after assault, the bushes had been cut down with bullets as if by a mowing machine; and so much small-arms fire had riddled the trees that their bark resembled a sieve. Long rows of mounds of fresh earth marked the spots where friend and foe lay buried side by side."[26]

Casualty lists from the major battles were reported quickly by the government and reached hometowns through their local newspapers. As a result it was not unusual for fathers or other family members to visit battle sites soon afterward, seeking to assist in the soldier's convalescence or, if necessary, return the body for final burial.

So it was with Shryock, the 87th Regiment's first colonel who had resigned in March and returned to Rochester. After the Battle of Chickamauga, Shryock was advised that his son-in-law, Adj. Ryland of the 87th, had been wounded and so he left for Chattanooga in late September to find and help him.

Ryland, in fact, had been killed at Chickamauga on the second day. Shryock never got to Chattanooga to learn this, for on the way he unluckily joined the wagon train that Wheeler's men so joyously attacked. Surviving that harrowing experience, he then narrowly missed his own death or winding up in a Confederate prison pen.

At Stevenson, Ala., on Wednesday, September 30, he was allowed to walk along with the slow-moving supply train. Two days later five freed Negroes, or "contrabands," appeared to warn that Rebel cavalry had attacked the train two miles ahead. Capt. Anthony R. Ravenscroft, in charge of that section, refused to believe them and ordered his wagons to continue. Soon frightened teams began appearing from the front. The captain organized his guard for defense but then, inexplicably, disappeared. Shryock took command.

It was a short fight. The Rebel cavalry flanked the train and came up on its rear in a gallop, "yelling like devils incarnate," said Shryock. After looting the wagons, destroying stores and ammunition, burning wagons and killing mules, the Rebels were anxious to leave an area where so many Federals were sure to be after them quickly. Prisoners, consisting of 583 teamsters and Shryock, were mounted on mules so as not to delay their captors and were hurried off to the northeast. For the next two days, Shryock and his fellow prisoners traveled without food, water or sleep.

Reaching McMinnville, Tenn., 50 miles away, early on a Sunday morning, Shryock found that the Rebels had taken charge of the town and were burning all the stores they could find. There the prisoners were made to suffer a final indignity, but not without a protest from the Hoosier colonel.

"After having marched our men 48 hours without anything to eat or allowing them to sleep they compelled them, under threat of murdering them, to carry stores from the Courthouse to the bonfire in the street. Against that I protested, asking 'for time to eat at least a hard cracker.' The reply of the captain in command was, 'God damn them; that was what they were brought here for.' My reply was, 'Very well, sir, *you* may be a prisoner some day.' Some of our men staggered and came near falling while carrying boxes of hard bread and throwing them on the fire."

Five miles northeast of McMinnville, Shryock and the other prisoners were released at last, but not before being relieved of all their possessions: money, overcoats, satchels, even their hats and boots. The Rebels informed us, said Shryock, "that we were getting off well at that."[27]

And so they were, particularly in the kind of war this was becoming.

The year of 1863 that now was playing out had been a momentous year for the Union: the year of Gettysburg, Vicksburg and Chattanooga. Veteran Union regiments were reenlisting, considering the Rebellion to be fading and the liberal bounties being offered too attractive to miss out on. In the South there were many who were ready to agree with the Louisiana father who wrote his son in the Confederate army that "this war was got up drunk but they will have to settle it sober."

It also was the year of the Emancipation Proclamation, which had gone into effect January 1 and freed all the slaves in territory still under Confederate control. The war had taken a new turn and, for the Union soldier, assumed a higher meaning than the obvious objective of simply killing all the butternuts he could find.

Capt. Troutman clearly was pondering this subject at year's end. He believed President Lincoln's Proclamation was being generally approved by the soldiers, including those in the 87th. His thoughts seemed to reveal an alteration in his own approach to the matter, as well:

"There has been a wonderful change in the popular sentiments of the soldiers in the last year in regard to the slavery question. Soldiers who could not bear the sight of a darky a year ago are ready to use him in any way to put down the rebellion. They begin to see that it is just as well to allow negroes to drive mules through the mud as for soldiers to do it; or that it is even as well to allow a darky to carry the musket and if it comes to the pinch, stop a rebel bullet, as for the white man to perform the delightful work alone. In a word, popular sentiment is being educated (I say educated, laugh who will) to the noble position enunciated in the President's Proclamation of September 1862, as fast as even the most fastidious could desire."[28]

Not only was the country changing, but the war soon would take a new turn as well. Indiana's 87th Infantry Regiment, resplendent with the respect it bravely won in battle, believed it was ready for whatever would be asked of it.

14

Jonas Gets a Diary

Jonas Myers was in a reflective mood at Chattanooga, now that the Confederate siege of the city was lifted and six months' hard campaigning finally had ended in a peaceful interlude. Jonas had survived on the front line at Perryville and inside the firestorm of Chickamauga. No longer a youth, he was approaching his 34th birthday and quite likely realized that as a sergeant of Company F, 87th Indiana Infantry Regiment, he was in the defining experience of his life.

So he welcomed the unexpected New Year's gift of a pocket-sized diary from his wife Annie. Now he would make a record of his military days that he, his family and perhaps even his descendants could recall. Jonas might not be certain of his future; nevertheless, past events were proof that the experiences still to come his way would be worth noting. The diary arrived 10 days into the new year of 1864 but Jonas got at it right away, filling in most of the preceding January activities.

There was time for this. The victorious Union army was at rest after its fateful Chattanooga campaign while supplies, equipment and recruits were gathered and plans laid for the next advance against the retreated, but still close by, Confederates. The army's newly lionized commander, Ulysses S. Grant, soon would be summoned to Washington to confer with President Abraham Lincoln and Secretary of War Edwin Stanton about these plans. When spring came, Sgt. Myers and the Army of the Cumberland would be on the move again.

It's worth knowing more about Jonas Myers, for in many ways he typified all the mechanics, tradesmen and farmers from the rural North who filled the Union army's ranks in the West.

We met him first in the opening fight at Chickamauga near Jay's Mill when he and fellow sergeant Clement Clay drew the admiration of their captain for the brave way they joined in the firing even though detailed to the rear as file-closers. Later, we saw Jonas as one of only four survivors of his company on Horseshoe Ridge. He saved Clay's life there by taking him to the rear, bandaging Clay's wound and seeing that he reached medical attention. Myers rejoined the regiment at Chattanooga but missed the Missionary Ridge assault because of a minor camp injury.

Jonas was a product of the American frontier who participated in its ever-westward expansion, like countless others of his day. The oldest of 11 children, he was born in 1829 among the hills of Washington County, Pa., south of Pittsburgh. With his family and that of an uncle, he traveled the 350 miles to Indiana when only 10 years old, settling first in the small village of Gilead in Miami County.

Northern Indiana in 1839 was not much more than a wilderness, heavily forested and full of wild game. The ground had to be cleared of shubs and trees before corn could be planted amidst the stumps. When the ears began to show, it was a constant battle with raccoons, squirrels and deer to get the crop to maturity. Squirrels particularly were a menacing pest. While it was not uncommon to shoot 75 squirrels a day, their numbers never seemed to diminish. Life did not hold many comforts; one summer Jonas lived with 22 others in a double log house served by one fireplace.

Like most of the soldiers in the western Union army, Jonas grew up with a gun. As a child he developed a fondness for night hunting, often staying out until morning or arising at 1 A.M. to begin his stalk.

In 1846 at the age of 17, he escaped from the incessant demands of frontier farming to learn the carpenter's trade in Rochester. He began an apprentice program for $100 a year and meals, persisting for three years and surviving attacks of the ague every summer. This malarial-like sickness was so rampant that "by fall there would not be enough well people to take care of the sick," remembered Myers. He remained four more years with this employer after finishing his apprenticeship.

In the summer of 1853, at age 24, Jonas yielded to the lure of a new frontier and went to northern Iowa where lands were being newly settled. He was hired to accompany another carpenter, Randall Wells, and erect a sawmill there for a LaPorte speculator, Leonard Cutler, who then made them a proposition. Cutler would take out a 320-acre claim for each of them and, if the two would agree to help make the necessary improvements and stay until the land became salable, Cutler would give them half the proceeds. Myers demurred; he missed his family and friends back in Indiana. In 1860 he returned to Iowa on a visit and wondered whether he'd made a mistake; "the country looked older than Indiana, except the orchards."

With the money made in the Iowa venture, Jonas stopped in Chicago long enough to buy his first personal set of tools. Returning to Rochester, he built a shop and began his own carpentry business. By the time he joined the 87th Regiment nine years later, Myers not only had become an enterprising contractor but also prominent in the town's affairs. Among his construction projects were the Odd Fellows Hall, several business buildings along Main Street, a hall for the firemen's hook and ladder company and many barns on the rapidly appearing farms thereabouts. His fellow citizens honored him with election as town marshal, a term which was just ending when he volunteered with many of his friends for a three-year hitch with Company F of the 87th.

Jonas was of average height for his time, 5 feet 7 inches, had a sandy complexion, blue eyes and brown hair. He had a gregarious personality and was somewhat of a practical jokester with his close friends. Although enlisting as a private in August 1862, he soon found himself a corporal and then began a rise through the sergeant rankings that would make him first sergeant of Company F in June of 1864. Jonas was a popular fellow; his captain, Horace Long, described him as "one of the best of men." Although occasionally put down briefly by camp fever or other illness, Jonas went through almost three years of battles and skirmishes without taking a wound or becoming seriously ill. His robust good health, he once said, was due to his decision early in life to abstain from both tobacco and intoxicating liquors.[1]

Afterward a contemporary called him a "man of iron nerve" and for Jonas that has the ring of truth as, indeed, it does for all those like him who now were caught up in war's white-hot crucible.

Some of its heat would have been welcomed in Chattanooga right then. The year 1864 came in cold and disagreeable, a daylong rain turning to ice overnight. Jonas was informed by some citizens that Friday, January 1, was "the coldest day that has been here in 15 years"; he found it only "comfortably cold but nothing to what it is in the north. We are very well fixed for soldiers."

Jonas evidently was a hardy sort. Temperatures of below zero were recorded in Memphis on New Year's Day; pickets were relieved every 10 minutes in East Tennessee to keep them from freezing.

The 87th Regiment teamster and diarist, Daniel Bruce, certainly did not find the weather as tolerable as did Jonas. When Bruce awoke on New Year's Day, he found his trousers frozen "so that I could not get them on for some time, working them and rubbing them. Coat froze stiff. I shivered like a dog." The next night and day were no better, Bruce recorded. "I could sleep but little on account of the cold. I thought sometimes I had frozen my feet. I never felt as cold as I did this date."

The inclement weather continued to plague the tented army for three weeks with intermittent rain, ice and an occasional snowfall. Then, paradoxically, it turned almost springlike. Myers and his comrades lapsed into what he called "the boring roteen" of camp duty.

Rations still were scarce and the idle troops were becoming impatient and out of sorts. Jonas and 11 of his friends "had quite a jolly time" Wednesday, January 13, on an excursion around the Point at Lookout Mountain but "come very nigh into getting into a fight" with some other soldiers they encountered. His diary entry offers no details except to note that "all hands (are) out of humor." On another occasion, he and his comrades of Company F "come very nigh getting into a muss" with Company A when men from A were caught stealing some of F's wood supply.

Things began looking up on Thursday, January 14, when the railroad which the Confederates had destroyed finally was rebuilt and the first locomotive arrived in Chattanooga with "a couple of cars." Food and supplies would begin piling up more rapidly now, easing the Spartan conditions of camp. Jonas recorded "quite an excitement" among the men. Two days later a full train of cars came after dark with hardtack flour and meat, bringing some of the hungry troops out to forage among the cars for themselves. "Stole any amount," wrote Jonas, but added that he "took no part myself." A guard detail from the 87th Regiment, including four from Company F, was set up immediately to guard the rations. Another week brought a decided change in the spirits of the men as their stomachs began to be filled on a regular basis.

A visitor from home arrived Tuesday, January 19, on a sad mission. Lemuel Shelton of Rochester appeared to claim the body of his son David. A private in Company D, David fell during the regiment's Chickamauga action at Kelly Field on Sunday, September 20, and died of his wounds at Chattanooga on October 9. The elder Shelton remained four days, taking comfort at dinner with Jonas and other friends of his son before departing.

Arrival of mail was a happy time in camp and Jonas records it faithfully. His wife's letters often would come two or three at a time. He answered them quickly. Mail from Rochester took nine to 10 days to reach camp, but a box of food and clothing required six weeks. Jonas was a prolific letter writer who kept in touch with his family and many of his friends. Besides frequent letters to his wife, son and daughter, he also wrote regularly to sisters Rachel and Rose Ann, to brothers Jacob and Lewis and to another brother in Minnesota, and to friends named G.C. Baumgardner, Susan Jane, Geny and Albert.

Jonas had plenty of time to investigate the camp's surroundings, seeing and recording sights the small-town Hoosier carpenter considered unusual. He often visited the Chattanooga railroad depot.[2] There, wrote Jonas, "I saw the first Negro soldier I ever saw doing duty." Late in January four companies of Negro soldiers arrived at the depot and Jonas recorded this revolutionary change in the Union army, still incomprehensible to many northerners. He recorded no objection to their appearance in the diary. Jonas also took note of the many "distressed women" (refugees) gathered at the depot awaiting transportation north. Another time he found more than 100 men, women and children, the latter crying from the cold, laying about the depot grounds awaiting a northbound train.

On Sunday, February 7, the diary's entry begins with news that the depot burned down between 4 and 6 A.M., causing a total loss of $150,000, including much stored clothing but no loss of life.

Jonas mentions going to headquarters shortly after the depot fire to see "a large grisley bear." How such a beast came to be in an army camp at wartime was not explained; perhaps it was a tame traveling bear, with trainer. He and friends also explored a cave in Lookout Mountain for over three hours late in January, when the weather was "warm enough to go barefoot."

The first recruits for the regiment's depleted companies arrived in late January and Jonas could not resist commenting on how young they looked. By the end of February, Company F had received eight of them.

Several of the notations in Jonas' diary reveal his sensitivity to and an appreciation for this unique time in his life. Three consecutive entries start with the notation that "today has been a splendid day." He records the sight of a rainbow in the western sky one morning, sees the stars "shining high and nice" after an 11 o'clock rain, finds the western sky turning red after another rain, notes the sudden warmth caused by a wind switch to the south, and one night comments that "the moon is flat on its back." Clearly, there was a contemplative side to his nature.

When Daniel Bruce, our teamster with the frozen pants, finally warmed up, he was ordered to take his mules and wagon to Bridgeport, one of the army's supply depots in Alabama. It's on the Tennessee River 23 miles southwest of Chattanooga and was reached by primitive wagon roads that wound through Sand and Raccoon mountains. Ten miles further on was Stevenson, site of another depot. On the way to Bridgeport, Bruce was surprised to find a cousin, L.B. Hoch, at work on replacing a creek bridge that had been destroyed by Confederates.

Bruce was sent to Bridgeport on Saturday, January 9, and remained there until the end of the month. He had little to do, so he spent most of his time splitting clapboards for a large shanty that the troops were building for shelter. Daniel split 471 clapboards in three days, helped lay some on the shanty's roof and later dragged in brush to hide the building from Rebel artillery spotters.

Ordered back to Chattanooga on Sunday, January 31, Bruce spent the entire Leap Year month of February there without specific orders, awaiting the next movement of the army. Restoration of the railroad was bringing a steady buildup of supplies, leaving little for the regimental wagons to do for the moment. He suffered through more cold nights, took his turn at barbering for the company, patched his clothing, chopped wood and had time to take a pleasure ride on one of his mules into Georgia on several occasions, once spending the night with a group of refugees. Daniel also had his silhouette cut to send to his wife, just as he had done at Camp Rose in South Bend.

There is a hint from a diary entry about this time that Jonas Myers applied for a command assignment with a Negro regiment. Such a transfer might have brought him a commission and it apparently was approved. On Wednesday, February 10, he described his dilemma: "hardly know whether to report or not dont like to back off." In the end, back off he did.

The following day, his regiment got marching orders and Jonas must have decided it would be best to stick with friends in his company to face the fighting that he knew was coming.

As was often the case in this army, the orders were countermanded and it was not until Monday, February 22, that the regiment marched off, at 7 A.M. with three days' rations in their haversacks. Action was anticipated, because all the baggage and tents were left behind. So was Jonas.

The previous Wednesday night was so cold it "froze our ink hard," wrote Jonas, and afterward he was stricken with three hours of severe chills, followed by a high fever and splitting headache. He called for the company surgeon, Dr. Vernon Gould, who prescribed quinine powders and confined him to bed. When the regiment left camp, Jonas was not considered fit to go along.

Five days later Col. Newell Gleason, the regimental commander, returned to order the 87th and its equipment moved south 14 miles to a new base at Ringgold, in north Georgia. Jonas was up and ready, as was Bruce, who had moved into the tent vacated by his brother-in-law, Alfred Hizer, a private in Company E. Jonas and Daniel toiled in a persistent rain to get the gear packed. On Tuesday, March 1, they left behind them Chattanooga and 28 men from the 87th who had died of illnesses in its hospitals since Chickamauga.

They were off to join the regiment, which on that February 22 had moved out with Maj. Gen. John Palmer and the XIV Corps to probe the Confederate army's positions around Dalton, 14 miles south of Ringgold. The 87th's Third Division led the corps into Ringgold, which was practically deserted, its buildings abandoned. Five miles on toward Dalton, Rebels were found in considerable strength behind fortifications along Rocky Face Ridge. The division probed the Rebel works with reconnaissance in force for two days, finding them too strong to be tackled by a single division and so withdrew to Ringgold to establish base camp. The 87th's brigade was at the center of the Federal line during this heavy skirmishing but fired no shots and took no casualties.[3]

The Federals were getting into position to challenge the Army of Tennessee in combat once more, but were not quite ready yet to launch a full-scale assault. The Union forces were neither completely reprovisioned nor at top strength. Many three-year regiments were on 30-day furloughs as a condition of their reenlistment. The Second Minnesota was one of these regiments that was "veteranizing" and would not to return to the 87th's brigade until April 10.[4]

For the men of the 87th Infantry Regiment, the change of camps would bring an end to the informal, rather lazy days of Chattanooga and return them to military drill, discipline and protocol. There would be only minor action against the waiting enemy. Fighting would come in two months, with the beginning of the campaign to reach and capture Atlanta.

The immediate concern of the troops was bodily comfort at their camp along Taylor's Ridge on the east side of Ringgold, where the 87th's entire Third Division of three brigades was pleasantly situated. Most of the men had run out of patience with shivering in tents, so they demolished almost every unoccupied house in Ringgold for materials to build huts, or shanties as most were called.

Henry W. Hoober, sergeant in Company E, found only the courthouse, two churches and a few dwellings still standing in Ringgold when he returned April 17 from a furlough to Blue Grass in Fulton County. Only two white families were brave enough to remain through the Yankees' occupation, Hoober stated. When the Second Minnesota got back in late April, the regiment razed one of the two remaining churches for the boards and beams to make its shelter.[5]

Jonas Myers, the carpenter, was in the thick of such construction, as one might imagine. The first three days after arriving at Ringgold, Myers was occupied with helping his comrades erect their shanties or in gathering lumber, bricks and building materials for others. He complained that the work was hampered by a lack of tools, for he could find only a single axe and two hatchets. Nevertheless, he made a cook stove for his own shanty and put up a chimney so the Company F captain, Horace Long, could use his. A floor was laid in the shed and a ditch dug around it for drainage. Later Jonas' talents were called upon by a sergeant to design him a plan for a postwar house.

Daniel Bruce no sooner had arrived at Company E's camp than he was assigned as the company's cook, duties he performed for a week while his mates were getting their own sheds in order. The shelters were worth the work, for the March weather was most unpredictable: intermittent rainstorms, a hailstorm and a day-long snowfall of seven inches. The temperature dropped so quickly one night that Jonas couldn't get his morning coffee made before the water froze in his tin cup. Not until late April did the weather become dependably moderate.

Meanwhile, for Jonas and his fellow 87th infantrymen, it was back to the military basics that are necessary when within range of the enemy and on the edge of a campaign. There was picket duty to stand on a regular basis, sometimes by the entire regiment, but on the whole this was rather easy duty. There were inspections, company drill every morning, brigade drill at least once a week. There were dress parades, sometimes by regiments, sometimes by brigades and once, by the entire Third Division. The latter was a Grand Review before Maj. Gen. George H. Thomas, commanding the Army of the Cumberland, on Thursday, April 7. Jonas sometimes was detailed for duty as sergeant of the guard, or as a night camp guard.

Sgt. Hoober recalled that the encamped troops were in good health as well as spirits. The monotony of the camp routine soon was leavened when the troops organized musical concerts and gymnastic exhibitions at the courthouse nightly except Sunday. There was little indication of the enemy's presence, just an occasional dash by Rebel cavalry at the outposts, which were easily turned aside.

Once, however, the 87th was sent out on a reconnaissance with the Ninth Ohio and 35th Ohio, accompanied by wagon teams that brought three displaced families back into the Union lines. The brigade closed within rifle range of the Rebel pickets, who got off a couple of meaningless shots before the scouting mission retreated.

On Sunday, March 20, Jonas takes note it was "six months today since the Battle of Chicamauga. How soon the time has passed." He confides no other memory of those fearsome two days. Three weeks later, though, he records that Company D went to the battleground with George Moore of Rochester to seek the remains of Moore's son. Nothing identifiable was found, although the search party "found a part of the remaines of some one near where he was last seen."

It appears that the senior Moore was tragically misinformed about the fate of his son. Corp. James Moore of Company D was listed as severely wounded in the leg at Chickamauga on a list of casualties published two weeks after the battle of September 19–20, 1863. He died in an army hospital at Madison, Ind., on March 24, 1864.[6] That was 18 days before his father appeared at Chickamauga, believing him killed on the battlefield and seeking his body there.

It was 10 days after the troops arrived at Ringgold before their knapsacks were brought from Chattanooga and, as usual, in the accounting some clothing had disappeared. Two of Jonas' friends lost their blankets, another his overcoat.

As the weather warmed in April, the Baptist preachers began to stop by on Sundays to evangelize and purify the lives of those piously inclined among the Federal host. There were sermons, distribution of religious tracts and, most importantly, baptisms to calm the spirits of those become apprehensive about their immediate future.

Chickamauga Creek was nearby and at 2 o'clock in the afternoon of Sunday, April 10, Jonas said "their was 45 baptised in Chicamauga Creek and on the banks, 25 by immersion, 19 by sprinkling and 2 by pouring." Daniel Bruce was there as a spectator, too; he counted 44 taking the waters, all of them afterwards returning to the church to take the sacrament. The next Sunday 47 more joined in the ceremony, 27 by immersion and 20 by sprinkling, wrote Myers. Bruce evidently had other things to do that day, but the following Sunday he counted 57 baptisms. Myers commented on the same day that the church services had become so popular, two of his friends, Asa Batchelor and Clark Hickman, could find no seats.

There also were evening church services during the week, which Daniel attended from time to time. Jonas makes no mention of being present. He and Capt. Peter Troutman of Company E evidently were more interested in a personal project: organizing within the regiment a Knights Templars Lodge, a branch of Freemasonry. Nine men later were initiated into the order, including Capt. James Burnham of Rensselaer, Company A; Dr. Gould, company surgeon, and Henry Weller of LaPorte, regimental chaplain. "Co. F well represented" as well, noted Jonas.

He had become a bit of an entrepreneur during these camp days. As a popular, resourceful and talented sergeant, he used these attributes and his position to launch some moneymaking enterprises within the regiment.

For one thing, he was selling photographs to his fellow soldiers. There are 13 entries in his diary of such sales, at prices ranging from 50 cents to $2.75. A Philadelphia photographic concern, probably the supplier, is mentioned twice. He also seemed to be lending money. One entry records that a G.D. Middleton gave him a note for $10, payable on or before the next regular payday; no interest rate was noted. Capt. Long of Company F is credited with paying him 18 cents by postage stamps; Corp. J.J. Babcock was lent 25 cents, Lt. Jacob Leiter 50 cents. He was selling pencils, three for 15 cents each, two for 20 cents; and also shoes. J.T. Gaines bought a pair from him on February 1 for $1 and paid in cash on March 5.

Clearly, Jonas was a man of many parts.

As April days lengthened toward May, the last of the recruits arrived to fill the regiment's vacancies created by illness and death. By the time the Atlanta campaign was launched, the regiment had integrated 142 new men into its 10 companies. Company A enrolled 33, while there were 20 in Company B, two in Company C, seven in Company D, 14 in Company E, 28 in Company F, seven in Company G, 20 in Company H, six in Company I and five in Company K.[7]

Almost all the newcomers were the result of recruitment by company officers during furloughs to their home counties for that purpose. Thus, on April 14 Bruce welcomed to Company E eight acquaintances, all of whom had enlisted March 8. He listed them: John Anderson, Theodore Baker, Martin Brown, William Dukes, James Harvey, James Hurst, James Kilmer and Jesse Oldham. All were from Kewanna except Brown, Star City, and Oldham, Logansport.

The replacements were welcomed, but still fell 50 short of replacing the 192 men the regiment had lost in killed, wounded and missing at Chickamauga. The 87th's strength never again would come up to the 366 effectives who went into that frightful battle.

Sgt. Hoober's five-month furlough home had left him troubled. Hoober considered those who opposed the war with their votes for Democratic candidates "second only to those who oppose us in the field." Don't these men understand, he wondered, that the only protection they have for their property is the soldier in the field? If a Rebel army invaded the North, these Copperheads would receive little sympathy from Southerners "for they are looked upon by the Rebels in nearly the same light as they are by us." Hoober went on:

"The story of the drowning man illustrates the case of Northern traitors exactly. A man was in the act of drowning but was rescued by a friend and because that friend did not attempt to save his hat, he kicked him severely. Their best friend, the Government, is attempting to save their property and protect their homes, but because that friend does not try to save their hat (the Negro in bondage) they kick at him by casting all their influence in that side of the balance containing treason and everything opposed to liberty and freedom, the great principles upon which our Republic is founded."[8]

After his stint as company cook, Daniel Bruce returned to his mules and soon was busy hauling materials for the construction of troop shanties. When that was finished, he and five teamsters from other regiments combined to transport boards and posts to put up a 48-foot-long shed to house their mules. Bringing loads of wood to the soldiers' camp stoves, sometimes even chopping it, took up much of his time, also.

On Monday, April 4, the 87th Regiment opened seven barrels of potatoes, the second such shipment of food and other comforts received at Ringgold from Indiana's governor. "Morton is the best man of all governors to the soldiers," wrote Bruce, and he was right. Oliver P. Morton was noted for his constancy in looking after the welfare of Indiana's volunteer soldiers, both materially and politically.[9]

Daniel had a spell of sickness four days in early April, shaking it off with help from some of Dr. Gould's medicines. Then he got into trouble while caring for his mules. Teamsters spent a lot of their time herding the animals during grazing but many would wander past the picket lines and had to be rounded up, much to the annoyance of the nervous pickets. On Monday, May 2, Bruce was rounding up some young, untrained mules beyond the lines when picketing soldiers of the 92nd Ohio Infantry stopped and arrested him "as a rebel spy" and sent him under guard to the nearest provost marshal's office. He was rescued by the 87th's quartermaster, Jerome Carpenter, and was issued a pass to continue his mule-herding without such inconveniences. Bruce saved the document with his diary; it read:

"Ringgold, Georgia, May 2, 1864. Guards and pickets: Pass Lt. J. Carpenter, Q.M. 87th Ind. Inf., and Daniel E. Bruce, teamster, to look for mules that broke through picket lines this morning. By Command of Brig. Gen. Baird, Maj. James A. Lewis, Adj."

On Tuesday, May 3, the day after Daniel's run-in with the pickets, the character of the camp changed radically. Additional troops began arriving from Chattanooga and on Wednesday Jonas recorded that "soldiers (were) coming in by the thousands all day." All extra baggage was sent to the rear on Thursday and on Friday knapsacks and haversacks were packed, ready to march at daylight.

Over five months of waiting and preparing had ended. Jonas and the 87th Indiana Infantry were going back to war Saturday morning, May 7. From now on there would be no rest until the Confederates had given up the fight.

15

A Running
Fight for Atlanta

In May 1864, there was no question about who was in charge of the Union's war with the rebellious South. Ulysses Simpson Grant had been called to Washington in early March, promoted to the revived rank of lieutenant general and given command of all Federal armies.[1]

This quiet 42-year-old Ohioan, Sam to his old Regular Army friends, had rocketed to success in the three years since he entered the war as colonel of an Illinois regiment. Grant was close to a failure in civilian life after resigning from the prewar army, but war brought him to his destiny. At Forts Henry and Donelson, at Shiloh, in the Vicksburg campaign and by the relief of Chattanooga, he had proved he was a resourceful fighter of grim determination, with a remarkable ability to lead and inspire troops.

Grant's straightforward, keen military mind grasped intuitively that the single, most important Northern objective in the war was not to occupy the Confederacy's territory or capture its cities, but to destroy its main armies. Without them the Confederacy could not exist. He had a grand strategic plan to implement this strategy, and the government was giving him a free hand with it.

And so, on Wednesday, May 4, Grant sent 118,000 men of the Army of the Potomac across the Rapidan River in northern Virginia and with them he headed toward Richmond, the Southern capital. Their real purpose was the destruction of Gen. Robert E. Lee's Army of Northern Virginia that stood in the way.

This was half of a ruthless strategy by Grant that in 11 months would end the South's four-year experiment in secession.

The other half was a simultaneous invasion of the Confederate heartland. It got underway from Chattanooga three days later, on Saturday, May 7, when Grant's close friend and trusted lieutenant, Maj. Gen. William Tecumseh Sherman, launched 98,000 men toward Atlanta, the South's most important city and military base after Richmond. Sherman wanted Atlanta, to be sure, but he really was out to shatter the Army of Tennessee, now reorganized and revitalized under a new and more competent Rebel commander.[2]

It was the beginning of an 800-mile march that would bring undying fame to all who participated in it, including the 87th Indiana Infantry Regiment.

As the 87th left its base at Ringgold, its place within the organization of George Thomas' Army of the Cumberland remained the same as it was at the Missionary Ridge assault. The Hoosiers of Col. Newell Gleason were in the Second Brigade, commanded by Col. Ferdinand Van Derveer, along with the Second Minnesota, 35th Ohio, Ninth Ohio, 75th Indiana, 101st Indiana and 105th Ohio regiments. Their brigade was a part of Brig. Gen. Absalom Baird's Third Division of Maj. Gen. John Palmer's XIV Corps.[3]

Their caps now displayed the distinctive acorn badge of the XIV Corps. These cloth patches that identified the various Union Army corps first were ordered by Maj. Gen. Joseph Hooker when he took command of the Army of the Potomac in 1863. By now the practice had spread to the West.

Maj. Gen. Daniel Butterfield, who designed most of the badges while Hooker's chief of staff in the East, accompanied Hooker to Chattanooga with the reinforcements from the Army of the Potomac. Butterfield was asked by Maj. Gen. Thomas to suggest an appropriate patch for his old XIV Corps command.

"If I had command of the Fourteenth Corps, which stood firm as an oak at Chickamauga," Butterfield replied, "I would give it the acorn for a badge in honor of its bravery." Thomas agreed and so it was done.[4]

Some of the 87th's companies had new captains as the campaign got underway. James Burnham of Rensselaer replaced the resigned George Payne of Pleasant Grove in A. William Agnew of Winamac led B after George Baker of Star City fell at Chickamauga. John Elam of Rochester was in command of D because of the death of Lewis Hughes, Rochester, at Chickamauga. William Poole of Star City replaced the resigned Alanson Bliss of LaPorte in G. Company H's captain changed because Richard Sabin of Union Mills was promoted to major and was replaced by William Biddle of LaPorte. In Company K, Lyman Crosby of Cedar Falls, Iowa, had resigned and was succeeded by another Iowan, William Deacon, of Marion. Crosby himself had been a replacement for another Chickamauga casualty, James Holliday of Mishawaka.

In addition, James Crawley of LaPorte and Company I would resign shortly after the Atlanta campaign began and be replaced by John Catlin. That was to be the last of the changes in the regiment's company commanders.[5]

The men of the 87th now would follow Sherman, a supreme commander, who was one of the most singular personalities of the Civil War and, after Grant, its most renowned leader.

Cump to his family, Uncle Billy to his soldiers, the 44-year-old Sherman was a military genius who, it has been said, understood the art of war perhaps to a greater degree than any one of his contemporaries on either side. Quick to understand and move against major problems, this Ohioan had an inexhaustible energy that wore out those around him and he was remorseless against anyone who was not committed to total war. Militarily, he and Grant were peas in a pod.

Sherman inspired confidence among the hard-bitten veterans of his Western army, for his talk was rough like theirs and he even bore a physical resemblance to them. One of his soldiers described Sherman as "the most American-looking man I ever saw; tall and lank, not very erect, with hair like thatch which he rubs up with his hands, a rusty beard trimmed close, a wrinkled face, sharp, prominent red nose, small bright eyes, coarse red hands; black felt hat slouched over his eyes, dirty dickey (collar) with the points wilted down, black old-fashioned stock (scarf), brown field officer's coat with high collar and no shoulder straps, muddy trowsers and one spur. He carries his hands in his pockets, is very awkward in his gait and motions, talks continually and with immense rapidity."[6]

Above all, Sherman tolerated neither fools nor nonsense. He was the perfect man for the job that now had to be done.

He was not so lucky, however, in drawing a Confederate counterpart as Grant had been at Chattanooga. The Army of Tennessee, so badly led by Braxton Bragg at Perryville, Murfreesboro, Chattanooga and even in the victory at Chickamauga, was now restored in numbers and morale under a new, greatly respected commander, Gen. Joseph E. Johnston. President Jefferson Davis had removed his good friend Bragg, finally admitting that Bragg was incapable of winning campaigns. Inexplicably, Davis then brought him to Richmond as chief military adviser to the president.

Johnston was extremely capable and canny as an army leader, but in this situation he was working under a monumental handicap: Davis had little confidence in him and the two men disliked one another intensely.

Nevertheless, Johnston had his 62,000 troops strongly entrenched along the heights of Rocky Face Ridge northwest of Dalton and would be hard to deal with. A 57-year-old Virginian, Johnston was a West Point classmate of Lee, whom he preceded as commander of the Army of Northern Virginia. Johnston was wounded at Seven Pines before Richmond in 1862, presenting Lee with a path to glory. Johnston most recently had led Confederate forces in a failed effort to prevent Grant from besieging Vicksburg.

Johnston had spent a lifetime in the military, serving in the Black Hawk expedition, on the Indian frontier, in the Seminole War and in Mexico, where he was wounded five times, won three brevets for bravery and led the storming column at Chapultepec. A small, gray, neat-appearing man of brisk and touchy temperament, Johnston was described as "having a certain gamecock jauntiness." He also was a consummate soldier, possessing a sharp strategic sense.

Johnston and Sherman posed a good match for the coming struggle. The two men became good friends after the war and it is ironic that Johnston died of pneumonia contracted from standing hatless in the rain at Sherman's 1891 funeral.[7]

The area over which this campaign now was to be fought presented formidable geographical obstacles to the invaders. The route to Atlanta covered 120 miles of Appalachian mountain spurs, swift rivers, deep valleys with thick forests and dismal swamps, every bit of it easily defended by the Rebels. Johnston had 62,000 men in the corps of Lt. Gens. William Hardee, John Hood and Leonidas Polk, plus cavalry.

Sherman's overpowering 98,000-man force was divided into three armies: Thomas had 60,000 in his Army of the Cumberland, which included the 87th Indiana's XIV Corps, the IV Corps, the XX Corps and cavalry. Sherman's old Army of Tennessee was led by promising young Maj. Gen. James McPherson with 24,000 in the XV, XVI and XVII Corps. Smallest was the 14,000-man Army of the Ohio, really just the XXIII Corps and cavalry. Its commander was Maj. Gen. John Schofield, who briefly commanded the 87th Indiana's division while it was at Triune, Tenn., in the spring of 1862.[8]

Sherman's tactical plan was easily understood. The line of attack was along his supply line, which was the Western and Atlantic Railroad connecting Chattanooga and Atlanta. Thomas' Cumberlanders with the 87th Indiana formed the center, confronting the Rebels down the railroad while McPherson on the right and Schofield on the left traveled in wide flanking paths to threaten Johnston's rear.

That approach determined the course of the campaign for the first 10 weeks. Johnston, outnumbered, would find a strong defensive position and invite attack, only to be flanked by a turning movement and forced to retreat, first from Dalton, then successively from Resaca, Allatoona Pass, New Hope Church and Kennesaw Mountain until finally reaching the outskirts of Atlanta. There, as we shall see, the campaign's character changed dramatically.[9]

For Jonas Myers and the 87th Indiana, the struggle for Atlanta began at 6:30 A.M. on Saturday, May 7. The regiment left camp at Ringgold with the Third Division of the XIV Corps for Tunnel Hill seven miles out. There the Rebs had outposts ahead of steep Rocky Face Ridge, where the main line protected their base at Dalton seven miles further south. The sentinels were brushed aside easily for, as Jonas recorded, some were only dummies of coats and trousers stuffed with straw. Sherman then attacked up Rocky Face's quartz mountainside as a feint while sending the XIV Corps and the rest of the army through Snake Creek Gap on the right. There they joined McPherson coming in from the west, threatening Johnston's communications and forcing him to evacuate Dalton.

It was a nerve-wracking start for Jonas, and didn't get any better with time. "We found the Johnnies in less than two hours" after leaving Ringgold, he recalled after the war, and every day for the next four months there was a fight or skirmish with the butternuts.[10] Three months after leaving

Ringgold, Jonas remarked in his diary that the 87th had been under fire all but 18 days of that time.

At Resaca, 19 miles closer to Atlanta, Johnston halted and deployed along a four-mile ridge anchored on both ends by rivers. On two weekend days, May 14 and 15, Sherman tried without success to break the Confederate lines. Once again he ordered a turning movement and when McPherson's Army of Tennessee got over the Oostanaula River into Johnston's left, the Southern commander again disengaged and headed down the railroad toward the pass through the Allatoona Mountains, 35 miles away.[11]

Van Derveer's brigade was on the left of the Union line at Resaca. The 87th Indiana was not engaged on Saturday, although Myers experienced a constant barrage of artillery and musket fire from 12:15 P.M. until after 7 o'clock. It was "of the heaviest kind and seemingly nothing gained on either side." On Sunday, he recorded, Saturday's smoke had not disappeared when the guns began again at 6 A.M. Minié balls from Rebel sharpshooters were "occasionally flying over our heads (and) a Capt. of the Second Minn. just wounded in the head by one." In the afternoon the regiment moved into the front line but still did not engage; "having a mery time" seeing shells explode in the air as butternut artillery tried to find a Federal battery behind the regiment.

On Monday with Johnston's forces gone, Jonas and the 87th gathered Rebel trophies from the battleground, which presented a grim appearance: "Quite a number of dead Rebbels laying scattered over the ground. Bushes all shot to pieces. Every elevation is fortified. Dont look possible as though men could be drove out of such works but right must triumph," wrote Jonas. The regiment then entered Resaca just as a train arrived from Chattanooga to replenish the army's supplies.

The 87th took up the pursuit at 4 o'clock Tuesday morning, May 17, and around noon passed through the town of Calhoun in bravado style, with "colors flying and band playing." Some townspeople came out to see the Yankees. They were mostly quiet and unsmiling women, Jonas noticed. He got his first indication of how this Northern invasion affected the natives when he caught sight of "quite a small boy (who) sat in a gateway making faces at the Yanks." Nevertheless, Jonas considered Calhoun "quite a nice town and the nicest country I have saw in Georgia."

The march resumed at 3 o'clock Wednesday morning, when the 87th rejoined its brigade and continued 10 miles to Adairsville, whose citizens also were presented with a brisk military show of flying colors and martial music as the troops went through the town. "The Rebs were fleeing and the Yanks pursuing and in fine spirits," wrote an obviously contented Jonas.

On Thursday, May 19, the regiment advanced nine miles along the railroad to Kingston, where it was held for the next three days. During this pause, the Ninth Ohio's three-year service expired and the tough all-German regiment, having resisted all blandishments to reenlist, went home to

Cincinnati to be mustered out. Gen. Thomas came to honor his comrades from the 1862 victory at Mill Springs, relieving the Ninth from picket duty himself and leading them back to camp.[12] The Second Brigade continued without a replacement for the Ninth. While at Kingston, the 87th engaged in some skirmishing along its front but still was removed from the major line of battle.

On Monday, May 23, the regiment moved out to join the rest of Thomas' army and advance on Allatoona Pass, where Johnston again had entrenched. Sherman found this position too difficult to assault, so ordered a wide turning movement to the southwest. Johnston followed from Allatoona.

Then, around the town of Dallas and the crossroads settlement of New Hope Church, the two sides slugged it out for three days in forest so dense that Union troops called it "the hell hole" for the nightmarish fighting that took place. The 87th was not involved, nor was the Army of the Cumberland; McPherson and Schofield had the honors. Neither side could gain the advantage, so McPherson again turned Johnston's flank, forcing him to withdraw to Kennesaw Mountain.[13]

Kennesaw is a 700-foot-high, steep, wooded and rocky peak north of Marietta and 30 miles from Atlanta; Johnston soon had it laced with trenches and bristling with cannon.

For some reason, Sherman here decided to abandon his flanking maneuvers and go at the Rebels with an all-out frontal assault. He launched it on Monday, June 27, and it was a disaster: 2,000 in killed and wounded against only 500 casualties for the Rebels. Among the Union dead was Col. Daniel McCook, who had figured so prominently in the development of the Perryville battle. He was the fourth of his family to be killed in action. The Confederates also suffered a serious loss about this time: Lt. Gen. Polk was killed June 14 by Union artillery while reconnoitering from nearby Pine Mountain.[14]

In the assault on Kennesaw, the 87th and its XIV Corps were held in reserve on the right and never committed. The regiment's brigade took one loss that day, however, when its longtime commander, Col. Van Derveer, was forced onto sick leave after an extended illness. The 87th Indiana proudly saw its own colonel, Gleason, succeed to the brigade command and in Gleason's place received Lt. Col. Edwin Hammond, a 28-year-old lawyer from Rensselaer.

Jonas Myers had been too busy dodging Minié balls to give daily attendance to his diary, but on the day of Polk's death, he was at Acworth, near Kennesaw, and made a significant entry:

"Tis now after 12. I have just eat some hard tac (and) are laying in line of battle. Moved towards the front at ten. Picketts have been fiering all morning. Occasionally a Rebble ball passes over us. Close enough to the last mountain to see the Rebble flag flying and a very good prospect of having a little muss before night.

"Some of the boys have been sleeping since laying here in line of battle. A novel place to sleep.

"Half after four we have just had a mail. Received a letter from my wife, all well. One of the co. A boys has just come in from the skirmish line and reports William Irvin of our co. killed (Irvin was from Rochester). Since been confirmed by one of the 35th Ohio. Since writing at 12 we have moved about the length of the regiment to the left where we now lay. A ball just passed by me three feet high."

On July 4 the 87th Regiment took its first head count since leaving Ringgold and found 289 effectives, 15 officers and 274 in the ranks. So far in this campaign, the 87th was holding its numbers; 316 had left Chattanooga with the regiment.

Johnston left his mountain redoubt to keep Sherman from getting between him and Atlanta, retreating to the Chattahoochee River only 10 miles from the city. But he allowed McPherson to get far to the east and cross the river unopposed. Now the Confederates had to fall back to the outskirts of Atlanta.

Whereupon, the axe fell. President Davis, angered by Johnston's refusal to fight the Yankees, took the army away from him and gave it to John Hood on Sunday, July 17.

"This act," a Rebel soldier recalled, "threw a damper over this army from which it never recovered." Sherman, after the war, wrote that by this decision "the Confederate government rendered us most valuable service." Immediately, Sherman alerted his men for battle, for Hood was an impetuous, gambling fighter. One of Sherman's officers recalled how, in a prewar army poker game, Hood "bet $2,500 with nary a pair in his hand."[15]

This 33-year-old Kentuckian had an eye for the ladies to whom he exhibited the effects of his battlefield bravery proudly: a leg lost at Chickamauga and a crippled arm from Gettysburg. A lieutenant when he entered the army, Hood now was a full general and had been in many of the war's toughest fights: the Peninsula, Second Manassas, Antietam and Fredericksburg besides Gettysburg and Chickamauga.[16]

Meanwhile, our regimental teamster followed in the wake of the 87th and its XIV Corps, encountering difficulties of his own. Daniel Bruce and his mules traveled through Tunnel Hill, Snake Creek Gap and into Resaca, where his wagon was filled with 35 boxes of hardtack and sent on to Calhoun. Six miles from there he camped for the night in an orchard, where surgeons had set up a hospital and Bruce "saw them taking arms and legs off wounded men." The unfortunates were Missourians of the IV Corps with the Army of the Cumberland, he noted.

He was sent back to Resaca for seven barrels of pork, then went on through Adairsville and met the regiment during its pause at Kingston, where he had a chance to visit cousin Joseph Troutman. For the next couple of weeks Daniel and his other teamsters foraged among surrounding homes and plantations for supplies, once finding 15 bushels of husking corn that he said would last the mule train "several evenings." By July 7 he was around Acworth, pulling up green wheat and rye and clover and cutting sugarcane to keep his mules fed.

Bruce caught up with the regiment and visited it on the battle line on June 14, the day Jonas Myers made his entry about the death of Pvt. Irvin. He remained within sound of the daily cannonading for two weeks. A week before the Kennesaw assault took place, Bruce brought a wagonload of supplies to the 87th Regiment's front line, where he stayed 10 minutes and found "boys in good spirits." His diary laconically notes that a shell burst near his wagon. Then he records that John Busey of Peru and Company C was killed while coming back from the front with his company. According to the Official Records, however, Busey was only wounded and received a discharge because of it on November 29.

Roads were so bad in the region and the half-rations for the mules so inadequate that the animals were giving out while in harness. Bruce remained in the area between Marietta and Big Shanty Station, north of Kennesaw on the railroad, hauling food for the troops and foraging for the mules. On Saturday, July 2, he drove his team to the top of Kennesaw and the next day drove along the battle line of June 27. He was astonished: "Such shooting effects I never saw in my life. Trees shot to pieces and holes shot through them. Houses full of holes."

By Tuesday, July 5, he was taking hardtack to the troops and close enough to Atlanta to see its buildings. The weather was getting quite hot and water was becoming scarce. When Johnston was sacked, on July 17, Bruce was in Marietta, foraging and provisioning the troops from that base.

Hood, the new Confederate commander, wasted no time before launching six weeks of furious contention for possession of Atlanta. His first attack was made just three days after he took charge, on Wednesday, July 20. On the northwest front he tried to crush advance units of the Army of the Cumberland as they crossed Peachtree Creek. The assault was made late and failed in the face of determined resistance. Darkness ended the battle; Hood had lost 3,000 men with no appreciable result.[17]

The 87th Indiana was on the right of the Union line in this engagement. Companies D and G formed the skirmish line as the regiment advanced in the morning to feel out the Rebel works. Four men, including Lt. Jacob Leiter and Pvt. Alfred Hizer, Bruce's brother-in-law, were wounded before the regiment was pulled back to the cover of a hill. Leiter would be discharged later because of his wound, but Hizer's proved to be fatal. The regiment was not in action again but suffered so from the extreme heat that Pvt. David Fisher of Gilead, a new recruit in Company F, wound up in the field hospital.

Nevertheless, the men of the 87th "were heartened by the presence of the locomotive whistle and Uncle Sam's mail," according to regimental surgeon Vernon Gould who visited them at this time. Other than the close presence of their supplies and assurance of regular delivery of news from home, the soldiers also took comfort in the breastworks they were huddling behind, Gould added.[18]

The next day, Hood saw a chance to smash McPherson's Army of Tennessee on the eastern front in the crucial Battle of Atlanta. A fierce Federal counterattack at the end of the day repulsed the Confederates this time with a loss of 5,000. In two days Hood had taken 8,000 casualties, more than Johnston had lost in 10 weeks. The second battle, however, cost Sherman the services of the brilliant young McPherson, who was killed by a Rebel skirmisher and replaced by Maj. Gen. O.O. Howard.[19]

Another 5,000 Confederates were left on the field at the Ezra Church fight on the west side a week later, July 28. The 87th Indiana was close enough to this action to help take care of the dead when it was finished. Pvt. Whitsel Lewis of Rensselaer and Company A, who as a hospital orderly had unique opportunities to observe events, recorded how it was done:

"Our men took sticks with hooks on them and they would hook it in the dead reb cloths and drage them up in piles together and then dig holes and throw them in and throw dirt on them . . . general macperson (has been) killed and a mornful loss he was to the soldiers he was."[20]

After Ezra Church, Hood became less aggressive, but still prevented Sherman from cutting Atlanta's last lifeline to the south, the Macon & Western Railroad. On his part, Sherman continued a persistent shelling of the city. Jonas noted on July 24 that a shell was being sent that way every 15 or 20 minutes.

During this time the 87th Indiana was southwest of the city facing the entrenched Confederates and enduring constant shelling along the line of Utoy Creek. There on Thursday, August 4, the Hoosiers distinguished themselves once again in a Second Brigade reconnaissance of the Rebel works led by Col. Gleason. The entire brigade moved out vigorously with skirmishers in front and two battle lines behind, the 87th and 105th Ohio in the first line. Two rows of the enemy's skirmish pits were captured and the advance continued in the face of heavy artillery and musket fire. Only when the Rebels' main line 400 yards away was located and its character determined, as ordered, did Gleason retire his men, with 25 prisoners. The 87th received from the division commander "highest praise for the manner in which the affair was conducted." The regiment counted 26 casualties in the action; killed was Pvt. Adam Deelman of Mishawaka and Company K.

Capt. Peter Troutman of Company E called this one of the most important events of his war career, stating in a postwar memoir that he prevented a stampede of the 87th Regiment's left wing during the reconnaissance. Unfortunately, he provided no further details. With the information thus gained, the entire Third Division assaulted the Rebels the next day and occupied the new line. The division captured 140 prisoners in this attack, 62 of them taken by the Second Brigade.[21]

It was not a healthy place to be. One of Company F's new recruits, Seymour Wertz of Rochester, was killed and Capt. Poole of Star City and Company G was wounded while on a skirmish line. Wrote Jonas:

"The Rebs . . . have a very good range on us. And yesterday while we were to work to fortify they give us some very close calls causing us to lay right close to the ground, occasionally topping the bushes and letting the limbs down on us causing some very odd expressions such as what a curious way of topping they have down in Dixie. Up in God's country they top the wheat, cut down the trees. But here they begin at the top of the tree and work down. . . . This morning the Rebel skirmishers got in a big way of fiering at ours, throwing any amount of balls over our camp. It is now 11 o'clock I have just been to the spring while their a ball passed my head."

Sometimes, though, the two sides called time-out, such as on Friday, August 12. Pvt. Lewis told how the brief camaraderie was conducted:

"On front line and trading with rebs, coffee for tobacco—our men hollowed to the rebs and offered coffee for tobacco—rebs agreed—they quit shooting—went halfway between the line, did trading, go back to rifle pits and went to shooting at each other again. I stood on the breastworks and seen them come together and trade—it was a sight to see—a good many went out to trade."

In August the brigade was reduced in size again when the 35th Ohio Regiment reached the end of its three-year enlistment and left for Hamilton to muster out. Remaining in Col. Gleason's Second Brigade were the 87th Indiana, Second Minnesota, 101st Indiana and 75th Indiana. The latter now was commanded by Maj. Cyrus McCole to replace Lt. Col. William O'Brien, who had lost two fingers from a hand wound on July 20.[22]

Also in August came a change in command for the XIV Corps. Maj. Gen. Palmer resigned in a tiff with Sherman over his place in the seniority rankings and was replaced August 22 by Brig. Gen. Jefferson Columbus Davis, that hot-headed Hoosier who had redeemed his honor in Louisville by shooting down "Bull" Nelson.[23] Thanks to the intercession of his good friend, Gov. Oliver P. Morton of Indiana, Davis escaped punishment for that intemperance. He since had compiled a distinguished record as a division commander at Stones River, Chickamauga and in this Atlanta campaign. Davis was to continue at the head of the XIV Corps until war's end.

Col. Gleason reported on August 16 that with the Ninth Ohio and 35th Ohio gone, the Second Brigade's strength was 1,120 instead of the 2,549 counted before leaving Ringgold. Casualties of the 87th Indiana since then totaled 27, with only three killed.[24]

During its stay on the lines southwest of the city, the 87th was under fire almost constantly. Jonas wrote on Sunday, August 7, that a rifle ball was passing over his head every minute. The day before, one passed through his gum blanket (poncho) that was hanging on a line, "but small balls dont scare much," he confided. Action occurring on August 22 took the life of Lt. John Demuth of Peru and Company C.

Skirmishers on the front lines dug what they called "gopher holes" to escape the death-dealing bullets. Their exposure to fire often was so intense that they had to remain crouched in them for 24 hours before being relieved, even then in the dark of night and at great peril.

Indeed, there was an almost continuous uproar of musketry and cannon fire during these weeks, coming from either near or far. The sound soon became so familiar that the soldiers began to ignore it. They went about their mundane habits of sleeping, eating, writing letters home, gambling at cards or chuck-a-luck, washing and mending clothes and cleaning rifles, indifferent to the deadly racket unless they had to make or repel an attack. If the din ceased, as it sometimes briefly did at night, sleeping soldiers would awaken with a start at the sudden silence.[25]

Capt. Troutman, writing in his tent on a cracker box, considered the hot places the regiment had been in during the campaign and listed some of the company's wounded, such as Sgt. Samuel Leavitt, shoulder; Hizer, scrotum (died August 9); Jesse Oldham, foot; and Isaac Cannon, shin. All in all, he thought, after 101 days of campaigning "the army is nearly as srong as the first day nothwithstanding the warm weather, hard work and hard fighting," and went on to comment that "vacant places have been filled by returned veterans, (those) returned from hospitals and hundred days men. Company E left Ringgold with 42 men and now has 38. Nine were sent back sick: E.M. Rans, Wm. E. Dukes, H.S. Ross, Sgt. (Samuel) Richey, Daniel Herrold (who died July 9), Martin Brunson, John Anderson, James Hurst and Alfred Hizer, (all) wounded. Gained from hospitals: Corporals (Judson) Bennett and J. W. Rush, J. R. Smith, J. G. Minton, James Shreves and Moses Heckart."[26]

Capt. Troutman also took time to vent his spleen against the Northern Copperheads who were speaking out against the war during the presidential campaign then going on between President Lincoln and the Republicans and former Gen. George McClellan and the Democrats:

"We of the army have more respect for the Rebels that are fighting us than for the Copperheads of the North. The former have defined their position and we know how to meet them, while the latter are, under the guise of friends, seeking to destroy the Government that protects them.

"Nor do we go very far to find a Copperhead. For instance, we regard Vallandigham *and all that affiliate with him* as Copperheads. (Clement Vallandigham of Ohio, leader of the antiwar faction in the North.) Should he be admitted to a seat in the Chicago Convention (Democratic nominating convention) to which he has been elected will it not be proof positive that that body recognize him, with all his *treason*, as one of their party!

Should that body adopt a peace platform, as it doubtless will, will it not tend to carry the war North, as well as prolong it in the South? O, consistency, what a jewel thou art!

"Stay at home, you cowardly traitors, until the rebellion is gasping in the agonies of a terrible death, under the firm tread of the powerful armies of the Union; then, with tender emotion come forward and clamor for peace! Don't you know your very acts give you the lie? Does not your clamor encourage the South and prolong the war? Is it your blood that is being spilt?

"O, if I could command the language, how I would like to describe my idea of a Copperhead! As it is I can only say that I hate them worse than the Devil; yes sir, worse than the Devil, because I expect by honestly serving my country to keep out of his clutches, but the Copperheads may get hold of me, as I stand ready to fight them if that kind of suasion becomes necessary."[27]

The end of the struggle for Atlanta came 20 miles south of the city on Thursday, September 1. Sherman decided that he could break the stalemate with Hood by concentrating his forces and sending them to Jonesboro to cut the last railroad into the city. On August 31 the Federals were attacked there suddenly by 24,000 Confederates but held them off until the next day, when Davis and the XIV Corps smashed through a salient and forced back the Rebels. This was enough for Hood; he ordered a general withdrawal from Atlanta and went further south to regroup.[28]

Gleason's Second Brigade was held in reserve by Davis at the Jonesboro fight, but the 87th had a good view of the action. Hospital corpsman Lewis wrote how the bluecoats ran up and over almost the entire Rebel line, bayoneting some who did not give up quickly enough. Afterward the 87th helped tear up 15 miles of the last railroad into Atlanta, the Macon & Western. Lewis and the brigade's hospital unit made camp four miles from Jonesboro with 250 patients.

Sherman entered Atlanta on Friday, September 2. Its capture sealed the fate of the Confederacy by assuring Lincoln's reelection, assuring that the war now would continue unimpeded until Northern victory.

On that day the 87th Indiana took a roll call and found 249 effectives in its ranks, 14 officers and 235 men. The regiment had lost 40 men since the last count on July 4.

Pvt. Lewis borrowed a mule and made his own tour of Atlanta four days after the Jonesboro battle, finding it "a pretty town" and noting that Yankee soldiers already were busy tearing down foundries and depots to send north.

Teamster Bruce of the 87th, who had been left behind when the regiment crossed the Chattahoochee, finally crossed it himself on July 20 and the next day got his first sight of Atlanta from a hillside 14 miles away. The next days were occupied hauling rations to all three brigades of the 87th's Third Division until, on Friday, August 5, he was arrested and sent to the guard house.

This news makes a surprise appearance in his diary, for there is no hint of its prompting in the preceding days' entries. Bruce writes it without passion, nor with any scorn for "being reported by Henry Croffard (Crawford?) and John Mackey." Neither men appear on the rolls of the 87th Indiana; perhaps they were fellow teamsters from other regiments.

In any event, Bruce writes that he was taken to division headquarters, turned over to the quartermaster, a Capt. Seely, who sent him to the guard house. There he languished for two weeks, reading the Bible, writing letters and greeting visitors, one of whom told him the sad news that his brother-in-law and good friend, Alfred Hizer, had died August 9 in the hospital at Kingston.

During his incarceration, Bruce wrote a letter to the captain of his company, Peter Troutman. Possibly this communication had to do with his offense, but he offers no further explanation. In any event, on August 19 he was summoned to Capt. Seely's tent, released "free of charge for good conduct heretofore and was sent to feed the convalescent mules." His first night out, he had to sleep on his wagon.

Whatever his transgression might have been, it apparently was not of any great consequence nor, it seems, of any particular concern to the even-tempered Bruce. By September 9 he and his mule team were camped in Atlanta, awaiting orders.

The 87th Indiana, after Hood's departure, went into camp at White Hall near Atlanta.

Expecting a pause in the campaign, Jonas Myers and friend Asa Batchelor of Company F applied for 30-day furloughs, their first, to visit Rochester. In his application filed on September 12, Jonas gave as his reason "some time before entering the service I leased some property in Rochester, State of Indiana, on which some valuable buildings were put up, the lease runs out this fall, and as the property has increased very much in value, I can by paying my personal attention to it, turn it very much to my interest."

Leaves were granted to both soldiers and Jonas would have begun his immediately except that Batchelor needed money for the trip. He asked Jonas to wait until the troops got their pay, expected any time, so the two could travel together. Jonas agreed.

As it turned out, the payroll did not arrive until November 4. It mattered little by then, because on Monday, October 3, the 87th Indiana was ordered into the field once more and all furloughs were canceled. Hood had reorganized the remains of his used-up army, reduced by a third to 40,000 men. While Sherman was making plans to burn his way across Georgia to the sea, Hood decided he would try to draw the Yankees out of Atlanta by disrupting their supply line to Chattanooga. So by the first week of October, Hood was north of Atlanta, tearing up the railroad track down which Sherman had come.

Sherman set out with the bulk of his army, including the 87th Indiana and its division. Hood's generals soon balked at the prospect of meeting the huge Yankee army again, so the Confederates withdrew westward into Alabama and thence toward Tennessee.

Sherman himself grew tired of the chase. He sent Thomas after Hood with part of the Army of the Cumberland, augmented by the corps of Schofield and Brig. Gen. John Stanley. The commanding general then returned to Atlanta to attend to a more pressing matter.[29]

By Monday, November 14, the 87th Indiana was back there, too, after reaching as far north as Kingston on the aborted chase of Hood. Teamster Bruce went along and while at Kingston visited the grave of his brother-in-law. The 87th's brigade, on this swing back into Georgia, built a bridge near Rome so the XIV Corps could cross the Chattooga River. On its return to Atlanta, the 87th also helped tear up much of the railroad track behind it, for Uncle Billy was cutting his connection to Chattanooga and the North.

Sherman was about to set out from Atlanta on one of the most daring moves in the history of warfare and was choosing the best 62,000 men of his army for the undertaking. Among those best were the men of the 87th Indiana Infantry.

16

The March to the Sea

Now that he was deep in the heart of the Confederacy and possessed its jewel of Atlanta, what was William Tecumseh Sherman to do next? His answer was as unprecedented as it was bold. When carried out, it brought to his name equal measures of immortality and obloquy.

Sherman decided to abandon Lt. Gen. Ulysses S. Grant's policy of chewing up the Confederate armies. He had done enough of that already; let Maj. Gen. George Thomas take some of the army and counter Lt. Gen. John Hood's invasion of Tennessee. Sherman would cut his fragile communications with the Northern supply bases and with the rest of his men strike out for Savannah on the Atlantic, where Union ships could bring him provisions.

That was 275 miles away through Georgia's hostile countryside, but it was November and the harvests were in. Smokehouses were full and there were hogs, cattle, turkeys and chickens to be had. Sherman was certain his army could subsist off the countryside.

Anyway, this gamble had a more strategically sinister purpose which was, in Sherman's words, "to make Georgia howl." If a Union army could go anywhere it wanted in the South's heartland, live off the countryside and ignore any force sent against it, then Southerners would have to admit that the Confederacy was too weak a government to survive.[1]

This, then, was the March to the Sea, which is unique in the annals of warfare not only for its audacity. It also introduced "total war" involving innocent civilians behind the lines, a concept that lamentably has been repeated many times since.

Those who took part in the march were forever marked by the experience. Many, such as Sgt. Jerome Carpenter of the 87th Indiana, also understood its importance. When he reached Savannah, Carpenter, the regimental quartermaster, wrote that "this is a new feature in the history of this war (and) the Rebel government does not know how to meet it. The idea of an invading army running promiscuously over the country, destroying everything that comes within their reach, is to them a terrible affair and I think will do more towards making them tired of war than anything our Government has ever done."[2]

Sherman's army was made up of 62,000 of his finest, fittest troops. He divided them equally into two wings, the Army of Tennessee on the right led by Maj. Gen. O.O. Howard and the 87th's Army of Georgia on the left, which Sherman accompanied. Commander of the Army of Georgia was Maj. Gen. Henry Slocum, a 37-year-old New Yorker who had led corps at Chancellorsville and Gettysburg. Brig. Gen. Jefferson C. Davis remained at the head of the 87th's XIV Corps and Brig. Gen. Absalom Baird continued in command of the Third Division. Col. Newell Gleason still was in charge of the Second Brigade, Lt. Col. Edwin Hammond of the 87th Regiment.[3]

Together the two wings would cut a path of destruction through Georgia varying from 30 to 60 miles wide.

Sherman also selected for the march 2,500 light wagons that could travel fast and carry only ammunition and some food.[4] Daniel Bruce of the 87th Indiana would drive one of them.

When this Yankee horde began leaving Atlanta on Tuesday, November 15, it left behind a city two-thirds destroyed. Some destruction was caused by the Confederates before they fled; the entire industrial area had been obliterated on September 1 when the Rebels blew up a long ordnance train filled with shells, causing frightful explosions.[5]

Sherman's torches took care of many of the buildings that remained. Sgt. Carpenter first saw the flames when he approached the Chattahoochee River with the 87th Regiment on its way back from Kingston on Monday. He wrote:

"Long before we crossed (the river) we could see the vast clouds of smoke ascending, as if the world was on fire, and when we arrived at the city it was still burning, and by the time we left on our march through the State of Georgia, it might have been very appropriately said, as of ancient Babylon, 'Atlanta, that great city, has fallen and has become the habitation of moles and bats.' I verily believe there have been few, more terribly grand and terrific sights than that which the city of Atlanta presented on the night of the 15th of Nov'r as witnessed by our troops. A whole city, as it were, on fire and the smoke and flame ascending and mingling with the clouds. Were I to live a thousand years I never should forget that scene."[6]

The 87th Indiana's turn to depart came Wednesday, November 16, and its first two days out were hard, daylong marching with no time for dinners. The route took them eastward toward Augusta as a feint to hide their real destination. They passed through Decatur and then Lithonia and Conyers on the railroad, which they were destroying as they went.

This "unbuilding" of the railroads had been refined into a rapid, efficient maneuver by the Federals. The procedure went something like this:

A regiment stacks arms and removes knapsacks, then forms in a single rank outside the track and faces inward. After removing the end joints of the length of line being destroyed, the men all seize the rail with their hands. Then, at the command "yo, heave!", they lift together and gradually raise the rail up until the entire track is overturned. When it falls on its back, the track is shaken up and loosened since its pieces are secured only by simple chairs, or metal blocks. The ties are knocked off the rails, piled together on the roadbed with a few dry fence rails for kindling and set afire.

The iron rails, placed across the burning piles, soon are red-hot at their centers. A lever and hook then is put on each end of a rail so the ends can be turned in opposite directions and the rail brought down to the ground, leaving it with a spiral twist along its middle. Sometimes the rails would be given extra heating along their length so they could be wound around trees alongside the roads, giving rise to the term "Sherman's Neckties." Another variation in this railroad sport was to bend the 50-pound rails into the shape of letters U S and set them up at mileposts along the line as a memento of the army's passage.[7]

Some 40 miles out of Atlanta, at Oxford, the 87th's route bent to the south toward Savannah. After passing Covington on Friday, November 18, they took their first casualties when two of their foragers were wounded by Confederate bushwhackers. That was the only opposition so far encountered. No significant Rebel force was available to contest the passing of this swarm of Federals, just some cavalry and local militia outfits.[8]

Each morning the 87th, like all the regiments, sent out an officer, sergeant and one man from each of the 10 companies to bring in the day's supplies from the countryside. The foraging team always returned with an enormous and nourishing haul, more than the troops could use. It had been a bountiful harvest season in this part of Georgia and the plantations and farms overflowed with appetizing things to eat. Corn, sweet potatoes and various vegetables were waiting to be gathered; fat cattle, pigs and poultry existed in abundance; smokehouses were filled with cured hams and bacon. There were other delights awaiting the foragers, too: butter, honey, sorghum syrup, apples, homemade jelly, preserves and pickles.

The foraging team, armed to hold off any Confederate cavalry that might come along, rode ahead of the regimental column for a couple of hours, then left the road to visit the plantations. The foragers loaded up carts or wagons with provisions, commandeered horses or oxen to pull them and returned to the road to wait for the regiment to come along.[9] They were doing as Sherman commanded, for he expected the army to find its own provisions by "foraging liberally off the country."

In addition to the foragers, however, were the infamous "bummers" that surrounded the army like a plague of locusts. Here's how historian Bruce Catton described them:

"(They were) a destructive horde of lawless stragglers. These included outright deserters . . . who were going along now on the fringe of the army just for the fun of it; they included, also, men temporarily absent without leave . . . and they included, oddly enough, certain numbers of deserters from the Confederate army who found kindred spirits among these lawless marauders and went with them for the sake of the loot. (Together) they made Georgia's lot far more grievous than Sherman's orders intended. They robbed and pillaged all the way from Atlanta to the sea, not because they had anything against the people they were afflicting, simply because they had gone outside of all normal controls, including their own."[10]

Jonas Myers, now the first sergeant of Company F, recorded some incidents as the regiment moved through Sandtown, Shady Dale and finally into camp on the outskirts of the state capital, Milledgeville, 85 miles from Atlanta.

"Contrabands," or freed slaves, had begun to attach themselves to the brigade in ever-increasing numbers and the spectacle caused him bemusement. At Savannah when the march was over, he recalled:

"Thousands of slaves left their masters, or rather homes, for their masters were gone, when we come a long. And Sambo had but to pack up a fiew bed clothes and go with the live Yankees. Old and young followed mothers with their beds on their heads, a baby in one arm and leading one a size larger. Them that were to old to come along with us would come out to the road and clap their hands together and laugh and cry for joy. Some said they had been praying for us for fifty years."

Col. Gleason put the brigade's band to work while passing through Shady Dale and the music brought out "25 or 30 Negro wenches dancing as the Yankeys passed."

Jonas reported that by now the 87th was destroying property other than railroads, beginning with a cotton press and cotton gin at Sandtown, adding that the plantation had furnished them with plenty of sorghum and pork to eat that evening.

Sgt. Carpenter found Milledgeville "a rather poor town, not as large as Peru, and situated in a very poor country." The citizens of the place were quite surprised to see the Yankees, never expecting them so far into Georgia. The capitol building was vacant, the legislature having fled, and so was the governor's mansion. Gov. Joseph Brown, before departing, had offered freedom to state prison convicts who would join the Confederate army. All but 12 did and Sherman freed those himself. Soldiers, on their own, burned down the penitentiary, ransacked the library and threw away the worthless currency they found in the treasurer's office.[11]

The 87th remained two days at Milledgeville, feasting on roast turkey twice on Thanksgiving Day, November 24. Their route then turned more easterly, taking them through Sandersville and Louisville over the next four days. A stop was made to destroy $100,000 worth of baled cotton and Jonas remarked that the march was being impeded now by "darkies, in fine spirits and all shouting happy." When the regiment passed through Louisville on Monday, November 28, the town was on fire and, for some reason unexplained by Jonas, a Negro woman was shot by a private in Company G.

During a day and a half resting in camp, the 87th got into the only real action of its picnic stroll through Georgia. Rebel cavalry came up on Wednesday, November 30, to clash with an 87th foraging party under command of Capt. Peter Troutman of Company E. The butternut horsemen were repulsed in the resulting skirmish although Pvt. James Lidyard of Oak, Company B, and Thomas Estis of Washington, Company I, were captured. Both later escaped. The next day the entire brigade went into line of battle to confront another appearance by cavalry, which declined to tangle with infantry and disappeared.[12]

Approaching Waynesboro near the Savannah River, the 87th reached a section of large plantations and was set to burning their cotton and destroying gins and presses. Jonas records three such instances until Monday, December 5, when the regiment and its brigade caught up with the rest of the XIV Corps and found the remaining miles to Savannah to be open. By Thursday, December 15, the 87th was in camp four miles west of Savannah along the railroad to Macon. Sherman's army had made contact with the Union fleet from Fort McAllister south of the city. The North was ecstatic; after a nervous month of silence, Sherman's army had emerged intact and victorious.

The March to the Sea was ending with but two deaths in the 87th Indiana Regiment. The first was Sgt. Kline Wilson of Company D, who died of the flux on Wednesday, December 7, and was buried in a field 35 miles from Savannah. Wilson had attended the death of Pvt. James Quigg while the 87th was in camp at Gallatin in 1862; now Sgt. Carpenter did the same for him:

"I went to the ambulance that was conveying him about a half hour before he died and found him perfectly rational but very weak, not able to speak above a whisper. I saw that he was dying and asked him if he wished to send any special word to his parents. He said he was too weak to talk but to say to his father that he died in a good cause. He did not seem to regret in the least that he had to die, but offered up his life a willing sacrifice on the alter of Liberty. Sergt. Wilson was a brave, good soldier and his loss is deeply regretted by the officers and soldiers of his regiment, and especially of his own company."[13]

Two days after Wilson's death, illness also claimed John McCullough of Columbus and Company C but the details of his passing are lost to history.

Carpenter wrote that Capt. John Elam of Rochester and Company D had been ill during most of the march. Elam survived and was mustered out with the regiment.

The 87th's XIV Corps ended the Savannah campaign with 13 killed, 30 wounded and 94 missing, a remarkably low number for a 275-mile march through enemy country.[14] Sherman's total casualties did not exceed 2,200.[15]

Carpenter was at a loss to convey to others what he had just passed through, but he could wax eloquently about the meaning of the march, for most of these Union soldiers knew exactly why they had taken up a musket:

"I wish I could give you something of an idea of the magnitude of this campaign, but I cannot, and can only say that the half will never be told. A man must have been present during its progress in order to appreciate it; suffice it to say that we have seen the Confederacy as it is and feel reassured that a few more decisive blows in the right direction and the Rebellion will be dead; then will justice be meted out to the instigators and they and their sympathizers branded with eternal disgrace and infamy. The day is already dawning and I trust the sun of Freedom will shine forth in all its glory, then will the Star Spangled Banner, which has been baptized with fire and blood on many a battle-field, float more proudly in the breeze, then will the Bird of Liberty take a more lofty flight, and peace and prosperity shall again crown this noble Republic."

Having said this, Carpenter then proceeded, after all, to give a pretty good description of what he had seen during the past month:

"We have done an immense amount of damage to the Southern cause during this campaign by way of destroying railroads, bridges and other property, and devastating the country generally. There is not a mile a railroad between Chattanooga and Augusta that is not totally destroyed. The road from Atlanta to Macon is destroyed, also the road running from Macon to Savannah; in fact, the system of railroads is done away with in the State of Georgia, the Empire State of the Southern Confederacy.

"We have captured thousands of horses and mules, and destroyed hundreds of thousands of dollars worth of cotton and corn. We found plenty of hogs, chickens, turkeys, molasses, honey, &c. I have no hesitancy in saying that there is, at this time, more provisions in the Southern States than ever before at any one time, and for this reason they have abandoned cotton raising and have turned their whole attention to raising stock and grain. They have had abundant harvests, as will be seen by passing through the country.

"We have had no trouble in subsisting either men or animals from the products of the country and we have lived better than if we had been in camps. There are nearly enough sweet potatoes along through this country to subsist a large army. I am well satisfied that there is no probability of starving out the rebellion. We must destroy their armies and when their present armies are destroyed, the work is done, for they have no reserve to fall back upon except their negroes, and if they are put into the ranks, who will raise corn upon which to subsist their army, and even if they had plenty of corn, how can they transport it without railroads, which it is very certain they cannot have while Gen. Sherman commands our forces."[16]

Teamster Daniel Bruce began his stroll through Georgia with more pants trouble, although not from freezing as at Chattanooga. The night before he left Atlanta, he took his trousers off before going to bed and a tentmate stole them while he slept, a danger one ran if he was so incautious. Daniel just shrugged and bought two new pairs for $5. He departed Atlanta at 10 A.M. on Wednesday, December 16, with a load of bacon and salt. His route was following the 87th with the food and, when it was unloaded, foraging off the country each day with the brigade's wagons to keep men and animals supplied. It was an easy job.

Bruce followed the regiment through Milledgeville and at Davisboro, just before reaching Louisville, he stopped to help build a corduroy road to get men and wagons through swampy ground. Approaching Waynesboro, he heard heavy cannonading but was thankful it did not threaten his passage; quicksand and swamps were making that tough enough already. By December 13 he was at the Savannah River and his part of the march was over. Compared to his earlier service in campaigns, this one had been a lark. Daniel took a bath, washed his clothes, read his Bible and for a week did practically nothing but "rise off the straw to feed the mules."[17]

All that remained for Sherman now was to occupy Savannah and that he soon accomplished. Lt. Gen. William Hardee had a force of only 10,000 regulars and militia to defend the city from the 60,000 bluecoats descending upon it. When Fort McAllister, on the coast 12 miles south, was taken December 13, Hardee was in danger of being bottled up and captured. On the night of December 20–21, he escaped over the Savannah River to South Carolina on a hastily constructed pontoon bridge.[18]

The following day, Friday, December 22, Sherman took possession of the city and immediately sent the following telegram to President Abraham Lincoln: "I beg to present you, as a Christmas gift, the city of Savannah, with 150 heavy guns and plenty of ammunition; also about 25,000 bales of cotton." Just a week before, Thomas had completed the destruction of Hood's Army of Tennessee at Nashville. It surely was a merry Christmas for Honest Abe.[19]

The Yankees moved into the lovely old coastal city of 20,000 but not to rest. Only one phase of the campaign was over and there was much work to be done before the next could begin. There was a sense of urgency about it all, for officers and men alike in the bluecoat army now knew that their long ordeal was nearing an end.

"We have orders to get ready for an active campaign," Jonas Myers wrote in a letter to his family a week after arriving in Savannah. "General Sherman dont believe in laying in camp long at a time. He believes in the maxim that a setting hen never gets fat. We have been having inspection review or something els every day almost since we have been here. Yesterday (Wednesday, December 27) he reviewed our Corps the 14th in the streets of Savannah. Today he is reviewing the 20th Corps. In a fiew days more I suppose he will be ready to move on the City of Charleston or Augusta and maby both. Dont know but something is a brewing. He has been here long enough."

Jonas and his Company F captain, Horace Long, were being kept so busy "we have no time to play," some of their workdays lasting until 11 P.M. He found the city a healthy place to be and occupied mainly by women, nine out of 10 being black and most of those slaves. Jonas was puzzled by the color of many of the freed slaves. "Their is hundreds . . . as white as you or me are and a great deal whiter than some I could name."

By and large, the city had been left intact by the retreating butternuts. Jonas described dry-goods stores and drugstores being left in good order. Many cannons were unspiked, their ammunition laying in piles around them. A railroad roundhouse contained 20 locomotives in good running order and nearby were stacks of British-made railroad iron.

Soldiers trying to deal on the open market were in for some surprises, however. Eggs were selling for $35 gold per dozen; it took 40 Confederate dollars to buy one Yankee greenback. Jonas knew a soldier who paid $20,000 in "their money" for a pair of boots. He asked his family to send two checked shirts, a pair of suspenders, a good gold pen and a good three-bladed pocket knife. Wool shirts were the best, but impractical, he wrote. They attract lice, he explained, so they have to be boiled and that shrinks them so they can't be worn.

As Jonas expected, the 87th Indiana did not have long to wait. On Friday, January 20, 1865, the army left Savannah. "Uncle Billy" Sherman's wrath now was to descend upon South Carolina, cradle of the Confederacy, instigator of the heresy of secession.

17
Retribution in South Carolina

Jonas Myers was a stoic man, a quality that had served him well in nearly three years of this terrible Civil War, but as 1865 approached, his yearning for his wife and family had become deep and troublesome.

He tried to write to them a couple of times after arriving in Savannah only to become "so choked down" that he quit. Their letters telling him how much he was missed and how worried they were about his survival caused his melancholy. "I must confess it gives me the blues some when I hear (such words) from them that are nearer to me than Father and Mother."

He finally composed a letter, as we have seen, in which he provided details of the march through Georgia and the look of Savannah. His closing words in that letter revealed the depth of his private anguish:

"Dont think my love less for home than when I left. For I never knew what a home was till since I have been in the service." This was Jonas' wartime valedictory; not until 44 years later did he again write about his wartime service.[1]

The hunger for home and an end to war doubtless was shared by many in the army which William Tecumseh Sherman was about to launch into the Carolinas to reach Virginia. There he meant to hook up with Ulysses S. Grant, finish off Robert E. Lee's Army of Northern Virginia and finally bring down the Confederacy.

Sherman anticipated this campaign would be no pleasant outing, as the already famous March to the Sea had turned out to be. He was right. The advance through the Carolinas became a continuous battle with the elements, for the winter of 1865 developed into the wettest seen there in 20 years. After the war, Sherman said that the Carolinas Campaign was "10 times more difficult" than the March to the Sea and, also, "10 times more important" to bringing an end to the war. Its success, say many war scholars, lay in Sherman's inflexible resolution and in the physical endurance and mechanical skills of the men of the Western army.[2]

The immediate goal was Goldsboro, N.C., where Maj. Gen. John Schofield's forces would join to give Sherman almost 90,000 men with which to confront Lee. Goldsboro was 425 miles from Savannah and the countryside in between was daunting. It was the dead of winter, first of all, and foraging was difficult because all the crops were in and livestock was scarce and shabby, not fat and appetizing as on the lush Georgia farms. The constant rains had filled the many rivers that must be crossed and left miles of swampy ground to traverse.

This was the Army of the West, though, filled with lumbermen from Michigan and railsplitters from Indiana and Illinois, resourceful men from the American backwoods. With them Sherman created the Pioneer Corps, whose axes and improvisational skills corduroyed the roads, built the bridges and forded the rivers. As a result, the army and the 2,500 wagons and 600 ambulances that came in its wake moved along at an astonishing rate of 12 miles a day.[3]

Confederate Gen. Joseph Johnston, who came from retirement to face Sherman in North Carolina for one last time, had been told that the South Carolina hinterland was impenetrable in that season of the year, all the roads being under water. He believed it, he said later, until "I learned that Sherman's army was marching through the Salk swamps, making its own corduroy roads at the rate of a dozen miles a day and more." Then, said Johnston, "I made up my mind that there had been no such army in existence since the days of Julius Caesar."[4]

In the end the 87th Indiana and the rest of Sherman's men covered the 425 miles in 50 days, only 10 of which were given to rest.[5] It was a remarkable wartime achievement and one that has been given too little attention and not enough credit in the history of the war.

As the army passed through South Carolina, the people of that state were to pay dearly for their vociferous championing of Secession, for leading the other states out of the Union and for bombarding Fort Sumter to begin this brotherly strife. Sherman's men had been on their best behavior in Savannah but he promised them full freedom to wreak their vengeance on the South Carolinians and, almost to a man, they complied.

What had happened in Georgia on the March to the Sea was minuscule compared to the destruction visited on South Carolina. The soldiers burned down almost everything in their path, leaving behind them continuous pillars of smoke and fire to mark their way. "Our track through the state is a desert waste," wrote one officer. The devastation was culminated by the burning of most of the state capital, Columbia.[6]

The vandalism was done less in hate than in a kind of righteous retribution for having originated the heretical doctrine of secession. Yet there were those who were appalled by its excesses. Wrote James Connolly, major of an Illinois regiment:

"I was perfectly sickened by the frightful destruction our army was spreading on every hand in its march through South Carolina. Oh! It was absolutely terrible! Every house except the church and negro cabin was burned to the ground; women, children and old men turned out into the mud and rain and their houses and furniture first plundered and then burned. I knew it would be so before we entered the state but had no idea how frightful the reality would be."[7]

All this was yet to come on Friday, January 20, when the 87th Indiana Volunteer Infantry Regiment strapped on its knapsacks and left Savannah for its final campaign.

Sherman was invading the Carolinas in the same manner he had left Atlanta, with 60,000 men in two wings. Maj. Gen. O.O. Howard's Army of Tennessee was on the right and Maj. Gen. Henry Slocum with the 87th and the Army of Georgia was on the left. Brig. Gen. Jefferson C. Davis remained in charge of the XIV Corps and Absalom Baird, now a brevet major general, retained its Third Division.

Col. Newell Gleason, however, left command of the Second Brigade for reassignment elsewhere, his place being taken by Lt. Col. Thomas Doan of Wabash and the 101st Indiana. The 87th Indiana also took on a new commander for this final campaign when Maj. Richard Sabin of LaPorte replaced Lt. Col. Edwin P. Hammond of Rensselaer. Hammond, like Gleason, was reassigned for duty elsewhere but returned to the regiment along with Gleason in April.[8]

The 87th first moved eight miles out on the Augusta road where, because of bad roads and worse weather, it remained for five days before marching on to Springfield. From there on Saturday, January 28, the regiment moved to Sister's Ferry to await a crossing of the Savannah River into South Carolina. That did not come until a week later, when a pontoon bridge had been laid and roads sufficiently repaired. On Tuesday, February 7, the 87th moved north through Robertsville to Brighton, where it camped and then received its orders for the march.

The 87th was designated as guard for the Third Division's wagon trains and would remain so until reaching Goldsboro on Saturday, March 25, six weeks later. This meant that the 87th would not be in the advance of the army but, rather, in its wake. Thus, it was removed from any major actions and from participating in any of the civilian depredations.

The assignment did not mean that the 87th Indiana's passage through the Carolinas would be any easier, though. The sparse language in Maj. Sabin's official report hints at the difficulties:

"While with the trains the duties were arduous and unpleasant during the greater portion of the time, the weather being inclement and the roads bad. The regiment was required to perform much labor and make many night marches."[9]

The assignment did mean, however, that teamster Daniel Bruce would end the war as he began it, traveling with the 87th Indiana Volunteer Infantry and the relatives and friends who remained there after almost three years of war. Bruce and his mules were with one of the Third Division wagons put under the 87th's charge; his daily diary entries chart the course of their journey and some of its perils and pitfalls.

The first two villages passed by the regiment were completely burned down and the going was hard from the very beginning because of the terrible road conditions. Four or five mule teams became mired in the swampy ground and it took until midnight to get them out. Days began at sunup and didn't end until after dark and the 87th often had to pitch in and corduroy the roads with rails, poles and brush.

On Saturday, February 11, the wagon trains passed through Barnwell, 45 miles from the river. Bruce's diary entry pictures the scene: "Courthouse here. Village destroyed, almost burned down. Orphaned children turned out of doors, sitting in the streets. Passed on three miles further. Dark, and camped in barns. Houses burned to ashes, people gone."

Traveling became a bit easier and on Friday, February 17, they were 50 miles further at Lexington and bypassing on the west the burning city of Columbia. After crossing the Saluda River a few miles north, Bruce saw railroad cars, corn fodder and houses burning while crying women stood nearby. The next day the camp was visited by a desperate woman. Bruce wrote:

"Woman came into camp this morning, begging for something to eat for herself and her children. Said that the Yankees had burned everything she had."

By Tuesday, February 21, the 87th and its wagon train had reached Winnsboro and began an easterly turn leading toward North Carolina. Heavy rains delayed the entire XIV Corps at the Catawba River, breaking its pontoon bridges several times. Much hard labor finally got the troops, the wagon train and its 87th Infantry guards to the other side on the 28th.[10]

The march resumed on Wednesday, March 1, and traveling got worse. "Roads awful. Made 15 miles in sand and mire," wrote Bruce, and the next day he complained that "mules fall in the mud."

The 87th Infantry's only brush with the enemy on this march came Saturday, March 4, near Chester(field) close to the North Carolina line. The train was having such hard going through the mud that a halt was called to build a bridge over the goo. During this pause Maj. Sabin sent out a foraging party that ran into Rebel cavalry and left five men behind as captives.[11]

Their course now took them to Cheraw and across the state line to the plank road leading through Laurinburg to Fayetteville in North Carolina. That was Thursday, March 9, and Bruce found the plank road "terrible, some planks missing and the road bumpy and rotten. . . . Big chuck holes and deep." He also passed "the largest fire I have ever seen," of a large warehouse of resin and turpentine.

Four days later they had cleared Fayetteville where, Bruce boasted, the 87th had captured "enough food and materials in this city for the whole division for some weeks." Bad roads returned, along with citizens both "colored and white" begging for food. Then the path became corduroyed for long stretches as they approached Goldsboro.

Ahead at Bentonville on March 20–21, the last battle of the Western theatre was being fought against the small force that Johnston had put together. The 87th and Bruce's wagon train left the corduroy road on Tuesday, March 21, to allow hospital wagons to get to the front. Other regiments of the 87th's Second Brigade were present at the Bentonville fight but were not engaged and sustained only two Second Minnesota wounded, from artillery fire.[12]

On Saturday, March 25, the 87th Indiana Infantry Regiment safely escorted its division's wagon train into Goldsboro and rejoined the Second Brigade, which had come through the campaign with only seven wounded and 19 missing.[13] On April 1, however, just a week later, Pvt. Alexander Hatton, a recruit from Spencer and Company K, died of disease at Goldsboro. He was the regiment's last casualty during the war.[14]

On Sunday, April 9, Lee surrendered to Grant at Appomattox; there was no need now for Sherman to reach Virginia. Five days later, Johnston realized his situation was hopeless and requested an armistice. He surrendered to Sherman on Wednesday, April 26, at Durham.

There would be no more war for the 87th Indiana Infantry Regiment. However, one duty still faced these Hoosiers before they could return to the bosoms of their families. On Wednesday, May 3, they began a march to Richmond and then to Washington, D.C., where they were to perform it.

18
A New Nation

It was Wednesday in Washington, D.C., and the morning sun came up in a brilliant blue sky, promising that this May 24, 1865, would be a warm spring day. The Americans' Civil War was over, their Union preserved for future generations. The 313 men who remained of the 87th Indiana Volunteer Infantry Regiment's original 945 now would be in the last march of the 90,000-man Army of the West that had just rampaged through the Carolinas.

Jonas Myers of Company F, only a private at his enlistment, was wearing the shoulder straps of a second lieutenant when he and the 87th took their place among the army's six corps that morning. The troops began assembling behind Capitol Hill from their camps surrounding Washington, the 87th's being at Alexandria. At 9 o'clock the signal gun boomed and the army started up Pennsylvania Avenue.

Leading the way on Lexington, his handsome bay Kentucky thoroughbred, was the commanding general of these roughneck Westerners, Maj. Gen. William Tecumseh Sherman. Crusty old Uncle Bill, conqueror of Atlanta, scourge of Georgia and South Carolina.

Wednesday was the second, concluding day of the glorious Grand Review of the Union Army when nearly 200,000 soldiers paraded at the nation's capital to hear cheers from the multitudes gathered along the avenue, to salute the President and to bask in the public adulation they had so dearly earned. It was a pageant worthy of those Rome gave to its conquering legions.

The first day had been dedicated to Maj. Gen. George Gordon Meade and the Army of the Potomac. Those Easterners, thoroughly drilled and neatly outfitted, were all spit-and-polish as they coursed along the streets of the city they had visited so often during the ebb and flow of the Eastern war. Now it was the turn of the wild and scruffy Westerners, whose exploits in the vast regions beyond the Alleghenies had so astonished capital residents and who now were to see this army for the first time.

Sherman hoped his rowdy farmers and backwoodsmen would appeal to the crowd, for there had been little time for them to practice military niceties like drilling since they left Chattanooga a thousand rugged, muddy and swampy miles before.

He needn't have worried. His lean, sunburned, whiskered marchers peeled onto Pennsylvania Avenue with a proud, long-striding swagger. Their columns were compact, their muskets held erect in solid masses of steel; their manner flaunted their invincibility. "They march like lords of the world!" spectators were heard to exclaim. So they must have done and probably, on that day, so they must have felt.

Marching 12 abreast, it took more than six hours for them to pass the White House reviewing stand before President Andrew Johnson, Lt. Gen. Ulysses S. Grant and other dignitaries. The 87th Indiana's turn came about noon and its Hoosiers never forgot the magnificence and the thrill of the sight that greeted them as they wheeled about the Capitol and looked down the long, broad avenue: endless troops, marching curb-to-curb to the rhythms of martial music, their bright uniforms and muskets glistening in the sunshine. It was a moment to savor for the rest of their lives.[1]

With this highly emotional military panoply did the weary veterans of the 87th Indiana Infantry end their personal 1,600-mile war journey that had begun nearly 34 months before at South Bend's Camp Rose.

The regiment left behind 268 dead, 48 of whom were killed in battle. The other 220 died in captivity, of disease or of wounds received in action. It was an impressive record of regimental sacrifice.

With the Grand Review behind them, men of the 87th remained impatiently in their camps around Washington for more than two weeks. Daniel Bruce had time to tour the city and on Tuesday, May 30, visited the White House. "We were shown into nearly every room, one of the greatest sights I ever saw in my life," the awestruck Hoosier farmer wrote in his diary entry for that date.

At last on Sunday, June 11, the 87th Indiana Volunteer Infantry passed into history as a part of the Second Brigade, Third Division, XIV Corps, Army of Georgia. Its men marched to division headquarters where they were mustered out of the U.S. Army, 2½ months shy of three years after enlistment.

Monday, June 12, the 87th boarded cars of the Baltimore & Ohio Railroad and left for Indianapolis. At Parkersburg, W.Va., the regiment was transferred to Ohio River boats for a fast ride to Cincinnati, the current sometimes speeding them to 30 mph. From Cincinnati it was by rail to Louisville and then to Indianapolis, which was reached at 6 A.M. Saturday, June 17. There the men turned in their muskets, moving another step closer to becoming civilians.

Although some took "French leave" upon reaching Indianapolis, most of the veterans were present for a final military ceremony at the State Capitol grounds Wednesday, June 21, where the 87th and two cavalry regiments were congratulated by Gov. Oliver P. Morton for patriotic service to state and country.[2] Also speaking on that day was Newell Gleason, the 87th's colonel and later its brigade commander who had been with the regiment from its recruitment. He wore the star of a brigadier general on that day.

Suddenly, there was nothing more to do. The Great Experience was over. "I want to go home," Jonas Myers said, and learned he could do so by signing a few papers. He did and soon was on his way. His train put him in Peru at midnight and since there yet was no railroad to Rochester, he set out alone on one final march on Thursday, June 22. This one, of 25 miles, would take him home.

He got his breakfast five miles out, in the town of Mexico, and then stopped two miles from Rochester at the William McMahan farm to greet his old Company F companion, 22-year-old Polk McMahan, who had been wounded in the eye at Kelly Field on the second day of Chickamauga. The whole family turned out, delighted to see him, and gave Jonas dinner.

Afterward, McMahan hitched up a wagon and took Jonas into Rochester. Their rig went north up Main Street, turned west into an alley, came up behind the Myers house and Jonas hopped out. He later recalled:

"I went in the back door and was within five feet of my wife before she recognized me. That was one time in my life I was glad to get home. I had been away two years and 10 months."[3]

During the next few days, the 10 companies of the 87th Indiana began arriving at their respective county seats in groups large enough to merit public welcomes. At courthouse squares from LaPorte to Peru, from Rensselaer to Rochester, citizens and government officials welcomed their returning heroes and made them feel appreciated.

Daniel Bruce's journey home also was rather private, like that of Jonas, but a bit easier. He and five companions from Company E boarded the 10 P.M. train at Indianapolis on Saturday, June 24. The others were Sgt. John Rush, Blue Grass; Henry Rairick, Rochester; Henry Lebo and Cpl. Galon Smith, both Bruce Lake, and Cpl. John Stamm, Winamac.

After changing trains at Kokomo, they arrived in Winamac at 6 o'clock Sunday morning to find Daniel's uncle, Stephen Bruce, waiting to treat them to breakfast. Afterward Uncle Stephen gave his indefatigable mule-driving nephew a ride to the farm at Bruce Lake and to Daniel's wife and daughter. Was he glad to be there? Daniel did not record in his diary the obvious answer to this question; instead, he ended that exceptional journal with words one might expect from a soldier just returning from almost three years in the field:

"The first time I slept in a bed since I left home."[4]

In similar manner did one million Union soldiers return to their families and again take up their plows and tools. It was a quick and befitting evaporation of a huge volunteer army that counted 2.3 million enlistments over the war's four-year course.[5]

Farmers comprised 48 percent of that 2.3 million, mechanics another 24 percent, making farmer Bruce and carpenter Myers genuine representatives of the whole.[6] And they, like their fellows, came home suffused with pride and showered with respect, the intangible but inestimable rewards for having served their country in its time of peril. The esteem of fellow citizens would follow these veterans of the country's most devastating and defining war for the rest of their lives.

"We cannot escape history," the martyred President Abraham Lincoln had said during the war. "We . . . will be remembered in spite of ourselves. . . . The fiery trial through which we pass will light us down, in honor or dishonor, to the latest generation."[7]

In honor did it come about, as the survivors of the 87th Indiana Infantry and all like them lived out their days in a new and reinvigorated America, a nation anxious to fulfill the destiny so long denied it by the controversy between North and South. The argument over slavery and expansion was resolved; freedom had won and the settlement of a continent beckoned.

The transcontinental railroad soon gave quick access to these new western lands, but not all veterans of the war were attracted to such adventure. Many were content to return to the hometowns they had left for war, to raise their families while building careers and contributing to the community's prosperity and growth.

Among these men were some we came to know in this narrative.

Jonas Myers brought to postwar civilian life the same vigor he had shown as a sergeant in Company F of the 87th Indiana. He lived almost 50 years after war's end, prominent and progressive in the civic affairs of Rochester, which he served as marshal and trustee. An ardent, active Republican and articulate patriot, he was appointed by President Benjamin Harrison to a four-year term as postmaster in 1889.

Upon his return, Jonas transferred his carpenter's training into the operation of a series of planing mills, offering, as one advertisement had it, "planing, matching, sawing, turning and scroll work done to order. He buys lumber and furnishes all kinds of building materials (and deals) in lath and shingles."

Jonas, who went through almost three years of a vicious war without taking a wound of any kind, was not so fortunate around the whirling blades of the planing businesses that he owned for 40 years.

In the summer of 1875 Jonas lost his right arm from near the shoulder when it was caught in a running belt that he was moving from one pulley to another. Dauntless as always, 10 days later he was out for a buggy ride with a friend and soon after was back at the mill. By autumn he had found a combined knife-and-fork designed for one-armed use and was able to "elevate his hash with as much ease as anybody." A similar accident a few years later cost him some of his left hand but, as a contemporary wrote, Jonas "persevered manfully with a part of a hand and made a success."[8]

The main preoccupations of Jonas' civilian life were the Odd Fellows Lodge, of which he was a member 63 years, and the GAR, or Grand Army of the Republic, the politically powerful organization of Union Army veterans. His leadership in these two groups, both of which were significant forces in the affairs of postwar Northern societies, had much to do with securing his local prominence.

Annie Stradley, the wife who provided Jonas with the diary he began keeping at Chattanooga, died barely four months following his return in 1865. They had been married 10 years. Two years later he married Elizabeth Clayton, sister of his first wife, Marion, who had died only a year after their marriage in 1851. Elizabeth survived him, along with two children.

Jonas Myers died peacefully at his home on May 17, 1914, at 85 years of age. He was buried in a coffin of quarter-sawed golden oak which he had made himself and fitted so "he would be comfortable in the other world," so granddaughter Margaret Bailey Shafer was told.[9]

Daniel Bruce remained on his land in Harrison Township near Bruce Lake in Pulaski County, prospering in his agricultural fortunes and earning the high regard of his peers over a similarly long lifetime of 84 years. Daniel began farming on his own in 1857 at age 21. At that time he rented some of his father Abraham's 1,000 acres and received two steers and a colt as his starting capital, along with $50. Daniel owned 40 acres by the time he joined the 87th Indiana. When he died of pneumonia July 19, 1920, he had increased that acreage over tenfold.

Daniel's wife of 62 years, the former Sarah Hizer of Union Township in neighboring Fulton County, survived him along with five of their nine children.[10]

Peter Keegan, the shoemaker from Peru, returned to that Miami County seat town after his discharge but later removed southward to Bunker Hill, where he opened the town's first shoe repair shop and operated it for many years. He kept in touch with his wartime comrades in Peru and Rochester. Keegan died August 1, 1904, at the age of 71 and was buried in Crown Hill Cemetery in Indianapolis.[11]

Gleason, the railroadman and colonel of the 87th who led it so bravely through Chickamauga, was elected to the Indiana Legislature by a grateful citizenry upon his return to LaPorte. After one term, he resumed his prewar occupation, surveying and locating the line of the Iowa and Lansing Railroad as its chief engineer. He later performed the same service for the Indianapolis and Peru Railroad that connected Peru with Chicago via LaPorte.

Poor health forced Gleason's retirement in 1873 and he lived in LaPorte until his unfortunate death July 6, 1886. During the relentless heat wave of that summer, Gleason arose during the night to seek relief. He intended to get wine from the cellar of his home, but accidentally fell to the bottom of the 12-foot deep stairwell onto a brick floor. He died instantly of a massive skull fracture. Brig. Gen. Gleason was 61 and he left behind his wife, Nancy Mitchell, and one daughter.[12]

The regiment's first colonel, Kline G. Shryock, also had a long life. He died at age 84 on December 26, 1895, but never succeeded in achieving the wider political offices he coveted. Shryock's blustery personality and rigid views on personalities and issues did not endear him to his Republican political colleagues. He was rebuffed for secretary of state in 1868 and for Congressional nomination in 1878. He was delegate to the National Republican Convention of 1876, which nominated the successful Rutherford B. Hayes for president. In 1879 he gave a series of lectures for the memorial fund of Oliver P. Morton, Indiana's wartime governor and friend of Shryock. President Chester Arthur appointed him postmaster of Rochester in 1882 and he finished his legal career there as justice of the peace. Four children survived him.[13]

Edwin P. Hammond, the Rensselaer lawyer who commanded the 87th during the closing weeks of the Atlanta campaign and through the March to the Sea, returned to his hometown and compiled an outstanding career as a jurist. An 1857 law graduate of Asbury (now DePauw) University in Greencastle, Hammond served 10 years as circuit court judge at Rensselaer and in 1883 was appointed to the Indiana Supreme Court. After leaving the state's high bench, he continued his legal career at Lafayette and still was in active practice at the time of his death, at age 80 in 1915. He sired five surviving children.[14]

Hammond had joined the 87th Regiment as a seasoned soldier. Shortly after Fort Sumter in April of 1861, he volunteered for three months' duty as a first lieutenant with the Ninth Indiana that was recruited and commanded by Col. (later Maj. Gen.) Robert Milroy, also a Rensselaer attorney. Hammond served in the West Virginia campaign of that season, then returned to his law practice before helping to recruit Company A of the 87th in August 1862.

James Burnham of Rensselaer, who was mustered out as captain of Company A, also took up the study of law when he returned to Jasper County. He became a prominent pension attorney, assisting many veterans in securing their government stipends. Burnham later was justice of the peace and active in the Rensselaer post of the Grand Army of the Republic, which he organized and served as first commander. In his youth, Burnham spent the years 1857–61 in "Bleeding Kansas," helping that territory's free-state forces in the struggle against their slave-state antagonists.[15]

George Martling, the 20-year-old Mishawaka private from Company K whose diary impressions included his experiences at Chickamauga, was mustered out with the regiment at the close of the war but he then disappears from Mishawaka's records. Perhaps he chose to go West to seek his fortune, as many others did.

George Morgan, the 14-year-old who lied about his age to get into Company A at Rensselaer, took up blacksmithing when he returned and then established a solid reputation as a carpenter, carriage maker and woodworker in his own shop. He lived to be 97 years old. Morgan often spoke of how happy he was to get home alive from his military adventures: "I struck out right for home across the fields at a dog trot and did not stop until I reached the house," shouting at the top of his voice. He got no answer, but found his mother picking strawberries. "I got me a great big bowl of the freshly picked berries, stopped at the milkhouse and got a pitcher of cream, helped myself out of the contents of the sugar bag, and went to work."[16]

There were war victims, too, like Pvt. Benjamin McElfresh of Company F, a farm boy from Richland Township in Fulton County. The malnutrition he suffered from months in Libby Prison at Richmond helped to kill him when, on his way home, he was allowed to overfeed himself at Camp Chase, near Columbus, Ohio. He died there April 3, 1865, the month the war ended, at age 21.

Some of the war's survivors never escaped its effects. Among these from the 87th were Pvt. McMahan, Lt. Joseph Beeber and Capt. Horace Long, all of Company F.

The Minié ball that struck McMahan's head in Kelly Field at Chickamauga left him with a painful, troubled life that ended in 1874 at the age of 32 in a soldiers' home at Dayton, Ohio. The bullet had struck a glancing blow, entering a corner of his eye, carrying away an eyebrow and fracturing his skull, for which he was granted a pension of $24 per month. As the years went by, McMahan was afflicted with spasms of increasing frequency and intensity. Five years before his death he submitted at Chicago to a radical surgical procedure for that day, in which portions of his skull were removed to relieve pressure. No relief resulted and a year before his death a similar operation in Logansport removed more of the skull. The pain McMahan suffered must have been immense; the constant discomfort created personality traits that often involved him in public disturbances.[17]

Lt. Beeber was shot in both legs at Chickamauga but overcame those wounds in time to rejoin Company F for the final campaigns of 1864–65. He then was taken prisoner during the march through South Carolina, but escaped his captors while being marched to one of the South's infamous prison pens. Thereafter he hid out and traveled through the miasmal South Carolinian swamps before finding his regiment. The effects of this experience, along with his later development of epilepsy, steadily eroded his health and he died at age 42 in 1880.[18]

Capt. Long's disability arose from a fondness for alcohol that he developed during the war, an affliction that many of the rural innocents who put on the uniform struggled against when taking up civilian life. In his peacetime years, Long's obsession often made him a public embarrassment to his family, also creating fits of derangement and an addiction to morphine as well as whiskey. The captain lived until age 72, however, dying of a heart ailment on December 9, 1908. A son survived him.[19]

Wartime handicaps were common among veterans of the war and the Federal government provided pensions for those with normal physical disabilities. Psychological problems, such as alcohol addiction or mental stress, were not yet recognized as casualties.

A list of 119 pensioners published in 1883 found William Surguy leading the payees with $72 a month for having been totally blinded. McMahan received $24 a month for his head wound. George Nichols was granted $24 for loss of a right arm, but Thomas Patly's left leg was worth only $18. Chronic diarrhea, the result of months of campaigning on bad food and worse water, appears often in the list of pensioners and brought from $10 to $4 per month. Diseased eyes, wounds in arms, hands or legs or other body parts resulted in similar monthly payments. The smallest pension being paid was $2 a month, to Clark Miller for "archy finger."

There also were benefits for the widows, minor children and mothers of slain soldiers, ranging from $17 monthly to Electra Ryland, widow of Adj. Fredus Ryland, killed at Chickamauga, to $8 for the widows of privates.[20]

For these participants the war did not end when the shooting stopped. Wars never do. They continue in the broken bodies and troubled minds of all who survive their dreadful courses, as citizens of the six Northern Indiana counties that had created the 87th Indiana Regiment discovered.

Other changes wreaked upon the 87th Infantry's survivors they could see in their mirrors. Myers, Bruce, Keegan, Benjamin Brown, Henry Hoober, Martling, Long, Peter Troutman, Jacob Leiter, Gleason, Jerome Carpenter and their comrades had been matured and sobered by the "incommunicable" experiences of war, memories of which could not fully be shared. Most of all, they no longer were innocent of the fury that lurks behind man's civilized facade; the knowledge of that forever separated them intellectually from friends who had stayed at home.

Veterans of the Civil War would live out their lives as respected, singular citizens of their home communities, honored each May with parades and orations on the Memorial Day holiday created especially for them, marching with ever slower steps and increasingly fewer numbers until at last there were none to march, none to recount tales of long-gone calls to arms.

As their lives wound down and the war receded into ever-distant frontiers of their memories, the veterans no doubt mourned that their fiery time had lost its value and its meaning to those in the present. How pleased they would be to know that succeeding generations have persisted in studying their wartime endeavors and gallantry. The veneration of the Civil War's participants and the analysis of its events never have been greater than it is today.

Why this is so is worth a thought or two. The nation has had many wars and battle deaths since 1865. The Spanish-American War of 1898 was too short and relatively bloodless to interest history much. The United States' part in World War I was equally brief, although much more costly, but its horrors were forgotten in the worse calamities brought on soon after by World War II. That war, with its clearly defined characteristic of good against evil, comes closest to our nation's Civil War experience, but World War II was global and is difficult to examine as a whole. Korea and Vietnam linger in our national memories in equal combinations of pride, embarrassment and controversy while Desert Storm turned out to be more shooting gallery than warfare.

The Civil War thus continues to absorb us as no other can because of the virtuosity of its appeal. There is a perpetual sense of wonderment in its study, an impression of always finding something new or unusual to marvel at, which is perhaps its greatest fascination.[21]

We yearn, for example to understand how Americans could slaughter other Americans with such sustained ferocity for four long years. The cost of the war was frightful: 618,000 deaths, 360,000 for the North, 258,000 for the South. This total is astonishingly high, for not until late in the Vietnam War did the nation's battle deaths from all other wars equal it.

There is another comparison that is yet more shocking: Our World War II deaths totaled 384,000 from a population of 135 million. To equal the North's ratio of deaths to population (23 million) the World War II total would have been 2.1 million! To reach the South's ratio of deaths to its nine million population, almost 4 million would have died![22]

Intertwined in the consideration of such appalling statistics is the consideration of the senseless killings ordered by the generals, such as Grant at Cold Harbor, Robert E. Lee in Pickett's Charge at Gettysburg, Sherman at Kennesaw Mountain, Ambrose E. Burnside at Fredericksburg, John Hood around Atlanta and again at Franklin. There often was a horrible stalemate, a standoff, in the battles. Most of the commanding officers on both sides had learned the art of war at West Point and their tactics were anticipated and easily countered by their opponents. Only at Chickamauga on the second day, and that by a freak accident, was a defensive line breached by an attacking force. Elsewhere, on other fields, scores of thousands died trying to prove it could be done.

The war's generals were a curious and often feckless lot, amateurs mixed with professionals, and all caught in a time warp between epochs. This was the first of the modern wars, using new weapons and devices and directed at civilians as well as at soldiers. Yet the generals did not fully comprehend either the change in tactics nor the power of the new devices. They persisted in placing men in long, straight lines and sending them on those charges that hardly ever succeeded.

And so the generals clung to their doomed romantic idea of war, while we who study it are transfixed by its waste and futility.

There also is the appeal of the war's curious anomaly: the idea that two separate nations should try to dominate the North American continent. By discrediting that principle, the war became the seminal experience in the creation of the powerful United States of today.

We are attracted, as well, to the many intriguing personalities that the war produced. Above all there is the towering figure of Abraham Lincoln, but also there are the intricate personalities of Grant, Sherman, Lee, Stonewall Jackson, J.E.B. Stuart, Edwin Stanton, George McClellan, Jefferson Davis and their like.

When all else pales in the study of this dreadful, almost maniacal war, there always remains consideration of the volunteer soldier, both blue and gray, and what made him participate, and sacrifice, so willingly.

In the North, 2.3 million volunteered over four years; in the South, probably a million. The Yankee was motivated by the abstract idea of the Union and, later, by the nobler principle of eradicating slavery. The Northern soldier not only accepted these ideas; for the most part, he was enthusiastically articulate in expressing them. The men in the ranks of the Confederate army were fearsome fighters, but the origin of their hatred of their Yankee counterpart seemed to lie less in abstraction than in resentment for the "Yankee" way of life, what they perceived as its material nature. Since few of the butternut soldiers had slaves and fewer still owned much property of value, their reason for fighting seemed to get down to keeping a way of life.

To be sure, these were diverse civilizations that had gone to war and it must be remembered that the inhabitants of each had come to thoroughly despise the other over the course of 40 years. Each side considered the other rather a lower order of human species and there had to be a clear-cut winner; no other result would be tolerated.[23]

This was "a strange, sad war," said poet Walt Whitman, who nursed its wounded. It also was a national tragedy—our only one, if it comes to that. Perhaps that is one reason that the Civil War has held such a firm grip on the generations that have come after, for the memory of two peoples so much alike who killed each other with so much savagery is a sorrow that lingers in our national conscience.

Our story of the 87th Indiana Volunteer Infantry Regiment's course through three-fourths of this dreadful, mesmerizing war has come to an end with the return of its survivors to the farms and the small towns of northern Indiana.

Proud of the honor they had gained for answering their government's call, they had an even greater pride in America when the war was finished because of what they had seen of it. This satisfaction has been most eloquently expressed by historian Shelby Foote:

"They knew now they had a nation, for they had seen it; they had been there, they had touched it, climbed its mountains, crossed its rivers, hiked its roads; their comrades lie buried in its soil, along with many thousands of their arms and legs."[24]

This now was a singular nation, as well, for no longer would the expression be "the United States are," but rather "the United States is."[25]

The satisfaction of such an achievement was a keepsake that nourished the souls of Jonas Myers and Daniel Bruce, and all other survivors of the 87th Indiana's fiery trial, for the rest of their days.

EPILOGUE

O ur last glimpse of the 87th Indiana's infantrymen comes on a spring day 40 years after the Grand Review in Washington. It is a scene that haunts the mind, not only for its purpose but because we yearn to know more about what took place, words that were spoken, emotions expressed.

The old soldiers have gathered in a cemetery in Rochester to bury a comrade. There are 30 of them, some having served in other regiments during The Great Civil War.

Their dead comrade was not an officer passed to his final reward, nor an old company friend with whom they had shared a breastwork or who accompanied them on a charge into a Rebel battle line.

He was John Patton, onetime Negro slave, who had come into the camp of the 87th Regiment's Company F at Triune, Tenn., sometime during the spring of 1863, after Emancipation. He remained as Capt. Horace Long's personal cook and body servant and the company's handyman during all the 87th's remaining campaigns.[1] At the invitation of his new soldier friends, he came to Rochester at the close of the war to live out his life among them.[2]

That life had lasted 40 more years and on this May day of 1905 those old soldiers were assembling to pay "Uncle Johnny" his last and most meaningful measure of respect, a Christian burial attended by people who cared for him.

We are told Patton's age was "over 80" but we know very little of his background. He once said that he married as a young slave and that his wife and three children later were sold away from him. He was sold himself to three different masters, he claimed, once for the handsome sum of $1,400.

Patton became genuinely admired by many of Company F's Rochester soldiers, a conclusion made obvious by the invitation for him to come North at war's end. Over succeeding years, he lived in a small frame house in the southeast part of the city and performed all manner of useful work for his fellow citizens. They treated him generally as one of their own and described him as "willing, honest and genteel." Late in his life they bought him a peanut and popcorn stand which he operated for many years in the downtown area.[3]

At the time of his final illness, Patton was living at the Fulton County Home, for indigents, while friends were renovating his own house. He did not appear to be in failing health and death came as rather a surprise to those friends.

Nevertheless, his passing was considered of some consequence, so there would be no pauper's grave for "Uncle Johnny." The veterans agreed to share funeral expenses; Jonas Myers of the 87th and a friend, Michael Essick, selected the cemetery lot and headstone and made burial arrangements.

The funeral ceremony at the County Home took the form of a Grand Army of the Republic campfire, granting Patton the ultimate cachet of soldier. A local minister gave the sermon and seven soldier sponsors spoke about Patton's life, glowingly we suppose. How we wish to know their words, particularly those of the 87th Regiment's Capt. Long and Sgt. Myers.

Finally, and fittingly, a local newspaper published a lengthy obituary of this former slave in which it was written that the funeral "was a tribute of respect to his faithfulness and integrity as a man. He possessed the noblest qualities of the colored race and his memory will abide in Rochester for many a day."[4]

And so it has. People still seek details of his life after they read the well-tended gray granite headstone in the Citizens Cemetery's extreme northwest corner that proclaims:

JOHN PATTON
DIED MAY 15, 1905[5]
PATRIOT OF CIVIL WAR, 1861–1865
COLORED

Johnny Patton's honored burial provides an appropriate end to our particular story of the Civil War. The intuitive respect shown by that humane act reassures us of the inherent nobility of the men of the 87th Indiana Infantry. They obviously had learned something more from three years of civil war than simply how to endure and survive it.

THE CIVIL WAR RECORD OF THE
87TH REGIMENT INDIANA VOLUNTEERS

The 87th Indiana Infantry Regiment was mustered into Federal service August 31, 1862, with 945 men (909 enlisted, 36 officers). During its 34 months of service, 317 more were added; 292 enlisted recruits and 25 officers.

Altogether, 1,262 men served in the regiment and 466, or 37 percent, were casualties: 48 killed in action, 198 wounded in action, 220 dead of wounds or disease. Deaths were 21 percent of those serving.

Only 313, or 33 percent, of the regiment's original members were present at mustering out June 10, 1865, the number consisting of 11 officers and 302 enlisted men. Original enlisted members remaining, by companies:

A—20 of 98; B—21 of 94; C—44 of 97; D—31 of 95; E—38 of 97; F—46 of 94; G—20 of 81; H—39 of 86; I—19 of 80; K—24 of 87.

Summary of Deaths in Regiment

12—Officers	27—Company D	13—Company H
26—Company A	31—Company E	22—Company I
32—Company B	19—Company F	28—Company K
24—Company C	34—Company G	Total: 268

Killed at Chickamauga (42)

Adj. Fredus Ryland, Rochester, 9-20-1863
Capt. George Baker, B, Star City, 9-20-1863
2nd Lt. Elisha Brown, C, Peru, 9-20-1863
Capt. Lewis Hughes, D, Rochester, 9-20-1863
2nd Lt. Franklin Bennett, E, Kewanna, 9-19-1863
1st Lt. Sloan Martin, H, Westville, 9-19-1863
2nd Lt. Abram Andrew, I, LaPorte, 9-20-1863
Capt. James Holliday, K, Mishawaka, 9-19-1863
A—1st Sgt. Elijah Israel, Rensselaer, 9-19-1863
A—Matthew Hopkins, Rensselaer, 9-20-1863
B—Jacob Evans, Bruce Lake, 9-20-1863
B—Lewis Griffith, Winamac, 9-20-1863
B—Alexander Waters, Winamac, 9-20-1863
B—Maluff Williamson, Winamac, 9-20-1863

C—William Haskell, Peru, 9-20-1863
C—Miles Petty, Peru, 9-20-1863
C—William Wickler, Peru, 9-20-1863
D—William Ewer, Rochester, 9-19-1863
D—James Osborne, Rochester, 9-20-1863
D—Franklin Smith, Rochester, 9-19-1863
E—Simon Fall, Kewanna, 9-20-1863
E—Aaron Smith, Blue Grass, 9-20-1863
E—Robert Tribbett, Rochester, 9-20-1863
F—John House, Rochester, 9-20-1863
G—Henry Baker, LaPorte, 9-19-1863
G—John Garner, no city listed, 9-20-1863
G—Michael Gilfoyle, New Carlisle, 9-19-1863
G—Sgt. Solomon Harding, LaPorte, 9-20-1863
G—Abraham Leiper, Callao, 9-20-1863
G—Patrick McCarty, Plainfield, 9-20-1863
G—William Pointer, LaPorte, 9-20-1863
G—Amos Prince, Rochester, 9-19-1863
G—John Rody, LaPorte, 9-20-1863
G—Peter Warberton, LaPorte, 9-20-1863
H—Eugene Pratt, Union Mills, 9-19-1863
H—John Turner, Bradford, 9-20-1863
I—Cyrus Hecox, no city listed, 9-20-1863
I—Lewis Lowe, LaPorte, 9-20-1863 (missing in action)
K—Peter Balder, Bremen, 9-19-1863
K—Peter Heminger, Mishawaka, 9-20-1863
K—Jacob Keifer, South Bend, 9-20-1863
K—Sgt. Lewis Simpson, Elkhart, 9-20-1863
Summary: 11 killed on 19th (3 officers), 31 killed on 20th (5 officers).

Killed at Missionary Ridge (2)

G—Thomas Fisher, LaPorte, 11-25-1863
K—Solomon Deacon, Marion, Iowa, 11-25-1863

Died of Wounds Received in Action (19)

1st Lt. Burr Russell, Peru, 11-29-1863 (from Missionary Ridge)
B—Henry Cory, Logansport, 10-22-1863, at Chattanooga
C—Sylvester Edwards, Peru, 10-11-1863
C—Asa Marine, Peru, 10-2-1863, Walden's Ridge, Tenn.
C—Herman Marshall, Peru, 12-14-1863, at Nashville
C—Isaiah Newby, Peru, 10-7-1863

D—Wagoner Josephus Collins, Rochester, 10-17-1863
D—David Shelton, Rochester, 10-9-1863 (from Chickamauga)
E—Alfred Hizer, recruit, Blue Grass, 8-9-1864 (at Kingston, Ga.)
F—Isaiah Webb, Rochester, wounds received 10-18-1863
H—Willard Brown, no city listed, 10-30-1863, at Stevenson, Ala.
I—Ephraim Evans, Wanatah, wounds received 6-26-1864
I—James Hathaway, Morgan Station, wounds received 1-1-1864
I—Henry Martin, Hannah Station, 10-6-1863
K—Henry Ashley, South Bend, 10-21-1863
K—Cpl. William Bulla, South Bend, 10-15-1863
K—Ebert Gay, Mishawaka, 1-14-1864
K—Benjamin Schmidt, Mishawaka, 11-7-1863
K—John Sumstine, Mishawaka, 1-14-1864

Killed in Action (4)

1st Lt. John Demuth, C, Peru, 8-22-1864
F—William Irvin, Rochester, 6-14-1864 (near Acworth, Ga.)
F—Seymour Wertz, Rochester, 8-5-1864 (near Atlanta)
K—Adam Deelman, Mishawaka, 8-4-1864 (near Atlanta)

Died in Prison (9)

A—Wilber Tatman, Rensselaer, Danville, Va., 1-26-1864
B—John Hodges, Winamac, Danville, Va., 3-18-1864
C—William Hoover, Peru, Richmond, Va., 12-15-1863
G—Joseph Cherry, Waterford, Richmond, Va., 1-1864
G—John Siddles, LaPorte, Danville, Va., 11-29-1864
I—1st Sgt. Elihu Billings, LaPorte, Danville, Va., 12-6-1863
I—Augustus Vail, Morgan Station, Danville, Va., 1-22-1863
K—Edwin Bartlett, South Bend, Richmond, Va., 11-18-1863
K—William Currier, Mishawaka, Andersonville, Ga., 5-30-1864

Died in Military Prison (1)

D—John Kelly, at Indianapolis, no date listed

Died of Disease, No Location Listed (23)

Chaplain Joseph Albright, South Bend, 12-5-1862
Surgeon Samuel Higginbotham, South Bend, 5-29-1863

D—William Cole, Rochester, 3-3-1864
D—John Newby, Rochester, 11-30-1862
D—James Quiggs, Rochester, 12-4-1862
D—Kline Wilson, Rochester, 12-6-1864
E—Jonas Clark, Blue Grass, 9-23-1863 (Chickamauga wounds, captured)
E—George Kaler, Kewanna, 5-15-1864
E—Adam Spotts, Fulton, 12-19-1862
F—Cpl. Jewell Califf, Rochester, 11-14-1862
F—Louis Berry, recruit, Rochester, 5-3-1865
F—John Cripe, recruit, Rochester, 12-13-1863
F—Benjamin Evans, recruit, Rochester, 8-2-1864
F—Jacob Leise, Rochester, 4-14-1863
F—Benjamin McElfresh, Rochester, 4-15-1865
F—James Mow, Rochester, 1-16-1863
F—William Pentz, Rochester, 3-24-1863
F—Harper Rodgers, Rochester, 4-17-1864
F—Dennis Smith, Rochester, 1-25-1863
F—William Swartz, Rochester, 6-24-1863
F—Musician Isaac Townsend, Rochester, 11-8-1863
F—John Walts, recruit, Rochester, 12-22-1863
F—Elias Zolman, Rochester, 12-14-1862 (in hospital)

Died of Disease, by Location

Nashville (28):
A—Sgt. Robert Williams, Rensselaer, 4-13-1863
A—James Beal, Rensselaer, 11-16-1863
A—Jehu Openchain, Rensselaer, 2-9-1864
A—John Reed, Rensselaer, 3-15-1863
A—James Webb, Rensselaer, 12-19-1862
B—Amos Rouse, Winamac, 3-12-1864
B—Samuel Sell, Winamac, 6-5-1863
C—George Derick, Peru, 3-15-1863
D—John Biggs, Rochester, 2-21-1864
D—Lewis Bootz, Rochester, 8-11-1864
D—Absalom Macy, Rochester, 9-12-1863
D—William Polk, Rochester, 7-8-1864
E—William Dixon, Kewanna, 4-11-1863
E—Alexander McCarter, Kewanna, 11-13-1863
E—John Minton, recruit, Kewanna, 9-16-1864
G—Cpl. William Prince, Rochester, 3-15-1863
G—Arthur Casgriff, LaPorte, 2-18-1864
G—Joseph Chronister, LaPorte, 3-17-1863

G—Isaac McNeal, no city, 1-2-1864
H—Henry Blodgett, Union Mills, 3-31-1863
H—Richard Herman, Burnettsville, 3-3-1863
H—Willis Kelley, Monticello, 4-3-1863
I—Orrin Craig, Bigelow's Mills, 11-5-1863
I—Nicholas Vert, LaPorte, 4-1-1863
I—Henry Wilson, Morgan Station, 2-24-1863
K—Francis Burns, Rensselaer, 1-4-1863
K—Herman Dirst, South Bend, 5-3-1863
K—George Guibert, Mishawaka, 3-31-1863

New Albany, Ind. (4):
A—John Brown, Francesville, 12-11-1862
D—John Whittenberger, Rochester, no date listed
K—William Chambers, Deep River, 7-12-1864
K—Irwin Kelsey, New Carlisle, 11-5-1862

Louisville (17):
A—Benjamin Parkison, Rensselaer, 11-10-1862
B—Cornelius Doremus, Winamac, 11-23-1863
B—John McCarty, Winamac, 11-30-1862
C—William Loyd, Peru, 12-19-1862
C—Benjamin Williams, Peru, 11-7-1862
D—George Whittenberger, Rochester, 12-2-1862
E—Sgt. Simon Myers, Bruce Lake, 10-2-1862
E—Jacob Dipert, Bruce Lake, 12-14-1862
E—John Heckert, Kewanna, 12-18-1862
E—Carrington Slight, Bruce Lake, 3-4-1864
E—Henry Ummensetter, Star City, 12-2-1862
E—Ephraim Warrick, Kewanna, 12-12-1862
G—Benjamin Sharp, LaPorte, 12-7-1862
H—Charles Hall, Westville, 10-2-1863
K—1st Sgt. George Richards, Lawrenceburg, 11-15-1862
K—Henry Greenleaf, Mishawaka, 9-15-1862
K—William Maugherman, South Bend, 7-23-1863

Lebanon, Ky. (2):
B—David Barnes, Winamac, 11-2-1862
C—George Hart, Peru, 2-21-1863

Danville, Ky. (1):
A—Charles Orcutt, Rensselaer, 11-21-1862

Bowling Green, Ky. (12):
A—Sgt. James Sale, Pleasant Grove, 12-7-1862
A—Wagoner Robert Cory, Rensselaer, 11-6-1862
A—William Holmes, Joliet, Ill., 11-19-1863

B—John Adams, Winamac, 11-29-1862
B—John Aikens, Winamac, 11-29-1862
B—George Little, Winamac, 11-30-1862
C—George Walter, Peru, 12-23-1862
D—Dennis Cuberly, Rochester, 1-18-1863
D—Rufus Shores, Rochester, 1-8-1863
E—Erasmus VanMeter, Star City, 11-16-1862
H—George Bare, Monticello, 12-13-1862
I—Sanford Carr, Hannah Station, 12-31-1862

Murfreesboro, Tenn. (2):
A—Henry Parker, Pleasant Grove, 10-26-1863
B—Andrew Birch, Winamac, 12-8-1862

South Tunnel, Tenn. (1):
H—William Miller, Union Mills, 11-13-1862

Triune, Tenn. (4):
A—David Baker, Rensselaer, 5-9-1863
B—William Waterhouse, Oak, 3-20-1863
C—Jacob Woolf, Peru, 5-2-1863
D—Milton Hall, Rochester, 4-4-1863

Gallatin, Tenn. (34):
A—Andrew Goodell, Rensselaer, 1-14-1863
A—Henry Isinghoff, no city listed, 12-30-1862
B—Sgt. John Murphy, Star City, 1-4-1863
B—Sgt. Benjamin Whissinger, Star City, 12-7-1862
B—Cpl. Sam Chamberlain, Winamac, 1-12-1863
B—Cpl. Luther Williams, Winamac, 12-6-1863
B—Isaac Bales, Oak, 1-9-1863
B—William Bridgeman, Winamac, 2-20-1863
B—Endrew Evans, Francesville, 1-12-1863
B—Samuel Miller, Star City, 12-5-1862
B—Andrew Williams, Winamac, 1-3-1863
C—Musician Joseph Kennedy, Peru, 11-23-1862
C—Ithamer Perkins, Peru, 11-12-1862
C—John Reese, Peru, 1-10-1863
C—William Saxon, Peru, 12-14-1862
D—Christopher Gould, Rochester, 1-18-1863
D—Benjamin Miller, Rochester, 1-24-1863
D—William Shields, Rochester, 1-25-1863
E—John Brown, Star City, 2-5-1863
E—Charles Ummensetter, Star City, 2-21-1863
E—Garvin Ward, Star City, 12-12-1862
G—Samuel McConeghey, no city listed, 1-18-1863

G—Ephraim Moffit, New Carlisle, 1-25-1863
G—Liman Prince, LaPorte, 12-10-1862
H—John Dunnick, Monticello, 1-2-1863
I—Moses Griselle, Crown Point, 12-15-1862
I—Jerome Lyons, LaPorte, 12-23-1862
I—David Pairot, Morgan Station, 2-4-1863
I—Andrew Rockhill, no city, 12-22-1862
I—John Xander, LaPorte, 1-2-1863
K—Joseph Albright, Goshen, 12-5-1862
K—John Beglin, Mishawaka, 12-25-1862
K—Jonas Odell, Mishawaka, 12-13-1862
K—John Vanriper, Mishawaka, 1-22-1863

Manchester, Tenn. (1):
G—Cpl. George Dunham, Michigan City, 7-4-1863

Chattanooga (28):
A—Eli Dillon, Rensselaer, 9-26-1863
A—Curtis Hayden, Monrovia, 11-3-1863
A—James Jacks, Cathcart, 10-11-1863
A—John Peterson, recruit, Rensselaer, 3-6-1864
B—Noah Bradlee, recruit, Winamac, 3-21-1864
B—Frank Lane, Winamac, 10-20-1863
B—Cpl. Jacob Lemasters, recruit, Star City, 1-20-1864
C—Martin Brown, Peru, 11-22-1863
C—James Foss, Peru, 11-10-1863
C—George Glaze, Peru, 11-8-1863
D—Charles Pearson, Rochester, 12-18-1863
D—Henry Yoke, Rochester, 11-2-1863
E—Daniel Cannon, recruit, Kewanna, 1-5-1865
E—John Farrell, Kewanna, 10-14-1863
E—Daniel Herrold, Blue Grass, 7-9-1864, typhoid fever
E—Richard Liming, Star City, 9-28-1863
E—Robert Smith, Kewanna, 1-18-1864
E—John Yagle, Star City, 10-14-1863
G—Andrew Cole, no city listed, 9-30-1863
G—Thomas Pointer, LaPorte, 12-3-1863
G—Lewis Powers, Rolling Prairie, 11-18-1863
G—Charles Smootzer, Michigan City, 9-25-1863
H—Cpl. Alonzo Pitcher, Westville, 10-11-1863
H—Jacob Brooks, Union Mills, 2-17-1864
I—Joseph Penoyer, LaPorte, 10-24-1863
I—Orlando Sabin, LaPorte, 11-2-1863
I—Lewis Woodburn, recruit, LaPorte, 9-5-1864
K—Derrick Coppick, Logansport, 2-14-1864

Camp Thomas, Tenn. (1):
E—John Carter, Kewanna, 7-2-1863

Ringgold, Ga. (2):
C—John Kepler, Peru, 4-12-1864
I—Richard Hathaway, Kankakee City, 4-7-1864

Stevenson, Ala. (2):
G—Henry Dunn, LaPorte, 1-30-1864
G—Enoch Lightfoot, LaPorte, 10-10-1863

Tunnel Hill, Ga. (1):
G—Cpl. James Burden, LaPorte, 12-9-1863

Kingston, Ga. (1):
A—Cpl. Caleb Hopkins, Rensselaer, 7-8-1864

Acworth, Ga. (1):
G—Alexander Pratt, Callao, 6-21-1864

Lookout Mountain, Tenn. (2):
A—Oliver Daugherty, Rensselaer, 8-1-1864
G—Jacob Miller, recruit, LaPorte, 8-28-1864

Cowan Station, Tenn. (1):
A—Joshua German, Rensselaer, 10-3-1864

On the March to the Sea (1):
C—John McCullough, recruit, Columbus, 12-9-1864

Savannah, Ga. (4):
A—Charles Post, New Castle, 12-28-1864
B—James Moore, Kendallville, 3-9-1865
G—Archibald Clemmons, substitute, no city listed, 1-25-1865
I—John Peterson, substitute, no city listed, 1-15-1865

New Bern, N.C. (1):
B—Rufus Brown, recruit, Winamac, 5-8-1865

Goldsboro, N.C. (1):
K—Alexander Hatton, recruit, Spencer, 4-1-1865

Jeffersonville, Ind. (1):
B—Jesse Elmore, recruit, Winamac, 7-22-1864

Madison, Ind. (2):
D—James Moore, Rochester, 3-24-1864
H—John Malony, Rensselaer, 4-5-1864

Indianapolis, Ind. (3):
D—Frederick Rowe, Rochester, 3-2-1863
G—Musician Benjamin Hooten, New Carlisle, 7-15-1863
K—James Kessler, Rensselaer, 7-17-1863

At Home (7):
B—Thomas Lemasters, Star City, 7-30-1864
D—George Pownell, Fulton, 12-31-1864
E—Henry Hudkins, Kewanna, 4-19-1864
E—Philip Obermayer, Bruce Lake, 10-16-1863
F—George Miller, recruit, Rochester, 3-20-1864
G—Cpl. David Scholts, LaPorte, 12-7-1863
I—Valentine Extelle, Warren County, Ohio, 8-1864

Cincinnati, Ohio (1):
E—Allen Collins, Kewanna, 3-22-1865

David's Island, New York Harbor (2):
C—Andrew Clendenin, Peru, 4-8-1865
E—Eli Detrick, Kewanna, 3-25-1865

Regiment's Deserters, by Companies:

A—2	B—6	C—3	D—3	E—3	
F—3	G—2	H—2	I—5	K—3	Total—32

Deserters apparently loved company. Three from Company B left on Oct. 31, 1862: Joseph Goble, Frederick Huffman and William Huffman, all of Winamac. Two from Company C departed Nov. 12, 1862: Cpl. George Bellew and John Swoverland, both of Peru. And on Jan. 30, 1863, Calvin and Erwin Jones of Rolling Prairie and Company I took their leave.

Four others left the regiment marching toward its first battle of Oct. 8, 1862, at Perryville. John Steely of Canada, Company A, and Josiah Bradley of Tyner City, Company K, both vanished on Oct. 1, followed by Company K's Luke Aldrich of South Bend the next day and Peter Witmer of Kewanna and Company E the day after that.

Samuel Torley of Savannah, Ga., mustered into Company E in August of 1864 but soon found the regiment's approach to his home city too much to take. He disappeared during the March to the Sea, on Nov. 16, 1864.

MUSTER OF THE 87TH REGIMENT INDIANA VOLUNTEERS

Source: Report of the Adjutant General of the State of Indiana, 1861–1865,
Volumes 3 and 6, Indianapolis, 1866.

Regimental and Staff Officers

Colonel

Kline G. Shryock, Rochester, commissioned Aug. 28, 1862, resigned March
21, 1863.

Newell Gleason, LaPorte, commissioned March 22, 1863, brevetted brigadier general, mustered out with regiment.

Lieutenant Colonel

Newell Gleason, LaPorte, commissioned Aug. 28, 1862, promoted colonel.

Thomas Sumner, Plymouth, commissioned March 22, 1863, resigned Nov.
20, 1863.

Edwin P. Hammond, Rensselaer, commissioned Nov. 21, 1863, brevetted
lieutenant colonel, to date March 13, 1865; mustered out with regiment.

Major

Thomas Sumner, Plymouth, commissioned Aug. 29, 1862, promoted lieutenant colonel.

Edwin P. Hammond, Rensselaer, commissioned March 22, 1863, promoted
lieutenant colonel.

Richard C. Sabin, LaPorte, commissioned Nov. 21, 1863, brevetted lieutenant colonel to date March 13, 1865; mustered out with regiment.

Adjutant

Thomas Sumner, Plymouth, commissioned Aug. 14, 1862, promoted major.

Fredus Ryland, Rochester, commissioned Aug. 29, 1862, killed at Chickamauga, Sept. 20, 1863.

John E. Selleck, Union Mills, commissioned Oct. 12, 1863, resigned Sept. 8,
1864.

Edward Molloy, New Carlisle, commissioned Oct. 30, 1864, mustered out
with regiment.

Quartermaster

Robert N. Rannells, Rochester, commissioned Aug. 14, 1862, resigned Nov.
24, 1863.

Jerome Carpenter, Rochester, commissioned Nov. 25, 1863, mustered out with regiment.

Chaplain Joseph R. Albright, South Bend, commissioned Sept. 6, 1862, died of disease Dec. 5, 1862.

Nicholas E. Manville, city unlisted, commissioned Jan. 8, 1863, resigned April 9, 1863.

Henry Weller, LaPorte, commissioned May 20, 1863, resigned July 21, 1864; cause, age.

Surgeon

Samuel R. Pratt, Crown Point, commissioned Aug. 30, 1862, resigned Feb. 17, 1863.

Samuel Higginbotham, South Bend, commissioned March 20, 1863, died May 29, 1863, of disease.

Charles E. Triplett, Morocco, commissioned July 15, 1863, mustered out with regiment.

Assistant Surgeon

Samuel R. Pratt, Crown Point, commissioned Aug. 14, 1862, promoted surgeon.

Charles E. Triplett, Morocco, commissioned Aug. 30, 1862, promoted surgeon.

Gordon A. Moss, Rensselaer, commissioned Aug. 30, 1862, resigned Feb. 13, 1863.

Vernon Gould, Rochester, commissioned Feb. 28, 1863, mustered out with regiment.

Company Officers and Enlisted Men

Company A

Captain

Edwin P. Hammond, Rensselaer, commissioned Aug. 5, 1862, promoted major.

George W. Payne, Pleasant Grove, commissioned March 22, 1863, resigned Dec. 6, 1863.

James A. Burnham, Rensselaer, commissioned Dec. 7, 1863, mustered out with regiment.

First Lieutenant

George W. Payne, Pleasant Grove, commissioned Aug. 5, 1862, promoted captain.

Marion L. Spitler, Rensselaer, commissioned March 22, 1863, resigned Sept. 9, 1863.

James A. Burnham, Rensselaer, commissioned Sept. 10, 1863, promoted captain.

David H. Yeoman, Rensselaer, commissioned March 1, 1864, mustered out with regiment.

Second Lieutenant

Marion L. Spitler, Rensselaer, commissioned Aug. 5, 1862, promoted first lieutenant.

James A. Burnham, Rensselaer, commissioned March 22, 1863, promoted first lieutenant.

David H. Yeoman, Rensselaer, commissioned April 8, 1863, promoted first lieutenant.

William H. Gwinn, Rensselaer, commissioned May 1, 1865, mustered out as first sergeant with regiment.

First Sergeant

Burnham, James A., Rensselaer, mustered Aug. 11, 1862, promoted first lieutenant.

Sergeants

Edgar, James, Pleasant Grove, mustered Aug. 9, 1862, transferred to Engineer Corps, July 18, 1864.

Henkle, Joseph C., Rensselaer, mustered Aug. 9, 1862, discharged Feb. 2, 1863.

Sale, James C., Pleasant Grove, mustered Aug. 9, 1862, died at Bowling Green, Ky., Dec. 7, 1862.

Williams, Robert, Rensselaer, mustered Aug. 9, 1862, died at Nashville, Tenn., April 13, 1863.

Corporals

Barkey, John C., Pleasant Grove, mustered Aug. 11, 1862, discharged Jan. 17, 1863.

Hopkins, Caleb C., Rensselaer, mustered Aug. 9, 1862, died at Kingston, Ga., July 8, 1864.

Irwin, Alfred, Rensselaer, mustered Aug. 11, 1862, discharged Feb. 12, 1863.

Lamborn, Isaac M., Remington, mustered July 21, 1862, mustered out June 10, 1865.

Payne, Furguson, Francesville, mustered Aug. 9, 1862, discharged Nov. 30, 1863.

Platt, Charles, Rensselaer, mustered Aug. 9, 1862, discharged May 12, 1864.

Steel, James M., Rensselaer, mustered Aug. 9, 1862, transferred to Engineer Corps July 18, 1864.

Waymire, John, Rensselaer, mustered Aug. 9, 1862, discharged Nov. 24, 1863.

Musicians

Dunlap, George M., Valparaiso, mustered Aug. 11, 1862, mustered out June 10, 1865.

Dunlap, Robert A., Rensselaer, mustered Aug. 11, 1862, mustered out June 10, 1865.

Wagoner

Cory, Robert Z., Rensselaer, mustered Aug. 11, 1862, died at Bowling Green, Ky., Nov. 6, 1862.

Privates

Adams, Henry I., Rensselaer, mustered Aug. 11, 1862, discharged Feb. 19, 1863.

Babcock, Henry O., Rensselaer, mustered Aug. 9, 1862, mustered out June 10, 1865, as sergeant.

Baker, David, Rensselaer, mustered Aug. 11, 1862, died at Triune, Tenn., May 9, 1863.

Ball, Cyrus A., Rensselaer, mustered Aug. 6, 1862, discharged Jan. 25, 1863.

Beal, James P., Rensselaer, mustered Aug. 11, 1862, died at Nashville, Tenn., Nov. 16, 1863.

Brodrick, John, Brook, mustered Aug. 2, 1862, deserted Oct. 12, 1862.

Brown, George, Rensselaer, mustered Aug. 11, 1862, discharged June 20, 1863.

Brown, John H., Francesville, mustered Aug. 11, 1862, died New Albany, Ind., Dec. 11, 1862.

Buchanan, George W., Rensselaer, mustered Aug. 11, 1862, mustered out May 25, 1865.

Canfield, Aaron, Pleasant Grove, mustered Aug. 11, 1862, transferred to V.R.C. Feb. 4, 1864.

Colton, Luther E., Rensselaer, mustered Aug. 11, 1862, mustered out May 10, 1865.

Comer, Jesse M., Rensselaer, mustered Aug. 11, 1862, mustered out June 10, 1865.

Cragun, Jonathan S., Kokomo, mustered Aug. 11, 1862, mustered out June 10, 1865, as corporal.

Crockett, Thomas A., Rensselaer, mustered Aug. 11, 1862, mustered out June 10, 1865.

Daugherty, Oliver M., Rensselaer, mustered Aug. 11, 1862, died at Lookout Mountain Aug. 1, 1864.

Dillon, Eli W., Rensselaer, mustered Aug. 11, 1862, died at Chattanooga, Tenn., Sept. 26, 1863.

Evans, Benjamin F., Adriance, mustered Aug. 21, 1862, mustered out June 10, 1865.

German, Joshua, Rensselaer, mustered Aug. 9, 1862, died at Cowan Station, Tenn., Oct. 3, 1864.

Glassford, John W., Monticello, mustered Aug. 11, 1862, discharged March 22, 1863.

Glover, Peter B., Rensselaer, mustered Aug. 9, 1862, mustered out June 10, 1865, as corporal.

Goodell, Andrew J., Rensselaer, mustered Aug. 9, 1862, died at Gallatin, Tenn., Jan. 14, 1863.

Grant, Shelby, Rensselaer, mustered Aug. 9, 1862, discharged April 21, 1864.

Guin, William H., Rensselaer, mustered Aug. 6, 1862, mustered out June 10, 1865, as first sergeant.

Hayden, Curtis M., Monrovia, mustered Aug. 11, 1862, died at Chattanooga, Tenn., Nov. 3, 1863.

Hemphill, Samuel, Rensselaer, mustered Aug. 8, 1862, mustered out June 15, 1865.

Holmes, William, Joliet, Ill., mustered July 21, 1862, died at Bowling Green, Ky., Nov. 19, 1863.

Hoover, William M., Rensselaer, mustered Aug. 11, 1862, mustered out June 10, 1865, as corporal.

Hopkins, Matthew P., Rensselaer, mustered Aug. 11, 1862, killed at Chickamauga Sept. 20, 1863.

Hough, Calvin R., Rensselaer, mustered Aug. 11, 1862, transferred to V.R.C. Jan. 15, 1864.

Howe, George W., Rensselaer, mustered Aug. 2, 1862, discharged Jan. 19, 1863.

Idle, Sanders, Rensselaer, mustered Aug. 11, 1862, discharged Feb. 14, 1863.

Isinghoff, Henry, no city listed, mustered Aug. 9, 1862, died at Gallatin, Tenn., Dec. 30, 1862.

Israel, Elijah W., Rensselaer, mustered Aug. 11, 1862, killed at Chickamauga Sept. 19, 1863; first sergeant.

Jacks, Hiram M., Rensselaer, mustered Aug. 11, 1862, mustered out June 10, 1865, as corporal.

Jacks, James M., Cathcart, mustered Aug. 9, 1862, died at Chattanooga, Tenn., Oct. 11, 1863.

King, Franklin T., Cathcart, mustered Aug. 9, 1862, transferred V.R.C., mustered out July 12, 1865.

King, Sidnial, Cathcart, mustered Aug. 11, 1862, discharged Jan. 29, 1863.

Lamborn, Josiah W., Remington, mustered July 30, 1862, discharged Feb. 17, 1863.

Lewis, Isaac R., Pleasant Grove, mustered Aug. 9, 1862, discharged May 7, 1863.

Lewis, Whitsel, Rensselaer, mustered Aug. 11, 1862, mustered out June 10, 1865.

Martin, William H., Rensselaer, mustered Aug. 11, 1862, discharged June 17, 1863.

McCulloch, Porter, Rensselaer, mustered Aug. 9, 1862, mustered out June 10, 1865, as corporal.

McGinnis, Joseph M., Rensselaer, mustered Aug. 11, 1862, discharged Nov. 10, 1862.

Moore, Benjamin L., Pleasant Grove, mustered Aug. 11, 1862, discharged May 24, 1863.

Moore, Samuel, Rensselaer, mustered Aug. 6, 1862, mustered out June 10, 1865.

Morgan, George L., Pleasant Grove, mustered Aug. 11, 1862, mustered out June 10, 1865.

Morlan, Edmund H., Rensselaer, mustered Aug. 11, 1862, transferred to Engineer Corps July 28, 1864.

Mowatt, Joseph V., Peekskill, N.Y., mustered Aug. 6, 1862, mustered out June 10, 1865, as sergeant.

Murray, William W., Pleasant Grove, mustered Aug. 9, 1862, discharged June 21, 1863.

Nichols, John L., Rensselaer, mustered Aug. 11, 1862, discharged Feb. 17, 1863.

Nichols, Solomon, Pleasant Grove, mustered Aug. 9, 1862, discharged Dec. 28, 1863.

Nichols, William H., Pleasant Grove, mustered Aug. 9, 1862, discharged May 11, 1863.

Noland, James W., Francesville, mustered Aug. 11, 1862, mustered out June 20, 1865.

Noland, Obed E., Francesville, mustered Aug. 11, 1862, discharged Dec. 21, 1862.

Openchain, Jehu, Rensselaer, mustered Aug. 11, 1862, died at Nashville, Tenn., Feb. 9, 1864.

Orcutt, Charles W., Rensselaer, mustered Aug. 9, 1862, died at Danville, Ky., Nov. 21, 1862.

Orcutt, Martin J., Rensselaer, mustered Aug. 6, 1862, transferred to V.R.C., mustered out June 22, 1865.

Parker, Henry J., Pleasant Grove, mustered Aug. 11, 1862, died at Murfreesboro, Tenn., Oct. 26, 1863.

Parkison, Benjamin F., Rensselaer, mustered Aug. 9, 1862, died at Louisville, Ky., Nov. 10, 1862.

Peacock, Erastus, Rensselaer, mustered Aug. 11, 1862, mustered out June 10, 1865.

Post, Milton, Black River Falls, Wis., mustered Aug. 11, 1862, discharged Jan. 25, 1863.

Poston, Henry H., Rensselaer, mustered Aug. 6, 1862, mustered out June 10, 1865.

Randle, John E., Pleasant Grove, mustered Aug. 11, 1862, transferred to V.R.C., mustered out June 30, 1865.

Reed, John W., Rensselaer, mustered Aug. 11, 1862, died at Nashville, Tenn., March 15, 1863.

Rhoades, Marshall D., Rensselaer, mustered Aug. 11, 1862, discharged April 21, 1863.

Ricketts, Thomas B., Rensselaer, mustered Aug. 9, 1862, discharged Dec. 22, 1862.

Ritchey, Oslander K., Rensselaer, mustered Aug. 16, 1862, discharged Dec. 4, 1864.

Sayers, Thomas J., Rensselaer, mustered Aug. 11, 1862, mustered out June 10, 1865.

Steely, John, Canada, mustered Aug. 11, 1862, deserted Oct. 1, 1862.

Stiers, Samuel, Rushville, mustered Aug. 11, 1862, mustered out June 10, 1865, as sergeant.

Tatman, Wilber P., Rensselaer, mustered Aug. 9, 1862, died in Danville, Va., prison, Jan. 26, 1864.

Thorn, George, Cathcart, mustered Aug. 9, 1865, mustered out June 10, 1865.

Thornton, Henry T., Rensselaer, mustered Aug. 11, 1862, discharged Feb. 2, 1863.

Timmons, Clement, Rensselaer, mustered Aug. 9, 1862, discharged April 8, 1864.

Timmons, John D., Rensselaer, mustered Aug. 6, 1862, mustered out June 10, 1865.

Wapler, Isaac O., Francesville, mustered Aug. 11, 1862, mustered out June 10, 1865.

Wapler, Otto, no city listed, mustered July 31, 1862, discharged Jan. 29, 1863.

Watson, Henry H., Rensselaer, mustered Aug. 11, 1862, mustered out June 10, 1865.

Weathers, James G., Rensselaer, mustered Aug. 9, 1862, discharged July 14, 1863.

Webb, James F., Rensselaer, mustered Aug. 11, 1862, died at Nashville, Tenn., Dec. 19, 1862.

Webb, Isaac F., Frankton, mustered Aug. 11, 1862, mustered out June 10, 1865.

Woosley, John, Kokomo, mustered Aug. 11, 1862, discharged April 20, 1863.

Recruits

Alter, John Q., Rensselaer, mustered Dec. 26, 1863, transferred to 42nd Regiment June 9, 1865; corporal.

Babcock, Robert, Indianapolis, mustered April 5, 1864, transferred to 42nd Regiment June 9, 1865.

Ball, Cyrus A., Indianapolis, mustered April 5, 1864, transferred to 42nd Regiment June 9, 1865.

Barnes, John W., Rensselaer, mustered Dec. 26, 1863, transferred to 42nd Regiment June 9, 1865.

Beake, Franklin W., Nineveh, mustered March 4, 1864, transferred to 42nd Regiment June 9, 1865.

Beam, William, Rensselaer, mustered Jan. 6, 1864, transferred to 42nd Regiment June 9, 1865.

Blymer, William S., LaPorte, mustered Sept. 19, 1863, transferred to 42nd Regiment June 9, 1865.

Bogue, Jonathan, no city listed, mustered Nov. 12, 1864, transferrd to 42nd Regiment June 9, 1865; substitute.

Casey, John, Rensselaer, mustered Dec. 26, 1863, transferred to 42nd Regiment June 9, 1865.

Casteel, Eli, Rensselaer, mustered Dec. 26, 1863, transferred to 42nd Regiment June 9, 1865; corporal.

Cissell, Benjamin W., Rensselaer, mustered Dec. 26, 1863, transferred to 42nd Regiment June 9, 1865.

Comer, Martin S., Rensselaer, mustered Dec. 26, 1863, transferred to 42nd Regiment June 9, 1865.

Cooper, George M., Rensselaer, mustered Dec. 26, 1863, transferred to 42nd Regiment June 9, 1865.

Downing, Thomas F., Rensselaer, mustered Dec. 26, 1863, transferred to 42nd Regiment June 9, 1865; corporal.

Fuller, John D., Rensselaer, mustered Dec. 26, 1863, transferrd to 42nd Regiment June 9, 1865.

Gerard, Edward M., Rensselaer, mustered Feb. 13, 1864, transferred to V.R.C. April 3, 1865.

Guthridge, William, Rensselaer, mustered Dec. 26, 1863, transferred to 42nd Regiment June 9, 1865.

Haskell, Allen C., Indianapolis, mustered Feb. 13, 1864, transferred to 42nd Regiment June 9, 1865.

Henkle, Joseph C., Rensselaer, mustered March 22, 1864, transferred to 42nd Regiment June 9, 1865.

Hopkins, Philander C., Rensselaer, mustered Dec. 26, 1863, transferred to 42nd Regiment June 9, 1865.

Hough, William T., Rensselaer, mustered Feb. 18, 1864, transferred to 42nd Regiment June 9, 1865.

Irwin, Richard B., Rensselaer, mustered April 8, 1864, transferred to 42nd Regiment June 9, 1865.

James, Henry A., Rensselaer, mustered Dec. 26, 1863, transferred to 42nd Regiment June 9, 1865.

Jenkins, Wesley, no city listed, mustered Oct. 10, 1864, transferred to 42nd Regiment June 9, 1865; substitute.

Jones, Morris A., Rensselaer, mustered Feb. 18, 1865, transferred to 42nd Regiment June 9, 1865.

Kelly, Daniel B., no city listed, mustered Oct. 13, 1864, transferred to 42nd Regiment June 9, 1865; substitute.

Kinckelson, John A., Rensselaer, mustered Dec. 26, 1863, transferred to 42nd Regiment June 9, 1865.

Lanham, Charles, Richmond, mustered Sept. 28, 1864, mustered out July 5, 1865; substitute.

Mead, Merrill C., Indianapolis, mustered Jan. 22, 1864, transferred to 42nd Regiment June 9, 1865.

Nowles, George S., Rensselaer, mustered March 22, 1864, transferred to V.R.C. April 13, 1865.

Peterson, John M., Rensselaer, mustered Dec. 26, 1863, died at Chattanooga, Tenn., March 6, 1864.

Post, Charles B., Newcastle, mustered Oct. 17, 1864, died at Savannah, Ga., Dec. 28, 1864; substitute.

Post, John M., Newcastle, mustered April 8, 1864, transferred to 42nd Regiment June 9, 1865.

'oston, Samuel, Rensselaer, mustered Jan. 6, 1864, transferred to 42nd Regiment June 9, 1865.

Sewell, George W., Rensselaer, mustered Dec. 26, 1863, transferred to 42nd Regiment June 9, 1865.

Smith, James H., no city listed, mustered Oct. 17, 1864, transferred to 42nd Regiment June 9, 1865; substitute.

Walker, James A., Fishersburg, mustered Sept. 28, 1864, mustered out June 10, 1865; substitute.

Willey, William H., Nineveh, mustered March 4, 1864, transferred to 42nd Regiment June 9, 1865.

Williams, Seth, Rensselaer, mustered Jan. 6, 1864, transferred to 42nd Regiment June 9, 1865.

Wilson, Andrew J., Medaryville, mustered Jan. 6, 1864, transferred to 42nd Regiment June 9, 1865.

Wright, Charles P., Rensselaer, mustered Dec. 26, 1863, transferred to 42nd Regiment June 9, 1865.

Yeoman, David H., Rensselaer, mustered Jan. 6, 1864, promoted first lieutenant.

Company B

Captain

James W. Selders, Winamac, commissioned Aug. 6, 1862, resigned Dec. 22, 1862.

George W. Baker, Star City, commissioned Dec. 23, 1862, killed at Chickamauga Sept. 20, 1863.

William W. Agnew, Winamac, commissioned Sept. 20, 1863, mustered out with regiment.

First Lieutenant

George W. Baker, Star City, commissioned Aug. 6, 1862, promoted captain.

William W. Agnew, Winamac, commissioned Dec. 23, 1862, promoted captain.

William Poole, Star City, commissioned Sept. 20, 1863, promoted captain Company G.

Richard M. Hathaway, commissioned May 1, 1864, mustered out with regiment.

Second Lieutenant

Enoch Benefiel, Winamac, commissioned Aug. 6, 1862, resigned Feb. 12, 1863; reentered in 151st Regiment.

William Poole, Star City, commissioned Dec. 23, 1862, promoted first lieutenant.

James R. Holmes, Winamac, commissioned May 1, 1865, mustered out as first sergeant with regiment.

First Sergeant

Agnew, William W., Winamac, mustered July 26, 1862, discharged March 24, 1863.

Sergeants

Meeker, Charles A., Winamac, mustered Aug. 2, 1862, discharged Dec. 15, 1863.

Murphy, John J., Star City, mustered Aug. 6, 1862, died at Gallatin, Tenn., Jan. 4, 1863.

Poole, William, Star City, mustered Aug. 6, 1862, discharged March 24, 1863.

Whissinger, Benjamin F., Star City, mustered July 26, 1862, died at Gallatin, Tenn., Dec. 7, 1862.

Corporals

Chamberlain, Samuel B., Winamac, mustered Aug. 1, 1862, died at Gallatin, Tenn., Jan. 12, 1863.

Dilts, Daniel, Winamac, mustered July 26, 1862, mustered out June 10, 1865, as private.

Doremus, Christopher J., Winamac, mustered Aug. 2, 1862, discharged Jan. 7, 1863.

Lemasters, Jacob, Star City, mustered Aug. 5, 1862, died at Chattanooga, Tenn., Jan. 20, 1864.

May, John, Star City, mustered Aug. 6, 1862, mustered out June 10, 1865, as sergeant.

Smith, Hugh, Winamac, mustered Aug. 4, 1862, discharged Dec. 15, 1863.

Williams, Luther H., Winamac, mustered Aug. 2, 1862, died at Gallatin, Tenn., Dec. 6, 1862.

Musicians

Hathaway, Richard M., Winamac, mustered Aug. 2, 1862, discharged June 30, 1863.

Tibbetts, William W., Winamac, mustered July 26, 1862, discharged June 3, 1863.

Wagoner

Smith, Conrad, Winamac, mustered July 26, 1862, transferred to V.R.C. Dec. 12, 1863.

Privates

Aikens, John W., Winamac, mustered July 26, 1862, died at Bowling Green, Ky., Nov. 29, 1862.

Allen, George R., Winamac, mustered Aug. 6, 1862, discharged Jan. 15, 1863.

Bales, Isaac, Oak, mustered Aug. 6, 1862, died at Gallatin, Tenn., Jan. 9, 1863.

Bales, Spencer, Oak, mustered Aug. 6, 1862, mustered out June 10, 1865.

Barnes, David A., Winamac, mustered Aug. 6, 1862, died at Lebanon, Ky., Nov. 2, 1862.

Beebe, David, Winamac, mustered Aug. 6, 1862, mustered out June 10, 1865.

Birch, Andrew, Winamac, mustered Aug. 6, 1862, died at Murfreesboro, Tenn., Dec. 8, 1862.

Bochtenkircher, David, Francesville, mustered July 30, 1862, mustered out June 10, 1865, as sergeant.

Bourne, Frederick, Winamac, mustered Aug. 6, 1862, discharged Jan. 14, 1863.

Bridgeman, William, Winamac, mustered July 26, 1862, died at Gallatin, Tenn., Feb. 20, 1863.

Budd, Robert W., Star City, mustered Aug. 2, 1862, mustered out June 10, 1865, as corporal.

Cappis, John, Winamac, mustered Aug. 2, 1862, mustered out June 10, l865.

Conn, Solomon, Winamac, mustered July 26, 1862, mustered out June 10, 1865, as corporal.

Corbitt, Joseph H., Winamac, mustered July 26, 1862, mustered out June 10, 1865.

Cory, Henry M., Logansport, mustered Aug. 6, 1862, died at Chattanooga, Tenn., Oct. 22, 1863; wounds.

Criam, Lewis, Winamac, mustered Aug. 6, 1862, discharged Feb. 14, 1863.

Crist, John G., Star City, mustered Aug. 6, 1862, discharged April 28, 1864.

Davis, Tillman, Winamac, mustered Aug. 6, 1862, discharged Dec. 30, 1863.

Doremus, Cornelius W., Winamac, mustered Aug. 2, l862, died at Louisville, Ky., Nov. 23, 1862.

Drake, Francis F., Francesville, mustered Aug. 6, 1862, discharged Feb. 7, 1863.

Dye, Horatio, Star City, mustered Aug. 6, 1862, mustered out May 26, 1865.

Ernsperger, Cyrus W., Winamac, mustered July 26, 1862, transferred to Mississippi Marine Brigade, Dec. 1862.

Essex, Lemuel J., Winamac, mustered Aug. 6, 1862, discharged 1863 (no date listed).

Evans, Endrew W., Francesville, mustered Aug. 2, 1862, died at Gallatin, Tenn., Jan. 12, 1863.

Evans, Jacob, Bruce Lake, mustered Aug. 2, 1862, killed at Chickamauga Sept. 20, 1863.

Falvey, Mark, Winamac, mustered July 26, 1862, transferred to V.R.C.; mustered out June 30, 1865.

Ganson, George W., Francesville, mustered Aug. 2, 1862, deserted December 1862 (no date given).

Gillmore, Conrad F., Winamac, mustered Aug. 6, 1862, discharged Jan. 16, 1863.

Glover, Samuel B., Winamac, mustered July 20, 1862, discharged Dec. 3, 1862.

Goble, Joseph F., Winamac, mustered Aug. 2, 1862, deserted Oct. 31, 1862.

Griffith, Lewis H., Winamac, mustered July 26, 1862, killed at Chickamauga, Sept. 20, 1863.

Heeter, Levi, Winamac, mustered Aug. 6, 1862, discharged Feb. 14, 1863.

Helm, John N., Winamac, mustered Aug. 6, 1862, discharged April 3, 1863.

Hight, George W., Winamac, mustered July 26, 1862, absent without leave since May 10, 1864.

Hinkle, Jeremiah G., Star City, mustered July 26, 1862, mustered out June 13, 1865.

Hodges, John W., Winamac, mustered Aug. 6, 1862, died in Danville, Va., prison, March 18, 1864.

Holman, Aaron, Winamac, mustered Aug. 6, 1862, transferred to V.R.C.; mustered out Aug. 5, 1865.

Holmes, James R., Winamac, mustered Aug. 2, 1862, mustered out June 10, 1865, as first sergeant.

Huffman, Frederick, Winamac, mustered Aug. 6, 1862, deserted Oct. 31, 1862.

Huffman, William, Winamac, mustered Aug. 6, 1862, deserted Oct. 31, 1862.

Hurley, Cornelius, Columbus, mustered July 31, 1862, mustered out June 10, 1865.

Kirkham, Edward, Winamac, mustered July 26, 1862, mustered out June 10, 1865.

Kitchen, Andrew J., Winamac, mustered Aug. 6, 1862, discharged Feb. 2, 1863.

Lakin, Thomas, Winamac, mustered July 26, 1862, discharged Jan. 12, 1864.

Lane, Frank T., Winamac, mustered July 26, 1862, died at Chattanooga, Tenn., Oct. 20, 1863.

Lane, Jerome J., Winamac, mustered July 31, 1862, transferred to V.R.C. Feb. 11, 1864.

Lemasters, James, Star City, mustered Aug. 6, 1862, discharged Feb. 14, 1863.

Lemasters, Thomas, Star City, mustered Aug. 6, 1862, died at home July 30, 1864.

Lidyard, James, Oak, mustered Aug. 2, 1862, mustered out June 13, 1865.

Little, George, Winamac, mustered Aug. 2, 1862, died at Bowling Green, Ky., Nov. 30, 1862.

McCoy, Joseph G., Winamac, mustered Aug. 6, 1862, discharged Feb. 11, 1863.

McCarty, Jacob, Winamac, mustered Aug. 6, 1862, discharged Feb. 7, 1863.

McCarty, John, Winamac, mustered Aug. 6, 1862, died at Louisville, Ky., Nov. 30, 1862.

McDaniel, Reuben, Francesville, mustered Aug. 2, 1862, discharged Feb. 3, 1863.

Markins, Charles D., Francesville, mustered Aug. 2, 1862, discharged Feb. 27, 1863.

Mattox, Warren J., Winamac, mustered July 30, 1862, deserted Oct. 31, 1862.

Miller, Henderson, Star City, mustered Aug. 2, 1862, discharged July 8, 1863.

Miller, Samuel B., Star City, mustered Aug. 2, 1862, died at Gallatin, Tenn., Dec. 5, 1862.

Miller, Van, Francesville, mustered Aug. 2, 1862, discharged Feb. 20, 1863.

Nichols, Samuel, Star City, mustered Aug. 2, 1862, discharged June 30, 1864.

Reader, Daniel, Francesville, mustered Aug. 6, 1862, discharged Oct. 15, 1862.

Rector, Isaac, Logansport, mustered Aug. 6, 1862, mustered out June 10, 1865.

Ryans, James, Francesville, mustered Aug. 6, 1862, transferred to V.R.C. Sept. 26, 1863.

Sell, Samuel, Winamac, mustered Aug. 6, 1862, died at Nashville, Tenn., June 5, 1863.

Shaffner, Thomas T., Winamac, mustered July 26, 1862, promoted hospital steward, Regular Army.

Sickmak, John J., Winamac, mustered Aug. 6, 1862, discharged April 29, 1863.

Stamm, John H., Winamac, mustered Aug. 2, 1862, mustered out June 10, 1865, as corporal.

Stevens, John W., Francesville, mustered Aug. 2, 1862, mustered out June 10, 1865, as sergeant.

Stewart, Newton, Star City, mustered Aug. 6, 1862, mustered out June 10, 1865.

Stewart, William, Star City, mustered Aug. 6, 1862, discharged Nov. 30, 1862.

Styre, George W., Winamac, mustered Aug. 6, 1862, discharged March 11, 1863.

Thompson, Lorenza F., Star City, mustered July 26, 1862, mustered out June 20, 1865.

Waterhouse, William H., Oak, mustered Aug. 6, 1862, died at Triune, Tenn., March 26, 1863.

Waters, Alexander C., Winamac, mustered Aug. 6, 1862, killed at Chickamauga Sept. 20, 1863.

Williams, Andrew P., Winamac, mustered July 26, 1862, died at Gallatin, Tenn., Jan. 3, 1863.

Williamson, Maluff, Winamac, mustered July 26, 1862, killed at Chickamauga Sept. 20, 1863.

Wilson, Leonard, Maxinkuckee, mustered Aug. 2, 1862, mustered out June 10, 1865, as corporal.

Young, John, Winamac, mustered Aug. 2, 1862, discharged Feb. 2, 1863.

Recruits

Baker, Abraham, Winamac, mustered Feb. 2, 1863, discharged Oct. 4, 1864.

Baker, William P., Star City, mustered Feb. 25, 1864, transferred to 42nd Regiment June 9, 1865.

Benefield, Isaac, Winamac, mustered Feb. 19, 1864, transferred to 42nd Regiment June 9, 1865.

Bradlee, Noah P., Winamac, mustered Feb. 3, 1864, died at Chattanooga, Tenn., March 21, 1864.

Brown, Rufus C., Winamac, mustered April 9, 1864, died at New Bern, N.C., May 8, 1865.

Cole, Nelson V., LaPorte, mustered Sept. 19, 1863, transferred to 42nd Regiment June 9, 1865.

Copeland, William, Winamac, mustered Aug. 4, 1863, transferred to 42nd Regiment June 9, 1865.

Counts, Joseph, Winamac, mustered Jan. 13, 1864, transferred to 42nd Regiment June 9, 1865.

Culbertson, Charles, Kendallville, mustered Oct. 12, 1864, transferred 42nd Regiment June 9, 1865, substitute.

Elmore, David, Winamac, mustered Jan. 13, 1864, transferred to 42nd Regiment June 9, 1865, substitute.

Elmore, Jesse, Winamac, mustered Jan. 13, 1864, died at Jeffersonville, Ind., July 22, 1864.

Enyart, Harrison, Winamac, mustered Feb. 19, 1864, discharged March 3, 1865.

Evans, George H., Bruce Lake, mustered Feb. 3, 1864, transferred to 42nd Regiment June 9, 1865, substitute.

Farmin, John W., Dayton, Ohio, mustered March 22, 1864, transferred to 42nd Regiment June 9, 1865.

Green, George, Winamac, mustered Feb. 3, 1864, transferred to 42nd Regiment June 9, 1865.

Heeter, Levi, Winamac, mustered Feb. 3, 1864, transferred to 42nd Regiment June 9, 1865.

Hight, George W., Winamac, mustered Aug. 31, 1864, mustered out June 17, 1865.

Lee, Amos, Winamac, mustered Jan. 13, 1864, transferred to 42nd Regiment June 9, 1865.

Maxey, Asa, Winamac, mustered Feb. 3, 1864, transferred to 42nd Regiment June 9, 1865.

Moore, James R., Kendallville, mustered Oct. 21, 1864, discharged March 9, 1865, substitute.

Morrison, Henry, Lafayette, mustered Oct. 15, 1864, transferred to 42nd Regiment June 9, 1865, substitute.

Parrott, George, Winamac, mustered July 26, 1864, transferred to Engineer Corps July 1, 1864.

Patterson, Jerome, Evansville, mustered Nov. 2, 1864, transferred to 42nd Regiment June 9, 1865, substitute.

Penny, Noah, Star City, mustered Aug. 6, 1862, discharged (no date listed).

Read, John W., Winamac, mustered Jan. 13, 1864, transferred to 42nd Regiment June 9, 1865.

Rhodes, Henry, Winamac, mustered Feb. 3, 1864, transferred to 42nd Regiment June 9, 1865.

Rhorbaugh, Charles, Kendallville, mustered Oct. 6, 1864, transferred to 42nd Regiment June 9, 1865, substitute.

Rouse, Amos, Winamac, mustered Feb. 3, 1864, discharged March 12, 1864.

Rouse, Charles B., Indianapolis, mustered Oct. 4, 1864, transferred to 42nd Regiment June 9, 1865, substitute.

Shields, Robert, Winamac, mustered Feb. 3, 1864, transferred to 42nd Regiment June 9, 1865.

Smith, John, Winamac, mustered Feb. 3, 1864, transferred to 42nd Regiment June 9, 1865.

Van Scoik, Thomas M., Star City, mustered Aug. 6, 1862, discharged Jan. 15, 1863.

Wiley, William W., Winamac, mustered Feb. 3, 1864, mustered out July 2, 1865.

Wood, John H., Indianapolis, mustered March 3, 1865, mustered out May 3, 1865.

Woodruff, Roswell, Winamac, mustered Aug. 31, 1864, transferred to 42nd Regiment June 9, 1865.

Company C

Captain

Henry Calkins, Peru, commissioned Aug. 9, 1862, resigned May 2, 1863.

Milo D. Ellis, Peru, commissioned May 3, 1863, brevetted major to date March 13, 1865, mustered out with regiment.

First Lieutenant

Milo D. Ellis, Peru, commissioned Aug. 9, 1862, promoted captain.

Burr Russell, Peru, commissioned May 3, 1863, died of wound received in action Nov. 29, 1863.

John Demuth, Peru, commissioned Dec. 1, 1863, killed in action Aug. 22, 1864.

Irvin Hutchison, Peru, commissioned Aug. 23, 1864, mustered out with regiment.

Second Lieutenant

Isaac H. Cochran, Peru, commissioned Aug. 9, 1862, resigned Feb. 13, 1863.

Burr Russell, Peru, commissioned Feb. 14, 1863, promoted first lieutenant.

Elisha Brown, Peru, commissioned May 3, 1863, killed at Chickamauga Sept. 20, 1863.

William H. Reyburn, Peru, commissioned May 3, 1865, mustered out with regiment as first sergeant.

First Sergeant
Russell, Burr, Peru, mustered July 18, 1862, promoted second lieutenant.

Sergeants
Brown, Elisha, Peru, mustered Aug. 7, 1862, promoted second lieutenant.
Keyes, Alexander, Peru, mustered Aug. 6, 1862, mustered out June 10, 1865.
Reyburn, William H., Peru, mustered July 30, 1862, mustered out June 10, 1865, as first sergeant.
Smith, William J., Peru, mustered Aug. 10, 1862, discharged March 11, 1863.

Corporals
Bellew, George W., Peru, mustered Aug. 11, 1862, deserted Nov. 12, 1862.
Bowen, Benjamin F., Peru, mustered July 21, 1862, discharged July 1, 1864, as first sergeant.
Brower, Noah, Mexico, mustered Aug. 9, 1862, mustered out June 17, 1865.
Cotterman, Aaron, Chili, mustered Aug. 11, 1862, mustered out June 10, 1865, as private.
Demuth, John, Peru, mustered Aug. 6, 1862, promoted first lieutenant.
Hand, John, Peru, mustered Aug. 6, 1862, discharged Jan. 15, 1863.
Keegan, Peter, Peru, mustered Aug. 11, 1862, mustered out June 10, 1865, as sergeant.
Steele, John B., Chili, mustered Aug. 11, 1862, mustered out June 10, 1865; absent, sick.

Musicians
Kennedy, Joseph J., Peru, mustered Aug. 9, 1862, died at Gallatin, Tenn., Nov. 23, 1862.
York, Nathaniel, Peru, mustered July 21, 1862, discharged Oct. 27, 1863.

Wagoner
Marshall, Herman, Peru, mustered Aug. 6, 1862, died at Nashville, Tenn., Dec. 14, 1863, wounds.

Privates
Addington, Thomas, Peru, mustered Aug. 22, 1862, discharged Dec. 29, 1862, as corporal.
Baker, John, Peru, mustered Aug. 2, 1862, discharged May 1, 1865.
Bell, Reyneer, Peru, mustered Aug. 11, 1862, discharged Dec. 22, 1862.
Berry, Benjamin F., Xenia, mustered July 21, 1862, mustered out June 10, 1865.
Berry, George N., Peru, mustered July 24, 1862, transferred to V.R.C. June 20, 1864.
Brown, Martin V., Peru, mustered Aug. 11, 1862, died at Chattanooga, Tenn., Nov. 22, 1863.
Busey, John F., Peru, mustered July 30, 1862, discharged Nov. 29, 1864, wounds.

Clendenin, Andrew P., Peru, mustered Aug. 3, 1862, died at David's Island, N.Y.H. (New York Harbor), April 8, 1865.

Cochran, Charles W., Peru, mustered Aug. 3, 1862, discharged March 12, 1863.

Conradt, Henry, Peru, mustered Aug. 7, 1862, mustered out June 10, 1865.

Coon, Philip R., Peru, mustered July 18, 1862, mustered out June 21, 1865.

Cover, Edward A., Peru, mustered Aug. 1, 1862, discharged Oct. 28, 1862.

Cypherd, Ezra J., Peru, mustered July 24, 1862, discharged May 1865, wounds.

Dangerfield, John N., Xenia, mustered Aug. 11, 1862, mustered out June 10, 1865.

Demuth, William, Peru, mustered Aug. 6, 1862, mustered out June 10, 1865, as sergeant.

Derick, David, Peru, mustered Aug. 3, 1862, mustered out June 30, 1865.

Derick, George, Peru, mustered Aug. 3, 1862, discharged July 1, 1863, as corporal.

Detamore, David W., Xenia, mustered Aug. 6, 1862, mustered out June 10, 1865.

Donlay, Solomon, Peru, mustered Aug. 6, 1862, discharged Nov. 12, 1862.

Eastridge, Leander G., Peru, mustered Aug. 11, 1862, discharged Jan. 15, 1863.

Edwards, Sylvester, Peru, mustered Aug. 9, 1862, died at Chattanooga, Tenn., Oct. 11, 1863, wounds.

Fisher, Peter, Peru, mustered Aug. 6, 1862, deserted Jan. 15, 1863.

Fites, James G., Peru, mustered Aug. 11, 1862, discharged Dec. 1, 1863.

Foss, James G., Peru, mustered Aug. 2, 1862, died at Chattanooga, Tenn., Dec. 10, 1863.

Glaze, George, Peru, mustered July 21, 1862, died at Chattanooga, Tenn., Nov. 8, 1863.

Gordon, Joseph, Peru, mustered Aug. 6, 1862, mustered out June 10, 1865, as corporal.

Hanks, Christopher, Peru, mustered Aug. 6, 1862, mustered out June 10, 1865.

Hart, George, Peru, mustered Aug. 6, 1862, died at Lebanon, Ky., Feb. 21, 1863.

Haskell, William, Peru, mustered July 21, 1862, killed at Chickamauga Sept. 20, 1863.

Hawver, William H., Peru, mustered Aug. 6, 1862, died at Richmond, Va., prison Dec. 15, 1863, wounds.

Hollingworth, Levi, Xenia, mustered Aug. 6, 1862, mustered out June 10, 1865, as corporal.

Hurlburt, John W., Peru, mustered Aug. 4, 1862, discharged Jan. 15, 1863.

Hurtt, Thomas B., Peru, mustered Aug. 6, 1862, transferred to Engineer Corps Aug. 20, 1864.

Hutchinson, Irvin, Peru, mustered Aug. 6, 1862, promoted first lieutenant.

Keim, Constantine, Peru, mustered June 21, 1862, discharged Feb. 9, 1863.

Keim, Israel, Chili, mustered Aug. 6, 1862, mustered out June 10, 1865.

Kepler, John, Peru, mustered Aug. 6, 1862, died at Ringgold, Ga., April 12, 1864.

Keyes, Thaddeus, Peru, mustered Aug. 6, 1862, mustered out June 10, 1865.

Leffel, William J., Peru, mustered Aug. 11, 1862, discharged Aug. 1, 1864.

Loyd, William J., Peru, mustered Aug. 6, 1862, died at Louisville, Ky., Dec. 19, 1862.

Marine, Asa W., Peru, mustered Aug. 6, 1862, died at Walden's Ridge, Tenn., Oct., 1863, wounds.

Marine, Daniel O., Xenia, mustered Aug. 4, 1862, mustered out June 10, 1865.

McBride, William R., Peru, mustered Aug. 11, 1862, transferred to V.R.C., mustered out June 13, 1865.

McGrew, Francis, Peru, mustered July 30, 1862, transferred to Engineer Corps Aug. 20, 1864.

Mendenhall, Oscar, Xenia, mustered Aug. 5, 1862, mustered out June 10, 1865.

Miller, James, Chili, mustered Aug. 11, 1862, mustered out June 10, 1865, as absent sick.

Moore, John C., Gilead, mustered Aug. 4, 1862, mustered out June 10, 1865.

Mote, David, Gilead, mustered Aug. 4, 1862, mustered out June 10, 1865, as absent sick.

Newby, Isaiah J., Peru, mustered Aug. 5, 1862, died at Chattanooga, Tenn., Oct. 7, 1863, wounds.

Parker, Milton B., Xenia, mustered Aug. 4, 1862, mustered out June 10, 1865, as sergeant.

Perkins, Ithamer, Peru, mustered Aug. 4, 1862, died at Gallatin, Tenn., Nov. 12, 1862.

Petty, Miles C., Peru, mustered Aug. 11, 1862, killed at Chickamauga Sept. 20, 1863.

Powell, Hiram S., Xenia, mustered Aug. 11, 1862, mustered out June 10, 1865, as corporal.

Ptomey, John, Peru, mustered Aug. 6, 1862, transferred to V.R.C., mustered out June 30, 1865.

Reese, John A., Peru, mustered Aug. 6, 1862, died at Gallatin, Tenn., Jan. 10, 1863.

Robbins, George, Peru, mustered Aug. 4, 1862, discharged July 11, 1864.

Robbins, Redin, Peru, mustered Aug. 4, 1862, discharged Jan. 17, 1863.

Robbins, William S., Xenia, mustered Aug. 4, 1862, mustered out June 10, 1865.

Saxon, William J., Peru, mustered Aug. 6, 1862, died at Gallatin, Tenn., Dec. 14, 1862.

Shaffer, Isaiah J., Peru, mustered July 21, 1862, mustered out June 10, 1865.

Smith, Charles H., Peru, mustered Aug. 11, 1862, transferred to V.R.C. March 22, 1864.

Smith, John A., Peru, mustered Aug. 6, 1862, mustered out June 10, 1865, as corporal.

Smith, Valentine, Peru, mustered Aug. 7, 1862, mustered out June 10, 1865.

Snyder, Valentine, Peru, mustered Aug. 6, 1862, mustered out June 10, 1865.

Stitsworth, John, Peru, mustered July 23, 1862, mustered out June 10, 1865.

Studebaker, Henry R., Peru, mustered Aug. 7, 1862, discharged Oct. 31, 1864.

Sullivan, Benson, Peru, mustered July 23, 1862, mustered out June 10, 1865, as corporal.

Swoverland, John, Peru, mustered Aug. 6, 1862, deserted Nov. 12, 1862.

Walker, John H., Peru, mustered July 22, 1862, mustered out June 10, 1865.

Wallick, Charles F., Peru, mustered July 17, 1862, mustered out June 10, 1865, as corporal.

Walter, George F., Peru, mustered Aug. 11, 1862, died at Bowling Green, Ky., Dec. 23, 1862.

White, Erastus, Peru, mustered Aug. 11, 1862, mustered out June 10, 1865.

Wickler, William, Peru, mustered July 21, 1862, killed at Chickamauga Sept. 20, 1863.

Wissinger, Jacob, Peru, mustered Aug. 11, 1862, mustered out June 10, 1865.

Williams, Benjamin, Peru, mustered July 22, 1862, died at Louisville, Ky., Nov. 7, 1862.

Wood, Thomas G., Gilead, mustered Aug. 4, 1862, mustered out June 10, 1865.

Woolf, Jacob, Peru, mustered Aug. 6, 1862, died at Triune, Tenn., May 2, 1863.

Wright, Clayborn, Peru, mustered Aug. 6, 1862, discharged Dec. 17, 1865.

Yike, Franklin, Chili, mustered Aug. 9, 1862, mustered out June 10, 1865.

Young, Benjamin G., Peru, mustered Aug. 4, 1862, discharged Jan. 9, 1863.

Zimmerman, Martin, Chili, mustered Aug. 7, 1862, mustered out June 10, 1865.

Recruits

Bloker, John H., LaPorte, mustered Sept. 19, 1863, transferred to 42nd Regiment June 9, 1865.

Crane, Benjamin, Greensburg, mustered Oct. 15, 1864, transferred to 42nd Regiment June 9, 1865, substitute.

Denny, Milton I., Indianapolis, mustered April 8, 1864, mustered out May 16, 1865.

Fowler, James, Greensburg, mustered Oct. 25, 1864, transferred to 42nd Regiment June 9, 1865.

Francis, Edward, Indianapolis, mustered Oct. 20, 1864, mustered out July 14, 1865, substitute.

Hart, Samuel, Kendallville, mustered Oct. 7, 1864, transferred to 42nd Regiment June 9, 1865, substitute.

Kizer, William, Peru, mustered April 8, 1864, mustered out June 4, 1865.

Knapp, Ezra, Greensburg, mustered Oct. 3, 1864, transferred to 42nd Regiment June 9, 1865, substitute.

Lake, Peter, Wabash, mustered Oct. 27, 1864, mustered out June 17, 1865, substitute.

Lambert, Sterling, Terre Haute, mustered Oct. 26, 1864, transferred 42nd Regiment June 9, 1865, substitute.

McCullough, John C., Columbus, mustered Sept. 20, 1864, died in the field in Georgia Dec. 9, 1864.

Miner, William, no city or muster date listed, transferred to 42nd Regiment June 9, 1865, substitute.

Small, Leander, Wabash, mustered Oct. 26, 1864, transferred to 42nd Regiment June 9, 1865, substitute.

Smith, Thomas, Evansville, mustered Oct. 29, 1864, transferred to 42nd Regiment June 9, 1865, substitute.

Titus, James K., no city or muster date listed, transferred to 42nd Regiment June 9, 1865, substitute.

Wright, Allen C., Indianapolis, mustered Oct. 6, 1864, transferred to 42nd Regiment June 9, 1865, substitute.

Company D

Captain

William H. Wood, Rochester, commissioned Aug. 9, 1862, resigned Nov. 13, 1862.

Lewis Hughes, Rochester, commissioned Nov. 14, 1862, killed at Chickamauga Sept. 20, 1863.

John W. Elam, Rochester, commissioned Sept. 21, 1863, mustered out with regiment.

First Lieutenant

Lewis Hughes, Rochester, commissioned Aug. 9, 1862, promoted captain.

Abel O'Blennis, Maxinkuckee, commissioned Nov. 14, 1862, mustered out with regiment.

Second Lieutenant

Mark C. McAfee, Rochester, commissioned Aug. 9, 1862, resigned Jan. 30, 1863.

John W. Elam, Rochester, commissioned Jan. 31, 1863, promoted captain.

Lewis M. Spotts, Rochester, commissioned May 1, 1865, mustered out with regiment as first sergeant

First Sergeant

Elam, John W., Rochester, mustered July 31, 1862, promoted second lieutenant.

Sergeants

Brown, Benjamin F., Rochester, mustered July 31, 1862, mustered out June 10, 1865.

Newby, John L., Rochester, mustered Aug. 9, 1862, died Nov. 30, 1862.

Oliver, John J., Rochester, mustered Aug. 9, 1862, discharged May 15, 1863.

Spotts, Lewis M., Rochester, mustered July 31, 1862, mustered out June 10, 1865, as first sergeant.

Corporals

Bitters, Andrew T., Rochester, mustered July 29, 1862, transferred to Mississippi Marine Brigade, April 17, 1863.

Frazier, William, Rochester, mustered July 29, 1862, discharged Jan. 18, 1863.

Graham, James, Rochester, mustered July 31, 1862, discharged Jan. 6, 1863.

Gunkle, Philip, Rochester, mustered July 31, 1862, discharged Dec. 2, 1862.

Huling, Alexander M., Rochester, mustered July 29, 1862, discharged Feb. 14, 1863.

Sheaffer, William, Rochester, mustered July 29, 1862, deserted April 1, 1863.

Spohn, Henry, Rochester, mustered Aug. 2, 1862, discharged Jan. 24, 1863.

Stradley, Luther, Rochester, mustered July 29, 1862, discharged Dec. 29, 1862.

Musicians

Horack, Alfred, Rochester, mustered July 22, 1862, transferred Mississippi Marine Brigade April 17, 1863.

Smith, Lafayette, Rochester, mustered July 22, 1862, mustered out June 10, 1865.

Wagoner

Collins, Josephus A., Rochester, mustered Aug. 9, 1862, died Oct. 17, 1863.

Privates

Adamson, Isaiah, Rochester, mustered Aug. 9, 1862, transferred to Mississippi Marine Brigade, Jan. 1, 1863.

Ball, Aaron M., Rochester, mustered July 29, 1862, discharged April 17, 1863.

Ball, Daniel N., Rochester, mustered Aug. 9, 1862, mustered out June 10, 1865.

Ball, George W., Rochester, mustered July 25, 1862, discharged Jan. 8, 1863.

Biggs, James, Rochester, mustered Aug. 9, 1862, discharged Jan. 15, 1863.

Biggs, John W., Rochester, mustered Aug. 9, 1862, died at Nashville, Tenn., Feb. 21, 1864.

Bozarth, Jasper W., Rochester, mustered Aug. 9, 1862, mustered out June 3, 1865.

Brocaw, William, Rochester, mustered Aug. 9, 1862, discharged Feb. 28, 1863.

Brock, John W., Rochester, mustered July 28, 1862, discharged Nov. 18, 1862.

Burch, Lorenzo, Rochester, mustered Aug. 9, 1862, mustered out June 10, 1865.

Carr, Anderson, Rochester, mustered Aug. 28, 1862, transferred to Engineer Corps.

Chesnut, Robert E., Rochester, mustered Aug. 10, 1862, mustered out June 10, 1865.

Clarke, John D., Rochester, mustered July 31, 1862, deserted April 1, 1863.

Clemens, Harvey, Rochester, mustered Aug. 9, 1862, discharged Aug. 19, 1863.

Cole, Daniel S., Rochester, mustered July 26, 1862, mustered out June 10, 1865.

Cole, William, Rochester, mustered Aug. 8, 1862, died March 3, 1864.

Cuberly, Dennis, Rochester, mustered July 28, 1862, died at Bowling Green, Ky., Jan. 18, 1863.

Daggett, Israel, Rochester, mustered Aug. 9, 1862, transferred to Engineer Corps.

Daugherty, William, Rochester, mustered Aug. 9, 1862, mustered out June 10, 1865.

Day, Joseph, Rochester, mustered Aug. 9, 1862, discharged Jan. 6, 1863.

Dwiggins, Israel, Rochester, mustered Aug. 19, 1862, discharged Jan. 14, 1863.

Ewer, William, Rochester, mustered July 26, 1862, killed at Chickamauga Sept. 19, 1863.

Gallion, John W., Rochester, mustered July 31, 1862, discharged Jan. 17, 1863.

Galtry, Elam, Rochester, mustered July 31, 1862, mustered out June 10, 1865, as corporal.

Goudy, Noah, Rochester, mustered Aug. 9, 1862, mustered out June 10, 1865.

Gould, Christopher, Rochester, mustered Aug. 9, 1862, died at Gallatin, Tenn., Jan. 18, 1863.

Gould, James, Rochester, mustered Aug. 9, 1862, mustered out June 10, 1865.

Hall, Milton, Rochester, mustered Aug. 9, 1862, died at Triune, Tenn., April 4, 1863.

Hatter, Andrew, Rochester, mustered July 28, 1862, mustered out June 10, 1865, as sergeant.

Holder, Chichester, Rochester, mustered July 26, 1862, mustered out June 10, 1865, as corporal.

Holder, Robert C., Rochester, mustered July 26, 1862, discharged Jan. 2, 1863.

Kelly, John, Rochester, mustered Aug. 2, 1862, died in military prison at Indianapolis.

Kibler, George, Rochester, mustered July 26, 1862, mustered out June 10, 1865.

Mackey, Horace, Rochester, mustered Aug. 9, 1862, mustered out June 10, 1865, as sergeant.

Macy, Absalom, Rochester, mustered Aug. 9, 1862, died at Nashville, Tenn., Sept. 12, 1863.

Miller, Benjamin, Rochester, mustered Aug. 9, 1862, died at Gallatin, Tenn., Jan. 24, 1863.

Moore, David, Rochester, mustered Aug. 9, 1862, transferred to V.R.C.

Moore, Henry H., Rochester, mustered Aug. 9, 1862, mustered out June 10, 1865.

Moore, James H., Rochester, mustered Aug. 9, 1862, died at Madison, Ind., March 24, 1864.

Monshour, David, Rochester, mustered Aug. 9, 1862, discharged Dec. 2, 1862.

New, Thomas J., Rochester, mustered July 26, 1862, discharged Feb. 20, 1863.

O'Blennis, Able, Rochester, mustered Aug. 12, 1862, promoted first lieutenant.

Oliver, David C., Rochester, mustered Aug. 9, 1862, mustered out June 10, 1865.

Oliver, William, Rochester, mustered Aug. 9, 1862, mustered out June 10, 1865.

Oren, James, Rochester, mustered July 26, 1862, transferred to V.R.C., mustered out July 6, 1865.

Oren, John, Rochester, mustered July 26, 1862, discharged March 11, 1863.

Osborne, James B., Rochester, mustered Aug. 12, 1862, killed at Chickamauga Sept. 20, 1863.

Packard, William B., Rochester, mustered July 22, 1862, mustered out June 10, 1865, as corporal.

Pearson, Charles M., Rochester, mustered Aug. 19, 1862, died at Chattanooga, Tenn., Dec. 18, 1863.

Polk, William H., Rochester, mustered July 26, 1862, died at Nashville, Tenn., July 8, 1864.

Porter, Benjamin F., Rochester, mustered Aug. 9, 1862, mustered out June 10, 1865.

Pownell, George H., Rochester, mustered Aug. 9, 1862, died at Fulton, Ind., Dec. 31, 1864.

Quiggs, James, Rochester, mustered Aug. 9, 1862, died Dec. 4, 1862.

Raeston, George W., Rochester, mustered Aug. 6, 1862, mustered out June 21, 1865.

Reschke, John, Rochester, mustered July 28, 1862, discharged Feb. 26, 1863.

Rice, Christian, Rochester, mustered Aug. 9, 1862, discharged April 25, 1864.

Roany, John, Rochester, mustered Aug. 9, 1862, discharged March 11, 1863.

Robbins, John, Rochester, mustered Aug. 9, 1862, mustered out June 10, 1865, as corporal.

Ross, Charles M., Rochester, mustered Aug. 9, 1862, mustered out June 10, 1865.

Rowe, Frederick, Rochester, mustered Aug. 9, 1862, died at Indianapolis, Ind., March 2, 1863.

Shelton, David D., Rochester, mustered Aug. 9, 1862, died Oct. 9, 1863, wounds.

Sherow, Levi, Rochester, mustered July 24, 1862, transferred to 42nd Regiment June 9, 1865.

Shields, William H., Rochester, mustered Aug. 9, 1862, died at Gallatin, Tenn., Jan. 25, 1863.

Shores, Oracle, Rochester, mustered Aug. 8, 1862, mustered out June 10, 1865.

Shores, Rufus A., Rochester, mustered Aug. 8, 1862, died at Bowling Green, Ky., Jan. 8, 1863.

Smith, Franklin M., Rochester, mustered Aug. 2, 1862, killed at Chickamauga Sept. 19, 1863.

Smith, Jesse, Rochester, mustered Aug. 2, 1862, mustered out June 10, 1865.

Steffy, Abraham, Rochester, mustered July 28, 1862, mustered out June 10, 1865.

Strong, Eli, Rochester, mustered Aug. 9, 1862, discharged Jan. 4, 1865.

Stull, John, Rochester, mustered July 28, 1862, discharged Feb. 3, 1863.

Vantrump, Jacob, Rochester, mustered Aug. 9, 1862, deserted Sept. 10, 1862.

Whittenberger, George, Rochester, mustered Aug. 9, 1862, died at Louisville, Ky., Dec. 2, 1862.

Whittenberger, John F., Rochester, mustered Aug. 9, 1862, died at New Albany, Ind., no date listed.

Wilson, Kline S., Rochester, mustered July 26, 1862, died Dec. 6, 1864.

Wright, George W., Rochester, mustered Aug. 2, 1862, mustered out June 10, 1865.

Wright, Jacob, Rochester, mustered Aug. 2, 1862, mustered out June 10, 1865.

Wright, John B., Rochester, mustered July 26, 1862, transferred to V.R.C., mustered out July 11, 1865.

Wright, William, Rochester, mustered Aug. 9, 1862, transferred to V.R.C., mustered out June 30, 1865.

Yoke, Henry, Rochester, mustered Aug. 8, 1862, died at Chattanooga, Tenn., Nov. 2, 1863.

Recruits

Biggs, Hugh S., Greensburg, mustered Sept. 26, 1864, mustered out June 10, 1865, substitute.

Bootz, Lewis, Rochester, mustered Feb. 28, 1864, transferred to 42nd Regiment June 9, 1865.

Brock, Milton, no city listed, mustered Oct. 26, 1864, transferred to 42nd Regiment June 9, 1865, substitute.

Childers, John A., Lafayette, mustered Oct. 15, 1864, transferred to 42nd Regiment June 9, 1865.

Denen, Thomas J., no city listed, mustered Dec. 19, 1863, transferred to 42nd Regiment June 9, 1865.

Grooms, Benjamin, Michigan City, mustered Oct. 28, 1864, transferred to 42nd Regiment June 9, 1865.

Grooms, James, Michigan City, mustered Oct. 28, 1864, transferred to 42nd Regiment June 9, 1865.

Izzard, Jabez, Indianapolis, mustered March 5, 1864, transferred to 42nd Regiment June 9, 1865.

Johnson, Henry, Terre Haute, mustered Oct. 27, 1864, transferred to 42nd Regiment June 9, 1865, substitute.

Kanuffle, Charles E., Lafayette, mustered Oct. 15, 1864, transferred to 42nd Regiment June 9, 1865, substitute.

Latchan, William T., Indianapolis, mustered Dec. 19, 1864, transferred to 42nd Regiment June 9, 1865.

Marshman, Alexander, Indianapolis, mustered Feb. 22, 1864, transferred to 42nd Regiment June 9, 1865.

McDaniels, Henry, Lafayette, mustered Oct. 24, 1864, transferred to 42nd Regiment June 9, 1865.

McKinney, James, Terre Haute, mustered Sept. 29, 1864, mustered out June 10, 1865; drafted.

O'Bennis, Sanford T., Indianapolis, mustered Feb. 26, 1864, transferred to 42nd Regiment June 9, 1865.

Osgood, Obiel P., Indianapolis, mustered Sept. 19, 1863, transferred to 42nd Regiment June 9, 1865.

Parsons, Joshua, Terre Haute, mustered Oct. 26, 1864, transferred to 42nd Regiment June 9, 1865, substitute.

Powell, James, no city or muster date listed, transferred to 42nd Regiment June 9, 1865.

Reed, John M., no city listed, mustered Oct. 12, 1864, mustered out Aug. 4, 1865.

Thomas, John Q., no city or muster date listed, transferred to 42nd Regiment June 9, 1865.

Wheatly, John H., Indianapolis, mustered Feb. 20, 1864, transferred to 42nd Regiment June 9, 1865.

Young, Lewis, Indianapolis, mustered Feb. 29, 1864, transferred to 42nd Regiment June 9, 1865.

Company E

Captain

Alfred T. Jackson, Kewanna, commissioned Aug. 12, 1862, resigned Nov. 13, 1862.

Peter S. Troutman, Kewanna, commissioned Nov. 19, 1862, mustered out with regiment.

First Lieutenant

Peter S. Troutman, Kewanna, commissioned Aug. 12, 1862, promoted captain.

Hamilton McAfee, Kewanna, commissioned Nov. 19, 1862, resigned Aug. 10, 1863.

John H. Vandever, Plymouth, commissioned Sept. 20, 1863, mustered out with regiment.

Second Lieutenant

Hamilton McAfee, Kewanna, commissioned Aug. 12, 1862, promoted first lieutenant.

Joseph Slick, Kewanna, commissioned Nov. 19, 1862, resigned May 25, 1863.

Franklin H. Bennett, Kewanna, commissioned May 26, 1863, killed at Chickamauga Sept. 19, 1863.

Henry W. Hoober, Blue Grass, commissioned May 1, 1865, mustered out with regiment as first sergeant.

First Sergeant

Slick, Joseph, Kewanna, mustered Aug. 31, 1862, promoted second lieutenant.

Sergeants

Bennett, Franklin H., Kewanna, mustered Aug. 31, 1862, promoted second lieutenant.

Carter, John J., Kewanna, mustered Aug. 31, 1862, mustered out June 10, 1865.

Levit, Samuel, Logansport, mustered Aug. 31, 1862, mustered out June 10, 1865.

Myers, Simon, Bruce Lake, mustered Aug. 31, 1862, died at Louisville, Ky., Oct. 2, 1862.

Corporals

Clark, Jonas, Blue Grass, mustered Aug. 31, 1862, died in the field Sept. 23, 1863.

Dukes, James R., Winamac, mustered Aug. 31, 1862, discharged Feb., 1863, no date listed.

Hart, Johnson M., no city listed, mustered Aug. 31, 1862, deserted Nov. 1, 1862.

Hoober, Henry W., Blue Grass, mustered Aug. 31, 1862, mustered out June 10, 1865, as first sergeant.

McCarter, Alexander, Kewanna, mustered Aug. 31, 1862, died at Nashville, Tenn., Nov. 13, 1863.

Richey, Samuel R., Kewanna, mustered Aug. 31, 1862, mustered out June 13, 1865.

Troutman, John G., Kewanna, mustered Aug. 31, 1862, discharged Jan. 5, 1864.

Vanmeter, Erasmus, Star City, mustered Aug. 31, 1862, died at Bowling Green, Ky., Nov. 16, 1862.

Musicians

Halstead, William, Kewanna, mustered Aug. 31, 1862, discharged Dec. 22, 1862.

Ummensetter, Henry, Star City, mustered Aug. 31, 1862, died at Louisville, Ky., Dec. 2, 1862.

Wagoner

Troutman, James H., Kewanna, mustered Aug. 31, 1862, discharged Jan. 21, 1863.

Privates

Anderson, Philip, Kewanna, mustered Aug. 31, 1862, transferred to Engineer Corps July 29, 1864.

Barber, Thomas, Star City, mustered Aug. 31, 1862, discharged Feb. 13, 1863.

Barker, Isaac H., Star City, mustered Aug. 31, 1862, mustered out June 10, 1865.

Barnett, William S., Kewanna, mustered Aug. 31, 1862, mustered out June 10, 1865, as corporal.

Bennett, Judson, Kewanna, mustered Aug. 31, 1862, mustered out June 10, 1865.

Blasser, John R., Kewanna, mustered Aug. 31, 1862, mustered out May 23, 1865.

Boyer, Edwin R., Kewanna, mustered Aug. 31, 1862, discharged Dec. 31, 1862.

Brown, John, Star City, mustered Aug. 31, 1862, died at Gallatin, Tenn., Feb. 5, 1863.

Brown, Martin, Star City, mustered Aug. 31, 1862, discharged Nov. 2, 1862.

Bruce, Daniel, Bruce Lake, mustered Aug. 31, 1862, mustered out June 10, 1865.

Burk, John G., Star City, mustered Aug. 31, 1862, mustered out June 10, 1865.

Cannon, Isaac H., Kewanna, mustered Aug. 31, 1862, mustered out June 10, 1865.

Carter, John N., Kewanna, mustered Aug. 31, 1862, discharged April 12, 1864.

Carter, John W., Kewanna, mustered Aug. 31, 1862, died at Camp Thomas, Tenn., July 2, 1863.

Davis, Joel H., Kewanna, mustered Aug. 31, 1862, discharged Nov. 21, 1863.

Davis, William R., Kewanna, mustered Aug. 31, 1862, discharged Jan. 27, 1862.

Dipert, Jacob, Bruce Lake, mustered Aug. 31, 1862, died at Louisville, Ky., Dec. 14, 1862.

Dipert, Samuel, Bruce Lake, mustered Aug. 31, 1862, transferred to Engineer Corps July 22, 1864.

Dixon, William, Kewanna, mustered Aug. 31, 1862, died at Nashville, Tenn., April 11, 1863.

Dukes, Andrew, Kewanna, mustered Aug. 31, 1862, transferred to V.R.C., March 12, 1864.

Fall, Simon, Kewanna, mustered Aug. 31, 1862, killed at Chickamauga Sept. 20, 1863.

Ferrell, John W., Kewanna, mustered Aug. 31, 1862, died at Chattanooga, Tenn., Oct. 14, 1863.

Green, Henry C., Bruce Lake, mustered Aug. 31, 1862, mustered out June 10, 1865.

Heckert, John, Kewanna, mustered Aug. 31, 1862, died at Louisville, Ky., Dec. 18, 1862.

Heckert, Moses, Bruce Lake, mustered Aug. 31, 1862, mustered out June 10, 1865.

Herrold, Daniel, Blue Grass, mustered Aug. 31, 1862, mustered out June 10, 1865.

Hizer, Alfred, Blue Grass, mustered Aug. 31, 1862, died at Kingston, Ga., Aug. 9, 1864, wounds.

Holiday, Robert, Blue Grass, mustered Aug. 31, 1862, mustered out June 10, 1865, as sergeant.

Hudkins, Elias V., Kewanna, mustered Aug. 31, 1862, mustered out June 10, 1865.

Hudkins, Henry L., Kewanna, mustered Aug. 31, 1862, died at Fulton County, Ind., April 19, 1864.

Hyson, John, Bruce Lake, mustered Aug. 31, 1862, discharged Jan. 15, 1863.

Jeffries, Bailey N., Kewanna, mustered Aug. 31, 1862, discharged March 19, 1863.

Jones, Zephaniah, Bruce Lake, mustered Aug. 31, 1862, discharged Dec. 11, 1863.

Kaler, George W., Kewanna, mustered Aug. 31, 1862, discharged Dec. 6, 1862.

Kingry, David M., Metea, mustered Aug. 31, 1862, mustered out June 10, 1865, as corporal.

Kiplinger, George H., Fulton, mustered Aug. 31, 1862, mustered out June 10, 1865.

Lebo, Henry, Bruce Lake, mustered Aug. 31, 1862, mustered out June 10, 1865.

Liming, Richard B., Star City, mustered Aug. 31, 1862, died at Chattanooga, Tenn., Sept. 28, 1863.

Miller, William H., Kewanna, mustered Aug. 31, 1862, mustered out June 10, 1865, as corporal.

Mohler, Alexander E., Kewanna, mustered Aug. 31, 1862, discharged Feb. 2, 1863.

Moler, William W., Kewanna, mustered Aug. 31, 1862, discharged Feb. 11, 1863.

Myers, John, Bruce Lake, mustered Aug. 31, 1862, mustered out June 10, 1865.

Myers, William, Bruce Lake, mustered Aug. 31, 1862, discharged Feb. 20, 1863.

Obermayer, Philip, Bruce Lake, mustered Aug. 31, 1862, died at home Oct. 16, 1863.

Powell, Jonas, Blue Grass, mustered Aug. 31, 1862, discharged Jan. 6, 1863.

Rairick, Henry, Rochester, mustered Aug. 31, 1862, mustered out June 10, 1865.

Rairick, William, Rochester, mustered Aug. 31, 1862, mustered out June 12, 1865.

Rans, Emanuel M., Blue Grass, mustered Aug. 31, 1862, mustered out May 29, 1865.

Rans, William, Blue Grass, mustered Aug. 31, 1862, mustered out June 10, 1865.

Rogers, Daniel M., Bruce Lake, mustered Aug. 31, 1862, transferred to Mississippi Marine Brigade, Jan. 1, 1863.

Ross, Henry S., Bruce Lake, mustered Aug. 31, 1862, mustered out June 10, 1865.

Rouch, George, Fulton, mustered Aug. 31, 1862, discharged Jan. 6, 1863.

Rush, Allen N., Blue Grass, mustered Aug. 31, 1862, mustered out June 10, 1865.

Rush, John W., Blue Grass, mustered Aug. 31, 1862, mustered out June 10, 1865, as sergeant.

Shreves, James, Plymouth, mustered Aug. 31, 1862, mustered out June 10, 1865.

Singer, George W., Kewanna, mustered Aug. 31, 1862, mustered out June 10, 1865.

Slight, Carrington G., Bruce Lake, mustered Aug. 31, 1862, died at Louisville, Ky., March 4, 1864.

Smith, Aaron, Blue Grass, mustered Aug. 31, 1862, killed at Chickamauga Sept. 20, 1863.

Smith, Austin B., Blue Grass, mustered Aug. 31, 1862, discharged Dec. 2, 1862.

Smith, Galon, Bruce Lake, mustered Aug. 31, 1862, mustered out June 10, 1865, as corporal.

Smith, George P., Blue Grass, mustered Aug. 31, 1862, discharged Dec. 24, 1862.

Smith, John R., Blue Grass, mustered Aug. 31, 1862, discharged Dec. 28, 1862.

Smith, Orlen, Bruce Lake, mustered Aug. 31, 1862, mustered out June 10, 1865.

Smith, Robert, Kewanna, mustered Aug. 31, 1862, died at Chattanooga, Tenn., Jan. 18, 1864.

Snider, Jacob, Blue Grass, mustered Aug. 31, 1862, discharged March 15, 1863.

Soper, Walter F., Bruce Lake, mustered Aug. 31, 1862, discharged Oct. 26, 1864, wounds.

Spotts, Adam, Fulton, mustered Aug. 31, 1862, died Dec. 19, 1862.

Spotts, William H., Fulton, mustered Aug. 31, 1862, mustered out June 10, 1865, as corporal.

Starr, Julius B., Logansport, mustered Aug. 31, 1862, mustered out June 10, 1865.

Thomas, James W., Bruce Lake, mustered Aug. 31, 1862, discharged Sept. 22, 1864.

Tribbett, Robert, Rochester, mustered Aug. 31, 1862, killed at Chickamauga Sept. 20, 1863.

Troutman, James T., Kewanna, mustered Aug. 31, 1862, mustered out June 10, 1865, as corporal.

Ummensetter, Charles, Star City, mustered Aug. 31, 1862, died at Gallatin, Tenn., Feb. 21, 1863.

Vandever, John H., Kewanna, mustered Aug. 31, 1862, promoted first lieutenant.

Ward, Garvin, Star City, mustered Aug. 31, 1862, died at Gallatin, Tenn., Dec. 12, 1862.

Warrick, Ephriam, Kewanna, mustered Aug. 31, 1862, died at Louisville, Ky., Dec. 12, 1862.

Williams, John E., Fulton, mustered Aug. 31, 1862, mustered out June 10, 1865.

Williams, Randolph, Kewanna, mustered Aug. 31, 1862, mustered out June 10, 1865.

Williams, Ransom T., Kewanna, mustered Aug. 31, 1862, transferred to V.R.C. April 10, 1864.

Witmer, Peter, Kewanna, mustered Aug. 31, 1862, deserted Oct. 3, 1862.

Yagle, John F., Star City, mustered Aug. 31, 1862, died at Chattanooga, Tenn., Oct. 14, 1863.

Recruits

Ackley, Jacob, LaPorte, mustered Sept. 19, 1863, transferred to 42nd Regiment June 9, 1865.

Aiken, Albert G., Kewanna, mustered Nov. 5, 1864, transferred to 42nd Regiment June 9, 1865.

Anderson, John, Kewanna, mustered March 8, 1864, transferred to 42nd Regiment June 9, 1865.

Baker, Theodore, Kewanna, mustered Feb. 22, 1864, transferred to 42nd Regiment June 9, 1865.

Ball, William J., Kewanna, mustered Nov. 12, 1863, mustered out July 18, 1865.

Bibler, Nathan, Kewanna, mustered Nov. 5, 1864, transferred to 42nd Regiment June 9, 1865.

Brown, Martin, Star City, mustered March 8, 1864, transferred to 42nd Regiment June 9, 1865.

Cannon, Daniel, Kewanna, mustered Nov. 12, 1864, died at Chattanooga, Tenn., Jan. 5, 1865.

Cannon, Joseph, Kewanna, mustered Nov. 12, 1864, transferred to 42nd Regiment June 9, 1865.

Collins, Allen, Kewanna, mustered Nov. 12, 1864, died at Cincinnati, Ohio, March 22, 1865.

Cooper, Alexander, Kewanna, mustered Nov. 5, 1864, transferred to 42nd Regiment June 9, 1865.

Detrick, Eli M., Kewanna, mustered Aug. 31, 1862, died at David's Island, N.Y.H., March 25, 1865.

Dukes, William D., Kewanna, mustered March 8, 1864, transferred to 42nd Regiment June 9, 1865.

Gherghwil, John, no city listed, mustered Nov. 12, 1864, transferred to 42nd Regiment June 9, 1865.

Harvey, James E., Kewanna, mustered March 8, 1864, transferred to 42nd Regiment June 9, 1865.

Hoover, Abraham, Blue Grass, mustered Sept. 3, 1864, mustered out June 10, 1865.

Hurst, James, Kewanna, mustered March 8, 1864, transferred to 42nd Regiment June 9, 1865.

Johnson, William F., Plymouth, mustered Sept. 22, 1864, discharged Aug. 3, 1865.

Kaler, George W., Kewanna, mustered Nov. 12, 1864, mustered out June 10, 1865.

Kilmer, James M., Kewanna, mustered March 8, 1864, transferred to 42nd Regiment June 9, 1865.

McCumber, Hiram, Blue Grass, mustered Feb. 16, 1864, transferred to 42nd Regiment June 9, 1865.

Minton, John G., Kewanna, mustered March 8, 1864, died at Nashville, Tenn., Sept. 16, 1864.

Oldham, Jesse D., Logansport, mustered March 8, 1864, transferred to 42nd Regiment June 9, 1865.

Pugh, Jared, Kewanna, mustered Nov. 12, 1864, transferred to 42nd Regiment June 9, 1865.

Seipert, Adam, Evansville, mustered Nov. 3, 1864, transferred to 42nd Regiment June 9, 1865.

Smith, Francis M., Blue Grass, mustered Feb. 10, 1864, transferred to 42nd Regiment June 9, 1865.

Smith, Jordan R., Blue Grass, mustered Feb. 10, 1864, mustered out July 19, 1865.

Torley, Samuel, Savannah, Ga., mustered Aug. 22, 1864, deserted Nov. 16, 1864.

Ulber, Ludwig, no city or muster date listed, transferred to 42nd Regiment June 9, 1865.

Ware, Philip, Blue Grass, mustered Feb. 10, 1864, mustered out July 26, 1865.

Wills, Philip H., LaPorte, mustered Sept. 19, 1863, transferred to 42nd Regiment June 9, 1865.

Wilson, Thomas, Kewanna, mustered Nov. 12, 1864, transferred to 42nd Regiment June 9, 1865.

Company F

Captain

Asa K. Plank, Rochester, commissioned Aug. 11, 1862, resigned Nov. 13, 1862.

George W. Truslow, Rochester, commissioned Nov. 14, 1862, resigned March 16, 1863.

Horace C. Long, Rochester, commissioned March 17, 1863, mustered out with regiment.

First Lieutenant

George W. Truslow, Rochester, commissioned Aug. 11, 1862, promoted captain.

David Mow, Rochester, commissioned Nov. 14, 1862, resigned Jan. 8, 1863.

Horace C. Long, Rochester, commissioned Jan. 9, 1863, promoted captain.

Jacob H. Leiter, Rochester, commissioned March 17, 1863, honorably discharged April 25, 1865; cause, disability from wounds.

Joseph W. Beeber, Indianapolis, commissioned April 26, 1865, mustered out with regiment.

Second Lieutenant

David Mow, Rochester, commissioned Aug. 11, 1862, promoted first lieutenant.

Horace C. Long, Rochester, commissioned Nov. 14, 1862, promoted first lieutenant.

Jacob H. Leiter, Rochester, commissioned Jan. 19, 1863, promoted first lieutenant.

Joseph W. Beeber, Indianapolis, commissioned March 17, 1863, promoted first lieutenant.

Jonas Myers, Rochester, commissioned May 1, 1865, mustered out with regiment as first sergeant.

First Sergeant

Long, Horace C., Rochester, mustered Aug. 9, 1862, promoted first lieutenant.

Sergeants

Beeber, Joseph W., Rochester, mustered Aug. 9, 1862, promoted second lieutenant.

Leiter, Jacob H., Rochester, mustered Aug. 9, 1862, promoted second lieutenant.

Pugh, Albert G., Rochester, mustered Aug. 9, 1862, mustered out June 10, 1865, as private.

Corporals

Califf, Jewell, Rochester, mustered Aug. 8, 1862, died Nov. 14, 1862.

Jewel, Silas C., Rochester, mustered Aug. 8, 1862, discharged Jan. 25, 1863.

Lawhead, Banner, Rochester, mustered Aug. 12, 1862, mustered out June 10, 1865, as sergeant major.

League, James H., Rochester, mustered Aug. 8, 1862, mustered out June 10, 1865, as private.

Patton, Benjamin B., Rochester, mustered Aug. 8, 1862, mustered out June 10, 1865, as private.

Squires, Jasper W., Rochester, mustered Aug. 8, 1862, mustered out June 10, 1865.

Storm, William H., Rochester, mustered Aug. 8, 1862, transferred to V.R.C., mustered out June 30, 1865.

Musicians

Ellis, James S., Rochester, mustered Aug. 11, 1862, deserted Oct. 20, 1862.

Townsend, Isaac S., Rochester, mustered Aug. 11, 1862, died Nov. 8, 1863.

Wagoner

Wilson, James N., Rochester, mustered Aug. 8, 1862, discharged April 10, 1863.

Privates

Alleman, William H., Rochester, mustered Aug. 9, 1862, mustered out June 10, 1865, as corporal.

Apt, John, Rochester, mustered Aug. 12, 1862, mustered out June 10, 1865.

Apt, Peter B., Rochester, mustered Aug. 12, 1862, mustered out June 10, 1865.

Apt, William, Rochester, mustered Aug. 12, 1862, mustered out June 10, 1865.

Babcock, James J., Rochester, mustered Aug. 12, 1862, mustered out June 10, 1865, as corporal.

Barnhart, Daniel, Rochester, mustered Aug. 12, 1862, discharged Feb. 1, 1863.

Barnhart, Thomas, Rochester, mustered Aug. 12, 1862, transferred to V.R.C. Feb. 15, 1864.

Barrett, James, Rochester, mustered Aug. 11, 1862, transferred to V.R.C. Feb. 15, 1864.

Batchelor, Asa E., Rochester, mustered Aug. 8, 1862, mustered out June 10, 1865, as sergeant.

Berrier, Samuel A., Rochester, mustered Aug. 12, 1862, mustered out June 10, 1865.

Berry, Samuel P., Rochester, mustered Aug. 11, 1862, mustered out June 10, 1865.

Beverly, Stanford, Rochester, mustered Aug. 8, 1862, transferred to V.R.C. Feb. 15, 1864.

Capp, George C., Rochester, mustered Aug. 9, 1862, discharged Sept. 21, 1863.

Carpenter, Hamlin, Rochester, mustered Aug. 8, 1862, mustered out June 10, 1865.

Cates, John E., Rochester, mustered Aug. 8, 1862, mustered out June 10, 1865.

Chinn, Edward B., Rochester, mustered Aug. 8, 1862, discharged Dec. 31, 1862.

Clay, Clement W., Rochester, mustered Aug. 8, 1862, mustered out June 10, 1865, as sergeant.

Clay, Jonathan, Rochester, mustered Aug. 8, 1862, mustered out May 31, 1865.

Crain, John, Rochester, mustered Aug. 12, 1862, mustered out May 23, 1865.

Drake, Franklin, Rochester, mustered Aug. 12, 1862, deserted March 20, 1863.

Dunlap, John N., Rochester, mustered Aug. 12, 1862, mustered out June 10, 1865.

Farry, William R., Rochester, mustered Aug. 11, 1862, transferred to V.R.C.

Frear, Simeon J., Rochester, mustered Aug. 12, 1862, mustered out June 10, 1865.

Gainer, James T., Rochester, mustered Aug. 12, 1862, mustered out June 10, 1865.

Goodrich, Alfred L., Rochester, mustered Aug. 11, 1862, mustered out June 10, 1865.

Gripp, Peter, Rochester, mustered Aug. 11, 1862, discharged Dec. 15, 1863.

Gylam, Frederick, Rochester, mustered Aug. 12, 1862, discharged Feb. 26, 1863.

Hatfield, Henry, Rochester, mustered Aug. 11, 1862, discharged April 27, 1863.

Heikman, Clarkson S., Rochester, mustered Aug. 11, 1862, mustered out May 27, 1865.

Heikman, Lemuel H., Rochester, mustered Aug. 11, 1862, mustered out June 10, 1865.

Hoffman, Peter, Rochester, mustered Aug. 12, 1862, mustered out June 10, 1865.

House, John, Rochester, mustered Aug. 12, 1862, killed at Chickamauga Sept. 20, 1863.

Hunter, William, Rochester, mustered Aug. 11, 1862, discharged May 14, 1863.

Jinkens, Levi, Rochester, mustered Aug. 12, 1862, mustered out June 10, 1865.

Kessler, George, Rochester, mustered Aug. 8, 1862, mustered out June 10, 1865.

Kessler, George W., Rochester, mustered Aug. 8, 1862, discharged April 11, 1863.

Kessler, John, Rochester, mustered Aug. 11, 1862, discharged March 21, 1863.

Kessler, Simeon, Rochester, mustered Aug. 8, 1862, mustered out June 10, 1865.

Leise, Jacob, Rochester, mustered Aug. 11, 1862, died April 14, 1863.

Loomis, George, Rochester, mustered Aug. 11, 1862, discharged Jan. 20, 1863.

Love, Joseph A., Rochester, mustered Aug. 11, 1862, mustered out June 10, 1865.

Mackey, Shannon, Rochester, mustered Aug. 11, 1862, mustered out June 10, 1865, as absent sick.

Martindale, Jesse L., Rochester, mustered Aug. 11, 1862, discharged Jan. 7, 1863.

McAlexander, Robert, Rochester, mustered Aug. 12, 1862, mustered out June 10, 1865.

McElfresh, Benjamin, Rochester, mustered Aug. 12, 1862, died April 15, 1865.

McFall, Austin W., Rochester, mustered Aug. 8, 1862, discharged Dec. 15, 1862.

McMahan, James L., Rochester, mustered Aug. 8, 1862, discharged Jan. 7, 1863.

Mickey, Hiram, Rochester, mustered Aug. 11, 1862, mustered out June 10, 1865.

Middleton, Lewis D., Rochester, mustered Aug. 12, 1862, mustered out June 10, 1865.

Mow, James E., Rochester, mustered Aug. 12, 1862, died Jan. 16, 1863.

Mow, John O., Rochester, mustered Aug. 11, 1862, discharged Dec. 10, 1862.

Myers, Jonas, Rochester, mustered Aug. 8, 1862, promoted second lieutenant.

Paschall, Henry, Rochester, mustered Aug. 8, 1862, mustered out June 10, 1865.

Pence, William, Rochester, mustered Aug. 12, 1862, discharged Dec. 10, 1862.

Pentz, William A., Rochester, mustered Aug. 12, 1862, died March 24, 1863.

Platt, Henry, Rochester, mustered Aug. 11, 1862, mustered out June 10, 1865, as sergeant.

Realstin, John, Rochester, mustered Aug. 8, 1862, discharged May 11, 1863.

Reid, John M., Rochester, mustered Aug. 11, 1862, discharged March 2, 1863.

Rhodes, Otho N., Rochester, mustered Aug. 11, 1862, discharged Jan. 1, 1863.

Rimenschneider, Adam, Rochester, mustered Aug. 12, 1862, mustered out June 10, 1865, as corporal.

Robbins, Jonathan H., Rochester, mustered Aug. 11, 1862, discharged March 9, 1865.

Rodgers, Harper, Rochester, mustered Aug. 8, 1862, died April 17, 1864.

Roth, John, Rochester, mustered Aug. 12, 1862, mustered out June 10, 1865, as corporal.

Rugh, Andrew J., Rochester, mustered Aug. 11, 1862, discharged Jan. 15, 1863.

Short, Edward, Rochester, mustered Aug. 8, 1862, mustered out June 10, 1865.

Smith, Benjamin F., Rochester, mustered Aug. 12, 1862, mustered out June 10, 1865.

Smith, Dennis R., Rochester, mustered Aug. 12, 1862, died Jan. 25, 1863.

Smith, Joseph J., Rochester, mustered Aug. 11, 1862, mustered out June 10, 1865.

Squires, James W., Rochester, mustered Aug. 11, 1862, mustered out June 10, 1865.

Stahl, Jacob M., Rochester, mustered Aug. 8, 1862, discharged Feb. 26, 1863.

Stoops, Madison, Rochester, mustered Aug. 12, 1862, mustered out June 17, l865.

Stotler, Harrison, Rochester, mustered Aug. 9, 1862, discharged Dec. 21, 1863.

Swartz, William W., Rochester, mustered Aug. 12, 1862, died June 24, 1863.

Taylor, Joseph B., Rochester, mustered Aug. 8, 1862, transferred to V.R.C. Jan. 10, 1865.

Toothman, George, Rochester, mustered Aug. 11, 1862, mustered out June 10, 1865.

True, Jasper, Rochester, mustered Aug. 12, 1862, no further information listed.

Walker, Harrison, mustered Aug. 12, 1862, discharged Feb. 25, 1863.

Webb, Isaiah D., Rochester, mustered Aug. 12, 1862, died of wounds received Oct. 18, 1863.

White, Samuel W., Rochester, mustered Aug. 12, 1862, discharged July 18, 1863.

Zolman, Elias, Rochester, mustered Aug. 11, 1862, died in hospital Dec. 14, 1862.

Recruits

Anderson, John B., Rochester, mustered March 30, 1864, deserted Aug. 15, 1864.

Antrim, Samuel, no city listed, mustered Oct. 13, 1864, mustered out July 27, 1865, substitute.

Apt, Frederick, Rochester, mustered Nov. 12, 1864, transferred to 42nd Regiment June 9, 1865.

Baker, Alfred S., Rochester, mustered March 5, 1864, transferred to 42nd Regiment June 9, 1865.

Berry, Louis E., Rochester, mustered March 5, 1864, died May 3, 1865.

Braman, James W., Rochester, mustered Jan. 25, 1864, transferred to 42nd Regiment June 9, 1865.

Branneller, Augustus, Gilead, mustered Jan. 12, 1864, transferred to 42nd Regiment June 9, 1865.

Carter, Thomas, Rochester, mustered March 5, 1864, transferred to 42nd Regiment June 9, 1865.

Collins, Joseph S., Rochester, mustered March 5, 1864, transferred to 42nd Regiment June 9, 1865.

Collins, Palmer, Rochester, mustered March 30, 1864, mustered out May 12, 1865.

Corey, William D., Rochester, mustered Feb. 9, 1865, transferred to 42nd Regiment June 9, 1865.

Cripe, John, Rochester, mustered July 17, 1863, died Dec. 13, 1863.

Davis, Lewis, Rochester, mustered March 5, 1864, transferred to 42nd Regiment June 9, 1865.

Deweese, James R., Rochester, mustered Jan. 10, 1864, mustered out June 10, 1865.

Evans, Benjamin F., Rochester, mustered March 30, 1864, died Aug. 2, 1864.

Evans, Ratcliff B., Rochester, mustered July 17, 1863, discharged Dec. 10, 1863.

Ferguson, John T., no city listed, mustered Sept. 28, 1864, transferred 42nd Regiment June 9, 1865, substitute.

Fisher, David C., Gilead, mustered Jan. 13, 1864, mustered out July 7, 1865.

Flippin, William, no city listed, mustered Nov. 1, 1864, transferred 42nd Regiment June 9, 1865, substitute.

Fobar, George W., no city listed, mustered Oct. 19, 1864, transferred 42nd Regiment June 9, 1865, substitute.

Henry, Michael, Rochester, mustered May 30, 1864, transferred to 42nd Regiment June 9, 1865.

Irvin, William, Rochester, mustered March 30, 1864, killed near Acworth, Ga., June 14, 1864.

McCarter, William, Rochester, mustered March 30, 1864, transferred to 42nd Regiment June 9, 1865.

Miller, George O., Rochester, mustered May 5, 1864, died at home March 20, 1865.

Moore, Theodore, Rochester, mustered March 30, 1864, transferred to 42nd Regiment June 9, 1865.

Rhodes, John S., Rochester, mustered March 5, 1864, transferred to 42nd Regiment June 9, 1865.

Richardson, James, Rochester, mustered March 5, 1864, transferred to 42nd Regiment June 9, 1865.

Robinson, Asa, Rochester, mustered March 5, 1864, transferred to 42nd Regiment June 9, 1865.

Ross, Benjamin F., Rochester, mustered March 5, 1864, transferred to 42nd Regiment June 9, 1865.

Shelpman, Robert D., Rochester, mustered March 5, 1864, transferred to 42nd Regiment June 9, 1865.

Stringham, Willard, Rochester, mustered March 5, 1864, transferred to 42nd Regiment June 9, 1865.

Thompson, John W., Gilead, mustered Jan. 13, 1864, transferred to 42nd Regiment June 9, 1865.

Toothman, Russell, Rochester, mustered Jan. 13, 1864, transferred to 42nd Regiment June 9, 1865.

Vanankin, Charles, LaPorte, mustered Sept. 19, 1863, transferred to 42nd Regiment June 9, 1865.

Wallace, Andrew E., Rochester, mustered March 5, 1864, transferred to 42nd Regiment June 9, 1865.

Walters, Henry, Rochester, mustered March 5, 1864, transferred to 42nd Regiment June 9, 1865.

Walters, John F., Rochester, mustered March 5, 1864, mustered out May 25, 1865.

Walts, John, Rochester, mustered July 17, 1863, died Dec. 22, 1863.

Wertz, Seymour, Rochester, mustered March 5, 1864, killed at Atlanta, Ga., Aug. 5, 1864.

Young, Daniel, Rochester, mustered March 30, 1864, mustered out July 28, 1865.

Company G

Captain

Alanson T. Bliss, LaPorte, commissioned Aug. 13, 1862, resigned Feb. 15, 1864.

William Poole, Star City, commissioned May 1, 1864, mustered out with regiment.

First Lieutenant

Theodore Woodward, LaPorte, commissioned Aug. 13, 1862, resigned July 22, 1863.

Isaac S. Stockman, Rolling Prairie, commissioned July 23, 1863, resigned April 6, 1864.

George Urquhart, LaPorte, commissioned May 1, 1864, mustered out with regiment.

Second Lieutenant

David W. Dratt, LaPorte, commissioned Aug. 13, 1862, resigned April 15, 1863.

Isaac S. Stockman, Rolling Prairie, commissioned April 16, 1863, promoted first lieutenant.

John F. Cannell, LaPorte, commissioned May 1, 1865, mustered out with regiment as first sergeant.

First Sergeant

Harding, Solomon E., LaPorte, mustered Aug. 31, 1862, killed at Chickamauga Sept. 20, 1863.

Sergeants

Dowd, John H., LaPorte, mustered Aug. 31, 1862, mustered out June 10, 1865.

Harding, Thomas D., LaPorte, mustered Aug. 31, 1862, discharged Nov. 13, 1863.

Stockman, Isaac S., LaPorte, mustered Aug. 31, 1862, discharged Nov. 3, 1863.

Corporals

Burden, James, LaPorte, mustered Aug. 31, 1862, died at Tunnel Hill, Ga., Dec. 9, 1862.

Dudley, Henry H., LaPorte, mustered Aug. 31, 1862, mustered out June 10, 1865.

Dunham, George A., Michigan City, mustered Aug. 31, 1862, died at Manchester, Tenn., July 4, 1863.

Miller, Jacob V., LaPorte, mustered Aug. 31, 1862, discharged March 20, 1863.

Prince, William C., Rochester, mustered Aug. 31, 1862, died at Nashville, Tenn., March 15, 1863.

Sales, Thomas A., LaPorte, mustered Aug. 31, 1862, discharged April 29, 1863.

Scholts, David, Door Village, mustered Aug. 31, 1862, died at LaPorte, Ind., Dec. 7, 1863.

Musicians

Culp, Johnson W., LaPorte, mustered Aug. 31, 1862, discharged July 30, 1863.

Hooten, Benjamin F., New Carlisle, mustered Aug. 31, 1862, died at Indianapolis July 15, 1863.

Wagoner

Closser, Jerome B., LaPorte, mustered Aug. 31, 1862, discharged Jan. 27, 1863.

Privates

Allen, Laren, Callao, mustered Aug. 31, 1862, transferred to V.R.C., mustered out June 30, 1865.

Andrews, Robert S., no city listed, mustered Aug. 31, 1862, deserted Feb. 2, 1863.

Baker, Henry, LaPorte, mustered Aug. 31, l862, killed at Chickamauga Sept. 19, 1863.

Berget, Charles, New Durham, mustered Aug. 31, 1862, mustered out June 10, 1865, as corporal.

Billman, William, LaPorte, mustered Aug. 31, 1862, discharged, no date listed.

Brown, Frank, Almond, N.Y., mustered Aug. 31, 1862, mustered out June 10, 1865 as commissary sergeant.

Campbell, Charles, LaPorte, mustered Aug. 31, 1862, discharged Feb. 2, 1863.

Cannel, John F., LaPorte, mustered Aug. 31, 1862, mustered out June 10, 1865, as first sergeant.

Casgriff, Arthur, LaPorte, mustered Aug. 31, 1862, died at Nashville, Tenn., Feb. 18, 1864.

Cherry, Joseph,Waterford, mustered Aug. 31, 1862, died in Richmond, Va., prison, Jan. (no date), 1864.

Chronister, Joseph A., LaPorte, mustered Aug. 31, 1862, died at Nashville, Tenn., March 17, 1863.

Cloper, Joseph A., LaPorte, mustered Aug. 31, 1862, transferred to V.R.C., mustered out June 30, 1865.

Cole, Andrew, no city listed, mustered Aug. 31, 1862, died at Chattanooga, Tenn., Sept. 30, 1863.

Cornell, Charles, LaPorte, mustered Aug. 31, 1862, discharged Jan. 20, 1863.

Croll, August, LaPorte, mustered Aug. 31, 1862, discharged March 17, l863.

Cruzen, William, LaPorte, mustered Aug. 31, 1862, discharged Feb. 28, 1863.

Dauphin, Nicholas, LaPorte, mustered Aug. 31, 1862, discharged Dec. 6, 1862.

Davis, James H., LaPorte, mustered Aug. 31, 1862, discharged Nov. 24, 1862.

Day, Alden E., Waterford, mustered Aug. 31, 1862, mustered out June 10, 1865, as corporal.

Dudley, Milton, LaPorte, mustered Aug. 31, 1862, mustered out June 10, 1865.

Dunn, Henry, LaPorte, mustered Aug. 31, 1862, died at Stevenson, Ala., Jan. 30, 1864.

Fessendon, Major, LaPorte, mustered Aug. 31, 1862, discharged Feb. 1, 1863.

Fisher, Thomas, LaPorte, mustered Aug. 31, 1862, killed at Chattanooga, Tenn., Nov. 25, 1863.

Fogle, Jacob R., LaPorte, mustered Aug. 31, 1862, discharged Jan. 17, 1863.

Garner, John, no city listed, mustered Aug. 31, 1862, killed at Chickamauga Sept. 20, 1863.

Gilfoyle, Michael, LaPorte, mustered Aug. 31, 1862, killed at Chickamauga Sept. 19, 1863.

Graves, William H., LaPorte, mustered Aug. 31, 1862, discharged July 27, 1863.

Jacobos, Andrew J., LaPorte, mustered Aug. 31, 1862, discharged Jan. 17, 1863.

Jones, Aaron S., LaPorte, mustered Aug. 31, 1862, mustered out June 10, 1865; absent without leave.

Jones, Adam B., LaPorte, mustered Aug. 31, 1862, mustered out June 10, 1865.

Knapp, Hiram, Callao, mustered Aug. 31, 1862, mustered out June 10, 1865.

Leiper, Abraham, Callao, mustered Aug. 31, 1862, killed at Chickamauga Sept. 20, 1863.

Lightfoot, Eli II, LaPorte, mustered Aug. 31, 1862, discharged March 29, 1863.

Lightfoot, Enoch, LaPorte, mustered Aug. 31, 1862, died at Stevenson, Ala., Oct. 10, 1863.

Lockwood, Morgan, Callao, mustered Aug. 31, 1862, mustered out June 10, 1865, as sergeant.

McCarty, Patrick, Plainfield, mustered Aug. 31, 1862, killed at Chickamauga Sept. 20, 1863.

McConeghey, Samuel, no city listed, mustered Aug. 31, 1862, died at Gallatin, Tenn., Jan. 18, 1863.

McDonald, Ebenezer, LaPorte, mustered Aug. 31, 1862, discharged Feb. 20, 1863.

McNeal, Isaac, no city listed, mustered Aug. 31, 1862, died at Nashville, Tenn., Jan. 2, 1864.

Moffit, Ephraim, New Carlisle, mustered Aug. 31, 1862, died at Gallatin, Tenn., Jan. 25, 1863.

Montgomery, Thomas, New Carlisle, mustered Aug. 31, 1862, mustered out June 10, 1865.

Moore, Robert, LaPorte, mustered Aug. 31, 1862, mustered out June 10, 1865.

Moore, Thomas, LaPorte, mustered Aug. 31, 1862, discharged Jan. 25, 1863.

Pointer, Thomas, LaPorte, mustered Aug. 31, 1862, died at Chattanooga, Tenn., Dec. 3, 1863.

Pointer, William, LaPorte, mustered Aug. 31, 1862, killed at Chickamauga Sept. 20, 1863.

Powers, Lewis, Rolling Prairie, mustered Aug. 31, 1862, died at Chattanooga, Tenn., Nov. 18, 1863.

Pratt, Alexander, Callao, mustered Aug. 31, 1862, mustered out June 10, 1865.

Prince, Amos M., Rochester, mustered Aug. 31, 1862, killed at Chickamauga Sept. 19, 1863.

Prince, Liman, LaPorte, mustered Aug. 31, 1862, died at Gallatin, Tenn., Dec. 10, 1862.

Rader, James H., Peru, mustered Aug. 31, 1862, mustered out June 10, 1865.

Rice, George, LaPorte, mustered Aug. 31, 1862, mustered out June 10, 1865.

Roach, Michael, Rolling Prairie, mustered Aug. 31, 1862, mustered out June 10, 1865.

Rody, John, LaPorte, mustered Aug. 31, 1862, killed at Chickamauga Sept. 20, 1863.

Rogers, Amos, New Carlisle, mustered Aug. 31, 1862, transferred to Veteran Engineer Corps.

Roof, John M., South Bend, mustered Aug. 31, 1862, transferred to V.R.C., mustered out July 8, 1865.

Sharp, Benjamin, LaPorte, mustered Aug. 31, 1862, died at Louisville, Ky., Dec. 7, 1862.

Siddles, John A., LaPorte, mustered Aug. 31, 1862, died at Danville, Va., Nov. 29, 1864.

Singleton, Stephen, Tyner City, mustered Aug. 31, 1862, mustered out June 10, 1865.

Smootzer, Charles, Michigan City, mustered Aug. 31, 1862, died at Chattanooga, Tenn., Sept. 25, 1863.

Stark, John, LaPorte, mustered Aug. 31, 1862, deserted Oct. 6, 1862.

Stillmen, Allen G., Williamsport, mustered Aug. 31, 1862, mustered out June 10, 1865, as sergeant.

Urquhart, George, LaPorte, mustered Aug. 31, 1862, discharged July 13, 1864.

Vantassel, Alonzo, LaPorte, mustered Aug. 31, 1862, mustered out June 10, 1865, as corporal.

Vantassel, Andrew, LaPorte, mustered Aug. 31, 1862, discharged Dec. 17, 1862.

Warberton, Peter, LaPorte, mustered Aug. 31, 1862, killed at Chickamauga Sept. 20, 1863.

Wariner, Ory, Rolling Prairie, mustered Aug. 31, 1862, transferred to Marine Brigade April 22, 1864.

Young, Martin, Waterford, mustered Aug. 31, 1862, mustered out June 10, 1865.

Recruits

Ames, James S., no city or muster date listed, transferred to 42nd Regiment June 9, 1865, substitute.

Brenion, Charles, no city listed, mustered Oct. 28, 1864, transferred to 42nd Regiment June 9, 1865, substitute.

Brown, William, Markle, mustered Feb. 15, 1864, transferred to 42nd Regiment June 9, 1865.

Burgett, Philip, LaPorte, mustered Dec. 25, 1863, transferred to 42nd Regiment June 9, 1865.

Clemmons, Archibald, no city listed, Oct. 20, 1864, died at Savannah, Ga., Jan. 25, 1865, substitute.

Easterday, John, no city listed, mustered Sept. 26, 1864, mustered out June 10, 1865, drafted.

Farmer, Harrison E., no city listed, mustered Oct. 10, 1864, transferred 42nd Regiment June 9, 1865, substitute.

Grow, William, no city listed, mustered Sept. 22, 1864, mustered out June 10, 1865, drafted.

Huey, Andrew J., no city listed, mustered Oct. 28, 1864, transferred to 42nd Regiment June 9, 1865, substitute.

Hughs, Andrew J., no city or muster date listed, transferred to 42nd Regiment June 9, 1865.

John, Charles F., no city or muster date listed, transferred to 42nd Regiment June 9, 1865, substitute.

Jones, Jacob, no city listed, mustered Oct. 15, 1864, mustered out June 10, 1865, as absent sick.

Keefe, Morris, no city listed, mustered Sept. 22, 1864, mustered out June 10, 1865, drafted.

Lang, Jacob, no city listed, mustered Nov. 3, 1864, mustered out June 10, 1865, substitute.

Marks, Thomas B., no city listed, mustered Oct. 28, 1864, mustered out June 10, 1865, absent sick, substitute.

Maulsby, George B., no city or muster date listed, transferred to 42nd Regiment June 9, 1865.

McAfferty, John, no city listed, mustered Sept. 22, 1864, mustered out June 10, 1865, drafted.

McClelland, William G., no city listed, mustered out Oct. 17, 1864, transferred to 42nd Regiment June 9, 1865, substitute.

Miller, Jacob V., LaPorte, mustered Dec. 25, 1863, died at Lookout Mountain, Tenn., Aug. 28, 1864.

Molter, William, no city or muster date listed, transferred to 42nd Regiment June 9, 1865, substitute.

Moulton, Levi, no city listed, mustered Oct. 17, 1864, transferred to 42nd Regiment June 9, 1865, substitute.

Mulanix, John, no city listed, mustered Oct. 13, 1864, transferred to 42nd Regiment June 9, 1865, substitute.

Oldham, Sanford H., no city listed, mustered Oct. 14, 1864, transferred to 42nd Regiment June 9, 1865, substitute.

Peachee, Benjamin, no city listed, mustered Sept. 22, 1864, mustered out June 10, 1865.

Sherley, Jack, no city listed, mustered Oct. 24, 1864, transferred to 42nd Regiment June 9, 1865, substitute.

Thomas, Morris, no city listed, mustered Oct. 17, 1864, transferred to 42nd Regiment June 9, 1865, substitute.

Wathers, William F., no city listed, mustered Sept. 26, 1864, mustered out June 10, 1865, drafted.

Young, John, no city listed, mustered Oct. 8, 1864, transferred to 42nd Regiment June 9, 1865, substitute.

Company H

Captain
Richard C. Sabin, LaPorte, commissioned Aug. 18, 1862, promoted major.
William B. Biddle, LaPorte, commissioned Jan. 21, 1864, brevetted major U.S. Volunteers May 13, 1865, mustered out with regiment.

First Lieutenant
Sloan D. Martin, Westville, commissioned Aug. 18, 1862, killed at Chickamauga Sept. 19, 1863.
Albert C. Logan, Union Mills, commissioned Sept. 20, 1863, mustered out with regiment.

Second Lieutenant
James S. Durett, Peru, commissioned Aug. 18, 1862, resigned Oct. 18, 1862.
John E. Selleck, Union Mills, commissioned Oct. 19, 1862, promoted adjutant.
Ira Way, Union Mills, commissioned May 1, 1865, mustered out with regiment as first sergeant.

First Sergeant
Selleck, John E., Union Mills, mustered Aug. 31, 1862, promoted second lieutenant.

Sergeants
Andrews, Amos B., Chili, mustered Aug. 31, 1862, mustered out June 10, 1865.
Bowman, John W., Chili, mustered Aug. 31, 1862, mustered out June 10, 1865.
Logan, Albert C., Union Mills, mustered Aug. 31, 1862, promoted first lieutenant.
Loomis, Henry B., Union Mills, mustered Aug. 31, 1862, discharged Jan. 10, 1863.

Corporals
Brown, Henry C., Union Mills, mustered Aug. 31, 1862, arm amputated, mustered out June 10, 1865, as sergeant.
Johnson, Elijah, Bradford, mustered Aug. 31, 1862, mustered out June 10, 1865, as private.
Martin, Alexander A., Westville, mustered Aug. 31, 1862, transferred to V.R.C.

Miller, George B., Pawpaw, mustered Aug. 31, 1862, mustered out June 10, 1865.

Moorehouse, Hiram B., Brookston, mustered Aug. 31, 1862, mustered out June 6, 1865.

Poston, John A., Westville, mustered Aug. 31, 1862, discharged Dec. 29, 1862.

Way, Ira, Union Mills, mustered Aug. 31, 1862, mustered out June 6, 1865, as first sergeant.

Weed, Chancellor, Westville, mustered Aug. 31, 1862, transferred to V.R.C.

Musicians

Powls, Levi W., no city listed, mustered Aug. 31, 1862, transferred to Company I Sept. 24, 1862.

Wagoner

Carter, Charles W., no city listed, mustered Aug. 31, 1862, discharged Dec. 6, 1862.

Privates

Allen, Silas, Westville, mustered Aug. 31, 1862, mustered out June 10, 1865, as sergeant.

Armantrout, John S., Chili, mustered Aug. 31, 1862, mustered out June 10, 1865.

Ash, James G., Union Mills, mustered Aug. 31, 1862, discharged Jan. 6, 1864.

Bare, George W., Monticello, mustered Aug. 31, 1862, died at Bowling Green, Ky., Dec. 13, 1862.

Blackman, Homer O., Union Mills, mustered Aug. 31, 1862, transferred to Engineer Corps July 29, 1864.

Blodgett, Henry H., Union Mills, mustered Aug. 31, 1862, died at Nashville, Tenn., March 31, 1863.

Bonsman, Foreman, Rensselaer, mustered Aug. 31, 1862, mustered out June 10, 1865.

Bonsman, George W., Rensselaer, mustered Aug. 31, 1862, discharged Feb. 7, 1863.

Brown, Andrew P., no city listed, mustered Aug. 31, 1862, discharged Feb. 12, 1863.

Brown, Willard A., no city listed, mustered Aug. 31, 1862, died at Stevenson, Ala., Oct. 30, 1863, wounds.

Bryson, Ephraim M., Westville, mustered Aug. 31, 1862, mustered out June 10, 1865, as corporal.

Carpenter, Emory, Union Mills, mustered Aug. 31, 1862, discharged Jan. 27, 1863.

Carpenter, Leonard, Union Mills, mustered Aug. 31, 1862, discharged Feb. 18, 1863.

Catlin, John B., Union Mills, mustered Aug. 31, 1862, promoted captain of Company I.

Dunham, Ambrose, no city listed, mustered Aug. 31, 1862, mustered out June 10, 1865.

Dunham, George B., no city listed, mustered Aug. 31, 1862, mustered out June 10, 1865.

Dunham, Jonathan O., no city listed, mustered Aug. 31, 1862, mustered out June 10, 1865.

Dunnick, John A., Monticello, mustered Aug. 31, 1862, died at Gallatin, Tenn., Jan. 2, 1863.

Ewing, William A., Westville, mustered Aug. 31, 1862, dropped as a deserter.

Fierce, Henry, Westville, mustered Aug. 31, 1862, transferred to V.R.C., mustered out June 29, 1865.

Fierce, William W., Westville, mustered Aug. 31, 1862, discharged, no date listed.

Finch, Eddy S., Union Mills, mustered Aug. 31, 1862, mustered out June 10, 1865.

Fires, David, Peru, mustered Aug. 31, 1862, mustered out June 10, 1865.

Fletcher, Franklin, Union Mills, mustered Aug. 31, 1862, discharged Jan. 22, 1863.

Gee, John F., Westville, mustered Aug. 31, 1862, discharged Feb. 27, 1863.

Gray, Robert, Monticello, mustered Aug. 31, 1862, discharged Jan. 8, 1864.

Hall, Charles H., Westville, mustered Aug. 31, 1862, died at Louisville, Ky., Oct. 2, 1863.

Harsen, Sylvester D., mustered Aug. 31, 1862, discharged, no date listed.

Hass, William, Westville, mustered Aug. 31, 1862, discharged Feb. 22, 1863.

Herman, Richard B., Burnettsville, mustered Aug. 31, 1862, died at Nashville, Tenn., March 3, 1863.

Jerome, Samuel, Burnettsville, mustered Aug. 31, 1862, mustered out June 10, 1865.

Jones, John M., Union Mills, mustered Aug. 31, 1862, mustered out June 13, 1865.

Kavanough, James, Logansport, mustered Aug. 31, 1862, mustered out June 10, 1865, as corporal.

Kelley, Willis H., Monticello, mustered Aug. 31, 1862, died at Nashville, Tenn., April 3, 1863.

King, George, Chili, mustered Aug. 31, 1862, mustered out June 10, 1865.

Lash, Simon P., Chili, mustered Aug. 31, 1862, discharged Jan. 2, 1863.

Leazenby, Jacob H., Monticello, mustered Aug. 31, 1862, discharged Aug. 3, 1863.

Linard, Daniel J., Union Mills, mustered Aug. 31, 1862, mustered out June 15, 1865.

Lynch, Webster, Union Mills, mustered Aug. 31, 1862, mustered out June 10, 1865, as hospital steward.

Mahanny, Daniel, Union Mills, mustered Aug. 31, 1862, discharged Feb. 17, 1863.

Malony, John, Rensselaer, mustered Aug. 31, 1862, died at Madison, Ind., April 5, 1864.

Manderville, Abram C., Westville, mustered Aug. 31, 1862, discharged March 29, 1865, wounds.

McNarry, Warren, Monticello, mustered Aug. 31, 1862, discharged April 18, 1863.

Miller, William S., Union Mills, mustered Aug. 31, 1862, died at South Tunnel, Tenn., Nov. 19, 1862.

Mincher, William, Brookston, mustered Aug. 31, 1862, mustered out July 12, 1865.

Neihardt, William, Union Mills, mustered Aug. 31, 1862, mustered out June 10, 1865.

Nelson, Isaac N., Union Mills, mustered Aug. 31, 1862, transferred to Engineer Corps July 24, 1864.

O'Brien, James, Union Mills, mustered Aug. 31, 1862, mustered out June 10, 1865.

Pierson, James W., Westville, mustered Aug. 31, 1862, mustered out June 10, 1865, as corporal.

Pitcher, Alonzo, Westville, mustered Aug. 31, 1862, died at Chattanooga, Tenn., Oct. 11, 1863.

Poston, Elias B., Westville, mustered Aug. 31, 1862, mustered out June 10, 1865.

Pratt, Eugene A., Union Mills, mustered Aug. 31, 1862, killed at Chickamauga Sept. 19, 1863.

Ramey, Isaac S., Brookston, mustered Aug. 31, 1862, mustered out June 10, 1865.

Ramey, Joseph N., Brookston, mustered Aug. 31, 1862, mustered out June 10, 1865.

Richards, Oren M., Union Mills, mustered Aug. 31, 1862, discharged Feb. 8, 1863.

St. Ledger, John, Logansport, mustered Aug. 31, 1862, mustered out June 10, 1865.

Schermehorn, Jacob E., Westville, mustered Aug. 31, 1862, dropped as a deserter.

Steele, Hugh H., Monticello, mustered Aug. 31, 1862, mustered out June 10, 1865.

Steele, Samuel S., Monticello, mustered Aug. 31, 1862, mustered out June 10, 1865.

Taylor, John S., Union Mills, mustered Aug. 31, 1862, discharged Feb. 19, 1863.

Titus, Nelson J., Union Mills, mustered Aug. 31, 1862, mustered out June 10, 1865.

Turner, John A., Bradford, mustered Aug. 31, 1862, killed at Chickamauga Sept. 20, 1863.

Weed, Pope C., Union Mills, mustered Aug. 31, 1862, transferred to V.R.C., mustered out July 7, 1865.

Wellman, Wilson R., Union Mills, mustered Aug. 31, 1862, discharged Dec. 28, 1863.

Westheffer, Elias, Chili, mustered Aug. 31, 1862, mustered out June 10, 1865.

Westheffer, Jacob, Chili, mustered Aug. 31, 1862, mustered out June 10, 1865, as corporal.

Wilhelm, Jacob V., Peru, mustered Aug. 31, 1862, mustered out June 10, 1865, as corporal.

Willis, William C., Union Mills, mustered Aug. 31, 1862, mustered out June 10, 1865.

Wilson, Jonathan H., Westville, mustered Aug. 31, 1862, mustered out June 10, 1865.

Wooley, Samuel, Union Mills, mustered Aug. 31, 1862, discharged Feb. 15, 1863.

Young, Andrew, Westville, mustered Aug. 31, 1862, mustered out June 10, 1865.

Recruits

Big, John, Union Mills, mustered Dec. 30, 1863, transferred to 42nd Regiment June 9, 1865.

Brooks, Jacob, Union Mills, mustered Dec. 30, 1863, died at Chattanooga, Tenn., Feb. 17, 1864.

Brown, Daniel L., LaPorte, mustered March 23, 1864, transferred to 42nd Regiment June 9, 1865.

Brown, William, Union Mills, mustered March 12, 1864, transferred to 42nd Regiment June 9, 1865.

Burnstead, William T., Union Mills, mustered Dec. 30, 1863, transferred to 42nd Regiment June 9, 1865.

Campbell, Benjamin F., Union Mills, mustered Dec. 30, 1863, transferred to 42nd Regiment June 9, 1865.

Carpenter, Daniel, LaPorte, mustered March 12, 1864, transferred to 42nd Regiment June 9, 1865.

Clark, Erskine C., Union Mills, mustered Dec. 30, 1863, transferred to 42nd Regiment June 9, 1865.

Dennison, George S., LaPorte, mustered Sept. 19, 1863, transferred to 42nd Regiment June 9, 1865.

Fessenden, George M., Union Mills, mustered Dec. 30, 1863, transferred to 42nd Regiment June 9, 1865.

Fessenden, Harrison C., LaPorte, mustered Sept. 19, 1863, transferred to 42nd Regiment June 9, 1865.

Freeman, Samuel, Lafayette, mustered Oct. 19, 1864, mustered out Aug. 1, 1865, drafted.

Goose, Nicholas, Rensselaer, mustered Sept. 12, 1862, mustered out June 10, 1865.

Green, Thomas, no city or muster date listed, mustered out Aug. 1, 1865.

Grover, Stephen K., Union Mills, mustered Dec. 30, 1863, transferred to 42nd Regiment June 9, 1865.

Harvey, Anson, Union Mills, mustered Dec. 30, 1863, transferred to 42nd Regiment June 9, 1865.

McKlveen, William, Union Mills, mustered Sept. 24, 1862, mustered out June 10, 1865.

Morris, Morton P., Westville, mustered Sept. 12, 1862, mustered out June 10, 1865.

Sellers, William, Lafayette, mustered Oct. 19, 1864, discharged, no date given.

Teeple, Charles B., Union Mills, mustered Dec. 30, 1863, transferred to 42nd Regiment June 9, 1865.

Titus, Horace W., LaPorte, mustered April 8, 1864, transferred to 42nd Regiment June 9, 1865, drafted.

Turner, Francis, Union Mills, mustered Dec. 30, 1863, transferred to 42nd Regiment June 9, 1865.

Wilson, Milden H., LaPorte, mustered March 12, 1864, transferred to 42nd Regiment June 9, 1865.

Wise, Bernard, Union Mills, mustered Dec. 30, 1863, transferred to 42nd Regiment June 9, 1865.

Worden, Charles G., Union Mills, mustered Dec. 30, 1863, mustered out Aug. 18, 1865.

Company I

Captain

James A. Crawley, LaPorte, commissioned Aug. 25, 1862, resigned May 10, 1864.

John B. Catlin, Union Mills, commissioned July 1, 1864, mustered out with regiment.

First Lieutenant

William B. Biddle, LaPorte, commissioned Aug. 25, 1862, promoted captain of Company H.

DeWitt C. McCollum, LaPorte, commissioned Jan. 21, 1864, mustered out with regiment.

Second Lieutenant

Abram C. Andrew, LaPorte, commissioned Aug. 25, 1862, killed at Chickamauga Sept. 20, 1863.

John W. Armstrong, LaPorte, commissioned May 1, 1865, mustered out with regiment as sergeant.

First Sergeant

Billings, Elihu M., LaPorte, mustered Sept. 12, 1862, died at Danville, Va., Dec. 6, 1863.

Sergeants

Fox, George G., Hannah Station, mustered Sept. 12, 1862, mustered out June 10, 1865, as first sergeant.

McCasky, Isaac W., LaPorte, mustered Sept. 12, 1862, discharged, wounds.

McCollum, DeWitt C., LaPorte, mustered Sept. 12, 1862, promoted first lieutenant.

Root, Edward, Lowell, mustered Sept. 12, 1862, discharged Jan. 2, 1863.

Corporals

Allen, William C., Hannah Station, mustered Sept. 12, 1862, mustered out June 10, 1865, as sergeant.

Bear, Benjamin E., LaPorte, mustered Sept. 12, 1862, transferred to V.R.C., mustered out June 10, 1865.

Copelin, James, LaPorte, mustered Sept. 12, 1862, discharged April 1, 1863.

Johnston, Samuel V., Hannah Station, mustered Sept. 12, 1862, discharged Jan. 20, 1863.

Learn, William, LaPorte, mustered Sept. 12, 1862, mustered out June 10, 1865.

Lowe, William F., LaPorte, mustered Sept. 12, 1862, mustered out June 10, 1865.

Robinson, Asa S., Hannah Station, mustered Sept. 12, 1862, no further information listed.

Sabin, Orlando W., LaPorte, mustered Sept. 12, 1862, died at Chattanooga, Tenn., Nov. 2, 1863.

Musicians

McNelly, Silas, LaPorte, mustered Sept. 12, 1862, transferred to V.R.C. April 28, 1864.

Wilkinson, Clinton C., Hannah Station, mustered Sept. 12, 1862, discharged May 1, 1863.

Wagoner

Christeon, Abram, Wanatah, mustered Sept. 12, 1862, mustered out June 10, 1865.

Privates

Armstrong, John W., LaPorte, mustered Sept. 12, 1862, mustered out June 10, 1865, as sergeant.

Caler, Peter, Wanatah, mustered Sept. 12, 1862, mustered out June 10, 1865.

Carr, Sanford, Hannah Station, mustered Sept. 12, 1862, died at Bowling Green, Ky., Dec. 31, 1862.

Carr, Smith, Hannah Station, mustered Sept. 12, 1862, mustered out June 10, 1865.

Coder, Andrew J., no city listed, mustered Sept. 12, 1862, mustered out May 27, 1865.

Coder, Sanford J., no city listed, mustered Sept. 12, 1862, transferred V.R.C., mustered out June 28, 1865.

Courtney, William, Tippecanoe, mustered Sept. 12, 1862, deserted Dec. 12, 1862.

Craig, Orrin, Bigelow's Mills, mustered Sept. 12, 1862, died at Nashville, Tenn., Nov. 5, 1863.

Crawly, James, LaPorte, mustered Sept. 12, 1862, mustered out June 10, 1865.

Crismore, George W., Knox, mustered Sept. 12, 1862, mustered out June 13, 1865.

Crosby, Lyman B., LaPorte, mustered Sept. 12, 1862, promoted second lieutenant of Company K.

Eldridge, Stephen, Francesville, mustered Sept. 12, 1862, mustered out June 10, 1865, as corporal.

Estis, Thomas, Washington, mustered Sept. 12, 1862, mustered out June 10, 1865.

Evans, Ephraim S., Wanatah, mustered Sept. 12, 1862, died of wounds June, 1865, no date listed.

Extelle, Valentine, no city listed, mustered Sept. 12, 1862, died in Warren County, Ohio, Aug., 1864.

Gauze, John H., no city listed, mustered Sept. 12, 1862, discharged June 15, 1863.

Goon, Nicholas, no city listed, mustered Sept. 12, 1862, transferred to Company H Sept. 15, 1862.

Griselle, Moses K., Michigan City, mustered Sept. 12, 1862, died at Gallatin, Tenn., Dec. 15, 1862.

Hathaway, James H., Morgan Station, mustered Sept. 12, 1862, died, wounds received Jan. 1, 1864.

Hathaway, Richard H., Kankakee City, mustered Sept. 12, 1862, died at Ringgold, Ga., April 7, 1864.

Heald, George F., LaPorte, mustered Sept. 12, 1862, mustered out June 10, 1865, as corporal.

Hecox, Cyrus S., no city listed, mustered Sept. 12, 1862, killed at Chickamauga Sept. 20, 1863.

Homer, Isaac, Hannah Station, mustered Sept. 12, 1862, discharged Jan. 14, 1863.

Irwin, James, LaPorte, mustered Sept. 12, 1862, discharged March 2, 1863.

Johnson, William, Wanatah, mustered Sept. 12, 1862, transferred to V.R.C. April 14, 1864.

Jones, Calvin, Rolling Prairie, mustered Sept. 12, 1862, deserted Jan. 30, 1863.

Jones, Erwin M., Rolling Prairie, mustered Sept. 12, 1862, deserted Jan. 30, 1863.

Kelly, Thomas, Hannah Station, mustered Sept. 12, 1862, discharged March 30, 1863.

Lane, Alonzo, Morgan Station, mustered Sept. 12, 1862, transferred to Pioneer Corps; died Nashville, Tenn., Nov. 6, 1863.

Lienen, John, Union Mills, mustered Sept. 12, 1862, discharged Jan. 1, 1864.

Long, Wright, Wanatah, mustered Sept. 12, 1862, discharged Dec. 13, 1862.

Lowe, Lewis M., LaPorte, mustered Sept. 12, 1862, missing in action at Chickamauga Sept. 20, 1863.

Lyons, Jerome, LaPorte, mustered Sept. 12, 1862, died at Gallatin Dec. 23, 1862.

Maple, Benjamin, LaPorte, mustered Sept. 12, 1862, discharged March 14, 1863.

Martin, Henry, Hannah Station, mustered Sept. 12, 1862, died Oct. 6, 1863, wounds.

Mason, Asa C., LaPorte, mustered Sept. 12, 1862, transferred to V.R.C. Feb. 15, 1864.

Matsol, Jacob, LaPorte, mustered Sept. 12, 1862, mustered out June 10, 1865, as corporal.

Mayer, Charles H., LaPorte, mustered Sept. 12, 1862, deserted June 12, 1863.

McClellan, Hiram M., Wanatah, mustered Sept. 12, 1862, discharged Jan. 1, 1863.

Mead, William H., Morgan Station, mustered Sept. 12, 1862, mustered out June 21, 1865.

Mills, Daniel S., Hannah Station, mustered Sept. 12, 1862, discharged Dec. 2, 1862.

Morris, Morton P., Westville, mustered Sept. 12, 1862, transferred to Company H.

Pairot, David W., Morgan Station, mustered Sept. 12, 1862, died at Gallatin, Tenn., Feb. 4, 1863.

Penover, Joseph, LaPorte, mustered Sept. 12, 1862, died at Chattanooga, Tenn., Oct. 24, 1863.

Phillip, Henry, LaPorte, mustered Sept. 12, 1862, deserted Feb., 1863, no date listed.

Pike, William, Hannah Station, mustered Sept. 12, 1862, mustered out June 10, 1865.

Proutsman, George W., Wanatah, mustered Sept. 12, 1862, transferred to V.R.C. Feb. 17, 1864.

Robinson, John H.,Wanatah, mustered Sept. 12, 1862, discharged March 11, 1863.

Rockhill, Andrew, no city listed, mustered Sept. 12, 1862, died at Gallatin, Tenn., Dec. 22, 1862.

Shellevitle, Joseph, Hannah Station, mustered Sept. 12, 1862, discharged March 1, 1864.

Shurte, Andrew J., Morgan Station, mustered Sept. 12, 1862, transferred to V.R.C. Jan. 10, 1864.

Smith, Samuel P., Wanatah, mustered Sept. 12, 1862, discharged Jan. 1, 1863.

Smith, Wilson P., LaPorte, mustered Sept. 12, 1862, mustered out June 10, 1865.

Taylor, John H., LaPorte, mustered Sept. 12, 1862, discharged Jan. 8, 1863.

Vail, Augustus W., Morgan Station, mustered Sept. 12, 1862, died at Danville, Ky., Jan. 22, 1863.

Vanduzen, Enoch, New Carlisle, mustered Sept. 12, 1862, discharged Jan. 31, 1863.

Vert, Nicholas, LaPorte, mustered Sept. 12, 1862, died at Nashville, Tenn., April 1, 1863.

Wilkinson, Chancy C., Morgan Station, mustered Sept. 12, 1862, discharged Jan. 8, 1863.

Wilson, Henry M., Morgan Station, mustered Sept. 12, 1862, died at Nashville, Tenn., Feb. 24, 1863.

Wilson, William, Hannah Station, mustered Sept. 12, 1862, discharged Dec. 27, 1862.

Wilson, William H., Morgan Station, mustered Sept. 12, 1862, deserted Feb., 1863, no date listed.

Wood, George W., Wanatah, mustered Sept. 12, 1862, discharged Feb. 3, 1863.

Xander, John, LaPorte, mustered Sept. 12, 1862, died at Gallatin, Tenn., Jan. 2, 1863.

Yost, Peter H., LaPorte, mustered Sept. 12, 1862, discharged Jan. 1, 1863.

Zeller, William B., North Bend, mustered Sept. 12, 1862, mustered out June 10, 1865, as corporal.

Recruits

Anspoch, Noah, Ditney Hill, mustered Sept. 26, 1864, mustered out June 10, 1865, drafted.

Arheit, Henry, LaPorte, mustered Feb. 18, 1864, mustered out May 30, 1865.

Buchanan, Benjamin, Versailles, mustered Oct. 13, 1864, transferred 42nd Regiment June 9, 1865, substitute.

Burnstead, John A., Union Mills, mustered Aug. 20, 1862, transferred to 42nd Regiment June 9, 1865.

Coleman, Benjamin F., LaPorte, mustered Jan. 7, 1864, transferred to 42nd Regiment June 9, 1865, as sergeant.

Conklin, John H., Knightstown, mustered Oct. 13, 1864, transferred to 42nd Regiment June 9, 1865, substitute.

Cross, Dallas P., LaPorte, mustered Feb. 11, 1864, transferred to 42nd Regiment June 9, 1865, as corporal.

Dunn, Austin, New Boston, mustered Nov. 3, 1864, transferred to 42nd Regiment June 9, 1865, substitute.

Duree, Daniel, no city listed, mustered Oct. 12, 1864, transferred to 42nd Regiment June 9, 1865, substitute.

Ford, David S., Washington, mustered Sept. 22, 1864, mustered out June 10, 1865, drafted.

Foster, John A., no city listed, mustered Oct. 17, 1864, transferred to 42nd Regiment June 9, 1865, substitute.

Fraedenburgh, Spencer, LaPorte, mustered Feb. 27, 1864, transferred to 42nd Regiment June 9, 1865.

Frazier, James W., Yelverton, mustered Oct. 31, 1864, transferred to 42nd Regiment June 9, 1865, substitute.

Gougarty, Edward, no city listed, mustered Nov. 1, 1864, transferred 42nd Regiment June 9, 1865, substitute.

Gustufson, Gustus, Calumet, mustered Oct. 16, 1864, transferred to 42nd Regiment June 9, 1865, drafted.

Hager, Francis M., Whitestown, mustered Oct. 27, 1864, transferred to 42nd Regiment June 9, 1865, substitute.

Myers, William, no city listed, mustered Sept. 22, 1864, mustered out May 26, 1865, drafted.

Osborn, Tence L., Greentown, no muster date listed, transferred to 42nd Regiment June 9, 1865.

Peterson, John A., no city listed, mustered Nov. 1, 1864, died at Savannah, Ga., Jan. 15, 1865, substitute.

Powels, Levi W., LaPorte, mustered Sept. 12, 1862, discharged Jan. 29, 1863.

Reitnour, Anthony, Deerfield, mustered Oct. 15, 1864, transferred to 42nd Regiment June 9, 1865, substitute.

Richards, Clark R., Union Mills, mustered Sept. 9, 1863, transferred to 42nd Regiment June 9, 1865.

Seifort, Adam, Evansville, mustered Nov. 3, 1864, transferred to 42nd Regiment June 9, 1865, substitute.

Shields, John, no city or muster date listed, mustered out June 27, 1865.

Smith, John W., Evansville, mustered Oct. 29, 1864, transferred to 42nd Regiment June 9, 1865, substitute.

Spurry, Samuel W., Knightstown, mustered Oct. 15, 1864, transferred to 42nd Regiment June 9, 1865, substitute.

Walgsen, Charles G., Calumet, mustered Oct. 16, 1864, mustered out Aug. 18, 1865, drafted.

Wernce, William, Auburn, no muster date listed, transferred to 42nd Regiment June 9, 1865, substitute.

Wolford, Alexander, Brazil, mustered Oct. 16, 1864, transferred to 42nd Regiment June 9, 1865, drafted.

Woodburn, Lewis N., LaPorte, mustered Feb. 29, 1864, died at Chattanooga, Tenn., Sept. 5, 1864.

Company K

Captain

John Q. Wheeler, Mishawaka, commissioned Aug. 6, 1862, resigned March 17, 1863.

James M. Holliday, Mishawaka, commissioned March 18, 1863, killed at Chickamauga Sept. 19, 1863.

Lyman B. Crosby, Cedar Falls, Iowa, commissioned Sept. 20, 1863, resigned April 23, 1864.

William H. Deacon, Marion, Iowa, commissioned July 1, 1864, mustered out with regiment.

First Lieutenant

George H. Niles, Mishawaka, commissioned Aug. 6, 1862, resigned June 23, 1863.

William H. Deacon, Marion, Iowa, commissioned Jan. 1, 1864, promoted captain.

Andrew J. Chrisman, South Bend, commissioned July 1, 1864, mustered out with regiment.

Second Lieutenant

James M. Holliday, Mishawaka, commissioned Aug. 6, 1862, promoted captain.

Lyman B. Crosby, Cedar Falls, Iowa, commissioned May 30, 1863, promoted captain.

Elijah J. Cooper, Hillsdale, Mich., commissioned May 1, 1865, mustered out with regiment as first sergeant.

First Sergeant

Richards, George B., Lawrenceburg, mustered Aug. 11, 1862, died at Louisville, Ky., Nov. 15, 1862.

Sergeants

Beglin, John A., Mishawaka, mustered July 23, 1862, died at Gallatin, Tenn., Dec. 25, 1862.

Boyd, John W., Mishawaka, mustered Aug. 16, 1862, mustered out June 10, 1865.

Deacon, William H., Marion, Iowa, mustered Aug. 17, 1862, promoted first lieutenant.

Simpson, Lewis A., Elkhart, mustered Aug. 11, 1862, killed at Chickamauga Sept. 20, 1863.

Corporals

Boston, Daniel, Mishawaka, mustered Aug. 15, 1862, transferred to Engineer Corps July 29, 1864.

Bulla, William H., South Bend, mustered Aug. 16, 1862, died Oct. 15, 1863, wounds.

Hiner, Abraham C., Nineveh, mustered Aug. 16, 1862, mustered out June 10, 1865.

Hutson, Charles E., Mishawaka, mustered Aug. 12, 1862, discharged Jan. 12, 1863.

Milliken, Francis M., no city listed, mustered July 23, 1862, never mustered into the service.

Stair, Charles C., Rensselaer, mustered Aug. 14, 1862, discharged Feb. 4, 1863.

Tutt, Charles E., South Bend, mustered Aug. 16, 1862, discharged March 16, 1863.

Williams, Alonzo S., Mishawaka, mustered Aug. 9, 1862, mustered out June 10, 1865, as private.

Musicians

Cobb, William, Mishawaka, mustered July 29, 1862, discharged Feb. 14, 1863.

Tidswell, William, Adrian, Mich., mustered Aug. 11, 1862, mustered out June 10, 1865.

Wagoner

Quinn, Robert, Jasper County, mustered Aug. 18, 1862, discharged April 9, 1863.

Privates

Abbett, Preston S., Rensselaer, mustered Aug. 15, 1862, discharged April 7, 1863.

Albright, Joseph R., Goshen, mustered Aug. 18, 1862, died at Gallatin, Tenn., Dec. 5, 1862.

Aldrick, John W., Pleno, Ill., mustered Aug. 15, 1862, mustered out June 10, 1865.

Aldrick, Luke A., South Bend, mustered Aug. 15, 1862, deserted Oct. 2, 1862.

Ashley, Henry J., South Bend, mustered Aug. 15, 1862, died Oct. 21, 1863, wounds.

Balder, Peter, Bremen, mustered Aug. 12, 1862, killed at Chickamauga Sept. 19, 1863.

Bartlett, Edwin A., South Bend, mustered Aug. 11, 1862, died at Richmond, Va., Nov. 18, 1863.

Bell, Jacob H., Mishawaka, mustered Aug. 9, 1862, mustered out June 10, 1865.

Best, John, no city listed, mustered Aug. 22, 1862, never mustered into the service.

Bradley, Josiah P., Tyner City, mustered Aug. 12, 1862, deserted Oct. 1, 1862.

Bradley, Philander, Mishawaka, mustered July 23, 1862, discharged June 18, 1863.

Burgner, John, South Bend, mustered Aug. 12, 1862, discharged Feb. 14, 1863.

Burns, Francis M., Rensselaer, mustered Aug. 15, 1862, died at Nashville, Tenn., Jan. 4, 1863.

Buyssee, Charles, Mishawaka, mustered July 28, 1862, mustered out June 10, 1865, as corporal.

Carrier, William, Mishawaka, mustered July 31, 1862, died in Andersonville, Ga., prison, May 30, 1864.

Chambers, William, Deep River, mustered Aug. 14, 1862, died at New Albany, Ind., July 12, 1864.

Chrisman, Andrew J., South Bend, mustered Aug. 15, 1862, discharged Dec. 20, 1864.

Cooper, Elijah W., Hillsdale, Mich., mustered Aug. 14, 1862, mustered out June 10, 1865, as first sergeant.

Coppick, Derrick M., Logansport, mustered Aug. 15, 1862, died at Chattanooga, Tenn., Feb. 14, 1864.

Crothers, Andrew J., no city listed, mustered Aug. 11, 1862, never mustered into the service.

Deacon, Solomon W., Marion, Iowa, mustered Aug. 7, 1862, died at Missionary Ridge Nov. 25, 1864.

Dealman, Adam, Mishawaka, mustered Aug. 15, 1862, killed at Atlanta, Ga., Aug. 4, 1864.

Dirst, Herman, South Bend, mustered Aug. 16, 1862, died at Nashville, Tenn., May 3, 1863.

Dressler, Daniel N., South Bend, mustered Aug. 14, 1862, discharged Jan. 9, 1863.

Duck, Benjamin, no city listed, mustered Aug. 14, 1862, never mustered into the service.

Ferris, John A., Mishawaka, mustered Aug. 11, 1862, discharged April 28, 1863.

Fleming, Peter, Mishawaka, mustered Aug. 11, 1862, mustered out June 10, 1865.

Gay, Ebert, Mishawaka, mustered Aug. 5, 1862, died Jan. 14, 1864, wounds.

Ghrist, Wallace S., Mishawaka, mustered Aug. 11, 1862, mustered out June 10, 1865.

Gordon, William H., South Bend, mustered Aug. 16, 1862, transferred to 22nd Regiment to make up time lost.

Greenleaf, Henry C., Mishawaka, mustered July 23, 1862, died at Louisville, Ky., Sept. 15, 1862.

Guibert, George, Mishawaka, mustered Aug. 9, 1862, died at Nashville, Tenn., March 31, 1863.

Harris, Henry C., South Bend, mustered Aug. 9, 1862, discharged Feb. 4, 1864.

Hays, Henry C., Mishawaka, mustered Aug. 8, 1862, mustered out June 10, 1865, as sergeant.

Heckathorn, Adam, Mishawaka, mustered Aug. 6, 1862, mustered out June 10, 1865.

Heminger, Peter, Mishawaka, mustered July 26, 1862, killed at Chickamauga Sept. 20, 1863.

Irwin, Albert C., Rensselaer, mustered Aug. 18, 1862, discharged Dec. 25, 1862.

James, Zebedee, North Liberty, mustered Aug. 17, 1862, discharged May 12, 1863.

Jones, Ira, Mishawaka, mustered Aug. 11, 1862, discharged Feb. 20, 1863.

Jones, John, no city listed, mustered Aug. 20, 1862, no additional information listed.

Keifer, Jacob H., South Bend, mustered Aug. 9, 1862, killed at Chickamauga Sept. 20, 1863.

Kelsey, Irwin H., New Carlisle, mustered Aug. 15, 1862, died at New Albany, Ind., Nov. 5, 1862.

Kessler, James S., Rensselaer, mustered Aug. 18, 1862, died at Indianapolis, Ind., July 17, 1863.

Lell, August, no city listed, mustered Aug. 11, 1862, never mustered into the service.

Leslie, Albert R., Mishawaka, mustered Aug. 16, 1862, mustered out June 10, 1865.

Leslie, Lawyous, South Bend, mustered Aug. 11, 1862, transferred to V.R.C. Dec. 30, 1864.

Long, Charles W., Mishawaka, mustered Aug. 8, 1862, mustered out June 10, 1865.

Long, George E., Mishawaka, mustered July 30, 1862, mustered out June 10, 1865.

Martin, John H., South Bend, mustered Aug. 2, 1862, discharged May 21, 1863.

Martling, George H., Mishawaka, mustered Aug. 13, 1862, mustered out June 10, 1865.

Maugherman, John G., Mishawaka, mustered Aug. 9, 1862, discharged May 7, 1864.

Maugherman, William H., South Bend, mustered July 29, 1862, died at Louisville, Ky., July 23, 1863.

McMichael, John A., Mishawaka, mustered Aug. 9, 1862, mustered out June 10, 1865.

Miller, Loren C., South Bend, mustered Aug. 13, 1862, mustered out June 10, 1865, as sergeant.

Molloy, Edward, New Carlisle, mustered Aug. 5, 1862, discharged Jan. 3, 1865.

Odell, Jonas, Mishawaka, mustered Aug. 16, 1862, died at Gallatin, Tenn., Dec. 13, 1862.

Partridge, Francis, no city listed, mustered Aug. 15, 1862, never mustered into the service.

Rice, Thomas, no city listed, mustered Aug. 18, 1862, never mustered into the service.

Russ, Nathan F., Mishawaka, mustered Aug. 11, 1862, mustered out June 10, 1865.

Schmidt, Benjamin, Mishawaka, mustered July 25, 1862, died Nov. 7, 1863, wounds.

248   APPENDIX

Sponsler, Alexander, Mishawaka, mustered July 26, 1862, deserted Sept. 20, 1862.

Stevens, George S., Mishawaka, mustered Aug. 4, 1862, discharged Feb. 16, 1863.

Stuckey, James A., South Bend, mustered Aug. 5, 1862, mustered out May 25, 1865.

Sumstine, John, Mishawaka, mustered Aug. 5, 1862, died Jan. 14, 1864, wounds.

Sweeney, George C., South Bend, mustered Aug. 11, 1862, mustered out June 10, 1865.

Terrill, Oscar, New Carlisle, mustered Aug. 15, 1862, mustered out June 10, 1865.

Turner, Asher, Mishawaka, mustered Aug. 9, 1862, transferred to V.R.C. Feb.16, 1864.

Van Nest, Lewis T., Mishawaka, mustered July 23, 1862, transferred to Mississippi Marine Brigade, Dec. 26, 1862.

Vanriper, Bradford, Mishawaka, mustered Aug. 9, 1862, mustered out June 10, 1865, as corporal.

Vanriper, Garrett, Mishawaka, mustered July 30, 1862, discharged Jan. 17, 1863.

Vanriper, John, Mishawaka, mustered Aug. 9, 1862, died at Gallatin, Tenn., Jan. 22, 1863.

Worl, John, no city listed, mustered Aug. 15, 1862, never mustered into the service.

Recruits

Adair, Washington, New Castle, mustered Oct. 3, 1864, transferred to 42nd Regiment June 9, 1865, substitute.

Baird, Marcus M., Newville, mustered Oct. 13, 1864, transferred to 42nd Regiment June 9, 1865, substitute.

Dressell, John, St. Wendle, mustered Nov. 3, 1864, transferred to 42nd Regiment June 9, 1865, substitute.

Ensighn, Benjamin, Newville, mustered Oct. 7, 1864, discharged, no date listed.

Everhart, Gabriel M., Carlisle, mustered Oct. 28, 1864, transferred to 42nd Regiment June 9, 1865, substitute.

Hatton, Alexander, Spencer, mustered Oct. 26, 1864, died at Goldsboro, N.C., April 1, 1865.

Johnson, Thomas S., Roanoke, mustered Oct. 26, 1864, transferred to 42nd Regiment June 9, 1865, substitute.

King, David, Mt. Vernon, mustered Oct. 14, 1864, transferred to 42nd Regiment June 9, 1865, substitute.

Knoop, Charles, Cumberland, mustered Nov. 3, 1864, transferred to 42nd Regiment June 9, 1865, substitute.

Knust, Bernard, Ferdinand, mustered Nov. 3, 1864, transferred to 42nd Regiment June 9, 1865, substitute.

Leslie, John H., Mishawaka, mustered Dec. 19, 1863, transferred to 42nd Regiment June 9, 1865, substitute.

Maus, Anton, Mt. Vernon, mustered Nov. 2, 1864, transferred to 42nd Regiment June 9, 1865, substitute.

May, Jackson, Greensburg, mustered Oct. 12, 1864, transferred to 42nd Regiment June 9, 1865, substitute.

McComas, John R., Dillsboro, mustered Oct. 7, 1864, transferred to 42nd Regiment June 9, 1865, substitute.

Peters, John, no city listed, mustered Nov. 2, 1864, transferred to 42nd Regiment June 9, 1865, substitute.

Ping, Jasper, New Bellville, mustered Oct. 24, 1864, transferred to 42nd Regiment June 9, 1865, substitute.

Presler, John, Newville, mustered Oct. 13, 1864, transferred to 42nd Regiment June 9, 1865, substitute.

Pyle, Abraham C., New Carlisle, mustered Aug. 20, 1863, transferred to 42nd Regiment June 9, 1865, substitute.

Shay, Morris, no city listed, mustered Nov. 12, 1864, transferred to 42nd Regiment June 9, 1865, substitute.

Shull, Oliver, no city listed, mustered Sept. 20, 1864, mustered out June 10, 1865.

Swiney, James, Mt. Vernon, mustered Oct. 5, 1864, transferred to 42nd Regiment June 9, 1865, substitute.

Walters, William, Evansville, mustered Nov. 1, 1864, transferred to 42nd Regiment June 9, 1865, substitute.

Unassigned Recruits
Corey, Barney J., Rochester, mustered March 22, 1864.
Hench, Samuel, Fort Wayne, mustered Dec. 12, 1864.
King, John, LaPorte, mustered Aug. 22, 1864.
Line, Andrew, no city listed, mustered Feb. 10, 1864.
Lynch, Patrick, LaPorte, mustered Aug. 22, 1864.
Nicholson, John A., Rensselaer, mustered Dec. 26, 1863.
Rufus, Rufus C., Winamac, mustered April 8, 1864.
Salisberry, Alfred B., LaPorte, mustered Sept. 19, 1863.
Wells, Theodore H., LaPorte, mustered Sept. 19, 1863.
Winchel, Edward D., Grant County, mustered April 8, 1864.

*V.R.C.—Veteran Reserve Corps. The Invalid Corps, to which were assigned officers and men who had become unfit for combat duty but who were able to perform limited military service. Able-bodied soldiers thus were freed for combat. Some of those in the V.R.C. were assigned to guard duty; those most severely crippled became nurses and cooks at army hospitals.

NOTES

Preface

1. The reader was Jack Hogan of Kewanna, Ind., a friend of the author's for many years. The photograph, enlarged to a full page in width, appeared in the *Rochester* (Indiana) *Sentinel*, July 19, 1991, along with a short history of the regiment's Civil War service that was written by the author.

2. Only the official reports of the regiment's service exist; they appear in Indiana War Records, *Report of the Adjutant General*, vol. 3, 84–85, and in *Indiana at Chickamauga*, 252–58.

3. Of particular value were the letters published during 1862–65 by the *Rochester* (Indiana) *Chronicle*, written by members of the regiment while in service, and the diaries of Jonas Myers, sergeant in Company F, and of Daniel Bruce, Company E teamster. Existence of the Myers diary was little known outside of the family. It was graciously provided for the author's study by Myers' great-grandsons, Robert and David Bailey of Rochester, Ind.

4. Unattributed document among the Civil War papers of LaPorte County Museum, LaPorte, Ind.

1. The Rebels Are Coming!

1. Foote, *Fort Sumter to Perryville*, 583–84.

2. The *Rochester* (Indiana) *Chronicle*, editorial, August 7, 1862.

3. Kentucky's divided loyalties and subsequent attempts at neutrality are discussed in McPherson, 293–97.

4. Catton, in *This Hallowed Ground*, 156, goes on to say that Bragg "was disputatious to a degree, and in the old army it was said that when he could not find anyone else to quarrel with he would quarrel with himself. A ferocious disciplinarian, he shot his own soldiers ruthlessly for violations of military law."

5. Warner, *Generals in Gray*, 279–80.

6. Boatner, 755–56.

7. Warner, *Generals in Blue*, 51–52.

8. Barnhart, 167.

9. Esarey, 754–55. General Order 71 placed the whole state under arms, subject to being called to the colors at notice. Business houses had to be closed while the owners met to drill.

10. 12th, 16th, 55th, 66th and 71st Indiana plus seven companies of the 69th Indiana. Boatner, 697–98.

11. This was Wilder's first military action and so he decided to visit Confederate headquarters under a flag of truce and ask, politely, to inspect the enemy's forces and count their cannon. Allowed to do so, he determined it was best to surrender, with a loss of 15 killed and 75 wounded. Later he became one of the Union's most outstanding field commanders. Boatner, 575.

2. An Army of Volunteers

1. Other counties of the Ninth District were Porter, Lake, Starke, Marshall, Newton, Benton, White and Cass.

2. Indiana War Records, vol. 3, 84.

3. There were 36 officers and 909 enlisted men at the regiment's formation and during its service 317 more joined to fill vacancies, 25 officers and 292 enlisted recruits. Casualties were 48 killed in action, 198 wounded in action, 220 dead of wounds or disease. Deaths were 21 percent of those serving. Of the regiment's original 945 members, 11 officers and 302 enlisted men were present at the final muster.

4. Hinman, 693.

5. Ibid., 693.

6. South Bend had 3,028, Peru 2,506, Mishawaka 1,488. Esarey, 981.

7. Jackson, 62; Grand Army of the Republic, *Descriptive Book*.

8. Indiana War Records, vol. 3, 79–83; vol. 6, 403–20.

9. Hinman, 693.

10. Boatner, 612.

11. *Rochester* (Indiana) *Chronicle*, Aug. 21, 1862.

12. Boatner, 858.

13. Dyer, vol. 1, 11.

14. Dornbusch, pt. 5, 17–40.

15. Barnhart, vol. 1, 405–406.

16. Lavender, 147, 168–69, 190–211; Johannsen, 64–65.

17. McFeely, xiii.

18. Grand Army of the Republic. *Personal War Sketches*.

19. 87th Regiment Archives, Jasper County Public Library, Rensselaer, Ind.

20. *Thru a Private's Eyes*, 1.

21. The site is marked today on Portage Avenue, near a former brick schoolhouse that houses a community theatre.

22. Keegan diaries.

23. Civil War Diary of Daniel Bruce, Jan. 3, 1935, recounts events following his enlistment that are detailed in this chapter.

24. A marker on Meridian Street at 19th Street tells of the camp's location today. Its actual boundaries were 19th, Talbot, 22nd and Central streets.

3. The Life They Left Behind

1. Miller, *Home Folks*, vol. 1, 14–15. The passenger pigeons eventually were completely obliterated. The last died in 1914, in a Cincinnati zoo.

2. Madison, 148.

3. *Illustrated Historical Atlas*, 388.

4. Esarey, 763.

5. Brackett family history compiled from: *Some Descendants of Joseph Brackett and John Ely* by J. W. Wheaton, Hingham, Mass., 1974, collection of Mrs. Hugh Moore, Rochester, Ind.; letter from Kevin Young, Society of Mexican War Historians, to Fulton County Historian Shirley Willard, 1983; Kingman, 82; *Rochester* (Indiana) *Sentinel* of Jan. 2, 1875; Miller, *Home Folks*, vol. 2, 87; autograph letter from Col. A. G. Brackett to Gen. James Grant Wilson, Sept. 17, 1862, Indiana Historical Society, Indianapolis.

6. Miller, *Home Folks*, vol. 2, 95.

7. *Rochester Chronicle*, Aug. 21, 1862.

8. *Illustrated Historical Atlas*, 455.

9. *Rochester Mercury*, March 1, 1860.

10. *Rochester Sentinel*, March 17, 1860.

11. Miller, *Home Folks*, vol. 1, 59–60.

12. Ibid., vol. 2, 8–9.

13. Ibid., vol. 2, 86–87.

14. *Rochester Sentinel*, June 21, 1862.

15. Madison, 202–203.

16. *Rochester Chronicle*, Feb. 26, March 12, May 7, 1863; *Rochester Sentinel*, April 4, 1863.

17. *History of Henry Township Schools*, Fulton County Historical Society Quarterly, August 1969, 15.

18. *Rochester Chronicle*, June 18, 1863.

19. Civil War History of Capt. Horace C. Long, undated letter fragment.

20. Miller, *Home Folks*, vol. 1, 59; Fulton County Historical Society Quarterly, February 1973, 10.

21. *Rochester Sentinel*, Jan. 17, 1863.

4. Soldiering in Louisville

1. Warner, *Generals in Blue*, 54–55.

2. *Rochester Chronicle*, Sept. 25, 1862.

3. Ibid.

4. War experiences of Cpl. Joseph Gillit Wheat, Tonica, Ill. Transcribed by Laura Emily Foster, his daughter, Mt. Vernon, Iowa. Copy in collection of her daughter, Ruth Davis, Talma, Ind.

5. *Rochester Chronicle*, Sept. 25, 1862.

6. Wheat war experiences, as cited above.

7. Hafendorfer, 59.

8. Ibid., 59–62.

9. Ibid., 66–67.

10. Grebner, xii, 24–25.

11. Boatner, 489.

12. Foote, *Fort Sumter to Perryville*, 179.

13. Warner, *Generals in Blue*, 473.

14. Ibid., 424–25.

15. Official Records, vol. 26, part 2, 594.

16. Warner, *Generals in Blue*, 343–44.

17. Hafendorfer, 67–68; Foote, *Fort Sumter to Perryville*, 714.

18. Hafendorfer, 68–71; Foote, 715.

19. Foote, 728.

20. Hinman, 224–26.

21. Bishop, *The Mill Springs Campaign*, 57.

5. The Walnut Crackers Find a Fight

1. Hafendorfer, 72.

2. Bruce diary for Oct. 1, 1862.

3. Hafendorfer, 77.

4. Ibid., 81.

5. Ibid., 94.

6. Hafendorfer, 369. Grebner, 259, note 21.

7. Hafendorfer, 119–20.

8. Warner, *Generals in Blue*, 294–95.

9. Boatner, 643.

10. Hafendorfer, 288–89.

11. Ibid., 369.

12. Bishop, *Minnesota*, 91–92.

13. "Letters Home to Minnesota," no. 58.

14. Hafendorfer, 374.

15. Ibid., 375.

16. Boatner, 2.

17. Hafendorfer, 368–69; Foote, 737. Kline Shryock of the 87th Indiana is identified by Foote as the Indiana colonel involved in this incident. That appears to be mistaken. The 87th was not on the front line during the Perryville action while Col. Keith's 22nd Indiana was, and took heavy casualties as a part of Gooding's brigade. Hafendorfer cites a collection of war stories edited by B.A. Botkin as his source. Foote's three-volume narrative of the war carries no end or foot notes of sources.

18. Bruce diary, entry of Oct. 11, 1862.

19. Hafendorfer, 438.

20. Boatner, 111; James Ogden III, Chickamauga Park chief historian.

6. Campaigning in Tennessee

1. *Rochester Chronicle,* Nov. 27, 1862.

2. Peter Keegan diaries, entry for Oct. 12, 1862.

3. Warner, *Generals in Blue,* 410–11.

4. Ibid., 163–64.

5. Official Records, vol. 20, part 1, 178.

6. Warner, *Generals in Blue,* 500–503; Foote, *Fredericksburg to Meridian,* 748.

7. Jerome Carpenter letter, *Rochester Chronicle,* Dec. 4, 1862; "Letters Home," no. 62.

8. Bruce Diaries, entry for Nov. 29, 1862.

9. Solomon M. Deacon letters, Chickamauga National Park archives.

10. *Rochester Chronicle,* Dec. 18, 1862.

11. *Thru a Private's Eyes;* 8–10. "Letters Home," no. 68.

12. Warner, *Generals in Gray,* 220–21. Boatner, 682.

13. Boatner, 567–68.

14. *Rochester Chronicle,* Nov. 6, 1862.

15. Boatner, 568.

16. Bruce diaries, entry for Dec. 8, 1862.

17. *Rochester Chronicle,* Feb. 26, 1863, letter signed only as "W."

18. Warner, *Generals in Blue,* 522–23; Middletown, Ohio, Journal, Oct. 14, 1990.

19. *Rochester Chronicle,* Feb. 26, 1863.

20. Ibid., March 5, 1863.

21. Indiana War Records, vol. 6, 411.

22. LaPorte County Museum, newspaper clipping of July 7, 1886, from museum's Civil War papers.

23. "Letters Home," no. 74.

24. Boatner, 266.

25. "Twelve Roads to Gettysburg," CD-ROM, Armies and Individuals, Weapons and Uniforms, Personal Firearms.

26. Warner, *Generals in Blue,* 42–43.

27. Davis, 163.

28. Civil War papers, Fulton County Historical Society.

29. Microfilmed letter of May 26, 1863, Indiana Historical Society.

30. Indiana War Records, vol. 3, 79; vol. 6, 408.

31. *Rochester Chronicle,* April 9, 1863.

32. Ibid., June 11, 1863.

33. Official Records, vol. 23, part 1, 411.

7. Over Mountains to a Georgia Creek

1. Cozzens, *This Terrible Sound*, 21–22, 30.
2. Ibid., 22.
3. *Echoes of Glory*, 190.
4. Catton, *Reflections*, 39–41.
5. Hinman, 243.
6. Ibid., 41.
7. Boatner, 850–51.
8. "Letters from Home," no. 90.
9. *Rochester Chronicle*, Aug. 6, 1863.
10. Letter to John Dawson Timmons, Rensselaer, private in Company A, 87th Indiana. Fulton County Historical Society Civil War collection.
11. *Rochester Chronicle*, Aug. 6, 1863.
12. Civil War History of Capt. Horace C. Long, 9.
13. Gangrene.
14. Boatner, 568–69.
15. Indiana War Records, vol. 3, 162, 189–90.
16. *Rochester Chronicle*, Aug. 27, 1863.
17. Civil War History of Capt. Horace C. Long, 12.
18. Official Records, vol. 30, part 3, 267.
19. Cozzens, *This Terrible Sound*, 33.
20. Bowman, 166.
21. Letters Home, no. 100.
22. Letters Home, no. 100; Martling, entry for Aug. 22, 1863.
23. Civil War Letters of Benjamin E. Bear, Co. I, LaPorte County Museum.
24. Letters Home, no. 101; Cozzens, *This Terrible Sound*, 45.
25. *Rochester Chronicle*, Sept. 24, 1863; Letters Home, no. 103; Martling, entry for Sept. 5, 1863.
26. *Rochester Chronicle*, Sept. 24, 1863, letter signed by "B."
27. Martling, entries for Sept. 16–17, 1863.
28. Miller, *Home Folks*, vol. 2, 70.

8. The Night March

1. *Rochester Chronicle*, Oct. 15, 1863.
2. Cozzens, *This Terrible Sound*, 115.
3. Bishop, *The Story of a Regiment*, 95–96.
4. Cozzens, 537–39.
5. Ibid., 118.
6. Ibid.
7. Bishop, 97.

8. *Rochester Chronicle*, May 19, 1864; written April 14, 1864.

9. *Rochester Chronicle*, Nov. 19, 1863; written Oct. 21, 1863.

10. Bishop, 97–98.

11. *Indiana at Chickamauga*, 257; Arnold, 87.

9. "We Waded in without Flinching"

1. Arnold, 28–31, 40; Boatner, 152; *Echoes of Glory*, 239; conversation with James Ogden III, Chickamauga National Park historian; Cozzens, *This Terrible Sound*, 204.

2. Warner, *Generals in Blue*, 104.

3. Cozzens, 127.

4. Benjamin Brown's account of Chickamauga appears in *Rochester Chronicle*, Oct. 15, 1863.

5. Cozzens, 129–31.

6. Ibid., 135.

7. Spruill, 30.

8. Peter Troutman's account of Chickamauga appears in *Rochester Chronicle*, May 19, 1864.

9. Horace Long's account of Chickamauga appears in *Rochester Chronicle*, Nov. 19, 1863.

10. *Thru a Private's Eyes*, 20.

11. Cozzens, 136; Spruill, 30.

12. Cozzens, 147–48; Bishop, *The Story of a Regiment*, 101.

13. Peter Keegan diaries.

14. Cozzens, 148–49; Spruill, 32–33.

15. Martling, entry for Sept. 19, 1863.

16. Cozzens, 149.

17. Conversation with James Ogden III; Bishop, 101.

18. Conversation with James Ogden III.

19. Cozzens, 290; Bishop, 103.

20. Spruill, appendix 1, 239.

21. Cozzens, 139–40.

22. Ibid., 251, 258.

23. Spruill, 34; Cozzens, 283; Bishop, 103–104.

10. The Bravest Deed in the Entire War

1. Bishop, *The Story of a Regiment*, 104; Cozzens, *This Terrible Sound*, 305.

2. Cozzens, 295–301.

3. Col. Newell Gleason report, Official Records, vol. 30, part 1, 1058.

4. Bishop, 105–106.

5. Cozzens, 327–28.

6. Following the war, Boynton and Van Derveer inspired and then led the effort to establish the Chickamauga and Chattanooga National Military Park, created in 1890 by Congress as the nation's first military park. It also is the largest. Boynton acted as the park's chief historian in its early years.

7. The *Rochester Sentinel*, Feb. 2, 1894.

8. Col. Ferdinand Van Derveer report, Official Records, vol. 42, part 1, 430.

9. Newspaper clipping of April 25, 1903, LaPorte County Museum.

10. Capt. Peter Troutman's account of Chickamauga, *Rochester Chronicle*, May 19, 1864.

11. Peter Keegan diaries.

12. Capt. Horace Long's account of Chickamauga, *Rochester Chronicle*, Nov. 19, 1863.

13. George Martling diary, entry for Sept. 20.

14. Sgt. Benjamin Brown's account of Chickamauga, *Rochester Chronicle*, Oct. 15, 1863.

15. Bishop, 107.

16. Spruill, 150.

11. Making a Stand to Save an Army

1. Boatner, 152; Cozzens, *This Terrible Sound*, 368–69.

2. Chickamauga and Chattanooga, "On Your Own," 12.

3. Cozzens, 359–67; Arnold, 60–61; Battlefield marker of Brannan's position.

4. Cozzens, 402–403; "On Your Own," 19.

5. Cozzens, 410; Spruill, 200.

6. Cozzens, 421–23.

7. James Ogden III, chief historian, Chickamauga National Park.

8. Foote, *Fredericksburg to Meridian*, 752.

9. Cozzens, 452–53; Spruill, 207, 210.

10. Miller, *Home Folks*, 99–100.

11. Bishop, *The Story of a Regiment*, 109.

12. Spruill, 212–13; Cozzens, 471–76; Foote, 753–54.

13. Spruill, 206, 216.

14. Foote, 752; Cozzens, 486; Bishop, 110.

15. Cozzens, 507–508.

16. Bishop, 111.

17. Watkins, 109.

18. *Rochester Chronicle*, May 19, 1864.

12. Reflections on a Disaster

1. Chickamauga and Chattanooga, "On Your Own," 22.

2. Cozzens, *This Terrible Sound*, 534.

3. *Indiana at Chickamauga,* 257. Arnold, 87.

4. Official Records, vol. 30, part 1, 173.

5. *Rochester Chronicle,* Oct. 8, 1863.

6. Official Records, vol. 30, part 1, 173.

7. *Rochester Chronicle,* Nov. 19, 1863.

8. Official Records, vol. 30, part 1, 1057–60.

9. Keegan diaries. *Rochester Chronicle,* Nov. 19, 1863.

10. Conversation with James Ogden III, chief historian, Chickamauga National Park.

11. To find where in the woods the 87th first went into action, walk 540 paces down the trail leading south from the Reed's Bridge markers to reach the 82nd Indiana Regiment monument on the left. Turn left past the monument for 100 paces to the 35th Ohio marker, then continue on for another 140 paces to a small granite cube that marks the 87th's position.

12. Cozzens, 516.

13. Grand Army of the Republic, *Personal War Sketches.*

14. *Rochester Sentinel,* Nov. 30, 1894.

15. Spruill, 246.

16. Ibid.

13. Redemption at Missionary Ridge

1. Foote, *The Civil War: Fredericksburg to Meridian,* 804.

2. Cozzens, *This Terrible Sound,* 528–34; *The Shipwreck of Their Hopes,* 23–26.

3. Hurst, 139–42.

4. Bishop, *The Story of a Regiment,* 117.

5. Cozzens, *The Shipwreck of Their Hopes,* 31–34.

6. Ibid., 17–19.

7. Civil War Diary of Daniel Bruce, entries for Oct. 1–5, 1863.

8. Martling, entries for Oct. 26–29, Nov. 1, 3, 17.

9. *Echoes of Glory,* 232.

10. He was given command of the Department of the Missouri during 1864 and then was left to await orders or placed on leave until he resigned his Regular Army commission March 28, 1867. Warner, *Generals in Blue,* 411.

11. Boatner, 142.

12. Warner, 358–59.

13. Ibid., 15.

14. Official Records, vol. 31, part 3, 555.

15. Foote, 853.

16. Official Records, Gleason Report, vol. 31, part 2, 531.

17. Ibid. and Chrisman letter dated Nov. 30, 1863, Chickamauga National Park archives.

18. Cozzens, 282.

19. Manchester, 28–30.

20. Miller, *Home Folks*, vol. 1, 100.

21. From tablet marker at Delong Reservation, located along Missionary Ridge road, north of the cut for Interstate 24. The state of Minnesota has erected a memorial column there for its Second Infantry, which was deployed as skirmishers for the 87th's brigade in the assault. The view into the valley now is obscured by a heavy growth of trees. Missionary Ridge today is filled with private homes, many elegant. Five small areas including the Delong Reservation have been set aside as parks where actions that took place there can be studied; markers, cannon and tablets marking unit positions are in the yards of some of the private residences.

22. Linderman, 75.

23. Ibid., 73.

24. Cozzens, *This Terrible Sound*, 536.

25. Troutman, *Rochester Chronicle*, Jan. 21, 1864; Martling diary, entry for Dec. 16, 1863.

26. Grebner, 168.

27. *Rochester Chronicle*, Oct. 22, 1863.

28. Ibid., Jan. 21, 1864.

14. Jonas Gets a Diary

1. Miller, *Home Folks*, vol. 1, 94–103.

2. Its location today is occupied by the Public Library, Krystal Building and Tennessee Valley Authority headquarters on West Ninth Street.

3. Official Records, vol. 32, part 1, 419; Grebner, 170–71 and footnote 4.

4. Bishop, *Minnesota*, 106–108.

5. *Rochester Chronicle*, May 12, 1864.

6. Indiana War Records, vol. 6, 409.

7. Ibid., 403–20.

8. *Rochester Chronicle*, May 12, 1864.

9. Thornbrough, 169.

15. A Running Fight for Atlanta

1. George Washington was the last person to hold that rank. McPherson, 718.

2. Foote, *The Civil War, Red River to Appomattox*, 13–21; *Echoes of Glory*, 248.

3. Official Records, vol. 38, part 1, 96.

4. Boatner, 37–38; Chickamauga and Chattanooga, "On Your Own," 9, from *History of the 75th Regiment of Indiana Infantry Volunteers*, by David B. Floyd, 1893.

5. Indiana War Records, vol. 3, 79–83.

6. Foote, 318–20.

7. Boatner, 441; Warner, *Generals in Gray,* 161–62; McPherson, 365–66.

8. *Echoes of Glory,* 248, 250.

9. Ibid., 249.

10. Miller, *Home Folks,* vol. 1, 100.

11. *Echoes of Glory,* 253.

12. Grebner, 175.

13. *Echoes of Glory,* 254–55.

14. Ibid., 256–57; Warner, 295; Foote, 356.

15. McPherson, 753.

16. Warner, 142–43.

17. *Echoes of Glory,* 260.

18. *Rochester Chronicle,* Aug. 18, 1864.

19. *Echoes of Glory,* 262–63.

20. "A Union Soldier's Diary."

21. Official Records, vol. 38, part 1, 788–92.

22. Ibid., vol. 39, part 2, 547.

23. Ibid. and Warner, 359.

24. Official Records, vol. 38, part 1, 791.

25. Bishop, *Minnesota,* 109–10.

26. *Rochester Chronicle,* Sept. 1, 1864.

27. Ibid.

28. *Echoes of Glory,* 269.

29. Ibid., 270–71.

16. The March to the Sea

1. McPherson, 808–809.

2. *Rochester Chronicle,* Jan. 12, 1865.

3. Boatner, 509.

4. *Echoes of Glory,* 280.

5. Ibid., 268.

6. *Rochester Chronicle,* Jan. 12, 1865.

7. Bishop, *Minnesota,* 112–13.

8. Myers diary, entry for Nov. 18, 1864.

9. Bishop, *Minnesota,* 113.

10. *American Heritage,* 547.

11. *Rochester Chronicle,* Jan. 12, 1865.

12. Grand Army of the Republic, *Personal War Sketches,* Troutman; Myers diary entries Nov. 30, Dec. 1, 1865.

13. *Rochester Chronicle,* Jan. 12, 1865.

14. Official Records, vol. 44, part 2, 167.

15. Boatner, 512.

16. *Rochester Chronicle,* Jan. 12, 1865.
17. Bruce diary entries.
18. *Echoes of Glory,* 282–83.
19. McPherson, 811.

17. Retribution in South Carolina

1. In 1909 for a collection of memoirs by pioneer residents of Fulton County, organized, edited and published as *Home Folks* by Marguerite Miller, associate editor of the *Rochester Daily Republican.* A second volume was published in 1911. The letter referred to here was written from Savannah on Dec. 28, 1865, and the original copy is in the possession of Robert Bailey of Rochester, Ind., Myers' great-grandson.
2. McPherson, 827; Boatner, 127.
3. Foote, *Red River to Appomattox,* 751–53.
4. McPherson, 827–28; Foote, 789.
5. Boatner, 127.
6. Foote, 787; McPherson, 829; *American Heritage,* 563–64.
7. Angle, 387.
8. Official Records, vol. 47, part 1, no. 98.
9. Ibid., vol. 47, part 1, 564.
10. Official Records, Lt. Col. Doan Report, vol. 47, part 1, 562; Bishop, *Minnesota,* 116.
11. Bruce diary entry.
12. Bishop, 117.
13. Official Records, vol. 47, part 1, 563.
14. Indiana War Records, vol. 6, 420.

18. A New Nation

1. Foote, *Red River to Appomattox,* 1013–17; Bishop, *Minnesota,* 119–20.
2. Bruce diary entries, June 11–17, 1865.
3. Miller, *Home Folks,* vol. 1, 100.
4. Bruce diary, June 24–25, 1865.
5. Boatner, 858.
6. Catton, *Reflections,* 41.
7. Annual Message to Congress, Dec. 1, 1862.
8. *Rochester Union Spy,* July 23–Nov. 5, 1875; *Rochester Sentinel,* Sept. 20, 1895.
9. Fulton County Historical Society Quarterly, no. 27, 5.
10. *The History of White and Pulaski Counties,* F.A. Battey, Chicago, 1883, 696.

11. Keegan's diaries of service with the 87th Indiana were transcribed into a handsome folio in 1938 by a descendant, Dwight Reynolds of Indianapolis, who dedicated the volume to "a resolute, noble man." The Indiana State Library in Indianapolis has a copy which, unfortunately, has had many of its pages removed by person or persons unknown.

12. LaPorte County Museum, Civil War archives.

13. *Rochester Sentinel*, Sept. 20, Dec. 27, 1895.

14. Battle, *Biographical*, 19–21.

15. Ibid., 109–12.

16. Jasper County Library, 87th Indiana Regiment papers.

17. *Rochester Union Spy*, Nov. 5, 1869, Dec.12, 1872, Nov. 20, 1873, May 17, 1874; *Rochester Sentinel*, Dec. 13, 1873.

18. *Rochester Sentinel*, Jan. 11, 1879, May 1, 1880.

19. *Rochester Union Spy*, April 30, 1875; *Rochester Sentinel*, Dec. 10, 1908.

20. *Rochester Sentinel*, Nov. 10, 1883.

21. Williams, *That Strange Sad War*, 32.

22. Ibid., 32–33.

23. Ibid., 36–38.

24. *Red River to Appomattox*, 1042.

25. Ibid.

Epilogue

1. *Rochester Weekly Republican*, May 18, 1905.

2. *Evening Sentinel*, May 13, 1905.

3. Ibid., June 23, 1953.

4. Ibid., May 16, 1905.

5. Patton's soldier friends must have wrongly remembered the date of Patton's death for the monument's inscription. According to the *Evening Sentinel*, it occurred on the morning of May 13. Funeral services were held on the tombstone's date, May 15, and were reported by the *Sentinel* in its issue of May 16.

BIBLIOGRAPHY

Books

Alexander, E.P. *Military Memoirs of a Confederate: A Critical Narrative*. New York: Scribner's, 1907. Dayton, Ohio: Morningside Bookshop, 1977.

American Heritage Picture History of the Civil War. New York: Doubleday, 1960.

Angle, Paul M., ed. *Three Years in the Army of the Cumberland: The Letters and Diary of Major James A. Connolly*. Bloomington: Indiana University Press, 1959.

Arnold, James R. *Chickamauga 1863: The River of Death*. Campaign Series 17. London: Osprey, 1992.

Barnhart, John D., and Donald F. Carmony. *Indiana: From Frontier to Industrial Commonwealth*. 2 vols. New York: Lewis Historical Publishing Co., 1954.

Bishop, Judson W. *The Story of a Regiment: Being a Narrative of the Service of the Second Regiment Minnesota Volunteer Infantry in the Civil War of 1861–65*. Chapters 8 and 9. St. Paul, Minn.: Pioneer Press, 1890.

———. *Minnesota in the Civil and Indian Wars 1861–1865: Narrative of the Second Regiment*. 2nd ed. St. Paul, Minn.: Pioneer Press, 1891.

———. *The Mill Springs Campaign, from Glimpses of the Nation's Struggle Second Series, Papers Read before Minnesota Commandery Military Order of the Loyal Legion of the United States 1887–89*. St. Paul, Minn.: St. Paul Book and Stationery Co., 1890.

Boatner, Mark Mayo III. *The Civil War Dictionary: Revised Edition*. New York: Vintage, 1991.

Bowman, John S., gen. ed. *Who Was Who in the Civil War*. New York: Crescent, 1994.

Catton, Bruce. *America Goes to War: An Introduction to the Civil War and Its Meanings to Americans Today*. New York: MJF Books, 1958, 1986.

———. *Reflections on the Civil War*. Edited by John Leekley. Garden City, N.Y.: Doubleday, 1981.

———. *This Hallowed Ground*. Garden City, N.Y.: Doubleday, 1956.

Coggins, Jack. *Arms and Equipment of the Civil War*. Wilmington, N.C.: Broadfoot, 1990.

Counties of Warren, Benton, Jasper and Newton Indiana, Historical and Biographical. Part IV, History of Jasper County by J. H. Battle and Biographical Sketches. Chicago: F.A. Battey, 1883.

Cozzens, Peter. *This Terrible Sound: The Battle of Chickamauga*. Urbana: University of Illinois Press, 1992.

———. *The Shipwreck of Their Hopes: The Battles for Chattanooga*. Urbana: University of Illinois Press, 1994.

Davis, Burke. *Our Incredible Civil War*. New York: Rinehart and Winston, 1960.

Dornbusch, C.E., comp. *Regimental Publications and Personal Narratives of the Civil War: A Checklist*. Vol. 1, Pts. 1–7. New York: New York Public Library, 1961.

Dyer, Frederick H., comp. *A Compendium of the War of the Rebellion.* Vols. 1 and 3. Dayton, Ohio: Morningside Bookshop, 1978.

Echoes of Glory: The Illustrated Civil War Atlas. Alexandria, Va.: Time-Life Books, 1991.

Esarey, Logan. *History of Indiana: From Its Exploration to 1922.* Vol. 2. Dayton, Ohio: Dayton Historical Publishing Co., 1923.

Foote, Shelby. *The Civil War: A Narrative, Fort Sumter to Perryville.* New York: Random House, 1958.

———. *The Civil War: A Narrative, Fredericksburg to Meridian.* New York: Random House, 1963.

———. *The Civil War: A Narrative, Red River to Appomattox.* New York: Random House, 1974.

———, ed. *Chickamauga and Other Civil War Stories.* New York: Dell, 1993.

Grebner, Constantin. Translated and edited by Frederic Trautmann. *We Were the Ninth: A History of the Ninth Regiment Ohio Volunteer Infantry April 17, 1861 to June 7, 1864.* Cincinnati: Rosenthal, 1897. Kent, Ohio: Kent State University Press, 1987.

Griffith, Paddy. *Battle Tactics of the Civil War.* New Haven: Yale University Press, 1989.

Hafendorfer, Kenneth A. *Perryville: Battle for Kentucky.* 2nd ed. Louisville: KH Press, 1991.

Hinman, Wilbur F. *Corporal Si Klegg and His Pard.* Cleveland: Hamilton, 1889.

Hurst, Jack. *Nathan Bedford Forrest: A Biography.* New York: Knopf, 1993.

Illustrated Historical Atlas of the State of Indiana. Chicago: Baskin, Forster, 1876.

Images of the Civil War: The Paintings of Mort Kuntsler, The Text of James M. McPherson. New York: Gramercy, 1992.

Indiana at Chickamauga 1863–1900. Report of the Indiana Commissioners, Chickamauga National Military Park. Indianapolis: Sentinel, 1900.

Indiana War Records. Report of the Adjutant General of the State of Indiana, 1861–65. Vols. 3 and 6. Indianapolis: Samuel M. Douglass, State Printer, 1866.

Jackson, Donald Dale. *Twenty Million Yankees: The Northern Home Front.* New York: Time-Life, 1985.

Johannsen, Robert W. *To the Halls of Montezuma: The Mexican War in the American Imagination.* New York: Oxford University Press, 1985.

Kingman, A.L. *New Historical Atlas of Fulton County Indiana Illustrated.* Chicago: Kingman, 1883.

Lavender, David. *Climax at Buena Vista: The American Campaigns in Northeastern Mexico 1846–47.* New York: Lippincott, 1966.

Linderman, Gerald F. *Embattled Courage: The Experience of Combat in the American Civil War.* New York: Free Press, 1987.

Madison, James H. *The Indiana Way: A State History.* Bloomington: Indiana University Press, 1986.

Manchester, William. *American Caesar: Douglas MacArthur 1880–1964.* New York: Dell, 1978.

McFeely, William S. *Grant: A Biography.* New York: Norton, 1981.

McPherson, James M. *The Battle Cry of Freedom.* New York: Oxford University Press, 1988.

Miller, Marguerite L., comp. *Home Folks: A Series of Stories by Old Settlers of Fulton County, Indiana.* 2 vols. 1909–1911. Rochester, Ind.: Fulton County Historical Society, 1973.

Neely, Mark E., Jr. *The Last Best Hope of Earth: Abraham Lincoln and the Promise of America.* Cambridge: Harvard University Press, 1993.

Official Records. *The War of the Rebellion, A Compilation of the Official Records of the Union and Confederate Armies.* 70 vols., 128 books. Washington: U.S. Government Printing Office, 1881–1900.

Pomeroy, Eric, and Paul Brockman. *A Guide to the Manuscript Collection of the Indiana Historical Society and the Indiana State Library.* Indianapolis: Indiana Historical Society, 1986.

Sandburg, Carl. *Abraham Lincoln: The War Years.* Vol. 2. New York: Harcourt Brace, 1939.

Sifakis, Stewart. *Who Was Who in the Civil War.* New York: Facts on File, 1988.

Spruill, Matt, ed. *Guide to the Battle of Chickamauga incl. Appendix I, Medical Practice and Handling of the Wounded in the Civil War.* Lawrence: University Press of Kansas, 1993.

Thornbrough, Emma Lou. *Indiana in the Civil War Era 1850–1880.* Indianapolis: Indiana Historical Bureau and Indiana Historical Society, 1965.

Tombaugh, Wendell C., and Jean Tombaugh, comp. *Fulton County Indiana Newspapers Abstracted, The Rochester Sentinel 1862.* Rochester, Indiana: Tombaugh House, 1975.

———. *Fulton County Indiana Newspaper Excerpts 1858–78.* 8 vols. Rochester, Ind.: Tombaugh House, 1982–90.

Tombaugh, Wendell C. *Fulton County Indiana Obits/Biogs 1880–1912.* 7 vols. Rochester, Ind.: Tombaugh House, 1992–94.

Tucker, Glenn. *Chickamauga: Bloody Battle in the West.* Indianapolis: Bobbs-Merrill, 1961.

Warner, Ezra J. *Generals in Gray: Lives of the Confederate Commanders.* Baton Rouge: Louisiana State University Press, 1959.

———. *Generals in Blue: Lives of the Union Commanders.* Baton Rouge: Louisiana State University Press, 1964.

Watkins, Sam R. *Co. Aytch.* New York: Collier Books, Macmillan, 1962.

Wert, Jeffry D. *General James Longstreet: The Confederacy's Most Controversial Soldier, A Biography.* New York: Simon and Schuster, 1993.

Wheeler, Richard. *Sherman's March.* New York: Crowell, 1978.

———. *Voices of the Civil War.* Charlotte, N.C.: Meridian, 1990.

Williams, T. Harry. *The Selected Essays of T. Harry Williams.* Baton Rouge: Louisiana State University Press, 1983.

Diaries, Journals, Manuscripts, Memoirs, Letters

Fulton County Historical Society, Rochester, Ind., quarterly publications of society: "Civil War Diary of Daniel Bruce." Published by the *Pulaski County Democrat,* Winamac, Ind., in weekly installments from Jan. 3, 1935, to March 5, 1936.

"Civil War History of Capt. Horace C. Long by Martha Thompson."

"Letters of Capt. Albert Brackett of 4th Indiana Regiment from Mexican War."

Grand Army of the Republic. Personal War Sketches. Descriptive Book. Minutes of Meetings. McClung Post 95. Rochester, Ind.: Fulton County Public Library

Indiana Historical Society, William Henry Smith Memorial Library, Indianapolis:

"A Union Soldier's Diary," Whitsel Lewis.

Letters of Benjamin F. Hooten.

"Indiana in the Mexican War," R.C. Buley.

"Daniel E. Bruce, Civil War Teamster."

Autograph Letter from Capt. A.G. Brackett.

Jasper County Public Library, Rensselaer, Ind.: Letters and papers relating to members of 87th Indiana Infantry Regiment.

Keegan, Peter. "Diaries." Dwight Reynolds, ed. Indiana Division Indiana State Library. Indianapolis: 1938.

LaPorte County Museum, LaPorte, Ind.: Civil War papers.

"Letters Home to Minnesota by Cpl. D.B. Griffin of 2nd Minnesota Volunteers." Joan W. Albertson, comp. Spokane, Wash.: P.D. Enterprises, 1992.

Martling, George H. "The Civil War Diary." Copshaholm Museum, Northern Indiana Historical Society, South Bend, Ind.

"Mishawaka during the Civil War." Ward Baker, 1961. South Bend, Ind., Public Library.

Myers, Jonas. Diary, Journal, Letters, Records. Private collection of Robert and David Bailey, Rochester, Ind.

Newspapers:

Rochester (Indiana) Chronicle.

Rochester (Indiana) Sentinel.

Rochester Weekly Republican.

"Thru a Private's Eyes: The Four Campaigns," by Henry Clay Green, journal of service with Company E of the 87th Indiana Infantry, 1871. Transcribed by Rodger Green, Whitehouse, Ohio.

Wheat, Cpl. Joseph Gillit. Experiences with 104th Illinois Infantry Regiment. Transcribed by Laura Foster, daughter.

Other Sources

Chickamauga and Chattanooga. "On Your Own, An Illustrated Guide to the Battlefields," 2nd ed., 1981. Chattanooga National Military Park, Tenn.

Chickamauga and Chattanooga. Tour Pamphlets. National Military Park, Georgia/ Tennessee, National Park Service, U.S. Department of Interior, 1983 and 1994.

"Twelve Roads to Gettysburg." Multi-media CD-ROM. Milpitas, Calif.: Ebook, 1992.

Maps

Military Map Showing the Theater of Operations in the Tullahoma, Chickamauga and Chattanooga Campaigns. Chickamauga and Chattanooga National Park Commission, 1896.

Maps of the Battlefield of Chickamauga: Movements Morning to Noon Sept. 19th 1863, Noon to Night Sept. 19th 1863, Morning to Noon Sept. 20th 1863, Noon to Night Sept. 20th 1863. Chickamauga and Chattanooga National Park Commission, 1896.

INDEX

See also the appendixes on pages 187–249.

JACK K. OVERMYER

is president and owner of the *Rochester Sentinel* and was its editor and publisher for more than 30 years. A fourth-generation Hoosier, he studied history and political science at Indiana University. He is a founder and first president of the Fulton County Historical Society. For most of his life he has studiously pursued an interest in the Civil War that has culminated in this, his first book.